THE BIG BOOK OF HELL

A CARTOON BOOK BY MATT GROENING

OTHER BOOKS BY THIS SAME CARTOONIST

LOVE IS HELL
WORK IS HELL
SCHOOL IS HELL
CHILDHOOD IS HELL
BOX FULL OF HELL
(CONTAINING LOVE, WORK, & SCHOOL)
AKBAR & JEFF'S GUIDE TO LIFE
GREETINGS FROM HELL

FORTHCOMING

THE BIGGER BOOK OF HELL
THE EVEN BIGGER BOOK OF HELL
THE EVEN BIGGER THAN THE PREVIOUS EVEN BIGGER BOOK OF HELL
ETC., ETC., ETC.

The cartoons in this work were originally published in LOVE IS HELL, WORK IS HELL, SCHOOL IS HELL, CHILDHOOD IS HELL, and AKBAR & JEFF'S GUIDE TO LIFE by Matt Groening and in the LIFE IN HELL® comic strip from Acme Features Syndicate.

I.S.B.N. 0-394-58779-0 (hardcover) 0-679-72759-0 (paperback)

L.C. 89-61958

DESIGNER: CINDY VANCE
INDEXER: MAX FRANCKE
LEGAL ADVISOR: SUSAN GRODE
PRODUCTION DIRECTOR: KATHY GRASSO
THANKS TO ROBERT HUGHES FOR FIRST LOCATING AND THEN RELOCATING THE ROBERT GRAVES QUOTE.

THANKS TO THE STAFF AT THE LIFE IN HELL CARTOON CO. AND ACME FEATURES SYNDICATE:
SONDRA ROBINSON, DIANE PIRRITINO, LORI ABRAMSON, GARY BUSHERT, LESLIE RIZZO, DALE REDMAN, MICHELLE SHIRES AND MARK GATEWOOD

THANKS TO THE PANTHEON STAFF THROUGH THE YEARS AND MY EDITOR, WENDY WOLF

LYNDA BARRY WAS, IS, AND SHALL ALWAYS BE FUNK QUEEN OF NORTH AMERICA

Manufactured in the United States of America

First Edition

For Deborah, who got me
from there to here.

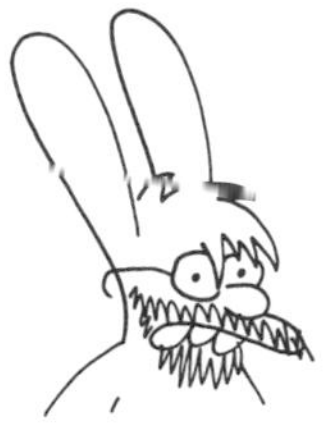

"Epitaph on an Unfortunate Artist"

He found a formula for drawing comic rabbits:
This formula for drawing comic rabbits paid,
So in the end he could not change the tragic habits
This formula for drawing comic rabbits made.

Robert Graves

All my life I've been torn between frivolity and despair, between the desire to amuse and the desire to annoy, between dread-filled insomnia and a sense of my own goofiness. Just like you, I worry about love and sex and work and suffering and injustice and death, but I also dig drawing bulgy-eyed rabbits with tragic overbites.

Hence "Life in Hell," an ongoing series of self-help cartoons--the self being helped being me. I don't know how helpful these cartoons have been, but drawing them over the last ten years has sure amused me. I hope the cartoons amuse you too, but if you're one of those people who finds my stuff annoying, that's OK. Luckily for me, being annoying is a blast, too.

Matt Groening
Los Angeles, California
September, 1990

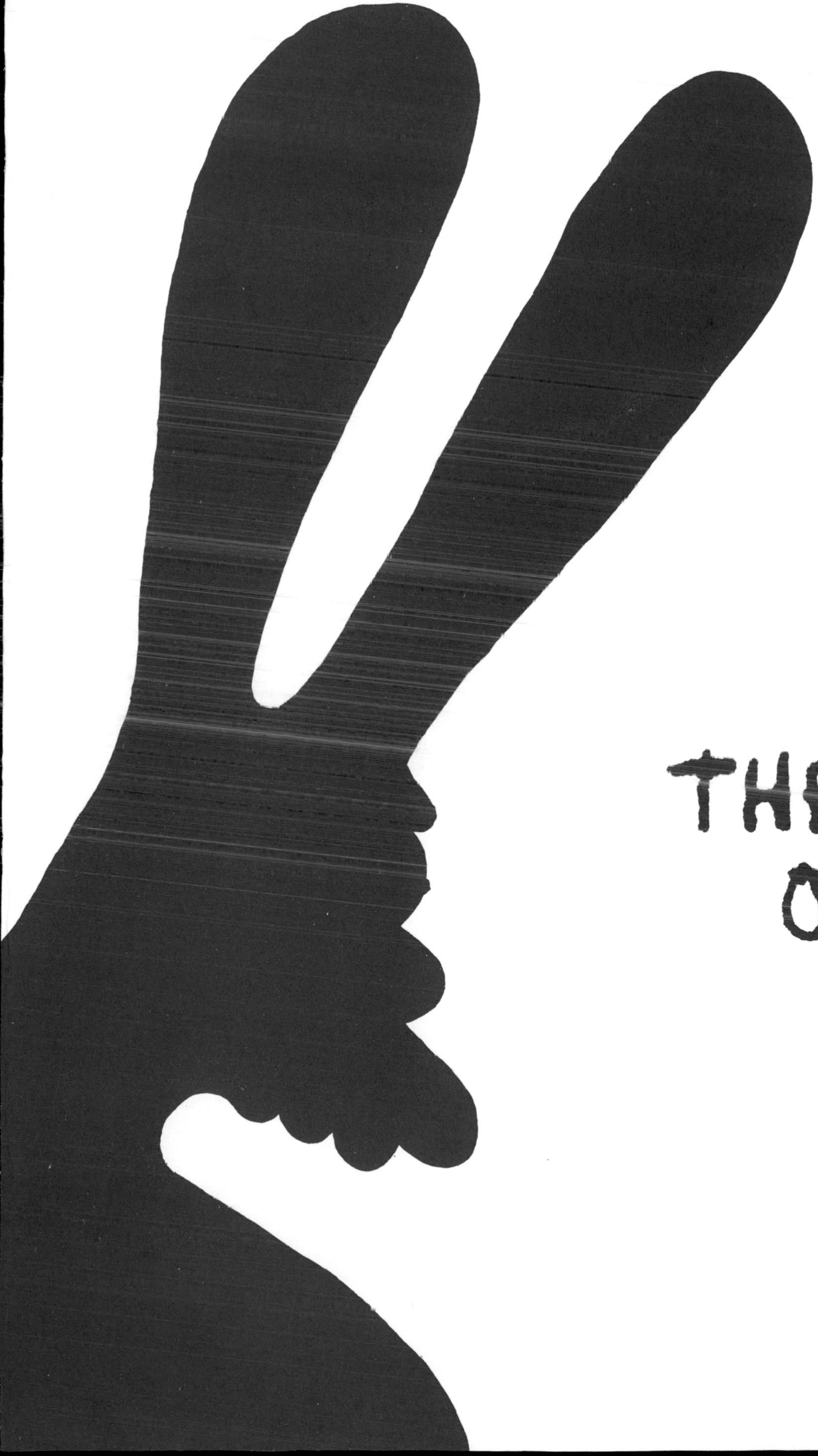

THE BIG BOOK OF HELL

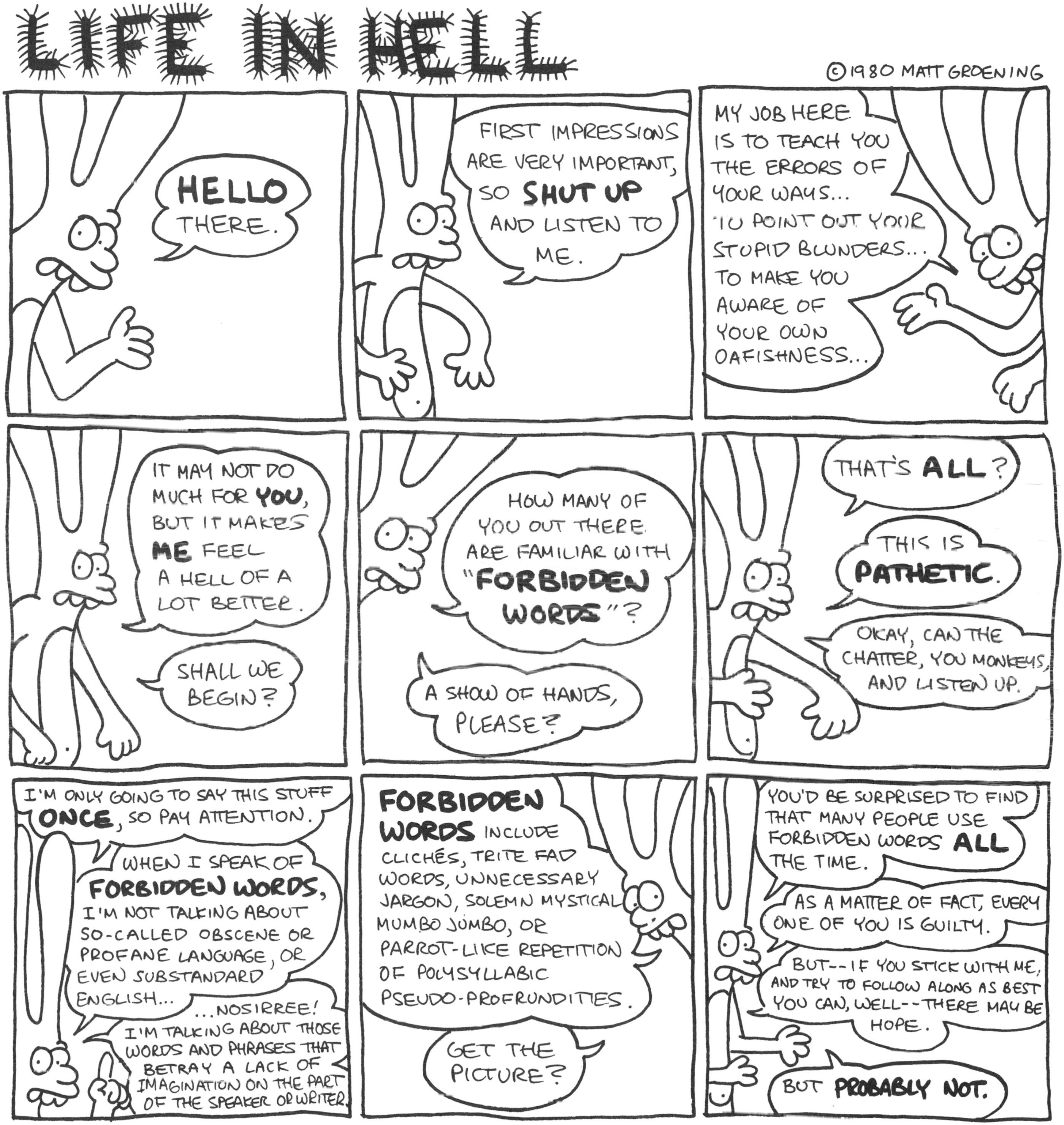
LIFE IN HELL
©1980 MATT GROENING
HELLO THERE.
FIRST IMPRESSIONS ARE VERY IMPORTANT, SO SHUT UP AND LISTEN TO ME.
MY JOB HERE IS TO TEACH YOU THE ERRORS OF YOUR WAYS... TO POINT OUT YOUR STUPID BLUNDERS... TO MAKE YOU AWARE OF YOUR OWN OAFISHNESS...
IT MAY NOT DO MUCH FOR YOU, BUT IT MAKES ME FEEL A HELL OF A LOT BETTER.
SHALL WE BEGIN?
HOW MANY OF YOU OUT THERE ARE FAMILIAR WITH "FORBIDDEN WORDS"?
A SHOW OF HANDS, PLEASE?
THAT'S ALL?
THIS IS PATHETIC.
OKAY, CAN THE CHATTER, YOU MONKEYS, AND LISTEN UP.
I'M ONLY GOING TO SAY THIS STUFF ONCE, SO PAY ATTENTION.
WHEN I SPEAK OF FORBIDDEN WORDS, I'M NOT TALKING ABOUT SO-CALLED OBSCENE OR PROFANE LANGUAGE, OR EVEN SUBSTANDARD ENGLISH...
...NOSIRREE!
I'M TALKING ABOUT THOSE WORDS AND PHRASES THAT BETRAY A LACK OF IMAGINATION ON THE PART OF THE SPEAKER OR WRITER.
FORBIDDEN WORDS INCLUDE CLICHÉS, TRITE FAD WORDS, UNNECESSARY JARGON, SOLEMN MYSTICAL MUMBO JUMBO, OR PARROT-LIKE REPETITION OF POLYSYLLABIC PSEUDO-PROFUNDITIES.
GET THE PICTURE?
YOU'D BE SURPRISED TO FIND THAT MANY PEOPLE USE FORBIDDEN WORDS ALL THE TIME.
AS A MATTER OF FACT, EVERY ONE OF YOU IS GUILTY.
BUT--IF YOU STICK WITH ME, AND TRY TO FOLLOW ALONG AS BEST YOU CAN, WELL--THERE MAY BE HOPE.
BUT PROBABLY NOT.

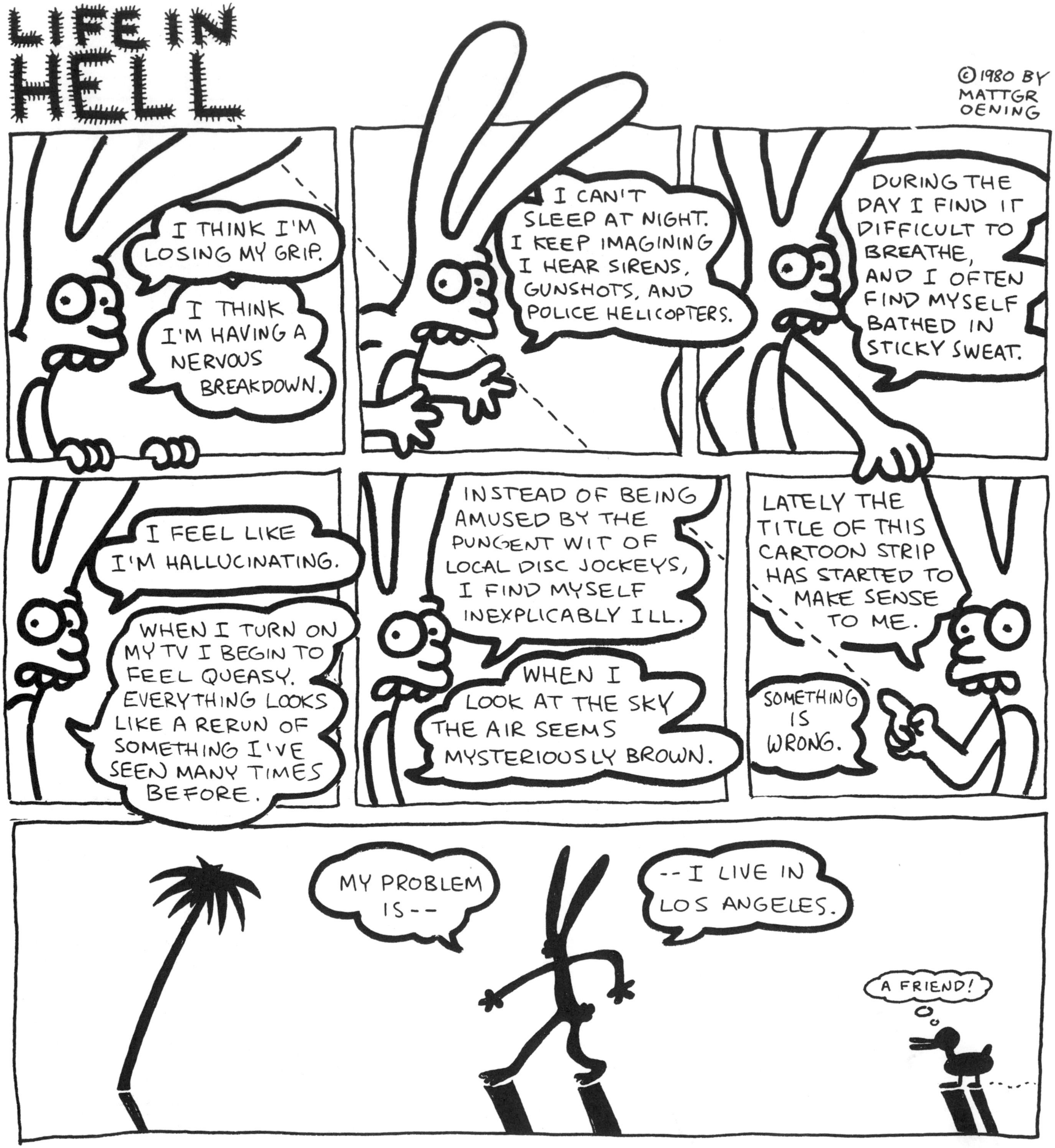

LIFE IN HELL
©1980 BY MATTGROENING
I THINK I'M LOSING MY GRIP.
I THINK I'M HAVING A NERVOUS BREAKDOWN.
I CAN'T SLEEP AT NIGHT. I KEEP IMAGINING I HEAR SIRENS, GUNSHOTS, AND POLICE HELICOPTERS.
DURING THE DAY I FIND IT DIFFICULT TO BREATHE, AND I OFTEN FIND MYSELF BATHED IN STICKY SWEAT.
I FEEL LIKE I'M HALLUCINATING.
WHEN I TURN ON MY TV I BEGIN TO FEEL QUEASY. EVERYTHING LOOKS LIKE A RERUN OF SOMETHING I'VE SEEN MANY TIMES BEFORE.
INSTEAD OF BEING AMUSED BY THE PUNGENT WIT OF LOCAL DISC JOCKEYS, I FIND MYSELF INEXPLICABLY ILL.
WHEN I LOOK AT THE SKY THE AIR SEEMS MYSTERIOUSLY BROWN.
LATELY THE TITLE OF THIS CARTOON STRIP HAS STARTED TO MAKE SENSE TO ME.
SOMETHING IS WRONG.
MY PROBLEM IS --
-- I LIVE IN LOS ANGELES.
A FRIEND!

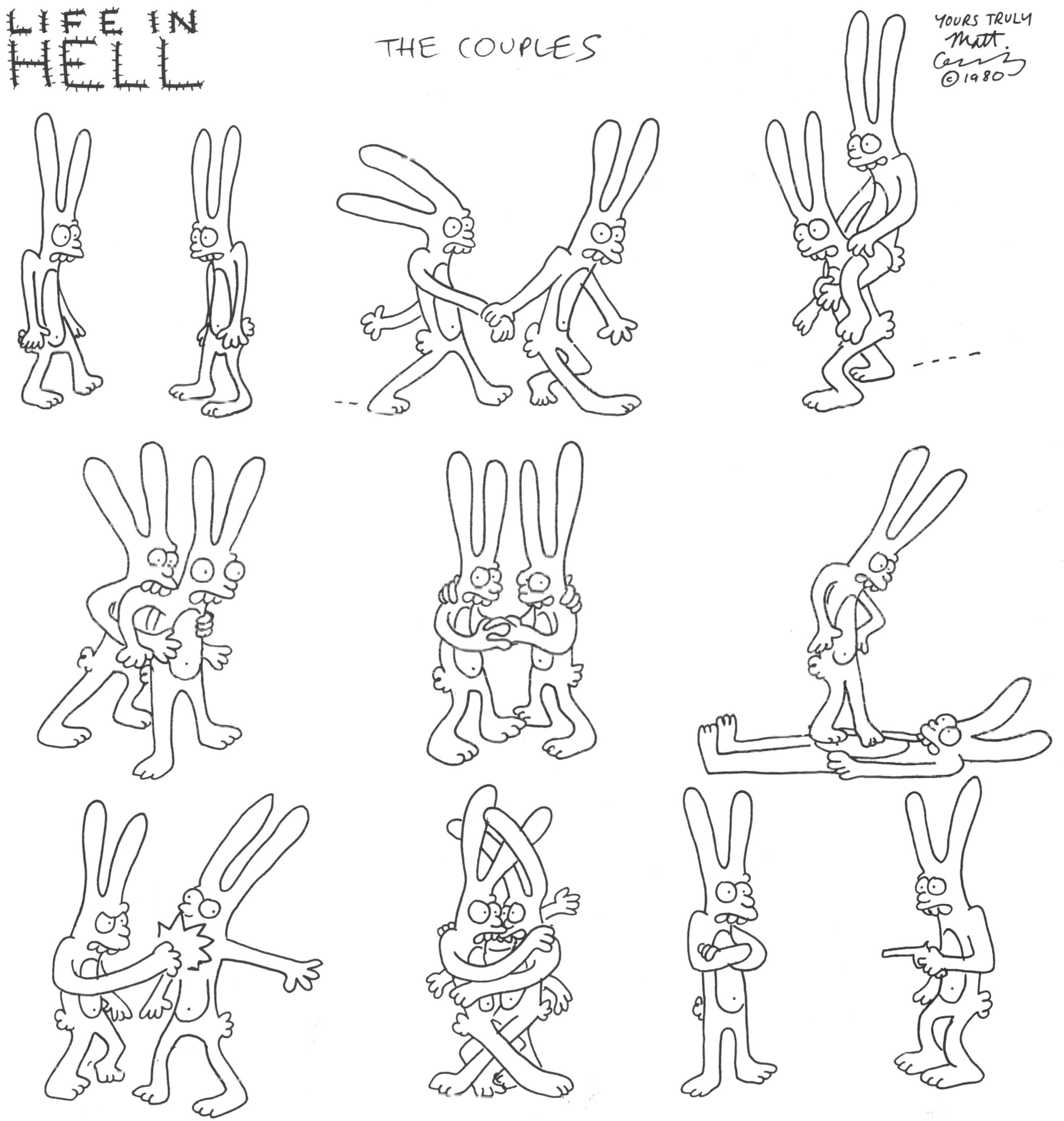
LIFE IN HELL
THE COUPLES
YOURS TRULY Matt Groening ©1980

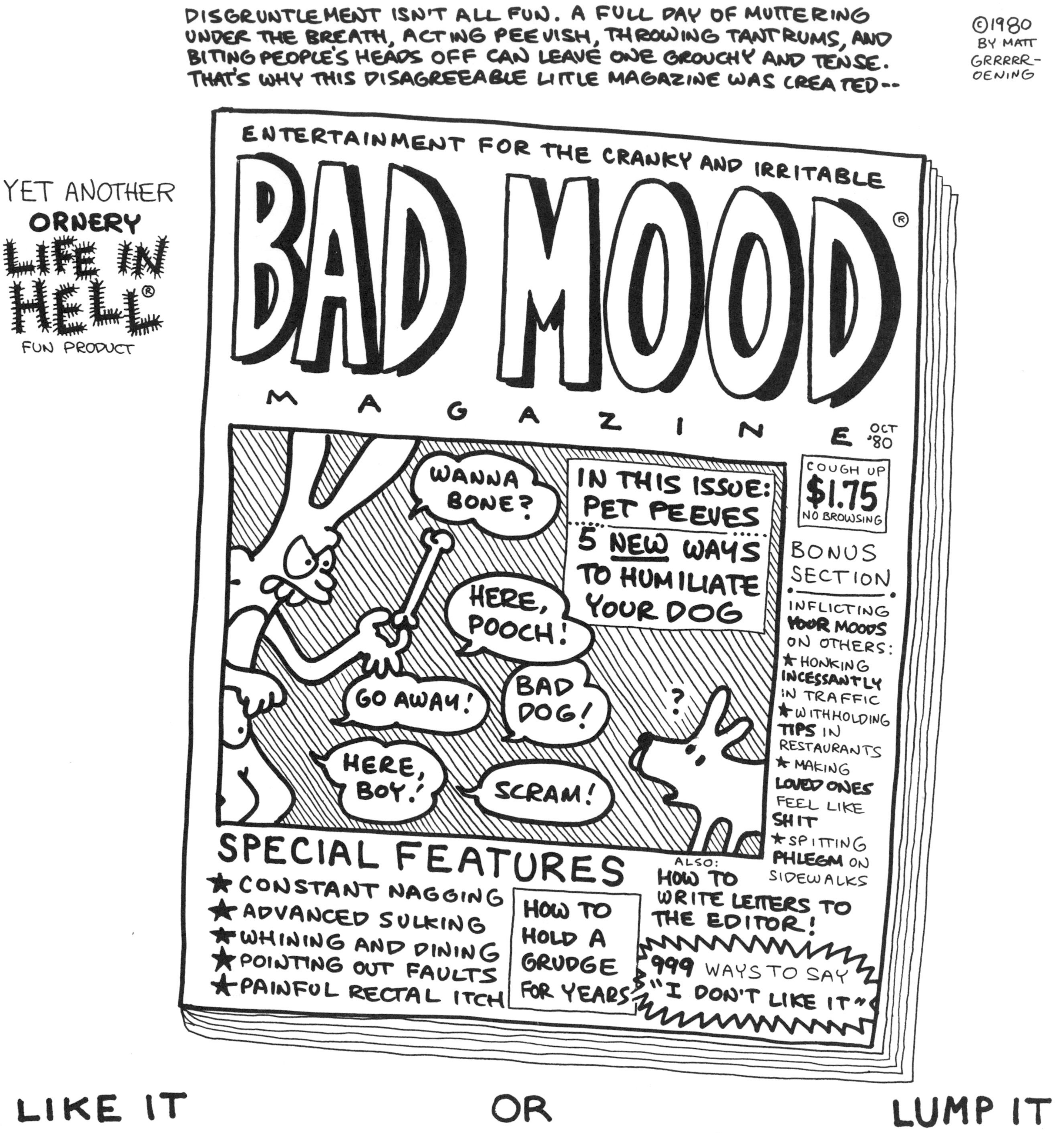
DISGRUNTLEMENT ISN'T ALL FUN. A FULL DAY OF MUTTERING UNDER THE BREATH, ACTING PEEVISH, THROWING TANTRUMS, AND BITING PEOPLE'S HEADS OFF CAN LEAVE ONE GROUCHY AND TENSE. THAT'S WHY THIS DISAGREEABLE LITTLE MAGAZINE WAS CREATED--
©1980 BY MATT GRRRRR-OENING
YET ANOTHER ORNERY LIFE IN HELL® FUN PRODUCT
ENTERTAINMENT FOR THE CRANKY AND IRRITABLE
BAD MOOD® MAGAZINE
OCT '80
COUGH UP $1.75 NO BROWSING
IN THIS ISSUE: PET PEEVES
5 NEW WAYS TO HUMILIATE YOUR DOG
WANNA BONE?
HERE, POOCH!
GO AWAY!
BAD DOG!
?
HERE, BOY!
SCRAM!
BONUS SECTION
INFLICTING YOUR MOODS ON OTHERS:
★ HONKING INCESSANTLY IN TRAFFIC
★ WITHHOLDING TIPS IN RESTAURANTS
★ MAKING LOVED ONES FEEL LIKE SHIT
★ SPITTING PHLEGM ON SIDEWALKS
SPECIAL FEATURES
★ CONSTANT NAGGING
★ ADVANCED SULKING
★ WHINING AND DINING
★ POINTING OUT FAULTS
★ PAINFUL RECTAL ITCH
HOW TO HOLD A GRUDGE FOR YEARS
ALSO: HOW TO WRITE LETTERS TO THE EDITOR!
999 WAYS TO SAY "I DON'T LIKE IT"
LIKE IT OR LUMP IT

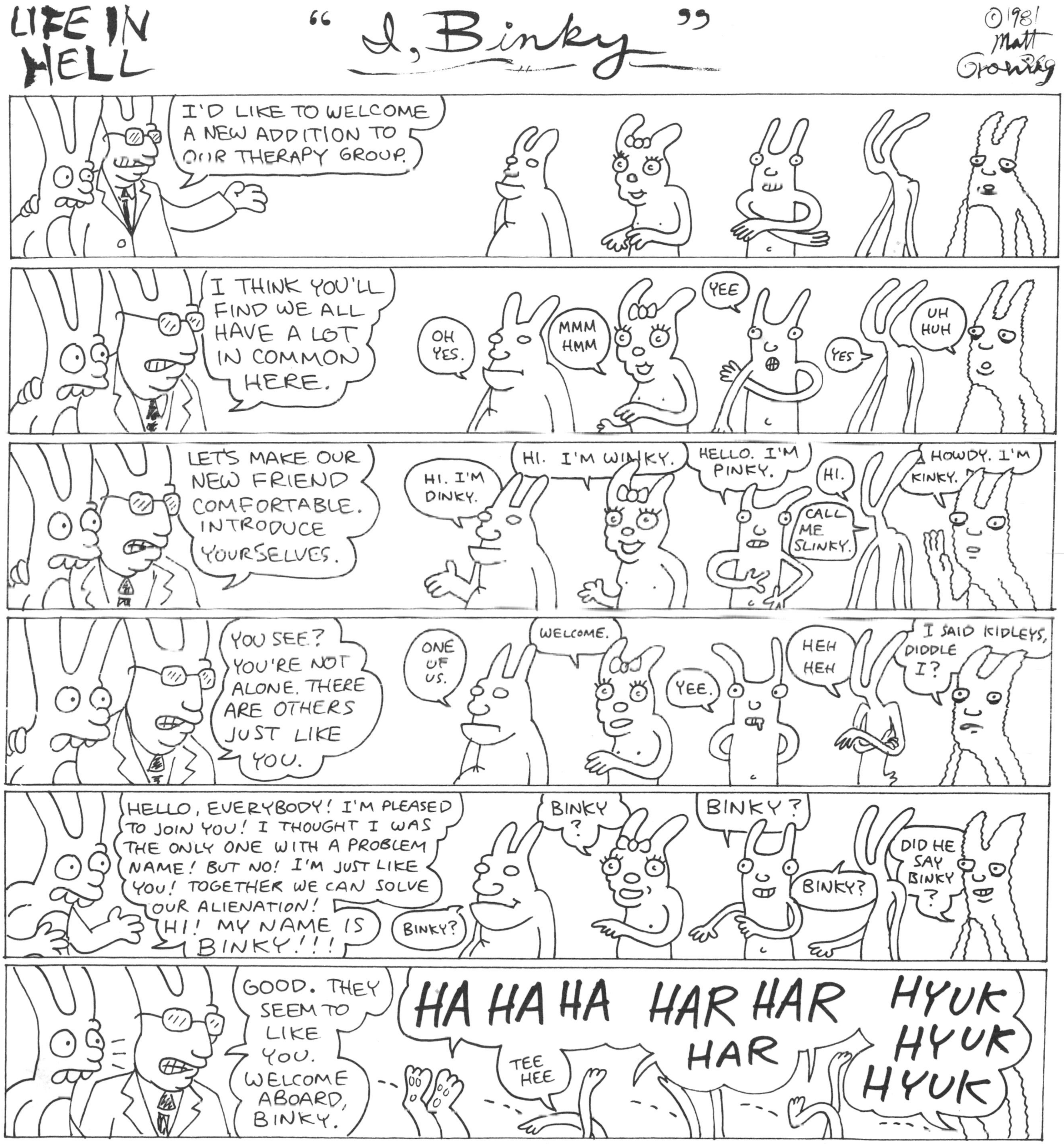
LIFE IN HELL
"I, Binky"
© 1981 Matt Groening
I'D LIKE TO WELCOME A NEW ADDITION TO OUR THERAPY GROUP.
I THINK YOU'LL FIND WE ALL HAVE A LOT IN COMMON HERE.
OH YES.
MMM HMM
YEE
YES
UH HUH
LET'S MAKE OUR NEW FRIEND COMFORTABLE. INTRODUCE YOURSELVES.
HI. I'M DINKY.
HI. I'M WINKY.
HELLO. I'M PINKY.
HI.
CALL ME SLINKY.
HOWDY. I'M KINKY.
YOU SEE? YOU'RE NOT ALONE. THERE ARE OTHERS JUST LIKE YOU.
ONE OF US.
WELCOME.
YEE.
HEH HEH
I SAID KIDLEYS, DIDDLE I?
HELLO, EVERYBODY! I'M PLEASED TO JOIN YOU! I THOUGHT I WAS THE ONLY ONE WITH A PROBLEM NAME! BUT NO! I'M JUST LIKE YOU! TOGETHER WE CAN SOLVE OUR ALIENATION! HI! MY NAME IS BINKY!!!
BINKY?
BINKY?
BINKY?
BINKY?
DID HE SAY BINKY?
GOOD. THEY SEEM TO LIKE YOU. WELCOME ABOARD, BINKY.
HA HA HA
TEE HEE
HAR HAR HAR
HYUK HYUK HYUK

LIFE IN HELL

BINKY'S BEACHFRONT BUNGALOW

©1981 BY Matt Groening

4·8·81 DRAWN UNDER PRESSURE

AFTER ROWLAND EMETT

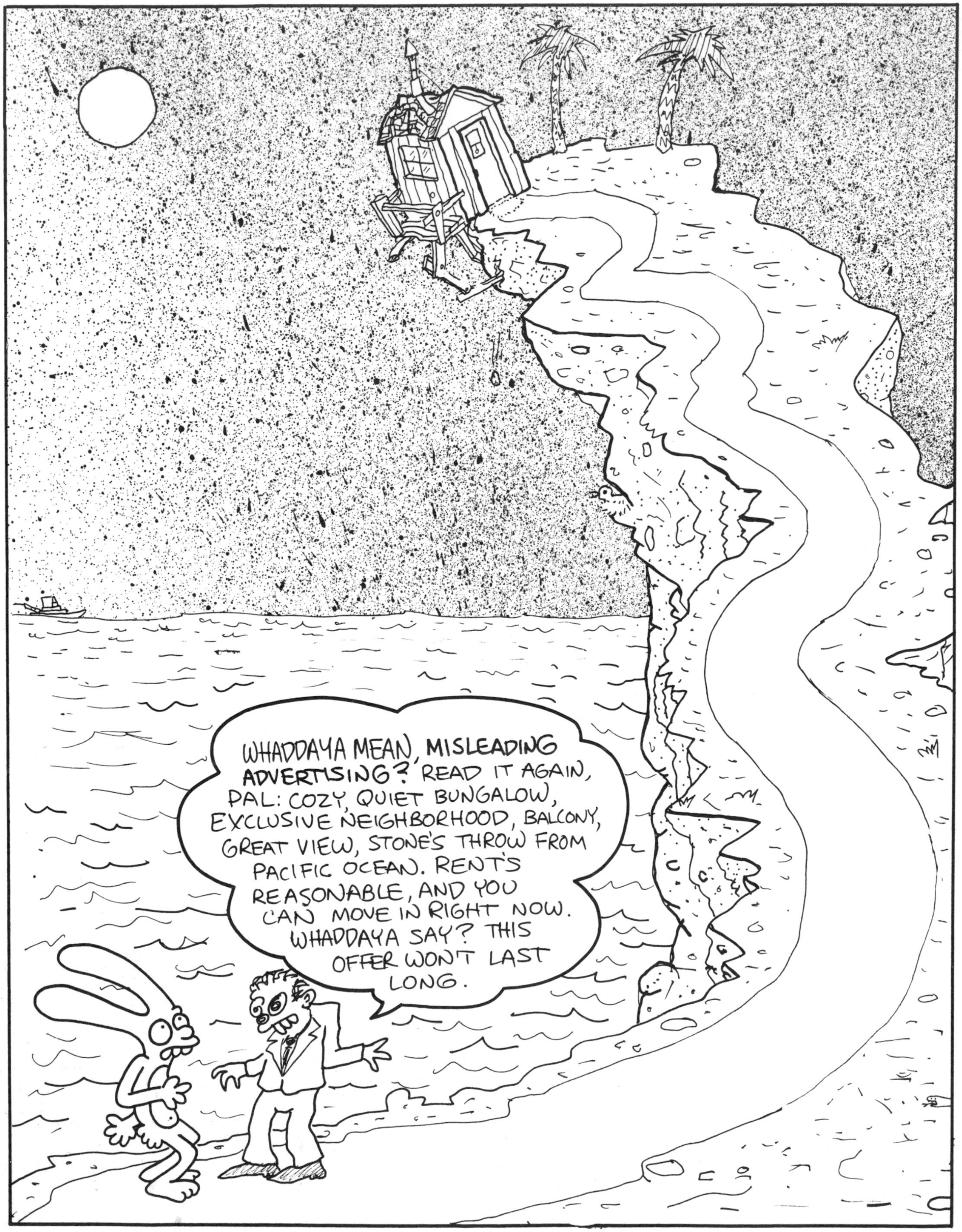
WHADDAYA MEAN, MISLEADING ADVERTISING? READ IT AGAIN, PAL: COZY, QUIET BUNGALOW, EXCLUSIVE NEIGHBORHOOD, BALCONY, GREAT VIEW, STONE'S THROW FROM PACIFIC OCEAN. RENT'S REASONABLE, AND YOU CAN MOVE IN RIGHT NOW. WHADDAYA SAY? THIS OFFER WON'T LAST LONG.

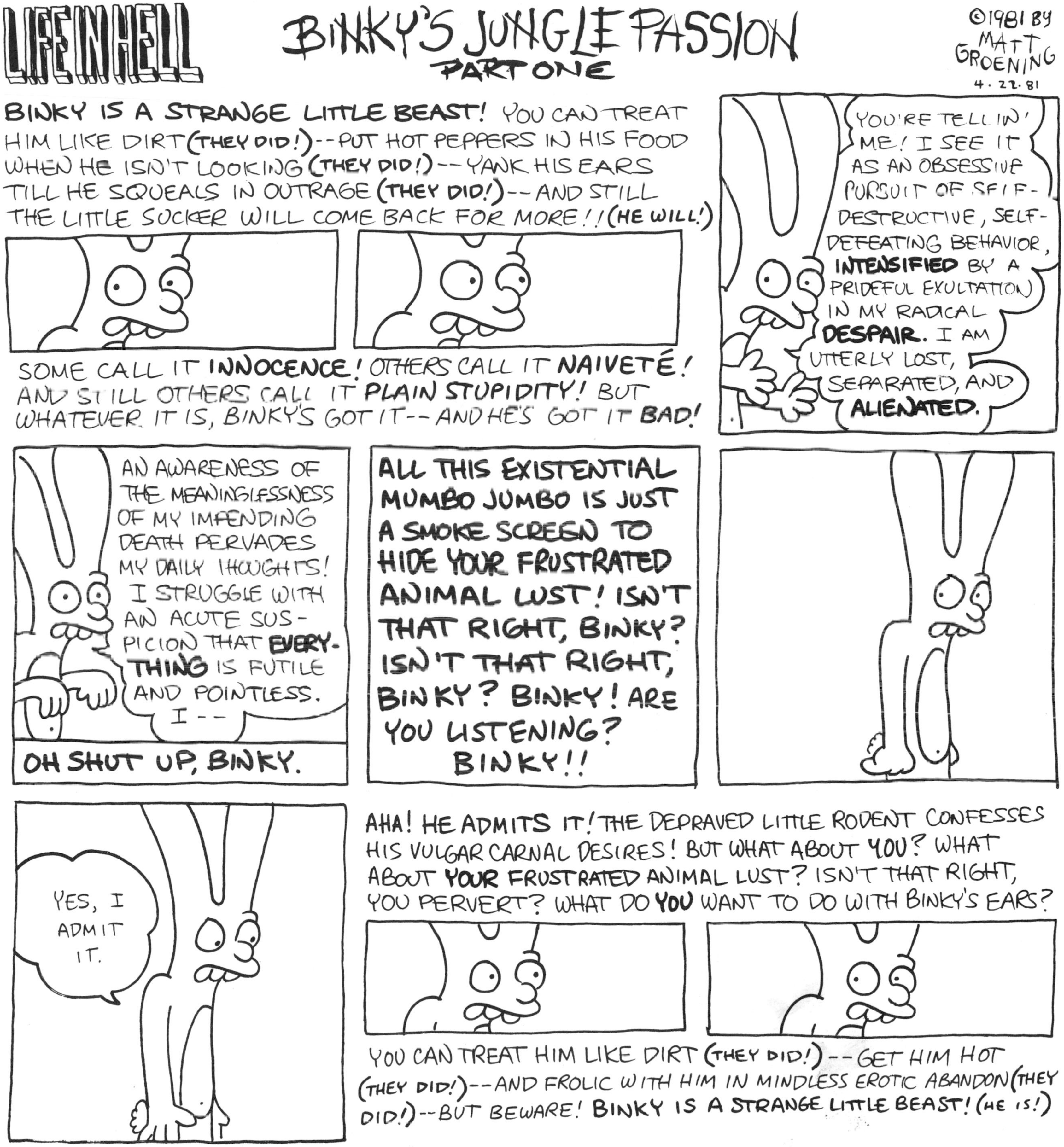
LIFE IN HELL
BINKY'S JUNGLE PASSION
PART ONE
©1981 BY MATT GROENING 4·22·81
BINKY IS A STRANGE LITTLE BEAST! YOU CAN TREAT HIM LIKE DIRT (THEY DID!) -- PUT HOT PEPPERS IN HIS FOOD WHEN HE ISN'T LOOKING (THEY DID!) -- YANK HIS EARS TILL HE SQUEALS IN OUTRAGE (THEY DID!) -- AND STILL THE LITTLE SUCKER WILL COME BACK FOR MORE!! (HE WILL!)
SOME CALL IT INNOCENCE! OTHERS CALL IT NAIVETÉ! AND STILL OTHERS CALL IT PLAIN STUPIDITY! BUT WHATEVER IT IS, BINKY'S GOT IT -- AND HE'S GOT IT BAD!
YOU'RE TELLIN' ME! I SEE IT AS AN OBSESSIVE PURSUIT OF SELF-DESTRUCTIVE, SELF-DEFEATING BEHAVIOR, INTENSIFIED BY A PRIDEFUL EXULTATION IN MY RADICAL DESPAIR. I AM UTTERLY LOST, SEPARATED, AND ALIENATED.
AN AWARENESS OF THE MEANINGLESSNESS OF MY IMPENDING DEATH PERVADES MY DAILY THOUGHTS! I STRUGGLE WITH AN ACUTE SUSPICION THAT EVERYTHING IS FUTILE AND POINTLESS. I --
OH SHUT UP, BINKY.
ALL THIS EXISTENTIAL MUMBO JUMBO IS JUST A SMOKE SCREEN TO HIDE YOUR FRUSTRATED ANIMAL LUST! ISN'T THAT RIGHT, BINKY? ISN'T THAT RIGHT, BINKY? BINKY! ARE YOU LISTENING? BINKY!!
YES, I ADMIT IT.
AHA! HE ADMITS IT! THE DEPRAVED LITTLE RODENT CONFESSES HIS VULGAR CARNAL DESIRES! BUT WHAT ABOUT YOU? WHAT ABOUT YOUR FRUSTRATED ANIMAL LUST? ISN'T THAT RIGHT, YOU PERVERT? WHAT DO YOU WANT TO DO WITH BINKY'S EARS?
YOU CAN TREAT HIM LIKE DIRT (THEY DID!) -- GET HIM HOT (THEY DID!) -- AND FROLIC WITH HIM IN MINDLESS EROTIC ABANDON (THEY DID!) -- BUT BEWARE! BINKY IS A STRANGE LITTLE BEAST! (HE IS!)

LIFE IN HELL

BINKY'S JUNGLE PASSION

PART TWO

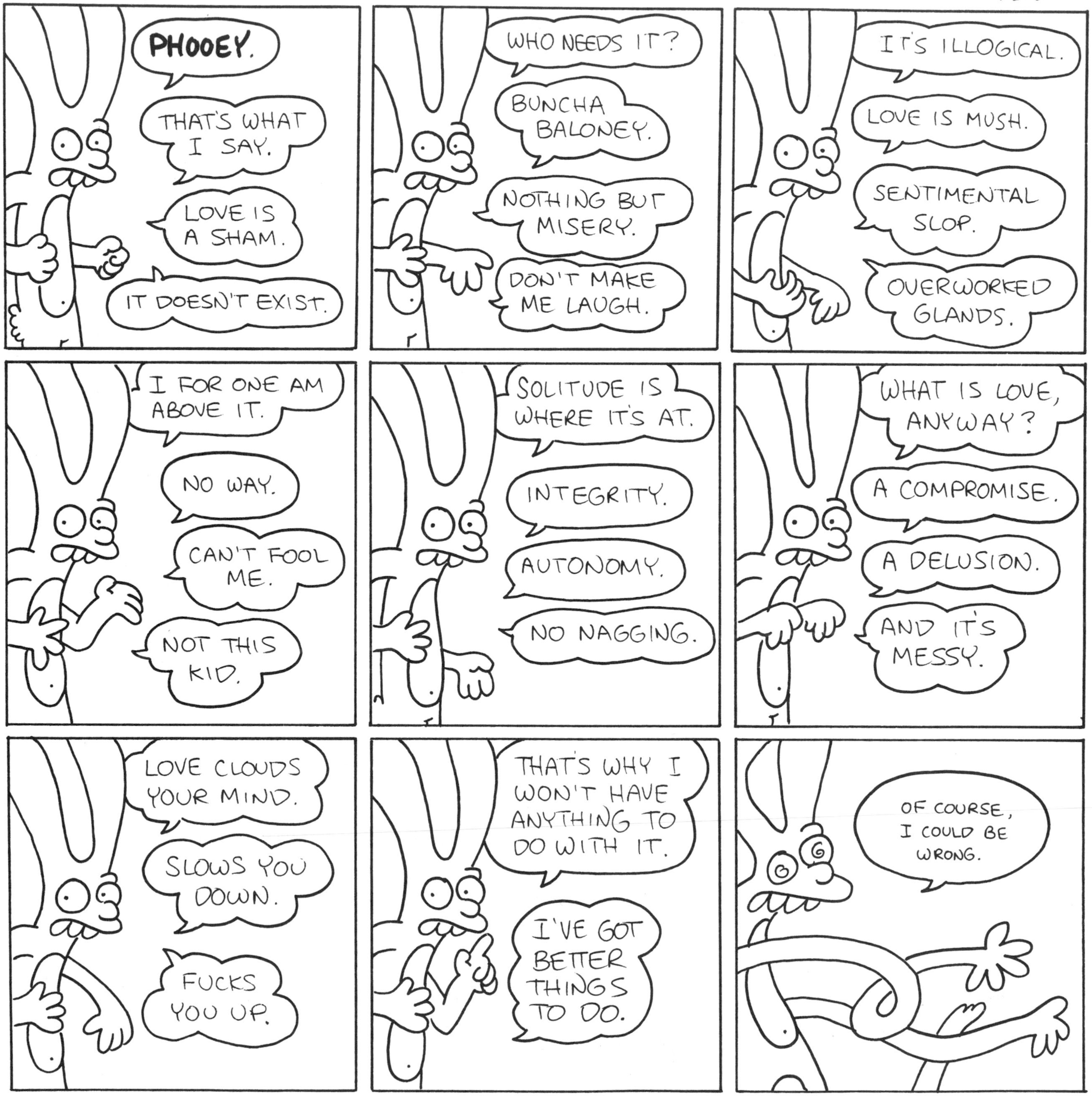
PHOOEY.
THAT'S WHAT I SAY.
LOVE IS A SHAM.
IT DOESN'T EXIST.
WHO NEEDS IT?
BUNCHA BALONEY.
NOTHING BUT MISERY.
DON'T MAKE ME LAUGH.
IT'S ILLOGICAL.
LOVE IS MUSH.
SENTIMENTAL SLOP.
OVERWORKED GLANDS.
I FOR ONE AM ABOVE IT.
NO WAY.
CAN'T FOOL ME.
NOT THIS KID.
SOLITUDE IS WHERE IT'S AT.
INTEGRITY.
AUTONOMY.
NO NAGGING.
WHAT IS LOVE, ANYWAY?
A COMPROMISE.
A DELUSION.
AND IT'S MESSY.
LOVE CLOUDS YOUR MIND.
SLOWS YOU DOWN.
FUCKS YOU UP.
THAT'S WHY I WON'T HAVE ANYTHING TO DO WITH IT.
I'VE GOT BETTER THINGS TO DO.
OF COURSE, I COULD BE WRONG.

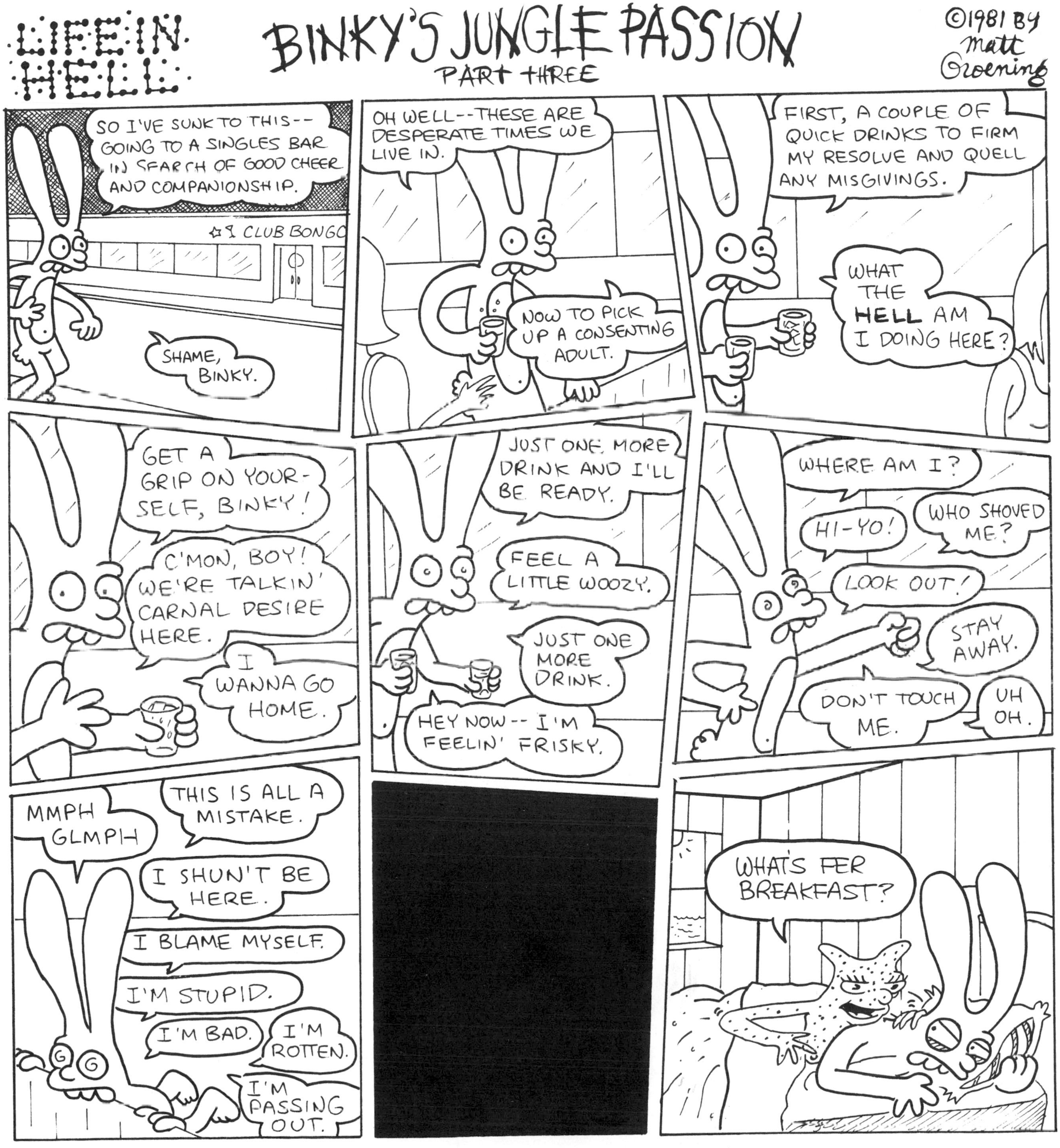
LIFE IN HELL
BINKY'S JUNGLE PASSION
PART THREE
©1981 BY Matt Groening
SO I'VE SUNK TO THIS-- GOING TO A SINGLES BAR IN SEARCH OF GOOD CHEER AND COMPANIONSHIP.
CLUB BONGO
SHAME, BINKY.
OH WELL--THESE ARE DESPERATE TIMES WE LIVE IN.
NOW TO PICK UP A CONSENTING ADULT.
FIRST, A COUPLE OF QUICK DRINKS TO FIRM MY RESOLVE AND QUELL ANY MISGIVINGS.
WHAT THE **HELL** AM I DOING HERE?
GET A GRIP ON YOURSELF, BINKY!
C'MON, BOY! WE'RE TALKIN' CARNAL DESIRE HERE.
I WANNA GO HOME.
JUST ONE MORE DRINK AND I'LL BE READY.
FEEL A LITTLE WOOZY.
JUST ONE MORE DRINK.
HEY NOW-- I'M FEELIN' FRISKY.
WHERE AM I?
HI-YO!
WHO SHOVED ME?
LOOK OUT!
STAY AWAY.
DON'T TOUCH ME.
UH OH.
MMPH GLMPH
THIS IS ALL A MISTAKE.
I SHUN'T BE HERE.
I BLAME MYSELF.
I'M STUPID.
I'M BAD.
I'M ROTTEN.
I'M PASSING OUT.
WHAT'S FER BREAKFAST?

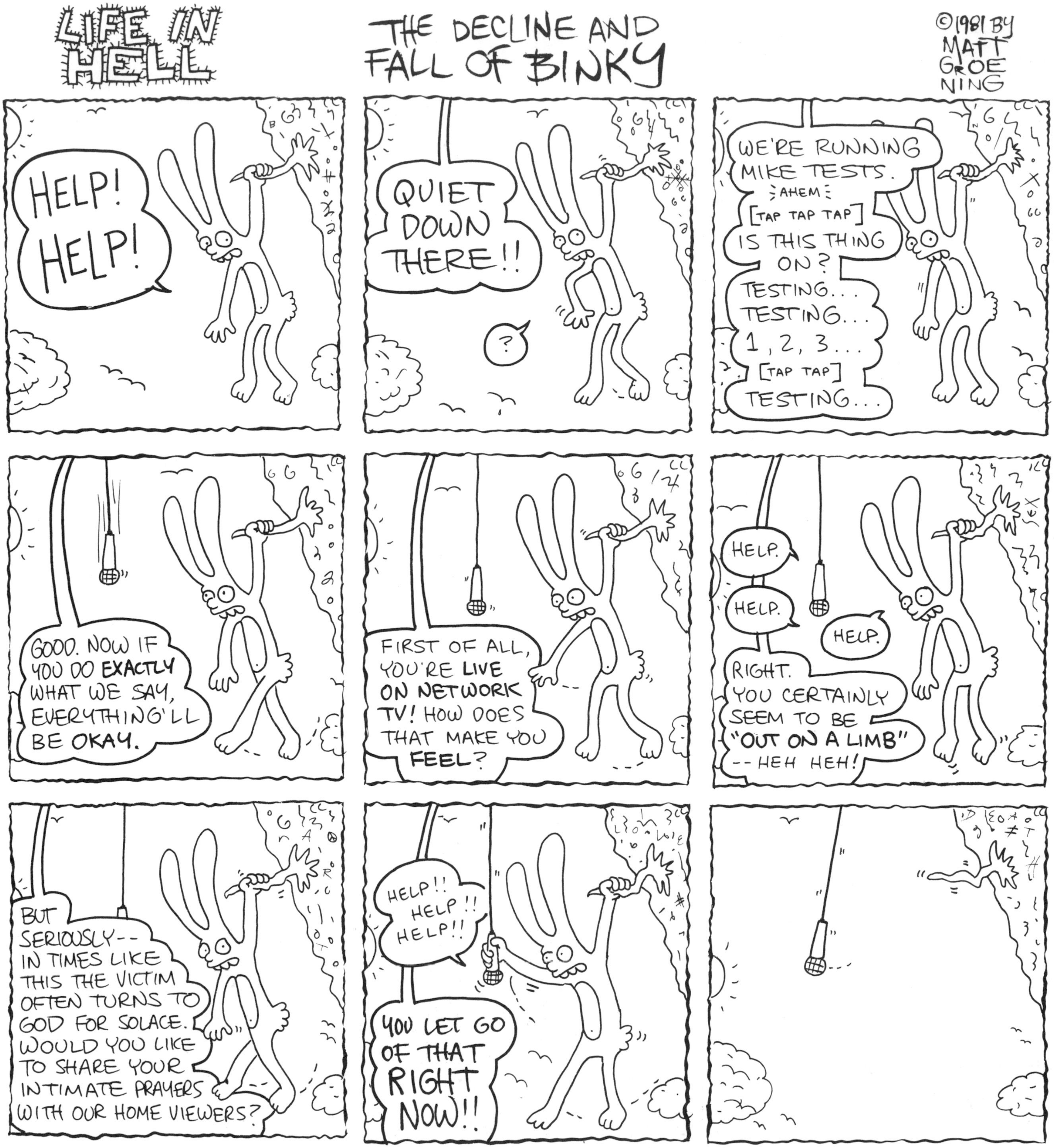
LIFE IN HELL
THE DECLINE AND FALL OF BINKY
©1981 BY MATT GROENING
HELP! HELP!
QUIET DOWN THERE!!
?
WE'RE RUNNING MIKE TESTS.
AHEM
[TAP TAP TAP]
IS THIS THING ON?
TESTING... TESTING... 1, 2, 3...
[TAP TAP]
TESTING...
GOOD. NOW IF YOU DO EXACTLY WHAT WE SAY, EVERYTHING'LL BE OKAY.
FIRST OF ALL, YOU'RE LIVE ON NETWORK TV! HOW DOES THAT MAKE YOU FEEL?
HELP.
HELP.
HELP.
RIGHT. YOU CERTAINLY SEEM TO BE "OUT ON A LIMB" --HEH HEH!
BUT SERIOUSLY-- IN TIMES LIKE THIS THE VICTIM OFTEN TURNS TO GOD FOR SOLACE. WOULD YOU LIKE TO SHARE YOUR INTIMATE PRAYERS WITH OUR HOME VIEWERS?
HELP!! HELP!! HELP!!
YOU LET GO OF THAT RIGHT NOW!!

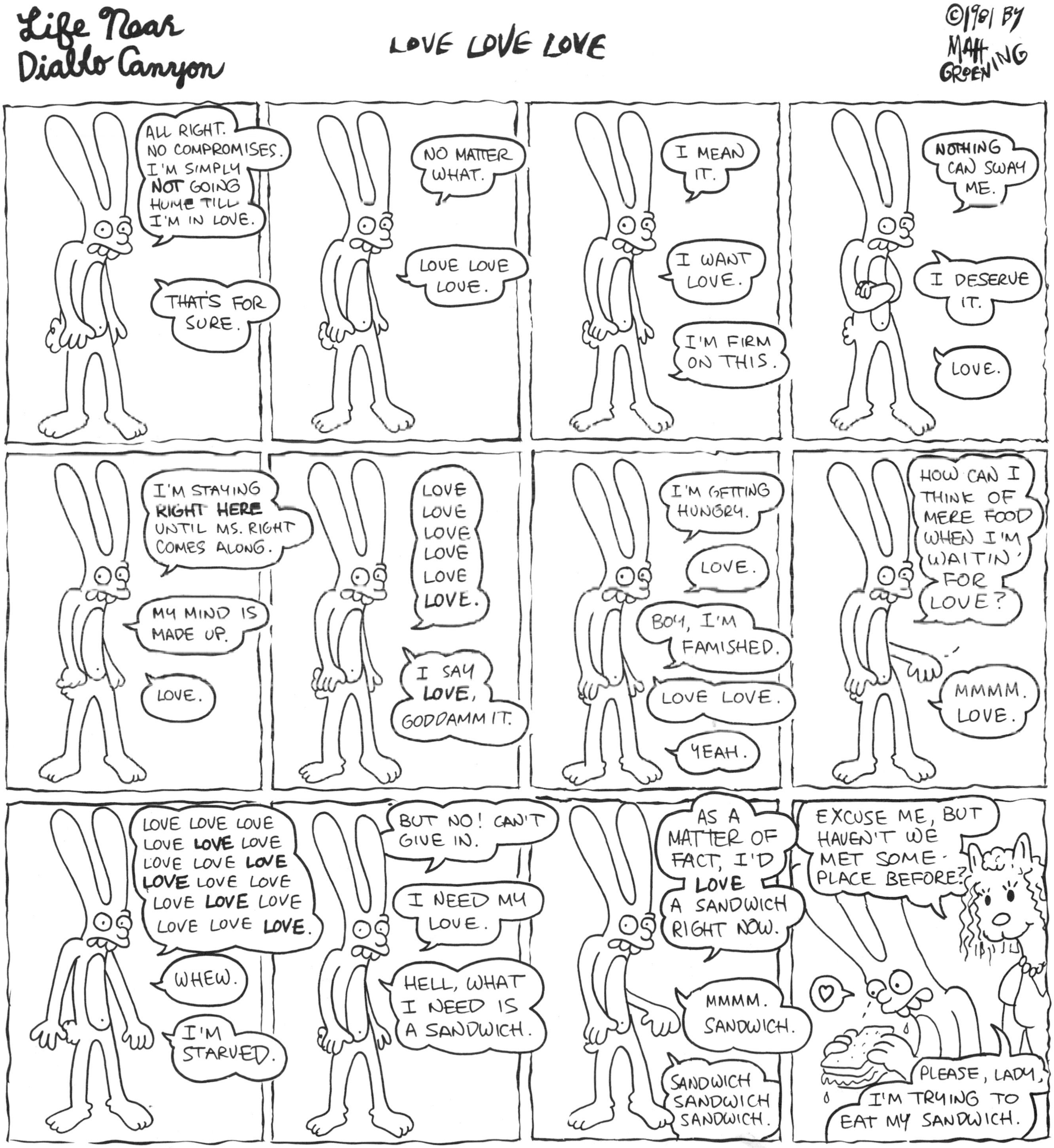
Life Near Diablo Canyon
LOVE LOVE LOVE
©1981 BY MATT GROENING
ALL RIGHT. NO COMPROMISES. I'M SIMPLY NOT GOING HOME TILL I'M IN LOVE.
THAT'S FOR SURE.
NO MATTER WHAT.
LOVE LOVE LOVE.
I MEAN IT.
I WANT LOVE.
I'M FIRM ON THIS.
NOTHING CAN SWAY ME.
I DESERVE IT.
LOVE.
I'M STAYING RIGHT HERE UNTIL MS. RIGHT COMES ALONG.
MY MIND IS MADE UP.
LOVE.
LOVE LOVE LOVE LOVE LOVE LOVE.
I SAY LOVE, GODDAMM IT.
I'M GETTING HUNGRY.
LOVE.
BOY, I'M FAMISHED.
LOVE LOVE.
YEAH.
HOW CAN I THINK OF MERE FOOD WHEN I'M WAITIN' FOR LOVE?
MMMM. LOVE.
LOVE LOVE LOVE LOVE LOVE LOVE LOVE LOVE LOVE LOVE LOVE LOVE LOVE LOVE LOVE LOVE LOVE LOVE.
WHEW.
I'M STARVED.
BUT NO! CAN'T GIVE IN.
I NEED MY LOVE.
HELL, WHAT I NEED IS A SANDWICH.
AS A MATTER OF FACT, I'D LOVE A SANDWICH RIGHT NOW.
MMMM. SANDWICH.
SANDWICH SANDWICH SANDWICH.
EXCUSE ME, BUT HAVEN'T WE MET SOME-PLACE BEFORE?
PLEASE, LADY, I'M TRYING TO EAT MY SANDWICH.

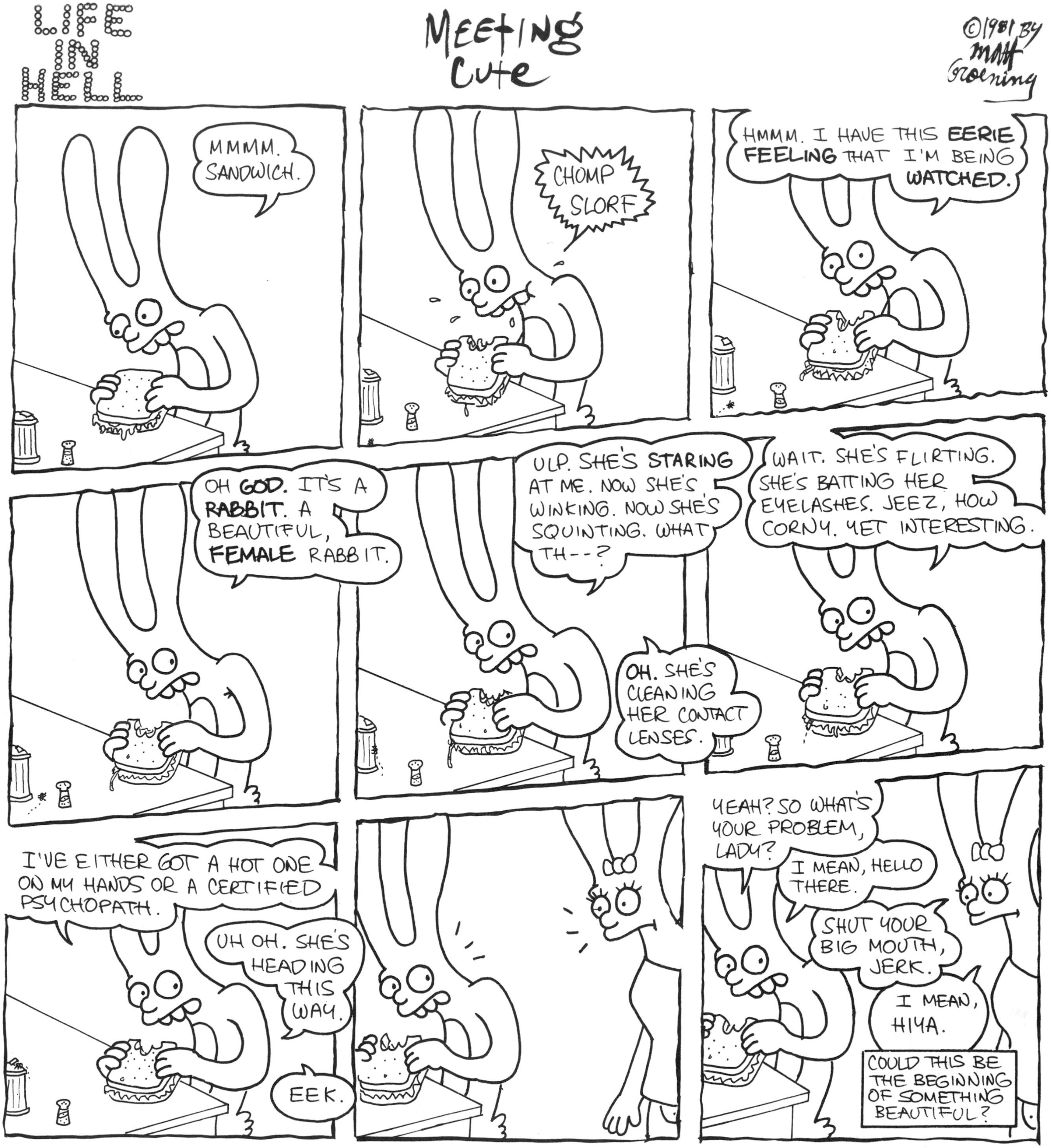
LIFE IN HELL
Meeting Cute
©1981 BY MATT GROENING
MMMM. SANDWICH.
CHOMP SLORF
HMMM. I HAVE THIS EERIE FEELING THAT I'M BEING WATCHED.
OH GOD. IT'S A RABBIT. A BEAUTIFUL, FEMALE RABBIT.
ULP. SHE'S STARING AT ME. NOW SHE'S WINKING. NOW SHE'S SQUINTING. WHAT TH--?
OH. SHE'S CLEANING HER CONTACT LENSES.
WAIT. SHE'S FLIRTING. SHE'S BATTING HER EYELASHES. JEEZ, HOW CORNY. YET INTERESTING.
I'VE EITHER GOT A HOT ONE ON MY HANDS OR A CERTIFIED PSYCHOPATH.
UH OH. SHE'S HEADING THIS WAY.
EEK.
YEAH? SO WHAT'S YOUR PROBLEM, LADY?
I MEAN, HELLO THERE.
SHUT YOUR BIG MOUTH, JERK.
I MEAN, HIYA.
COULD THIS BE THE BEGINNING OF SOMETHING BEAUTIFUL?

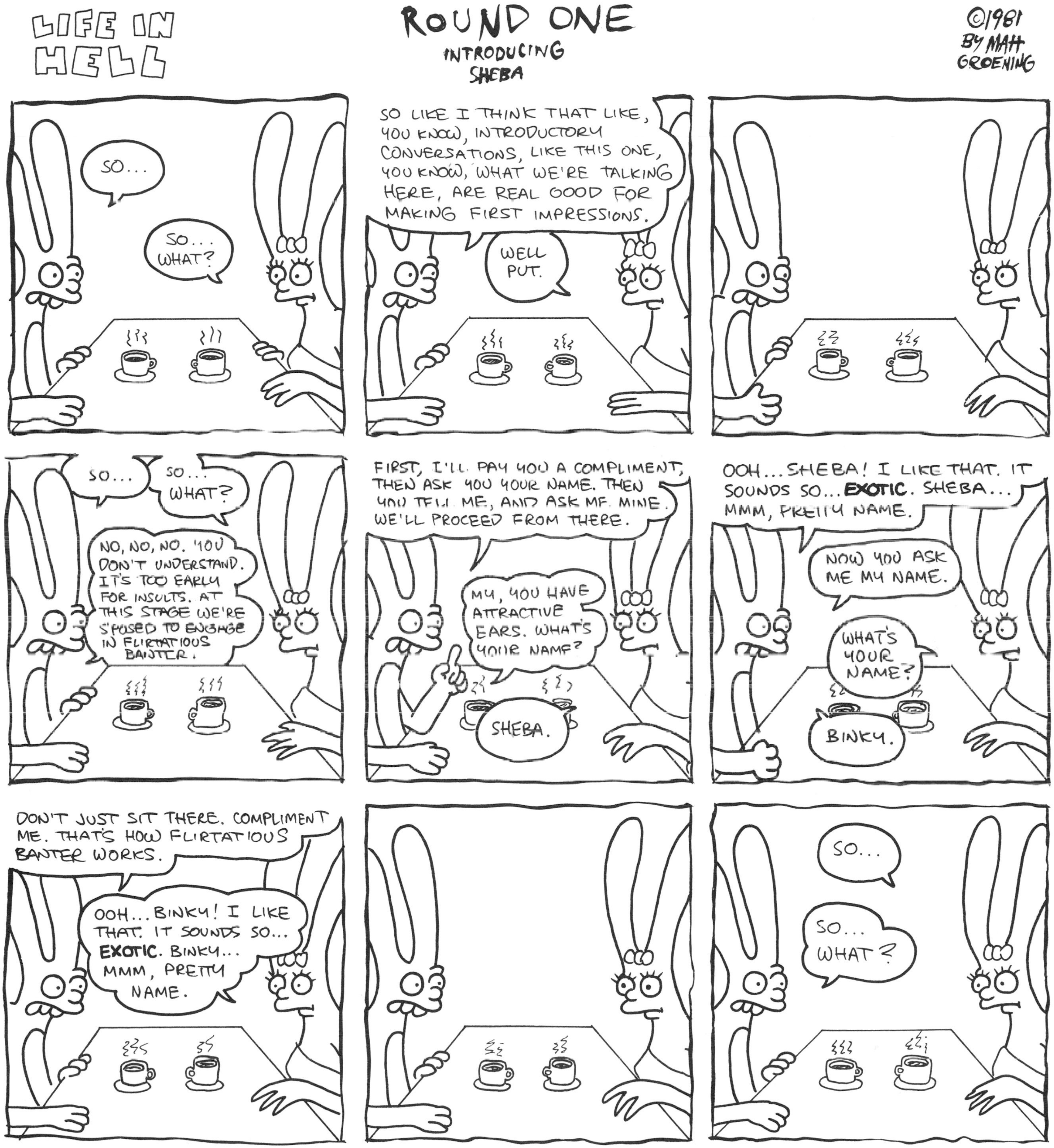
LIFE IN HELL
ROUND ONE
INTRODUCING SHEBA
©1981 BY MATT GROENING
SO...
SO... WHAT?
SO LIKE I THINK THAT LIKE, YOU KNOW, INTRODUCTORY CONVERSATIONS, LIKE THIS ONE, YOU KNOW, WHAT WE'RE TALKING HERE, ARE REAL GOOD FOR MAKING FIRST IMPRESSIONS.
WELL PUT.
SO...
SO... WHAT?
NO, NO, NO. YOU DON'T UNDERSTAND. IT'S TOO EARLY FOR INSULTS. AT THIS STAGE WE'RE S'POSED TO ENGAGE IN FLIRTATIOUS BANTER.
FIRST, I'LL PAY YOU A COMPLIMENT, THEN ASK YOU YOUR NAME. THEN YOU TELL ME, AND ASK ME MINE. WE'LL PROCEED FROM THERE.
MY, YOU HAVE ATTRACTIVE EARS. WHAT'S YOUR NAME?
SHEBA.
OOH... SHEBA! I LIKE THAT. IT SOUNDS SO... EXOTIC. SHEBA... MMM, PRETTY NAME.
NOW YOU ASK ME MY NAME.
WHAT'S YOUR NAME?
BINKY.
DON'T JUST SIT THERE. COMPLIMENT ME. THAT'S HOW FLIRTATIOUS BANTER WORKS.
OOH... BINKY! I LIKE THAT. IT SOUNDS SO... EXOTIC. BINKY... MMM, PRETTY NAME.
SO...
SO... WHAT?

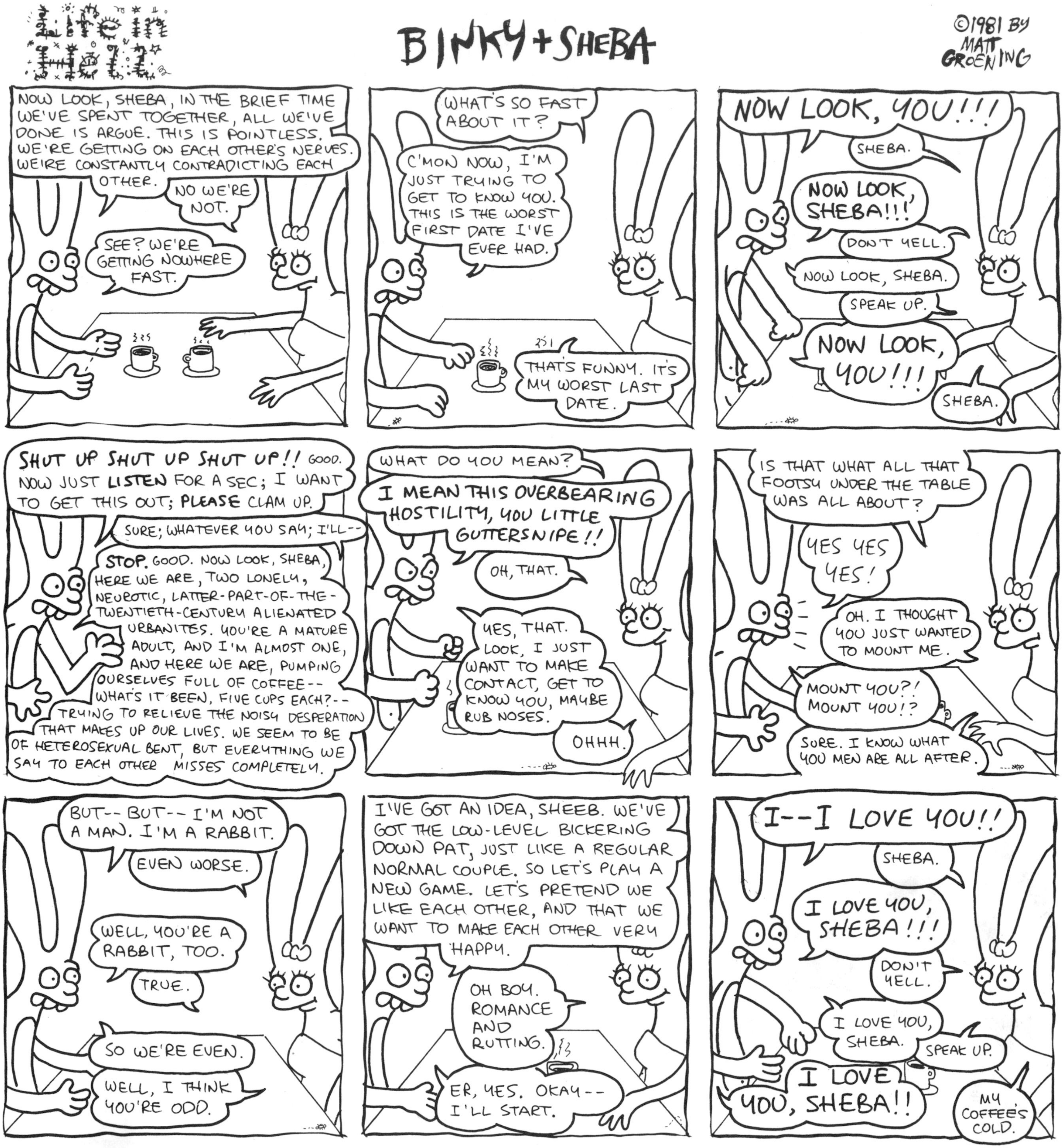
LIFE IN HELL
BINKY + SHEBA
©1981 BY MATT GROENING
NOW LOOK, SHEBA, IN THE BRIEF TIME WE'VE SPENT TOGETHER, ALL WE'VE DONE IS ARGUE. THIS IS POINTLESS. WE'RE GETTING ON EACH OTHER'S NERVES. WE'RE CONSTANTLY CONTRADICTING EACH OTHER.
NO WE'RE NOT.
SEE? WE'RE GETTING NOWHERE FAST.
WHAT'S SO FAST ABOUT IT?
C'MON NOW, I'M JUST TRYING TO GET TO KNOW YOU. THIS IS THE WORST FIRST DATE I'VE EVER HAD.
THAT'S FUNNY. IT'S MY WORST LAST DATE.
NOW LOOK, YOU!!!
SHEBA.
NOW LOOK, SHEBA!!!
DON'T YELL.
NOW LOOK, SHEBA.
SPEAK UP.
NOW LOOK, YOU!!!
SHEBA.
SHUT UP SHUT UP SHUT UP!! GOOD. NOW JUST LISTEN FOR A SEC; I WANT TO GET THIS OUT; PLEASE CLAM UP.
SURE; WHATEVER YOU SAY; I'LL--
STOP. GOOD. NOW LOOK, SHEBA, HERE WE ARE, TWO LONELY, NEUROTIC, LATTER-PART-OF-THE-TWENTIETH-CENTURY ALIENATED URBANITES. YOU'RE A MATURE ADULT, AND I'M ALMOST ONE, AND HERE WE ARE, PUMPING OURSELVES FULL OF COFFEE--WHAT'S IT BEEN, FIVE CUPS EACH?--TRYING TO RELIEVE THE NOISY DESPERATION THAT MAKES UP OUR LIVES. WE SEEM TO BE OF HETEROSEXUAL BENT, BUT EVERYTHING WE SAY TO EACH OTHER MISSES COMPLETELY.
WHAT DO YOU MEAN?
I MEAN THIS OVERBEARING HOSTILITY, YOU LITTLE GUTTERSNIPE!!
OH, THAT.
YES, THAT. LOOK, I JUST WANT TO MAKE CONTACT, GET TO KNOW YOU, MAYBE RUB NOSES.
OHHH.
IS THAT WHAT ALL THAT FOOTSY UNDER THE TABLE WAS ALL ABOUT?
YES YES YES!
OH. I THOUGHT YOU JUST WANTED TO MOUNT ME.
MOUNT YOU?! MOUNT YOU!?
SURE. I KNOW WHAT YOU MEN ARE ALL AFTER.
BUT-- BUT-- I'M NOT A MAN. I'M A RABBIT.
EVEN WORSE.
WELL, YOU'RE A RABBIT, TOO.
TRUE.
SO WE'RE EVEN.
WELL, I THINK YOU'RE ODD.
I'VE GOT AN IDEA, SHEEB. WE'VE GOT THE LOW-LEVEL BICKERING DOWN PAT, JUST LIKE A REGULAR NORMAL COUPLE. SO LET'S PLAY A NEW GAME. LET'S PRETEND WE LIKE EACH OTHER, AND THAT WE WANT TO MAKE EACH OTHER VERY HAPPY.
OH BOY. ROMANCE AND RUTTING.
ER, YES. OKAY-- I'LL START.
I--I LOVE YOU!!
SHEBA.
I LOVE YOU, SHEBA!!!
DON'T YELL.
I LOVE YOU, SHEBA.
SPEAK UP.
I LOVE YOU, SHEBA!!
MY COFFEE'S COLD.

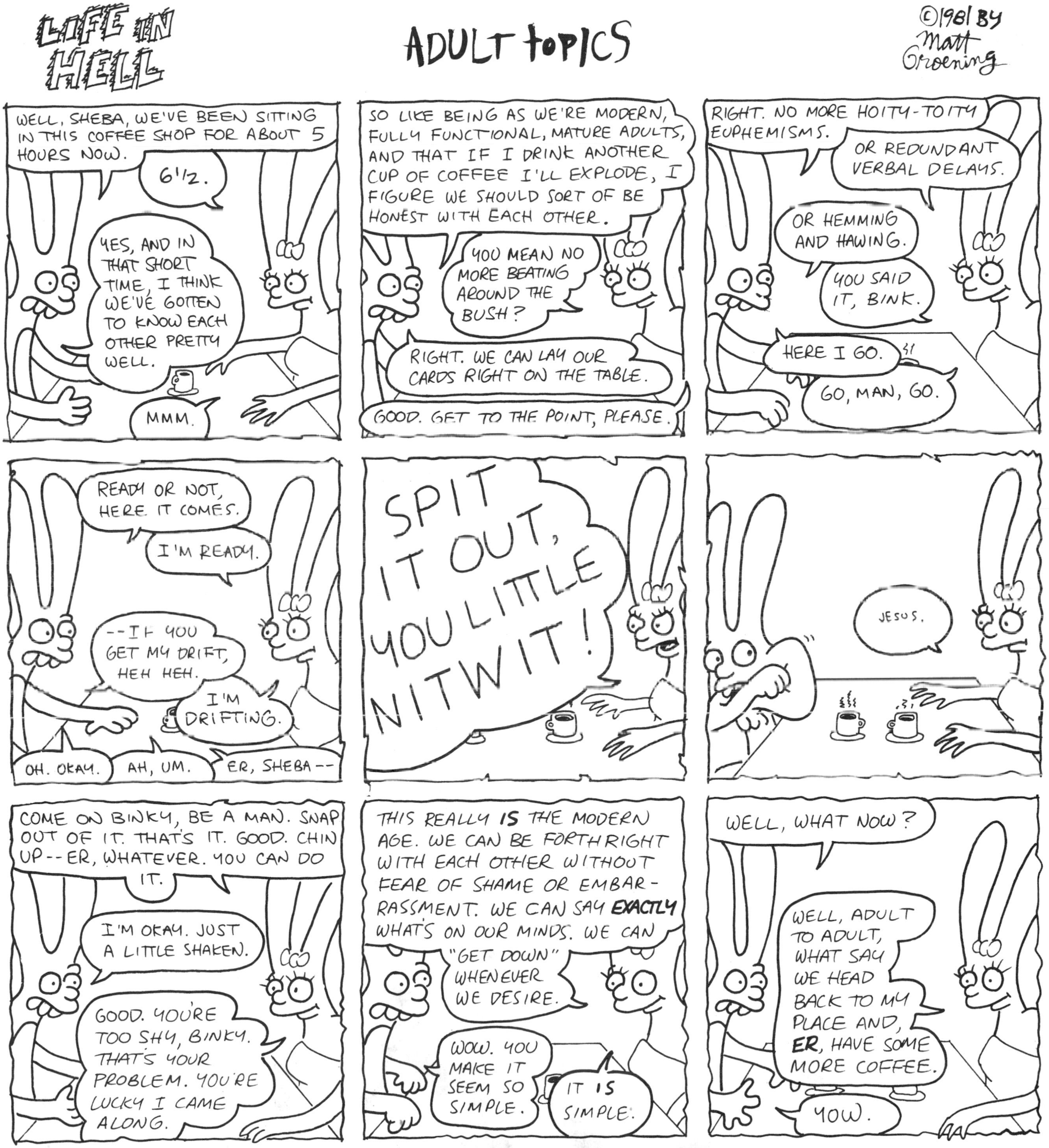
LIFE IN HELL
ADULT TOPICS
©1981 BY Matt Groening
WELL, SHEBA, WE'VE BEEN SITTING IN THIS COFFEE SHOP FOR ABOUT 5 HOURS NOW.
6½.
YES, AND IN THAT SHORT TIME, I THINK WE'VE GOTTEN TO KNOW EACH OTHER PRETTY WELL.
MMM.
SO LIKE BEING AS WE'RE MODERN, FULLY FUNCTIONAL, MATURE ADULTS, AND THAT IF I DRINK ANOTHER CUP OF COFFEE I'LL EXPLODE, I FIGURE WE SHOULD SORT OF BE HONEST WITH EACH OTHER.
YOU MEAN NO MORE BEATING AROUND THE BUSH?
RIGHT. WE CAN LAY OUR CARDS RIGHT ON THE TABLE.
GOOD. GET TO THE POINT, PLEASE.
RIGHT. NO MORE HOITY-TOITY EUPHEMISMS.
OR REDUNDANT VERBAL DELAYS.
OR HEMMING AND HAWING.
YOU SAID IT, BINK.
HERE I GO.
GO, MAN, GO.
READY OR NOT, HERE IT COMES.
I'M READY.
--IF YOU GET MY DRIFT, HEH HEH.
I'M DRIFTING.
OH. OKAY.
AH, UM.
ER, SHEBA--
SPIT IT OUT, YOU LITTLE NITWIT!
JESUS.
COME ON BINKY, BE A MAN. SNAP OUT OF IT. THAT'S IT. GOOD. CHIN UP--ER, WHATEVER. YOU CAN DO IT.
I'M OKAY. JUST A LITTLE SHAKEN.
GOOD. YOU'RE TOO SHY, BINKY. THAT'S YOUR PROBLEM. YOU'RE LUCKY I CAME ALONG.
THIS REALLY IS THE MODERN AGE. WE CAN BE FORTHRIGHT WITH EACH OTHER WITHOUT FEAR OF SHAME OR EMBARRASSMENT. WE CAN SAY EXACTLY WHAT'S ON OUR MINDS. WE CAN "GET DOWN" WHENEVER WE DESIRE.
WOW. YOU MAKE IT SEEM SO SIMPLE.
IT IS SIMPLE.
WELL, WHAT NOW?
WELL, ADULT TO ADULT, WHAT SAY WE HEAD BACK TO MY PLACE AND, ER, HAVE SOME MORE COFFEE.
YOW.

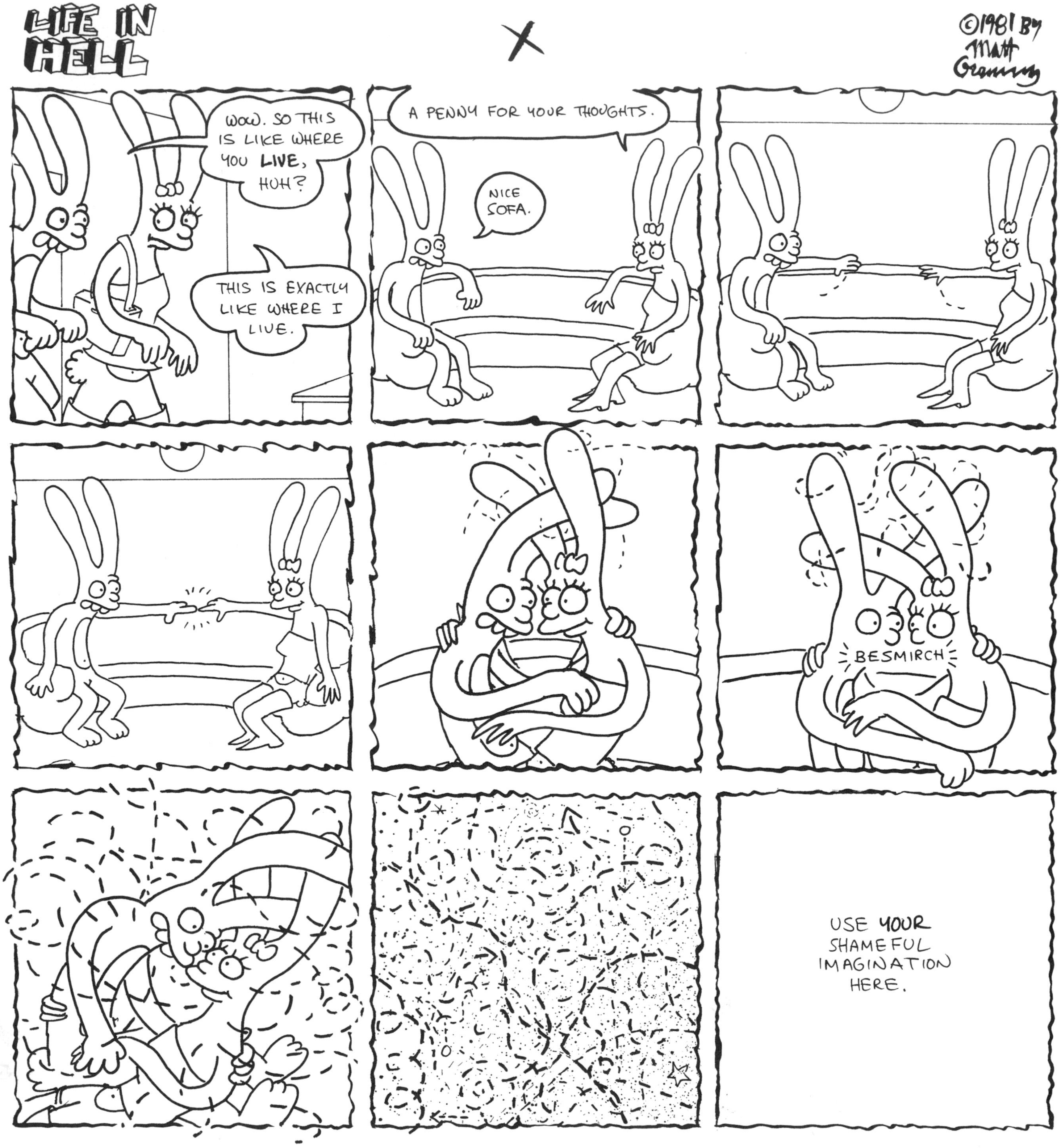
LIFE IN HELL
X
©1981 By Matt Groening
WOW. SO THIS IS LIKE WHERE YOU **LIVE**, HUH?
THIS IS EXACTLY LIKE WHERE I LIVE.
A PENNY FOR YOUR THOUGHTS.
NICE SOFA.
BESMIRCH
USE **YOUR** SHAMEFUL IMAGINATION HERE.

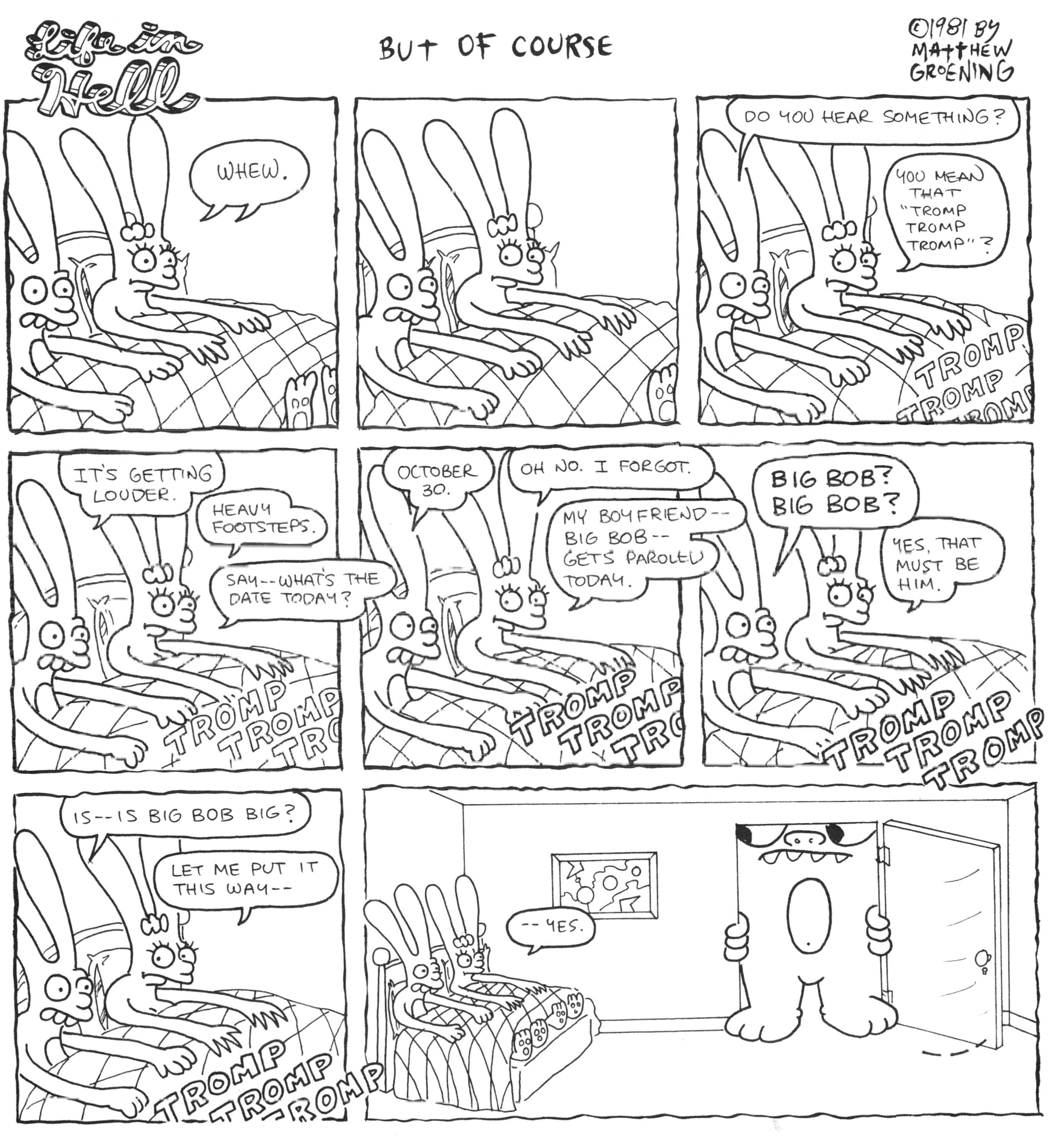
Life in Hell
BUT OF COURSE
©1981 BY MATTHEW GROENING
WHEW.
DO YOU HEAR SOMETHING?
YOU MEAN THAT "TROMP TROMP TROMP"?
TROMP TROMP TROMP
IT'S GETTING LOUDER.
HEAVY FOOTSTEPS.
SAY--WHAT'S THE DATE TODAY?
TROMP TROMP TRO
OCTOBER 30.
OH NO. I FORGOT.
MY BOYFRIEND--BIG BOB--GETS PAROLED TODAY.
TROMP TROMP TRO
BIG BOB? BIG BOB?
YES, THAT MUST BE HIM.
TROMP TROMP TROMP
IS--IS BIG BOB BIG?
LET ME PUT IT THIS WAY--
TROMP TROMP TROMP
--YES.

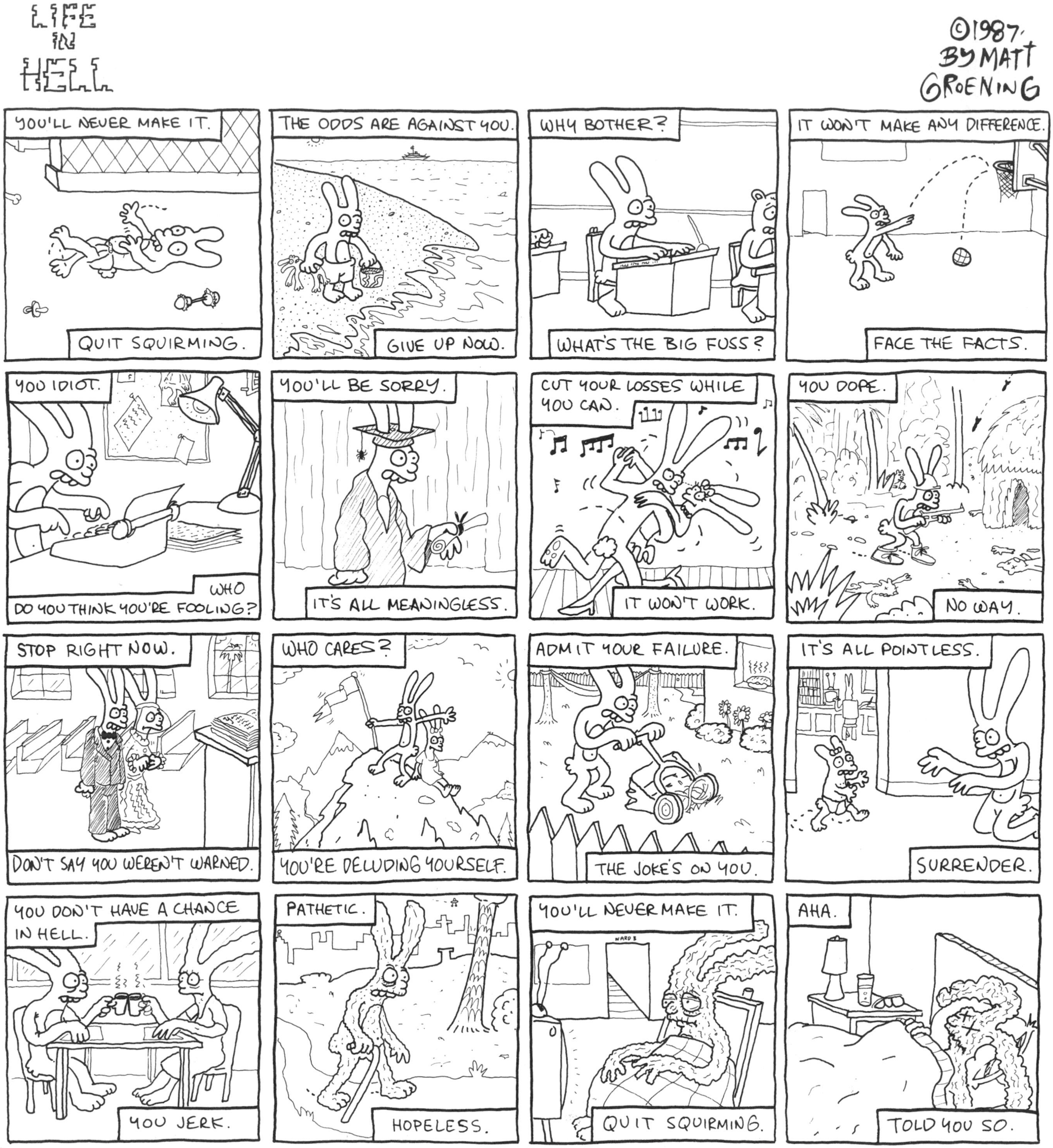
LIFE IN HELL
©1987 BY MATT GROENING
YOU'LL NEVER MAKE IT.
QUIT SQUIRMING.
THE ODDS ARE AGAINST YOU.
GIVE UP NOW.
WHY BOTHER?
WHAT'S THE BIG FUSS?
IT WON'T MAKE ANY DIFFERENCE.
FACE THE FACTS.
YOU IDIOT.
WHO DO YOU THINK YOU'RE FOOLING?
YOU'LL BE SORRY.
IT'S ALL MEANINGLESS.
CUT YOUR LOSSES WHILE YOU CAN.
IT WON'T WORK.
YOU DOPE.
NO WAY.
STOP RIGHT NOW.
DON'T SAY YOU WEREN'T WARNED.
WHO CARES?
YOU'RE DELUDING YOURSELF.
ADMIT YOUR FAILURE.
THE JOKE'S ON YOU.
IT'S ALL POINTLESS.
SURRENDER.
YOU DON'T HAVE A CHANCE IN HELL.
YOU JERK.
PATHETIC.
HOPELESS.
YOU'LL NEVER MAKE IT.
QUIT SQUIRMING.
AHA.
TOLD YOU SO.

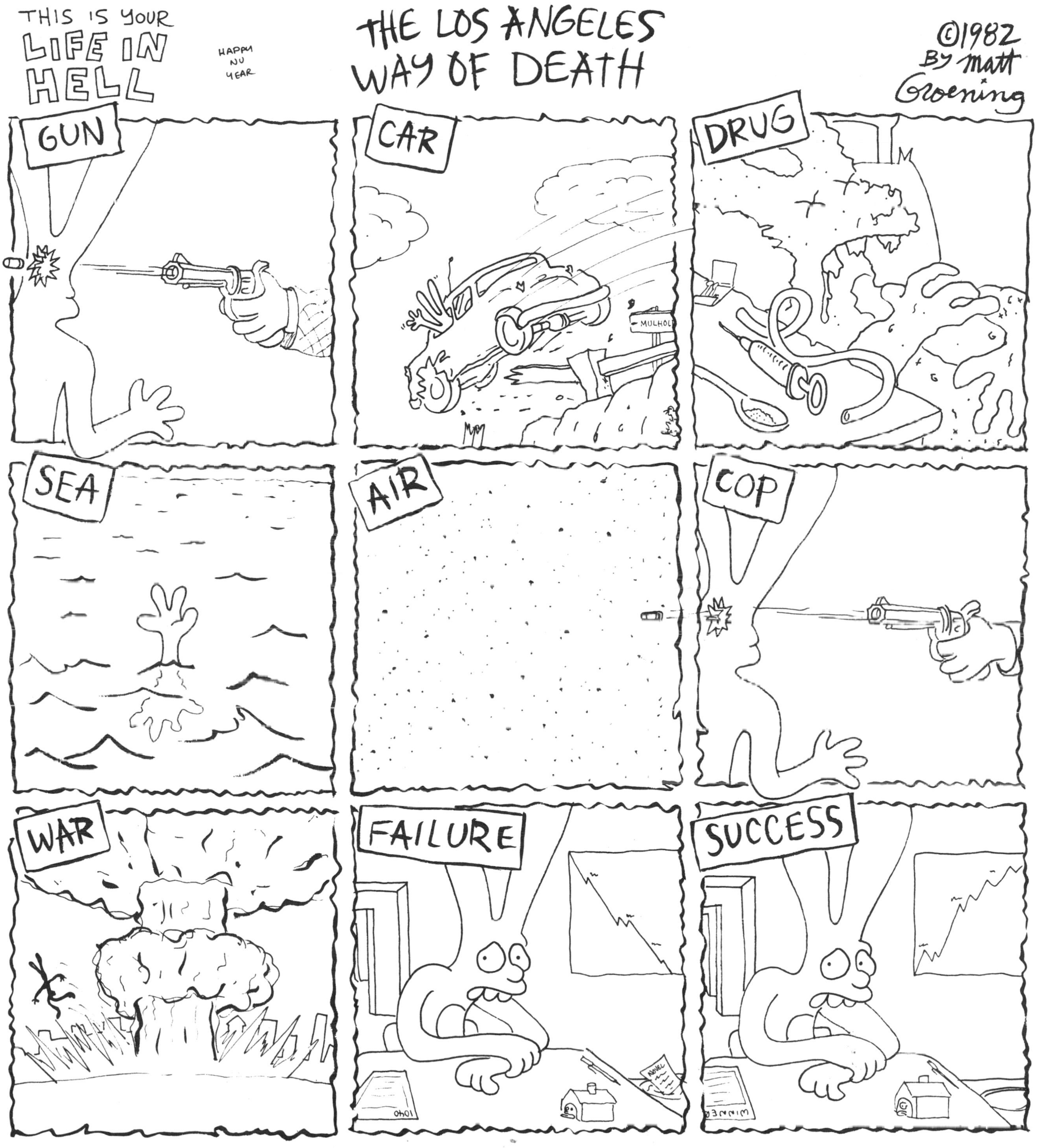
THIS IS YOUR LIFE IN HELL
HAPPY NU YEAR
THE LOS ANGELES WAY OF DEATH
©1982 BY Matt Groening
GUN
CAR
MULHOL
DRUG
SEA
AIR
COP
WAR
FAILURE
SUCCESS

TITLE: LIFE IN HELL

HOW TO KILL 8 HOURS A DAY AND STILL KEEP YOUR JOB

AUTHOR: MATT GROENING ©1982*

*IF YOU XEROX THIS AND STICK IT ON THE OFFICE BULLETIN BOARD YOU'RE IN BIG TROUBLE.

IT AIN'T THAT EASY, BUT IF YOU'VE GOT AN AVERAGE MIND AND A VAGUE, ILL-DEFINED SENSE OF RESENTMENT, YOU SHOULD BE ABLE TO FOLLOW THIS EASY GUIDE AND GET AWAY WITH MURDER.

THINGS YOU CAN DO W/O MOVING A MUSCLE

WATCH THE CLOCK.
HUM TUNELESSLY.
DAYDREAM.
STARE INTO SPACE.
BLANK OUT.
STEW IN YOUR OWN JUICES.
TAKE A BREATHER.
SIGH.

MEMOS:

WRITE 'EM.
READ 'EM.
IGNORE 'EM.

3 QUESTIONS TO ASK YOURSELF

- HAVE I CHECKED MY WORK?
- HAVE I DOUBLE-CHECKED MY WORK?
- HAVE I TRIPLE-CHECKED MY WORK?

NEVER

JUST WANDER AROUND.
ALWAYS HAVE A PIECE OF PAPER IN YOUR HAND AND LOOK LIKE YOU'RE GOING SOMEWHERE.

HANDY PHRASES

"GOOOOOOD MORNING."
"WHAT A DAY!"
"OHH, MY BACK."
"HAVE A GOOD ONE."

MINIMUM DAILY REQUIREMENTS

☐ A DESK SITUATED SO YOU CAN ESCAPE SCRUTINY.
☐ A WINDOW TO STARE OUT OF.
☐ A GOOD ACTING ABILITY.

1983
I ♥ TO SHIRK

PETTY BUT ODDLY SATISFYING OFFICE PRANKS

PUT ALL CALLERS ON HOLD FOREVER.
PRESS ALL THE BUTTONS IN THE ELEVATOR.
BORROW PENS AND NEVER RETURN THEM.

IT'S ALWAYS TIME FOR A COFFEE BREAK!

STEPS!!!

CHECK TO SEE IF THERE'S ANY COFFEE BREWING.

MR. KOFFEEMEISTER

RETURN TO DESK AND GET CUP. RINSE OUT CUP. POUR COFFEE. BLOW ON IT. SIP SLOWLY.

BE CREATIVE!

BECOMES THIS
PAPER CLIP
MODERN MINISCULPTURE

WHAT TO HAVE WITH YOUR COFFEE

☐ NONDAIRY CREME POWDER
☐ ARTIFICIAL SWEETENER
☐ DONUT
☐ ANOTHER DONUT-- WHY THE HELL NOT?

HANDY HINTS! E-Z & FUN!!

✓CLIP FINGERNAILS.
✓PAINT FINGERNAILS.
✓BITE FINGERNAILS.
✓SNIFF AT AIR.
✓MEMORIZE CALORIE CHART.
✓UNWRAP AND CHEW GUM.
✓SWIVEL HEAD ON NECK.

COFFEE-BREAK PROJECTS

BORED?

WHY NOT:
- XEROX YOUR HAND?
- THINK ABOUT YESTERYEAR?
- START VICIOUS RUMORS ABOUT A CO-WORKER?

→ WATCH GREASY FILM AT SURFACE OF COFFEE SWIRL AROUND.
MAKE WEIRD PATTERNS IN STYROFOAM CUP WITH THUMBNAIL.

FOR ADVANCED WORKERS ONLY:
HUNT AND KILL PESKY FLIES.
MAKE AND SAIL PAPER AIRPLANES.
KISS AND GROPE A CO-WORKER.

FANTASIZE ABOUT HAVING SEX WITH EACH PERSON WHO WALKS THROUGH THE DOOR.

UH OH! HERE COMES TROUBLE!

WHEN YOU GET CAUGHT:	YOU SAY:
SNOOPING	"I'M LOOKING FOR AN ERASER."
SLEEPING	"I'VE GOT IT!! A GREAT NEW IDEA FOR-- [THINK FAST]."
SHIRKING	"I THOUGHT I WAS S'POSED TO BE DOING THIS."

FOR A CHANGE OF PACE, ORGANIZE FREQUENT LITTLE OFFICE BIRTHDAY PARTIES!!

MAKE SURE EVERYONE ELSE IS JUST AS SLOW AS YOU ARE. A CONSISTENT WE'RE-ALL-IN-THIS-TOGETHER ATTITUDE CAN INSPIRE YOU ALL TO DEPTHS OF SLOTH AND INEFFICIENCY YOU NEVER KNEW EXISTED. IT'S EASY!!

MAKE YOUR OWN OFFICE TOYS

WITH PUSHPINS AND AN ERASER, YOU CAN MAKE A LITTLE PIG.

DON'T FORGET TO DOODLE!!!

SMILE!!!

THE KEY TO SUCCESS

RESTROOM

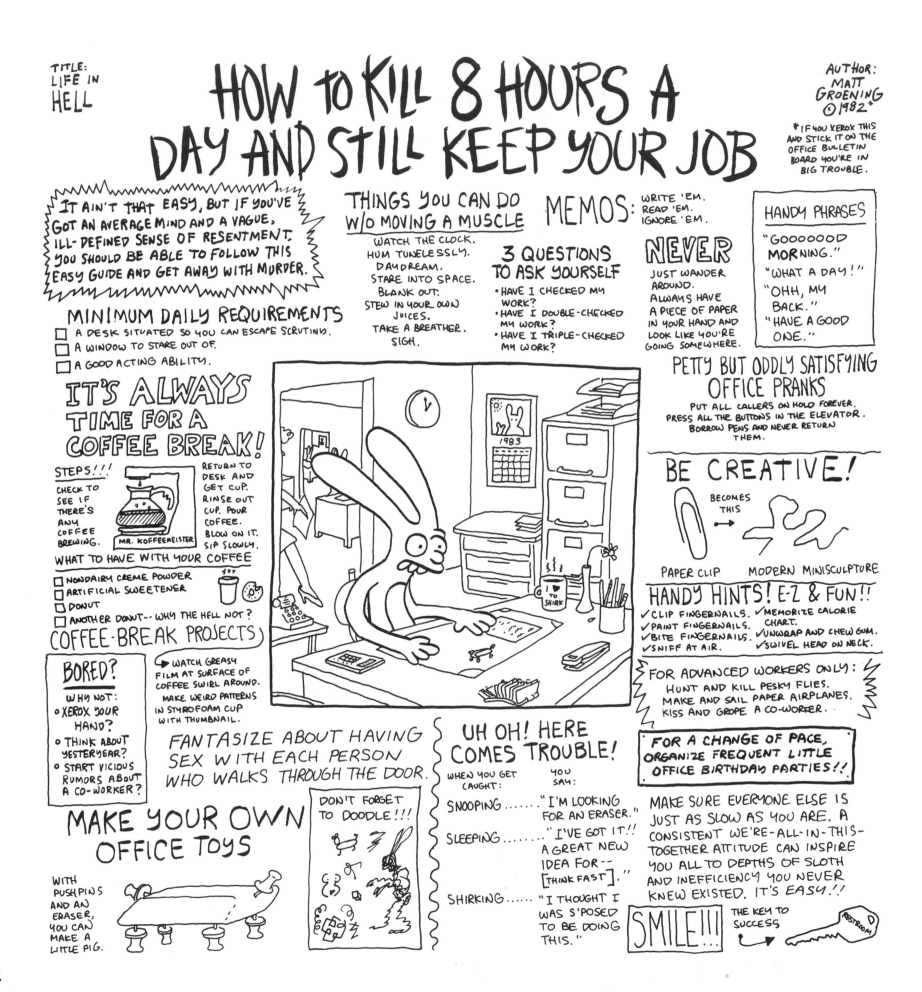

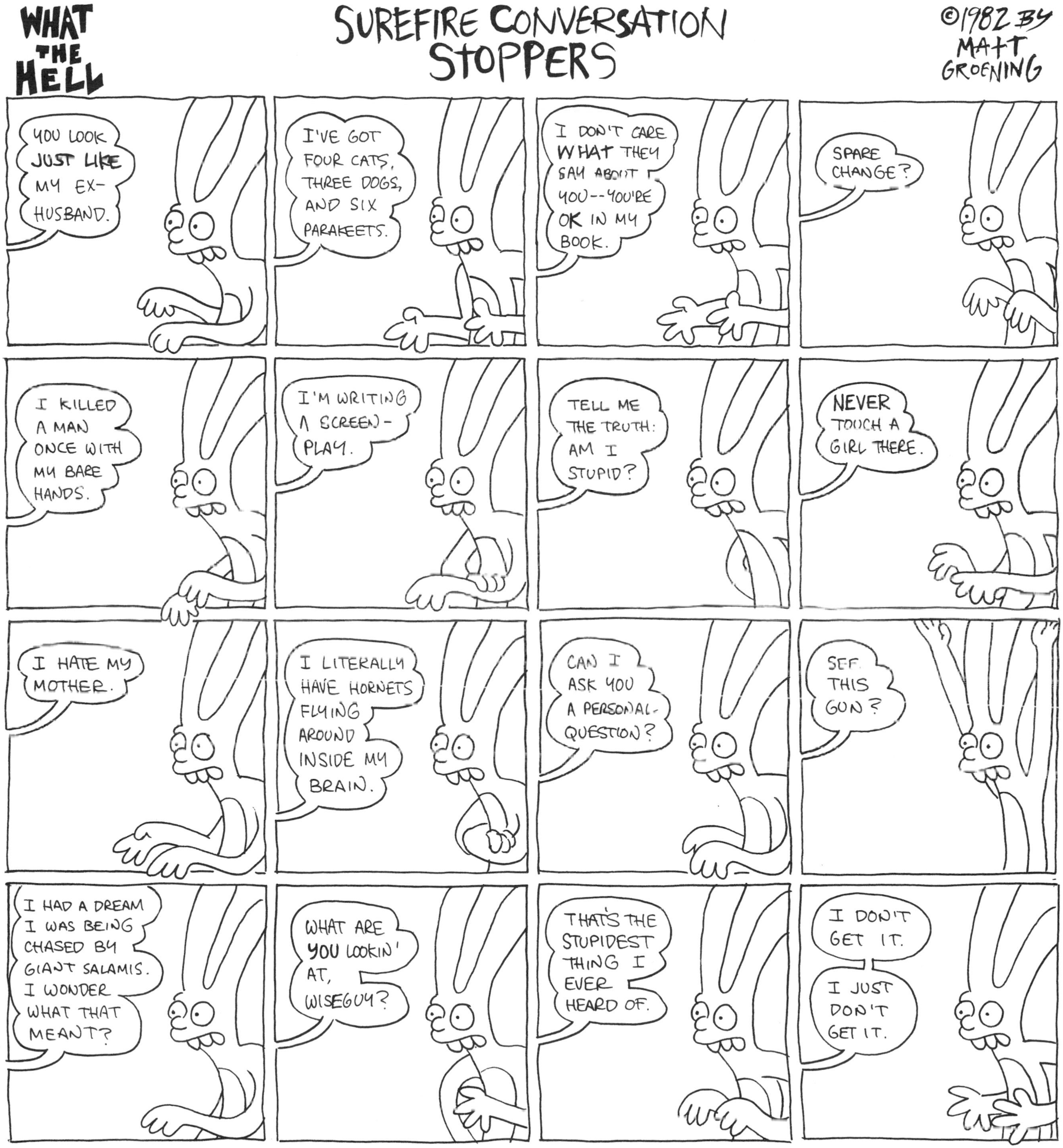
WHAT THE HELL
SUREFIRE CONVERSATION STOPPERS
©1982 BY MATT GROENING
YOU LOOK JUST LIKE MY EX-HUSBAND.
I'VE GOT FOUR CATS, THREE DOGS, AND SIX PARAKEETS.
I DON'T CARE WHAT THEY SAY ABOUT YOU--YOU'RE OK IN MY BOOK.
SPARE CHANGE?
I KILLED A MAN ONCE WITH MY BARE HANDS.
I'M WRITING A SCREEN-PLAY.
TELL ME THE TRUTH: AM I STUPID?
NEVER TOUCH A GIRL THERE.
I HATE MY MOTHER.
I LITERALLY HAVE HORNETS FLYING AROUND INSIDE MY BRAIN.
CAN I ASK YOU A PERSONAL QUESTION?
SEE THIS GUN?
I HAD A DREAM I WAS BEING CHASED BY GIANT SALAMIS. I WONDER WHAT THAT MEANT?
WHAT ARE YOU LOOKIN' AT, WISEGUY?
THAT'S THE STUPIDEST THING I EVER HEARD OF.
I DON'T GET IT.
I JUST DON'T GET IT.

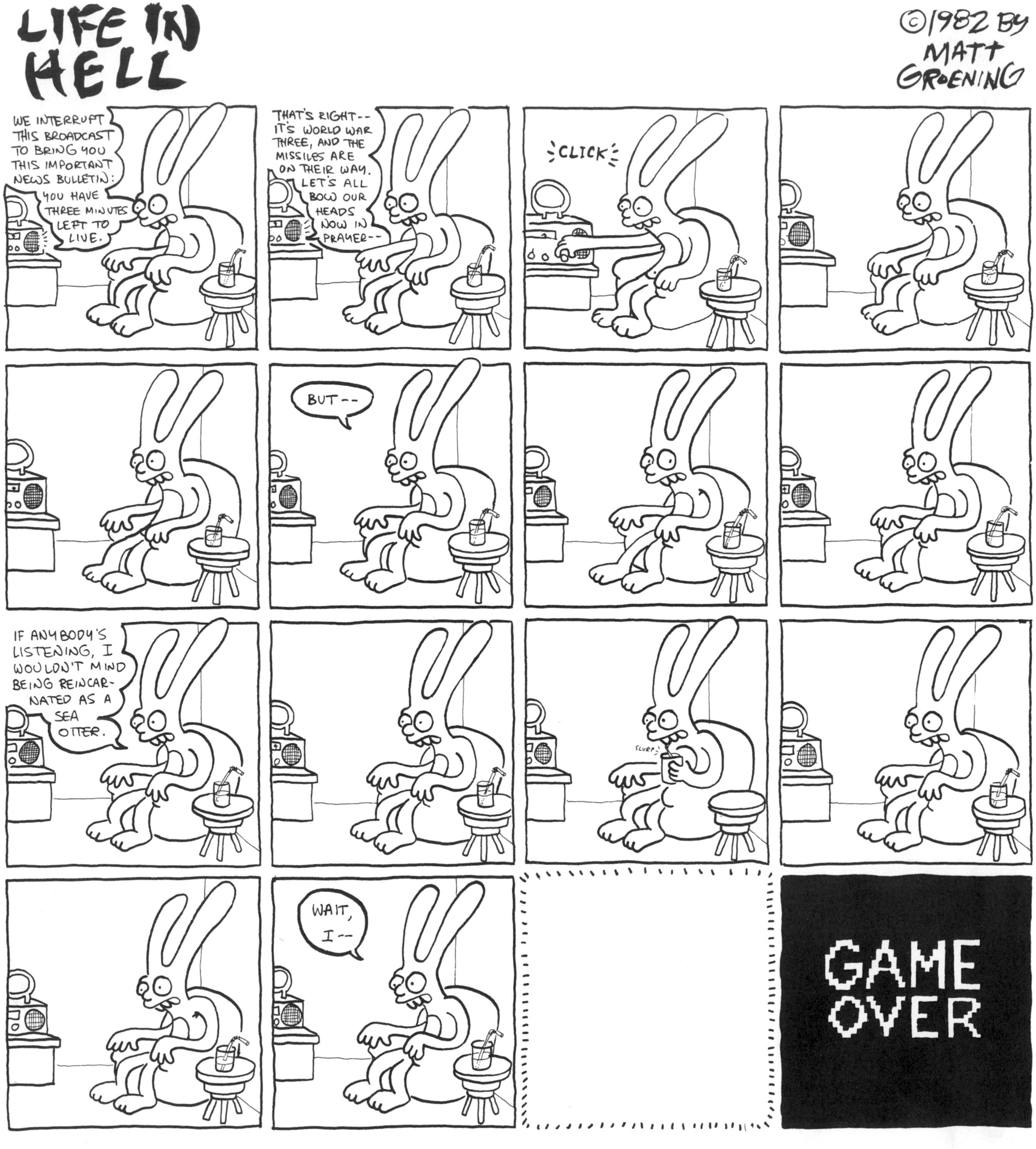
LIFE IN HELL
©1982 BY MATT GROENING
WE INTERRUPT THIS BROADCAST TO BRING YOU THIS IMPORTANT NEWS BULLETIN:
YOU HAVE THREE MINUTES LEFT TO LIVE.
THAT'S RIGHT-- IT'S WORLD WAR THREE, AND THE MISSILES ARE ON THEIR WAY.
LET'S ALL BOW OUR HEADS NOW IN PRAYER--
CLICK
BUT--
IF ANYBODY'S LISTENING, I WOULDN'T MIND BEING REINCARNATED AS A SEA OTTER.
SLURP
WAIT, I--
GAME OVER

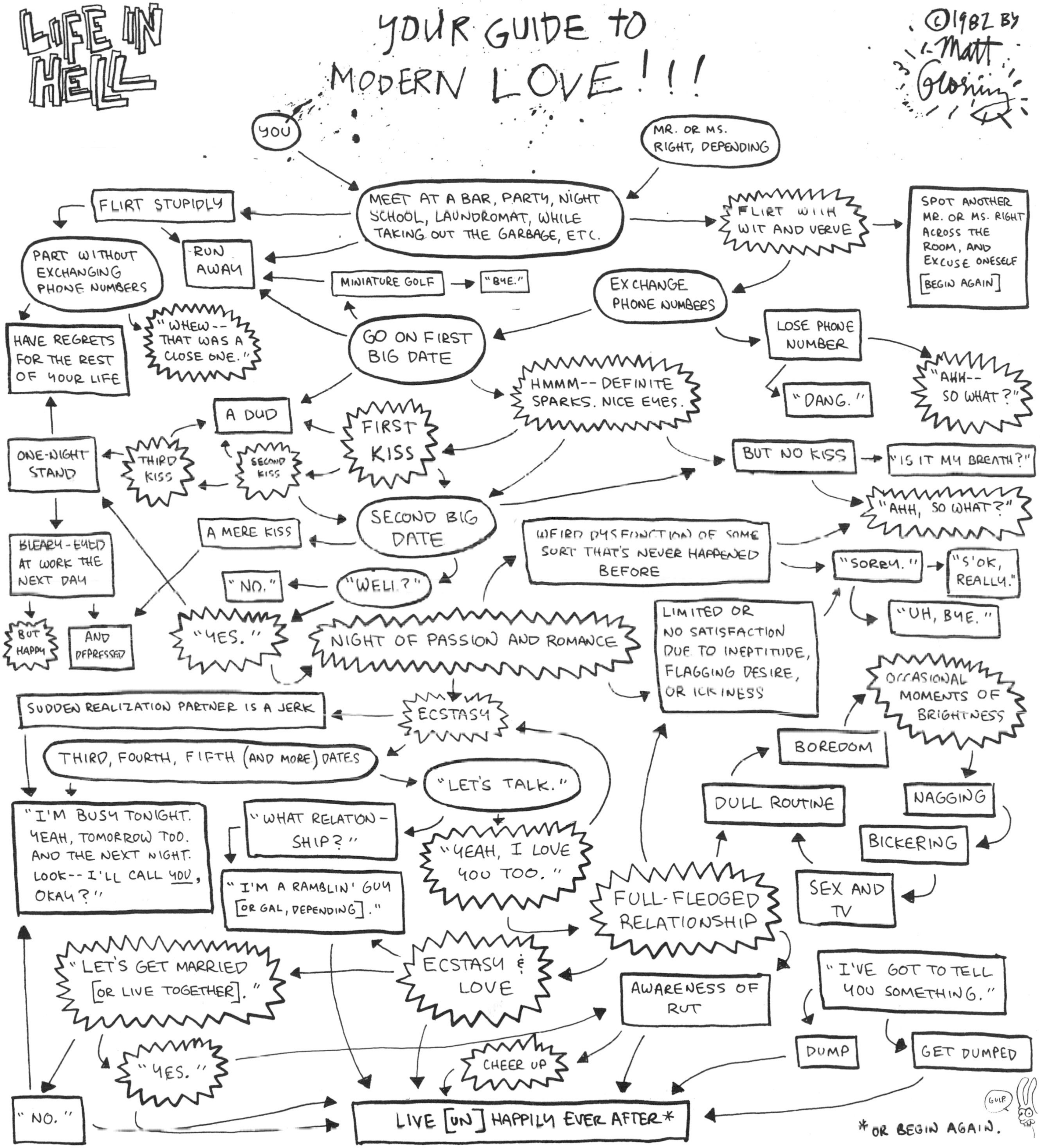
LIFE IN HELL
YOUR GUIDE TO MODERN LOVE!!!
©1982 BY Matt Groening
YOU
MR. OR MS. RIGHT, DEPENDING
MEET AT A BAR, PARTY, NIGHT SCHOOL, LAUNDROMAT, WHILE TAKING OUT THE GARBAGE, ETC.
FLIRT STUPIDLY
RUN AWAY
PART WITHOUT EXCHANGING PHONE NUMBERS
HAVE REGRETS FOR THE REST OF YOUR LIFE
"WHEW-- THAT WAS A CLOSE ONE."
FLIRT WITH WIT AND VERVE
SPOT ANOTHER MR. OR MS. RIGHT ACROSS THE ROOM, AND EXCUSE ONESELF [BEGIN AGAIN]
MINIATURE GOLF
"BYE."
EXCHANGE PHONE NUMBERS
LOSE PHONE NUMBER
"DANG."
"AHH-- SO WHAT?"
GO ON FIRST BIG DATE
HMMM-- DEFINITE SPARKS. NICE EYES.
A DUD
FIRST KISS
SECOND KISS
THIRD KISS
ONE-NIGHT STAND
BLEARY-EYED AT WORK THE NEXT DAY
BUT HAPPY
AND DEPRESSED
BUT NO KISS
"IS IT MY BREATH?"
"AHH, SO WHAT?"
SECOND BIG DATE
A MERE KISS
"WELL?"
"NO."
"YES."
WEIRD DYSFUNCTION OF SOME SORT THAT'S NEVER HAPPENED BEFORE
"SORRY."
"S'OK, REALLY."
"UH, BYE."
NIGHT OF PASSION AND ROMANCE
LIMITED OR NO SATISFACTION DUE TO INEPTITUDE, FLAGGING DESIRE, OR ICKINESS
OCCASIONAL MOMENTS OF BRIGHTNESS
ECSTASY
SUDDEN REALIZATION PARTNER IS A JERK
THIRD, FOURTH, FIFTH (AND MORE) DATES
"LET'S TALK."
BOREDOM
NAGGING
DULL ROUTINE
BICKERING
"I'M BUSY TONIGHT. YEAH, TOMORROW TOO. AND THE NEXT NIGHT. LOOK-- I'LL CALL YOU, OKAY?"
"WHAT RELATIONSHIP?"
"YEAH, I LOVE YOU TOO."
"I'M A RAMBLIN' GUY [OR GAL, DEPENDING]."
FULL-FLEDGED RELATIONSHIP
SEX AND TV
ECSTASY & LOVE
"LET'S GET MARRIED [OR LIVE TOGETHER]."
AWARENESS OF RUT
"I'VE GOT TO TELL YOU SOMETHING."
"YES."
CHEER UP
DUMP
GET DUMPED
"NO."
LIVE [UN] HAPPILY EVER AFTER*
GULP
*OR BEGIN AGAIN.

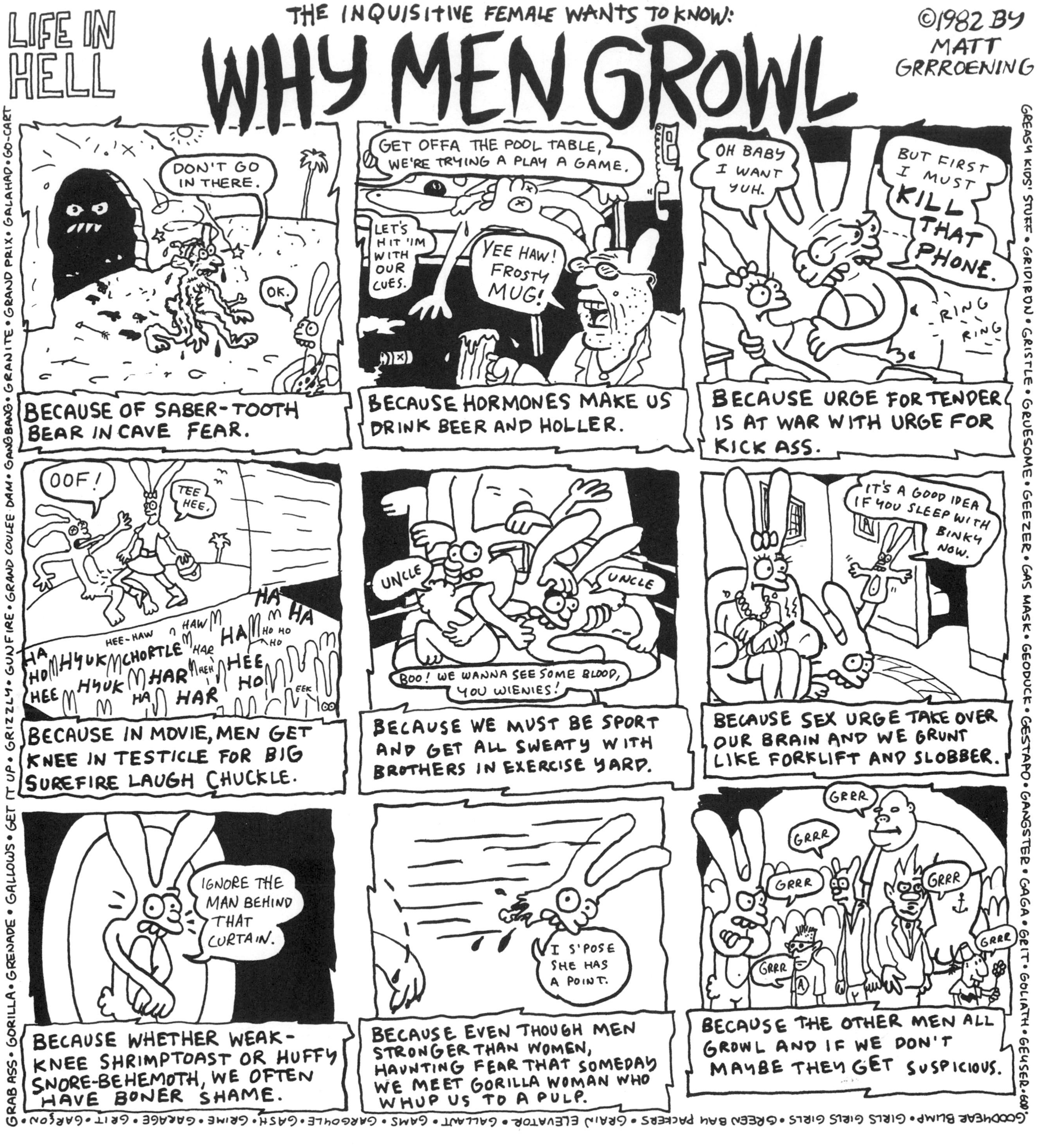

LIFE IN HELL
THE INQUISITIVE FEMALE WANTS TO KNOW:
WHY MEN GROWL
©1982 BY MATT GRRROENING
DON'T GO IN THERE.
OK.
BECAUSE OF SABER-TOOTH BEAR IN CAVE FEAR.
GET OFFA THE POOL TABLE, WE'RE TRYING A PLAY A GAME.
LET'S HIT 'IM WITH OUR CUES.
YEE HAW! FROSTY MUG!
BECAUSE HORMONES MAKE US DRINK BEER AND HOLLER.
OH BABY I WANT YUH.
BUT FIRST I MUST KILL THAT PHONE.
RING RING
BECAUSE URGE FOR TENDER IS AT WAR WITH URGE FOR KICK ASS.
OOF!
TEE HEE.
HA HA HA HEE-HAW HAW HA HO HO HO HAR HA HO HYUK CHORTLE HEH HEE HEE HYUK HAR HAR HO HA HAR EEK
BECAUSE IN MOVIE, MEN GET KNEE IN TESTICLE FOR BIG SUREFIRE LAUGH CHUCKLE.
UNCLE
UNCLE
BOO! WE WANNA SEE SOME BLOOD, YOU WIENIES!
BECAUSE WE MUST BE SPORT AND GET ALL SWEATY WITH BROTHERS IN EXERCISE YARD.
IT'S A GOOD IDEA IF YOU SLEEP WITH BINKY NOW.
BECAUSE SEX URGE TAKE OVER OUR BRAIN AND WE GRUNT LIKE FORKLIFT AND SLOBBER.
IGNORE THE MAN BEHIND THAT CURTAIN.
BECAUSE WHETHER WEAK-KNEE SHRIMPTOAST OR HUFFY SNORE-BEHEMOTH, WE OFTEN HAVE BONER SHAME.
I S'POSE SHE HAS A POINT.
BECAUSE EVEN THOUGH MEN STRONGER THAN WOMEN, HAUNTING FEAR THAT SOMEDAY WE MEET GORILLA WOMAN WHO WHUP US TO A PULP.
GRRR
GRRR
GRRR
GRRR
GRRR
GRRR
BECAUSE THE OTHER MEN ALL GROWL AND IF WE DON'T MAYBE THEY GET SUSPICIOUS.
GRAB ASS • GORILLA • GRENADE • GALLOWS • GET IT UP • GRIZZLY • GUNFIRE • GRAND COULEE DAM • GANGBANG • GRANITE • GRAND PRIX • GALAHAD • GO-CART
GREASY KIDS' STUFF • GRIDIRON • GRISTLE • GRUESOME • GEEZER • GAS MASK • GEODUCK • GESTAPO • GANGSTER • GAGA • GRIT • GOLIATH • GEYSER • GOD
GOODYEAR BLIMP • GIRLS GIRLS GIRLS • GREEN BAY PACKERS • GRAIN ELEVATOR • GALLANT • GAMS • GARGOYLE • GASH • GRIME • GARAGE • GRIT • GARÇON •

LIFE IN HELL

WHAT DO YOU WANT TO BE IF YOU GROW UP?

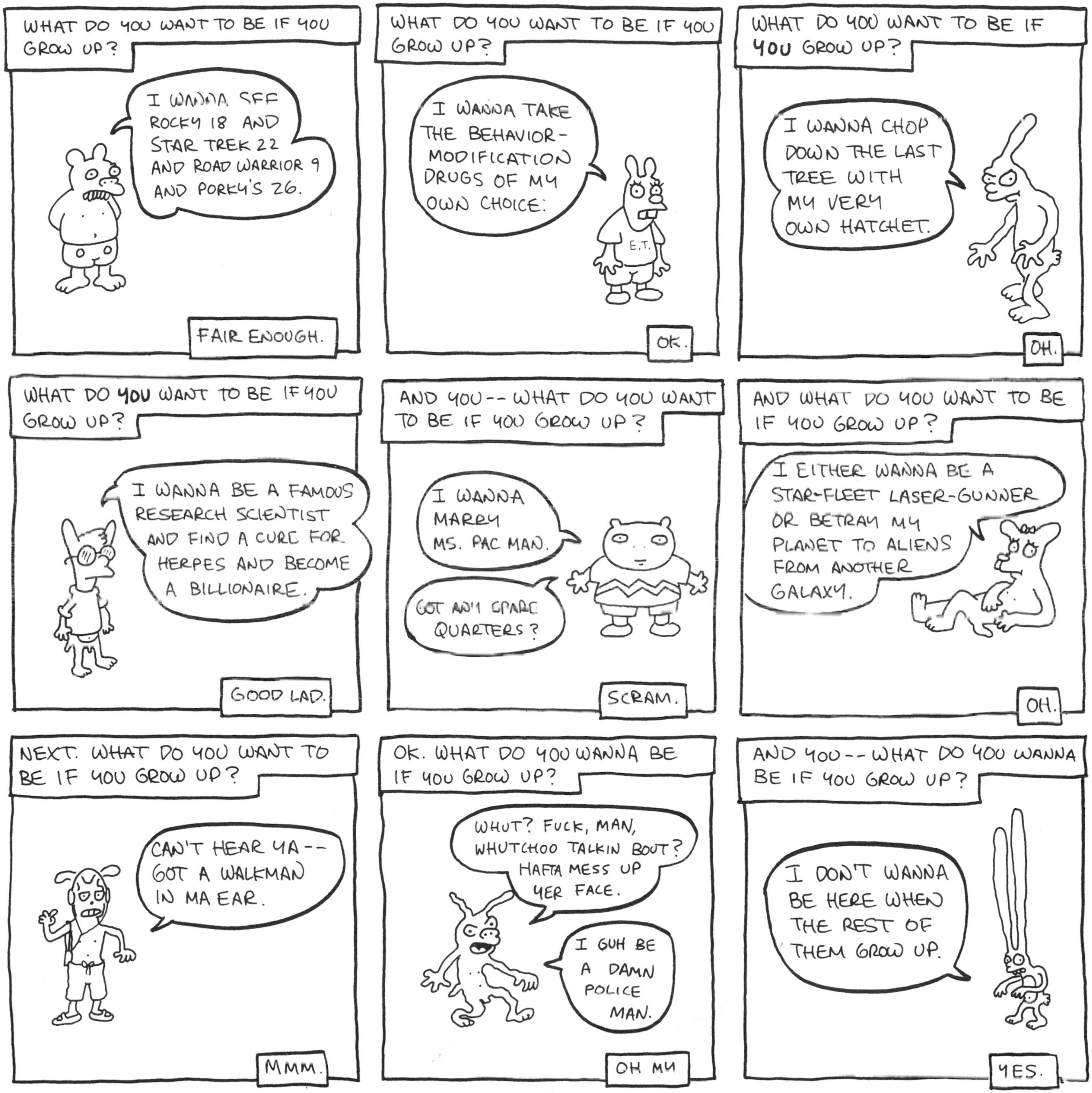
WHAT DO YOU WANT TO BE IF YOU GROW UP?
I WANNA SEE ROCKY 18 AND STAR TREK 22 AND ROAD WARRIOR 9 AND PORKY'S 26.
FAIR ENOUGH.
WHAT DO YOU WANT TO BE IF YOU GROW UP?
I WANNA TAKE THE BEHAVIOR-MODIFICATION DRUGS OF MY OWN CHOICE.
E.T.
OK.
WHAT DO YOU WANT TO BE IF YOU GROW UP?
I WANNA CHOP DOWN THE LAST TREE WITH MY VERY OWN HATCHET.
OH.
WHAT DO YOU WANT TO BE IF YOU GROW UP?
I WANNA BE A FAMOUS RESEARCH SCIENTIST AND FIND A CURE FOR HERPES AND BECOME A BILLIONAIRE.
GOOD LAD.
AND YOU -- WHAT DO YOU WANT TO BE IF YOU GROW UP?
I WANNA MARRY MS. PAC MAN.
GOT ANY SPARE QUARTERS?
SCRAM.
AND WHAT DO YOU WANT TO BE IF YOU GROW UP?
I EITHER WANNA BE A STAR-FLEET LASER-GUNNER OR BETRAY MY PLANET TO ALIENS FROM ANOTHER GALAXY.
OH.
NEXT. WHAT DO YOU WANT TO BE IF YOU GROW UP?
CAN'T HEAR YA -- GOT A WALKMAN IN MA EAR.
MMM.
OK. WHAT DO YOU WANNA BE IF YOU GROW UP?
WHUT? FUCK, MAN, WHUTCHOO TALKIN BOUT? HAFTA MESS UP YER FACE.
I GUH BE A DAMN POLICE MAN.
OH MY
AND YOU -- WHAT DO YOU WANNA BE IF YOU GROW UP?
I DON'T WANNA BE HERE WHEN THE REST OF THEM GROW UP.
YES.

9 SECRET LOVE TECHNIQUES THAT COULD POSSIBLY TURN MEN INTO PUTTY IN YOUR HANDS

©1982 BY M. GROENING

WOMEN: MEN! WHAT A WORLD, HUH? IN THE OLD DAYS EVERYTHING WAS EASY, WITH TRUE LOVE AND HEARTS AND FLOWERS AND FRILLY DRESSES AND LIGHT PETTING AND SING-ALONG HAYRIDES -- BUT NOWADAYS EVERYTHING IS SCREWY. YOU ALWAYS GOTTA BE ON GUARD, BECAUSE NO ONE CAN BE TRUSTED -- NOT EVEN YOUR FAVORITE LOVER. IT'S SAD IN A WAY. BUT WE CAN'T JUST GIVE UP. A MAN WITHOUT A WOMAN IS LIKE A TUGBOAT IN A LOGJAM. A WOMAN WITHOUT A MAN IS LIKE A FISH RUN OVER BY A BICYCLE. HENCE THIS HERE GUIDE, TO HELP WOMEN HELP MEN TO SEE THE LOVE LIGHT.

① DAZZLE 'EM.

FACE IT. MEN ARE DOPES -- GORILLAS -- SWEATY, LUMBERING BEASTS -- AND TO GET THEIR ATTENTION YOU HAVE TO FOOL 'EM -- TRICK 'EM -- PRACTICALLY WHACK 'EM ON THE NOSE WITH A ROLLED UP NEWSPAPER.

HEY -- WHAT FOR YOU WHACK ME ONNA NOSE WITH A ROLLED UP NEWSPAPER?

SAY -- WHAT IS THAT INTRIGUINGLY PROVOCATIVE PERFUME YOU'RE WEARING?

② FEIGN INTEREST IN THEIR TEDIOUS JABBER.

MEN DIG IT WHEN THEY CAN BABBLE ON ENDLESSLY YEAR AFTER YEAR ABOUT GUNS, BLIMPS, AND CIGARS WITHOUT BEING CHALLENGED TO CHANGE THE SUBJECT. ALL YOU HAVE TO DO IS LEARN A FEW SIMPLE WORDS AND DEVELOP A CAPACITY FOR LENGTHY MONOLOGUES ON CARBURETORS, HOME COMPUTERS, AND CURLY OF THE THREE STOOGES.

RILLY?

MY GOODNESS.

RILLY?

③ ACT PETULANT.

FOR SOME WEIRD REASON, MEN GET A CHARGE OUT OF SEEING WOMEN GETTING REALLY STEAMED -- PARTICULARLY WHEN IT'S ABOUT SOMETHING TRIVIAL, LIKE A RUN IN YOUR STOCKING OR EQUAL PAY FOR EQUAL WORK. JUST STOMP YOUR FOOT ON THE FLOOR, STICK OUT YOUR LOWER LIP, UTTER A LIGHT OBSCENITY, AND LISTEN FOR THAT CONDESCENDING, INDULGENT MALE CHUCKLE THAT SAYS, "WHATSAMATTA, BABY?"

MY YOU LOOK PRETTY WHEN YOU'RE PSYCHOPATHIC.

④ BE UNFATHOMABLE.

ONE THING THAT KEEPS MEN HOOKED IS WHEN THEY CAN'T FIGURE OUT WHAT THE HELL IS GOING ON. THIS IS EASY -- JUST THINK OF YOURSELF AS A FAUCET THAT RUNS BOILING HOT OR ICY COLD WITHOUT WARNING. MEN WON'T LIKE IT, BUT THEY HAVE BEEN KNOWN TO SPEND ENTIRE LIFETIMES TRYING TO UNDERSTAND IT.

I LOVE YOU.

I LOVE YOU TOO.

YOU DON'T KNOW WHAT LOVE IS.

HUH?

PLEASE -- LET'S NOT FIGHT. I LOVE YOU.

⑤ SLIP INTO SOMETHING A BIT MORE COMFORTABLE.

GET ALL DOLLED UP AND COME ON LIKE GANGBUSTERS. NOTHING CAN SWAY A WOULD-BE DREAMBOAT LIKE RUBY RED LIPS, THREE-INCH PAINTED FINGERNAILS, A PEEK-A-BOO BLOUSE, AND SEE-THRU PANTIES. WORKS LIKE A VOODOO CHARM.

YIKES.

⑥ ACCEDE TO THEIR SICKO EROTIC REQUESTS.

MEN CAN BE LIKENED TO RUTTING GRIZZLY BEARS, SNURFLING WOLVERINES, OR SEX-CRAZED WHITE RABBITS WITH JUST ONE THING ON THEIR DISGUSTING MINDS. ACTUALLY, YOU CAN PLAY IT TWO WAYS: EITHER FUCK THEIR BRAINS OUT, FOR WHICH YOU WILL BE REWARDED WITH DOGLIKE DEVOTION, OR WITHHOLD ALL SEXUAL FAVORS TILL LATER, FOR WHICH YOU WILL BE REWARDED WITH DOGLIKE DEVOTION.

OOH BABY I LOVE IT WHEN WE CUDDLE.

MMM HMM.

LISTEN MISTER KEEP YER GRUBBY PAWS TO YERSELF.

⑦ MAKE 'EM WHISTLE A DIFFERENT TUNE.

MEN ARE BASICALLY QUIVERING, SPINELESS JELLYFISH JUST FLOATING ALONG IN LIFE -- BUT WITH THE RIGHT AMOUNT OF PUSHING, PRODDING, AND NAGGING, YOU CAN IMPROVE THEM -- FROM HOPELESSLY INSENSITIVE OAFS INTO HOPELESSLY SENSITIVE OAFS. REMEMBER: KEEP AT IT.

STRAIGHTEN UP, HONEY -- YOU'RE SLOUCHING.

TAKE THAT TOOTHPICK OUT OF YOUR MOUTH. IT'S VULGAR.

YOU'LL THANK ME FOR THIS SOMEDAY.

DON'T GIVE ME THAT LOOK. IT'S UNBECOMING.

⑧ DEFLATE 'EM.

IT'S SURPRISINGLY EASY TO PUNCTURE THE EGOS OF SLOW-WITTED MALE BEHEMOTHS WITH A QUICK VERBAL JAB OR AN UNYIELDING MORAL/POLITICAL EXHORTATION. CURIOUSLY, MEN FEEL A TREMENDOUS AMOUNT OF GUILT THAT IS HELD IN CHECK ONLY BY AN EQUALLY HEFTY LOAD OF UNFOCUSED RAGE -- AND YOU CAN WORK THIS TO YOUR ADVANTAGE.

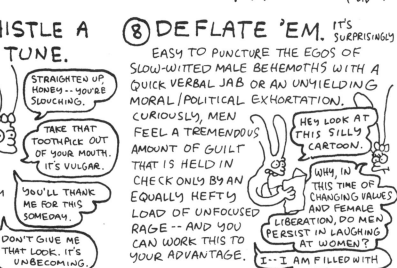

HEY LOOK AT THIS SILLY CARTOON.

WHY, IN THIS TIME OF CHANGING VALUES AND FEMALE LIBERATION, DO MEN PERSIST IN LAUGHING AT WOMEN?

I -- I AM FILLED WITH SHAME.

⑨ PUT YOUR ARM AROUND YOUR HONEY, READ THIS CARTOON ALOUD TOGETHER, AND SAY: "AREN'T YOU GLAD WE'RE BEYOND ALL THIS?"

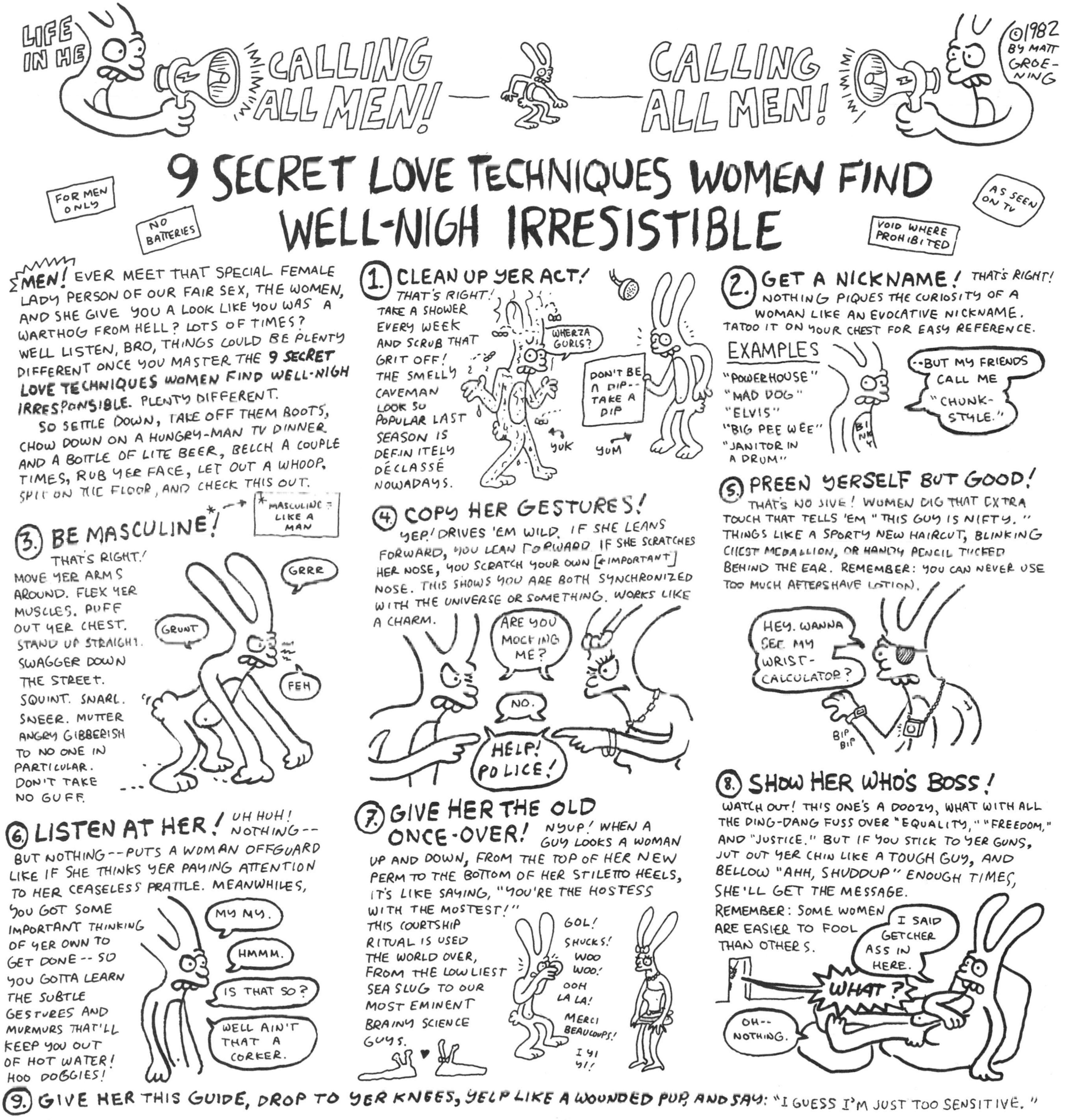
LIFE IN HELL
CALLING ALL MEN! — CALLING ALL MEN!
©1982 BY MATT GROENING
9 SECRET LOVE TECHNIQUES WOMEN FIND WELL-NIGH IRRESISTIBLE
FOR MEN ONLY
NO BATTERIES
AS SEEN ON TV
VOID WHERE PROHIBITED
MEN! EVER MEET THAT SPECIAL FEMALE
LADY PERSON OF OUR FAIR SEX, THE WOMEN,
AND SHE GIVE YOU A LOOK LIKE YOU WAS A
WARTHOG FROM HELL? LOTS OF TIMES?
WELL LISTEN, BRO, THINGS COULD BE PLENTY
DIFFERENT ONCE YOU MASTER THE 9 SECRET
LOVE TECHNIQUES WOMEN FIND WELL-NIGH
IRRESPONSIBLE. PLENTY DIFFERENT.
SO SETTLE DOWN, TAKE OFF THEM BOOTS,
CHOW DOWN ON A HUNGRY-MAN TV DINNER
AND A BOTTLE OF LITE BEER, BELCH A COUPLE
TIMES, RUB YER FACE, LET OUT A WHOOP,
SPIT ON THE FLOOR, AND CHECK THIS OUT.
1. CLEAN UP YER ACT! THAT'S RIGHT! TAKE A SHOWER EVERY WEEK AND SCRUB THAT GRIT OFF! THE SMELLY CAVEMAN LOOK SO POPULAR LAST SEASON IS DEFINITELY DÉCLASSÉ NOWADAYS.
WHERZA GURLS?
DON'T BE A DIP-- TAKE A DIP
YUK
YUM
2. GET A NICKNAME! THAT'S RIGHT! NOTHING PIQUES THE CURIOSITY OF A WOMAN LIKE AN EVOCATIVE NICKNAME. TATOO IT ON YOUR CHEST FOR EASY REFERENCE.
EXAMPLES
"POWERHOUSE"
"MAD DOG"
"ELVIS"
"BIG PEE WEE"
"JANITOR IN A DRUM"
BINKY
..BUT MY FRIENDS CALL ME "CHUNK-STYLE."
3. BE MASCULINE!* THAT'S RIGHT! MOVE YER ARMS AROUND. FLEX YER MUSCLES. PUFF OUT YER CHEST. STAND UP STRAIGHT. SWAGGER DOWN THE STREET. SQUINT. SNARL. SNEER. MUTTER ANGRY GIBBERISH TO NO ONE IN PARTICULAR. DON'T TAKE NO GUFF.
*MASCULINE = LIKE A MAN
GRRR
GRUNT
FEH
4. COPY HER GESTURES!
YEP! DRIVES 'EM WILD. IF SHE LEANS
FORWARD, YOU LEAN FORWARD. IF SHE SCRATCHES
HER NOSE, YOU SCRATCH YOUR OWN [←IMPORTANT]
NOSE. THIS SHOWS YOU ARE BOTH SYNCHRONIZED
WITH THE UNIVERSE OR SOMETHING. WORKS LIKE
A CHARM.
ARE YOU MOCKING ME?
NO.
HELP! POLICE!
5. PREEN YERSELF BUT GOOD! THAT'S NO JIVE! WOMEN DIG THAT EXTRA TOUCH THAT TELLS 'EM "THIS GUY IS NIFTY." THINGS LIKE A SPORTY NEW HAIRCUT, BLINKING CHEST MEDALLION, OR HANDY PENCIL TUCKED BEHIND THE EAR. REMEMBER: YOU CAN NEVER USE TOO MUCH AFTERSHAVE LOTION.
HEY. WANNA SEE MY WRIST-CALCULATOR?
BIP BIP
6. LISTEN AT HER! UH HUH! NOTHING-- BUT NOTHING--PUTS A WOMAN OFFGUARD LIKE IF SHE THINKS YER PAYING ATTENTION TO HER CEASELESS PRATTLE. MEANWHILES, YOU GOT SOME IMPORTANT THINKING OF YER OWN TO GET DONE -- SO YOU GOTTA LEARN THE SUBTLE GESTURES AND MURMURS THAT'LL KEEP YOU OUT OF HOT WATER! HOO DOGGIES!
MY MY.
HMMM.
IS THAT SO?
WELL AIN'T THAT A CORKER.
7. GIVE HER THE OLD ONCE-OVER! NYUP! WHEN A GUY LOOKS A WOMAN UP AND DOWN, FROM THE TOP OF HER NEW PERM TO THE BOTTOM OF HER STILETTO HEELS, IT'S LIKE SAYING, "YOU'RE THE HOSTESS WITH THE MOSTEST!" THIS COURTSHIP RITUAL IS USED THE WORLD OVER, FROM THE LOWLIEST SEA SLUG TO OUR MOST EMINENT BRAINY SCIENCE GUYS.
GOL! SHUCKS! WOO WOO! OOH LA LA! MERCI BEAUCOUPS! I YI YI!
8. SHOW HER WHO'S BOSS! WATCH OUT! THIS ONE'S A DOOZY, WHAT WITH ALL THE DING-DANG FUSS OVER "EQUALITY," "FREEDOM," AND "JUSTICE." BUT IF YOU STICK TO YER GUNS, JUT OUT YER CHIN LIKE A TOUGH GUY, AND BELLOW "AHH, SHUDDUP" ENOUGH TIMES, SHE'LL GET THE MESSAGE.
REMEMBER: SOME WOMEN ARE EASIER TO FOOL THAN OTHERS.
I SAID GETCHER ASS IN HERE.
WHAT?
OH-- NOTHING.
9. GIVE HER THIS GUIDE, DROP TO YER KNEES, YELP LIKE A WOUNDED PUP, AND SAY: "I GUESS I'M JUST TOO SENSITIVE."

Life is Swell!

MY SIMPLE FORMULA FOR HAPPINESS

By ©1982 MATT GROENING

A HANDY GUIDE.

THERE'S NOT A JOY THE WORLD CAN GIVE LIKE THAT IT TAKES AWAY,
WHEN THE GLOW OF EARLY THOUGHT DECLINES IN FEELING'S DULL DECAY.
-- BYRON

$$X+O \;\downarrow\; \otimes \rightarrow \frac{x+o}{A\overline{)\;C\overline{)\;B\overline{)\otimes}}}} + \frac{x+o}{\dfrac{F+G+H^{10}+J+K+\$}{(L^{(F)}+1+M)}} + \frac{\dfrac{x+o}{(D)^{12}}}{(D+D^{2})} = \frac{H}{\quad}$$

- X = YOUR DAD
- O = YOUR MAMA
- ⊗ = YOU
- A = SCHOOL
- B = TOILET TRAINING
- C = BAMBI
- F = MARRIAGE
- G = CHURCH
- H = HAPPINESS
- J = HOBBIES
- K = BAD HABITS
- L = JOB
- M = TAXES
- D = DESPAIR, DECAY

THINGS TO AVOID

- ☐ THE WRATH OF GOD
- ☐ DELUSIONS OF GRANDEUR
- ☐ KIERKEGAARD
- ☐ BULLETS
- ☐ HERPES SIMPLEX II
- ☐ FISHSTICKS
- ☐ COLD SHOWERS
- ☐ RADIOACTIVE SMOKE ALARMS
- ☐ DARK ALLEYS
- ☐ LAUNDROMATS
- ☐ LIFESTYLES
- ☐ RECTAL THERMOMETERS
- ☐ NONDAIRY CREME
- ☐ MEN WITH GOATEES
- ☐ GIANT STUFFED DAY-GLO POODLES
- ☐ BREAKFAST AT 24-HR. CONVENIENCE STORES
- ☐ COAL MINES

BANANA PEEL
WHOOPS.

FIG. ONE
THE ROLLING DONUT OF LIFE...

THINGS TO GET

- ☐ LOVE
- ☐ WEALTH
- ☐ POWER
- ☐ ACCLAIM
- ☐ MINDLESS PLEASURES
- ☐ JOLLITY
- ☐ ROMANCE
- ☐ ADVENTURE
- ☐ THRILLS
- ☐ BAUBLES
- ☐ EXACT CHANGE
- ☐ TOASTER OVEN
- ☐ ICE CREAM
- ☐ PROPERTY
- ☐ EDUCATION OR GUSTO
- ☐ COSMETIC SURGERY
- ☐ PORTABLE STEREO
- ☐ NOBEL PRIZE

HANDY PHRASES

"HOT ENOUGH FOR YOU?"
"MMM-MMM GOOD."
"HOO BOY!"
"YEE HAW!"
"DON'T CALL BEFORE NOON."
"I'M INNOCENT."
"I DIDN'T DO IT."
"NO WAY."
"OH, IT'S YOU."
"HAVE A NICE DAY."
"NO. I REPEAT--NO."

POINTS TO PONDER

FINDERS KEEPERS, LOSERS WEEPERS.

A WO/MAN'S BEST FRIEND IS HIS/HER DOG.

MONEY DOESN'T GROW ON TREES.

HAPPINESS ISN'T EVERYTHING.

THE REST IS UP TO YOU.

SO BUCK UP. IT'S NOT THE END OF THE WORLD. SURE YOU'RE CONFUSED. WHO ISN'T? QUIT YER WHINING. SHUT UP. YER GOOFING OFF. YOU GOT NOBODY TO BLAME BUT YERSELF. SO CHEER UP.

THANK YOU.

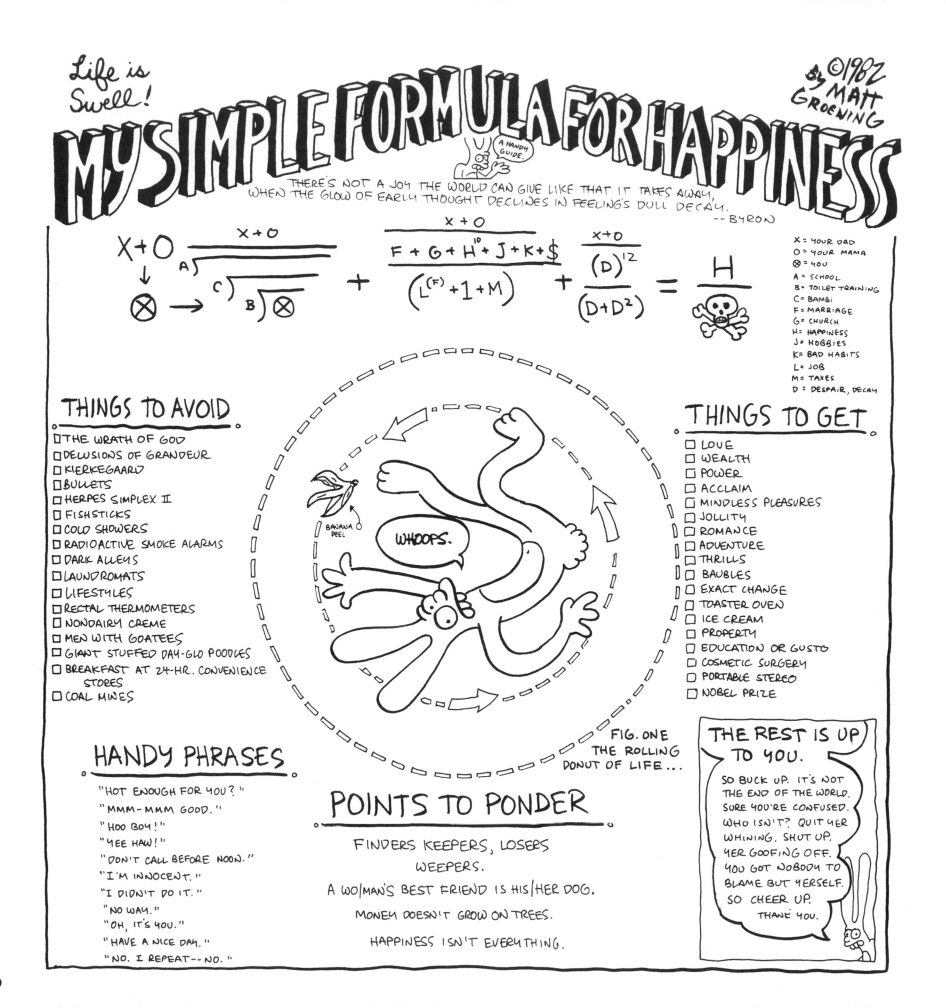

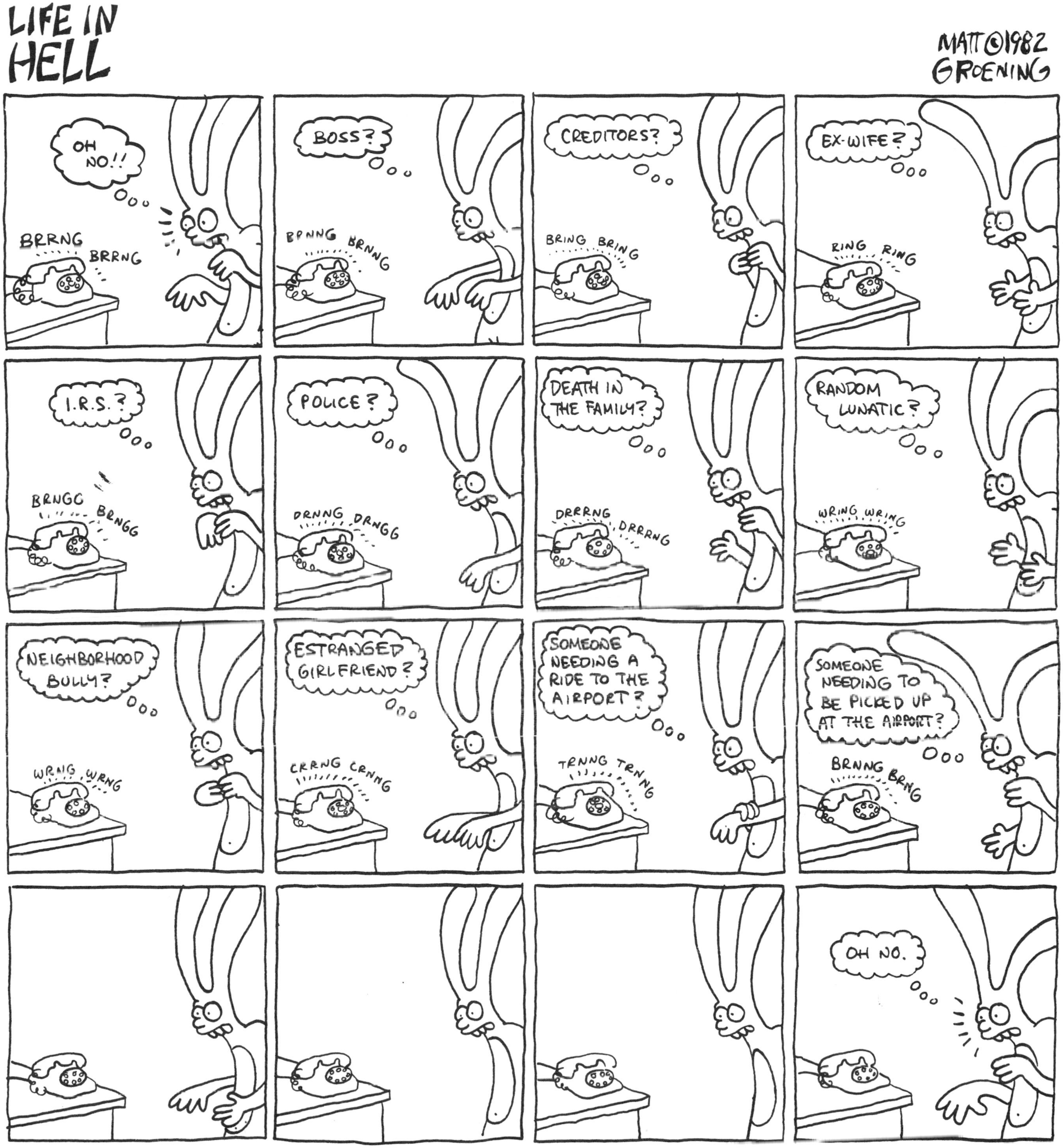
LIFE IN HELL
MATT ©1982 GROENING
OH NO!!
BRRNG BRRNG
BOSS?
BRNNG BRNNG
CREDITORS?
BRING BRING
EX-WIFE?
RING RING
I.R.S.?
BRNGG BRNGG
POLICE?
DRNNG DRNGG
DEATH IN THE FAMILY?
DRRRNG DRRRNG
RANDOM LUNATIC?
WRING WRING
NEIGHBORHOOD BULLY?
WRNG WRNG
ESTRANGED GIRLFRIEND?
CRRNG CRNNG
SOMEONE NEEDING A RIDE TO THE AIRPORT?
TRNNG TRNNG
SOMEONE NEEDING TO BE PICKED UP AT THE AIRPORT?
BRNNG BRNG
OH NO.

HOW MUCH ARE YOU WORTH?

©1982 BY MATT GROENING

HELLO THERE, YOU LITTLE BUNDLE OF GUILT, SHAME, AND SELF-AGGRANDIZEMENT. HOW YOU DOING? YOU EVER LIE THERE IN THE DARK LATE AT NIGHT, UNABLE TO SLEEP, THINKING TO YOURSELF, HOW MUCH AM I WORTH? I MEAN TRUE WORTH -- STRIPPED DOWN BUCK NAKED, WITHOUT ANY FAMILY HEIRLOOMS, DESIGNER JEANS, OR PERSONALIZED LICENSE PLATES TO HIDE BEHIND. WELL, NOW YOU NEED WONDER NO LONGER. NOW YOU CAN **KNOW FOR SURE** WITH THIS HANDY POCKET TEST. HERE YOU GO.

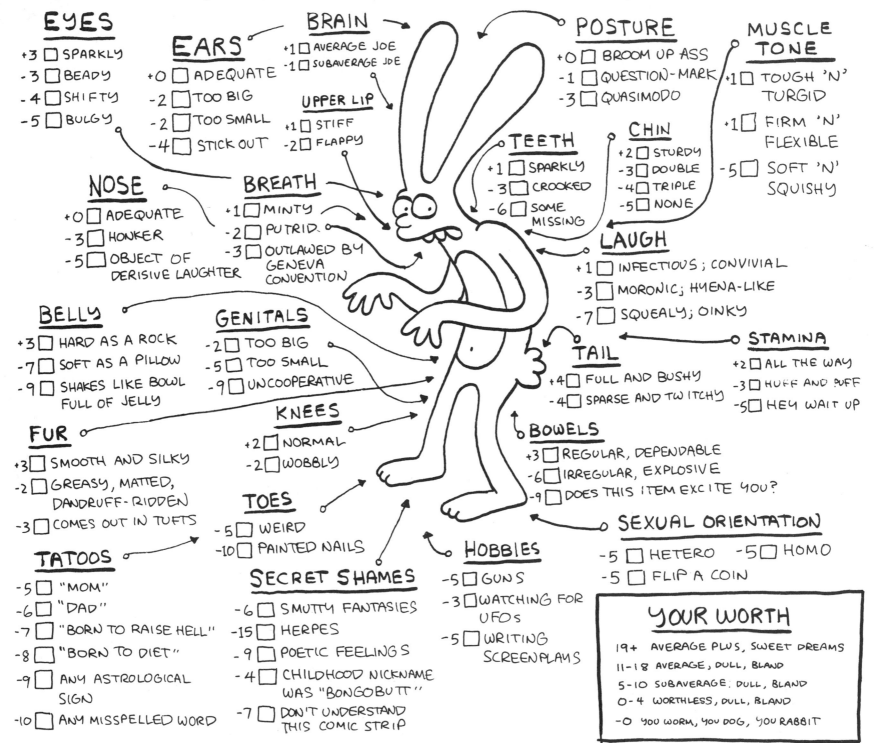

EYES
- +3 SPARKLY
- -3 BEADY
- -4 SHIFTY
- -5 BULGY

EARS
- +0 ADEQUATE
- -2 TOO BIG
- -2 TOO SMALL
- -4 STICK OUT

BRAIN
- +1 AVERAGE JOE
- -1 SUBAVERAGE JOE

UPPER LIP
- +1 STIFF
- -2 FLAPPY

NOSE
- +0 ADEQUATE
- -3 HONKER
- -5 OBJECT OF DERISIVE LAUGHTER

BREATH
- +1 MINTY
- -2 PUTRID
- -3 OUTLAWED BY GENEVA CONVENTION

TEETH
- +1 SPARKLY
- -3 CROOKED
- -6 SOME MISSING

CHIN
- +2 STURDY
- -3 DOUBLE
- -4 TRIPLE
- -5 NONE

POSTURE
- +0 BROOM UP ASS
- -1 QUESTION-MARK
- -3 QUASIMODO

MUSCLE TONE
- +1 TOUGH 'N' TURGID
- +1 FIRM 'N' FLEXIBLE
- -5 SOFT 'N' SQUISHY

LAUGH
- +1 INFECTIOUS; CONVIVIAL
- -3 MORONIC; HYENA-LIKE
- -7 SQUEALY; OINKY

BELLY
- +3 HARD AS A ROCK
- -7 SOFT AS A PILLOW
- -9 SHAKES LIKE BOWL FULL OF JELLY

GENITALS
- -2 TOO BIG
- -5 TOO SMALL
- -9 UNCOOPERATIVE

KNEES
- +2 NORMAL
- -2 WOBBLY

TAIL
- +4 FULL AND BUSHY
- -4 SPARSE AND TWITCHY

STAMINA
- +2 ALL THE WAY
- -3 HUFF AND PUFF
- -5 HEY WAIT UP

FUR
- +3 SMOOTH AND SILKY
- -2 GREASY, MATTED, DANDRUFF-RIDDEN
- -3 COMES OUT IN TUFTS

TOES
- -5 WEIRD
- -10 PAINTED NAILS

BOWELS
- +3 REGULAR, DEPENDABLE
- -6 IRREGULAR, EXPLOSIVE
- -9 DOES THIS ITEM EXCITE YOU?

TATOOS
- -5 "MOM"
- -6 "DAD"
- -7 "BORN TO RAISE HELL"
- -8 "BORN TO DIET"
- -9 ANY ASTROLOGICAL SIGN
- -10 ANY MISSPELLED WORD

SECRET SHAMES
- -6 SMUTTY FANTASIES
- -15 HERPES
- -9 POETIC FEELINGS
- -4 CHILDHOOD NICKNAME WAS "BONGOBUTT"
- -7 DON'T UNDERSTAND THIS COMIC STRIP

HOBBIES
- -5 GUNS
- -3 WATCHING FOR UFOs
- -5 WRITING SCREENPLAYS

SEXUAL ORIENTATION
- -5 HETERO
- -5 HOMO
- -5 FLIP A COIN

YOUR WORTH
- 19+ AVERAGE PLUS, SWEET DREAMS
- 11-18 AVERAGE, DULL, BLAND
- 5-10 SUBAVERAGE, DULL, BLAND
- 0-4 WORTHLESS, DULL, BLAND
- -0 YOU WORM, YOU DOG, YOU RABBIT

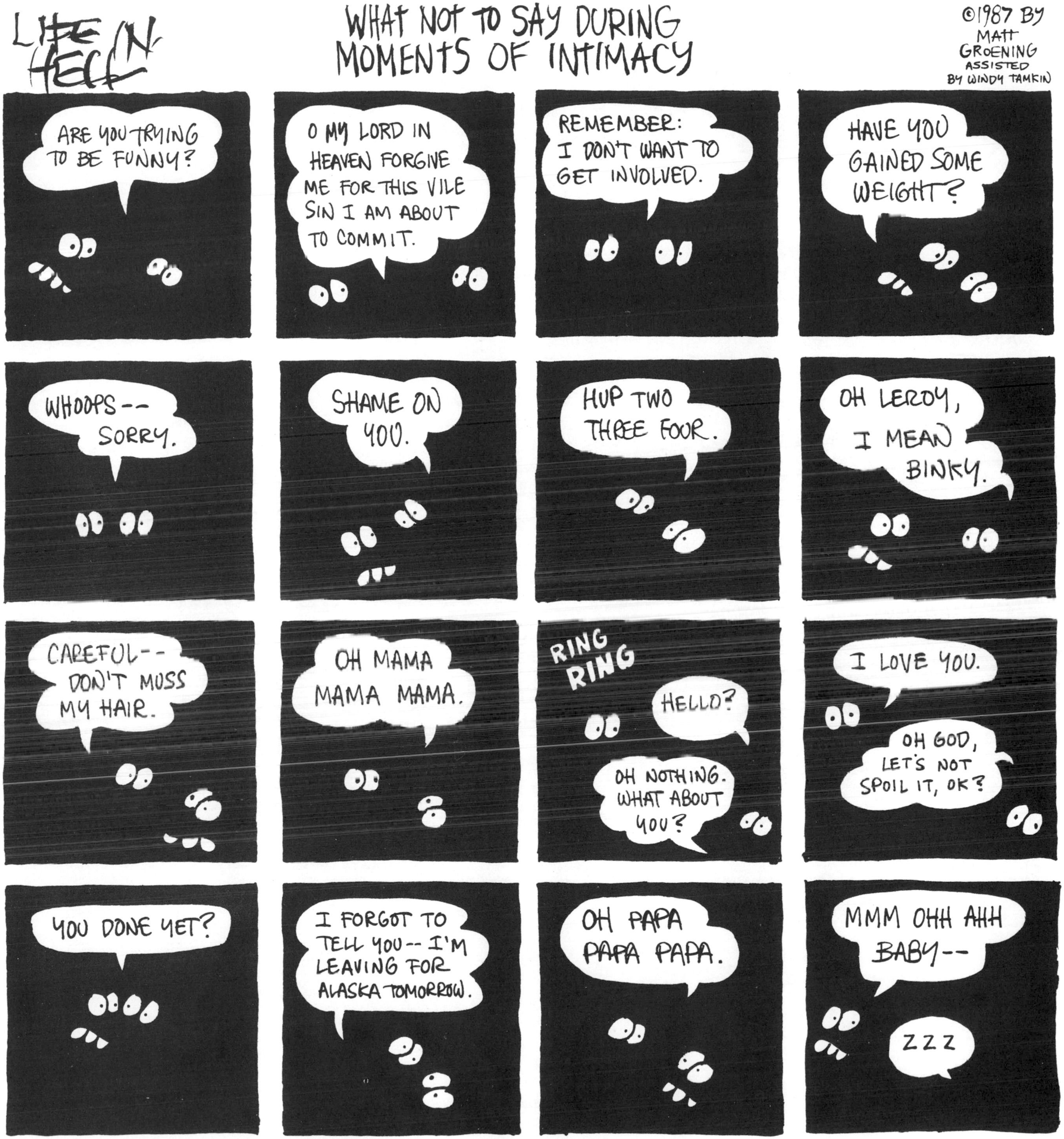
LIFE IN HELL
WHAT NOT TO SAY DURING MOMENTS OF INTIMACY
©1987 BY MATT GROENING ASSISTED BY WINDY TAMKIN
ARE YOU TRYING TO BE FUNNY?
O MY LORD IN HEAVEN FORGIVE ME FOR THIS VILE SIN I AM ABOUT TO COMMIT.
REMEMBER: I DON'T WANT TO GET INVOLVED.
HAVE YOU GAINED SOME WEIGHT?
WHOOPS -- SORRY.
SHAME ON YOU.
HUP TWO THREE FOUR.
OH LEROY, I MEAN BINKY.
CAREFUL -- DON'T MUSS MY HAIR.
OH MAMA MAMA MAMA.
RING RING
HELLO?
OH NOTHING. WHAT ABOUT YOU?
I LOVE YOU.
OH GOD, LET'S NOT SPOIL IT, OK?
YOU DONE YET?
I FORGOT TO TELL YOU -- I'M LEAVING FOR ALASKA TOMORROW.
OH PAPA PAPA PAPA.
MMM OHH AHH BABY --
ZZZ

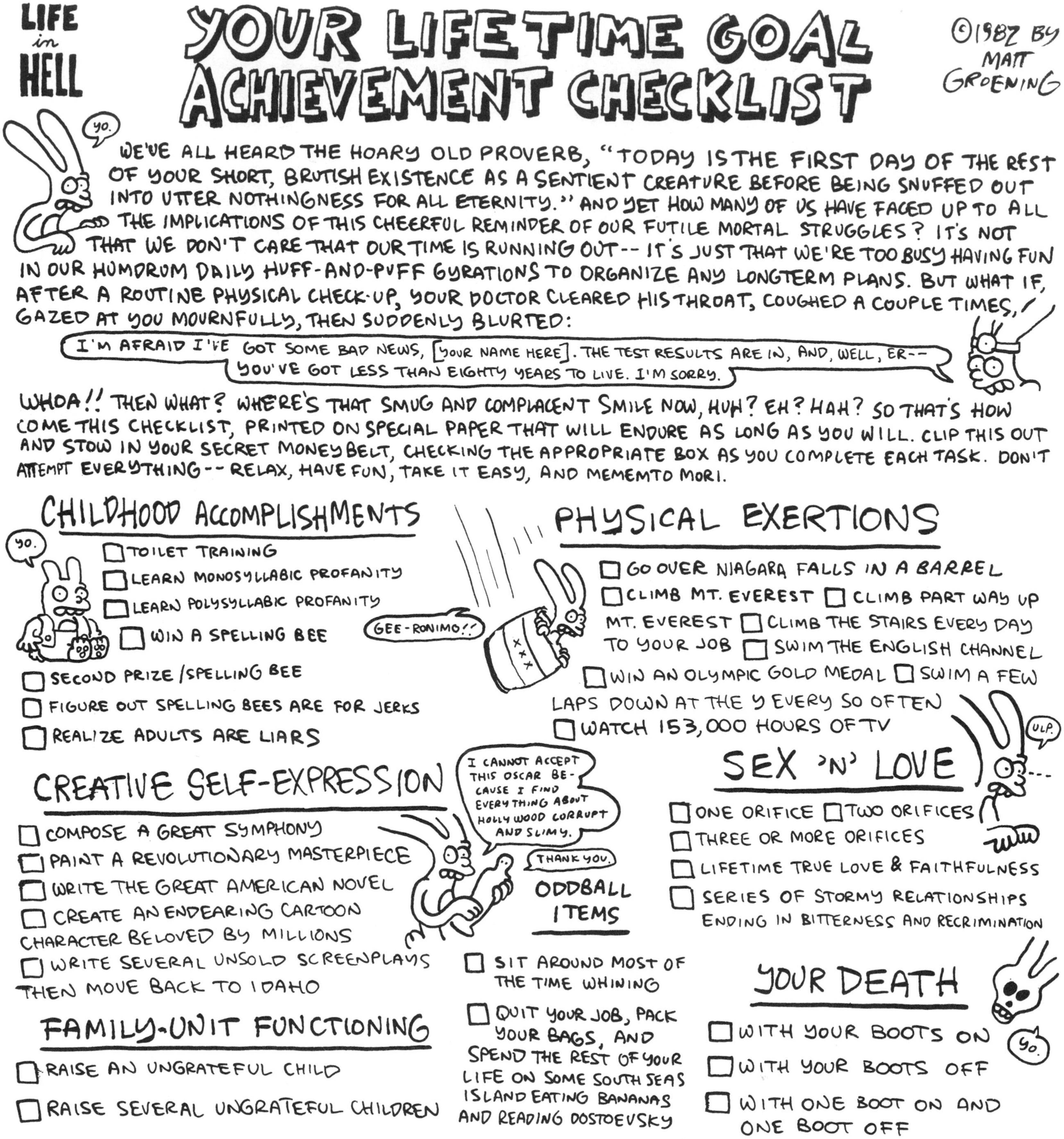
LIFE in HELL
YOUR LIFETIME GOAL ACHIEVEMENT CHECKLIST
©1982 BY MATT GROENING
YO.
WE'VE ALL HEARD THE HOARY OLD PROVERB, "TODAY IS THE FIRST DAY OF THE REST OF YOUR SHORT, BRUTISH EXISTENCE AS A SENTIENT CREATURE BEFORE BEING SNUFFED OUT INTO UTTER NOTHINGNESS FOR ALL ETERNITY." AND YET HOW MANY OF US HAVE FACED UP TO ALL THE IMPLICATIONS OF THIS CHEERFUL REMINDER OF OUR FUTILE MORTAL STRUGGLES? IT'S NOT THAT WE DON'T CARE THAT OUR TIME IS RUNNING OUT-- IT'S JUST THAT WE'RE TOO BUSY HAVING FUN IN OUR HUMDRUM DAILY HUFF-AND-PUFF GYRATIONS TO ORGANIZE ANY LONGTERM PLANS. BUT WHAT IF, AFTER A ROUTINE PHYSICAL CHECK-UP, YOUR DOCTOR CLEARED HIS THROAT, COUGHED A COUPLE TIMES, GAZED AT YOU MOURNFULLY, THEN SUDDENLY BLURTED:
I'M AFRAID I'VE GOT SOME BAD NEWS, [YOUR NAME HERE]. THE TEST RESULTS ARE IN, AND, WELL, ER-- YOU'VE GOT LESS THAN EIGHTY YEARS TO LIVE. I'M SORRY.
WHOA!! THEN WHAT? WHERE'S THAT SMUG AND COMPLACENT SMILE NOW, HUH? EH? HAH? SO THAT'S HOW COME THIS CHECKLIST, PRINTED ON SPECIAL PAPER THAT WILL ENDURE AS LONG AS YOU WILL. CLIP THIS OUT AND STOW IN YOUR SECRET MONEY BELT, CHECKING THE APPROPRIATE BOX AS YOU COMPLETE EACH TASK. DON'T ATTEMPT EVERYTHING-- RELAX, HAVE FUN, TAKE IT EASY, AND MEMEMTO MORI.
CHILDHOOD ACCOMPLISHMENTS
YO.
☐ TOILET TRAINING
☐ LEARN MONOSYLLABIC PROFANITY
☐ LEARN POLYSYLLABIC PROFANITY
☐ WIN A SPELLING BEE
☐ SECOND PRIZE / SPELLING BEE
☐ FIGURE OUT SPELLING BEES ARE FOR JERKS
☐ REALIZE ADULTS ARE LIARS
GEE-RONIMO!!
XXX
PHYSICAL EXERTIONS
☐ GO OVER NIAGARA FALLS IN A BARREL
☐ CLIMB MT. EVEREST
☐ CLIMB PART WAY UP MT. EVEREST
☐ CLIMB THE STAIRS EVERY DAY TO YOUR JOB
☐ SWIM THE ENGLISH CHANNEL
☐ WIN AN OLYMPIC GOLD MEDAL
☐ SWIM A FEW LAPS DOWN AT THE Y EVERY SO OFTEN
☐ WATCH 153,000 HOURS OF TV
ULP.
CREATIVE SELF-EXPRESSION
☐ COMPOSE A GREAT SYMPHONY
☐ PAINT A REVOLUTIONARY MASTERPIECE
☐ WRITE THE GREAT AMERICAN NOVEL
☐ CREATE AN ENDEARING CARTOON CHARACTER BELOVED BY MILLIONS
☐ WRITE SEVERAL UNSOLD SCREENPLAYS THEN MOVE BACK TO IDAHO
I CANNOT ACCEPT THIS OSCAR BECAUSE I FIND EVERYTHING ABOUT HOLLYWOOD CORRUPT AND SLIMY.
THANK YOU.
SEX 'N' LOVE
☐ ONE ORIFICE
☐ TWO ORIFICES
☐ THREE OR MORE ORIFICES
☐ LIFETIME TRUE LOVE & FAITHFULNESS
☐ SERIES OF STORMY RELATIONSHIPS ENDING IN BITTERNESS AND RECRIMINATION
FAMILY-UNIT FUNCTIONING
☐ RAISE AN UNGRATEFUL CHILD
☐ RAISE SEVERAL UNGRATEFUL CHILDREN
ODDBALL ITEMS
☐ SIT AROUND MOST OF THE TIME WHINING
☐ QUIT YOUR JOB, PACK YOUR BAGS, AND SPEND THE REST OF YOUR LIFE ON SOME SOUTH SEAS ISLAND EATING BANANAS AND READING DOSTOEVSKY
YOUR DEATH
☐ WITH YOUR BOOTS ON
☐ WITH YOUR BOOTS OFF
☐ WITH ONE BOOT ON AND ONE BOOT OFF
YO.

HELLABALOO

©1983 BY MATT GROENING

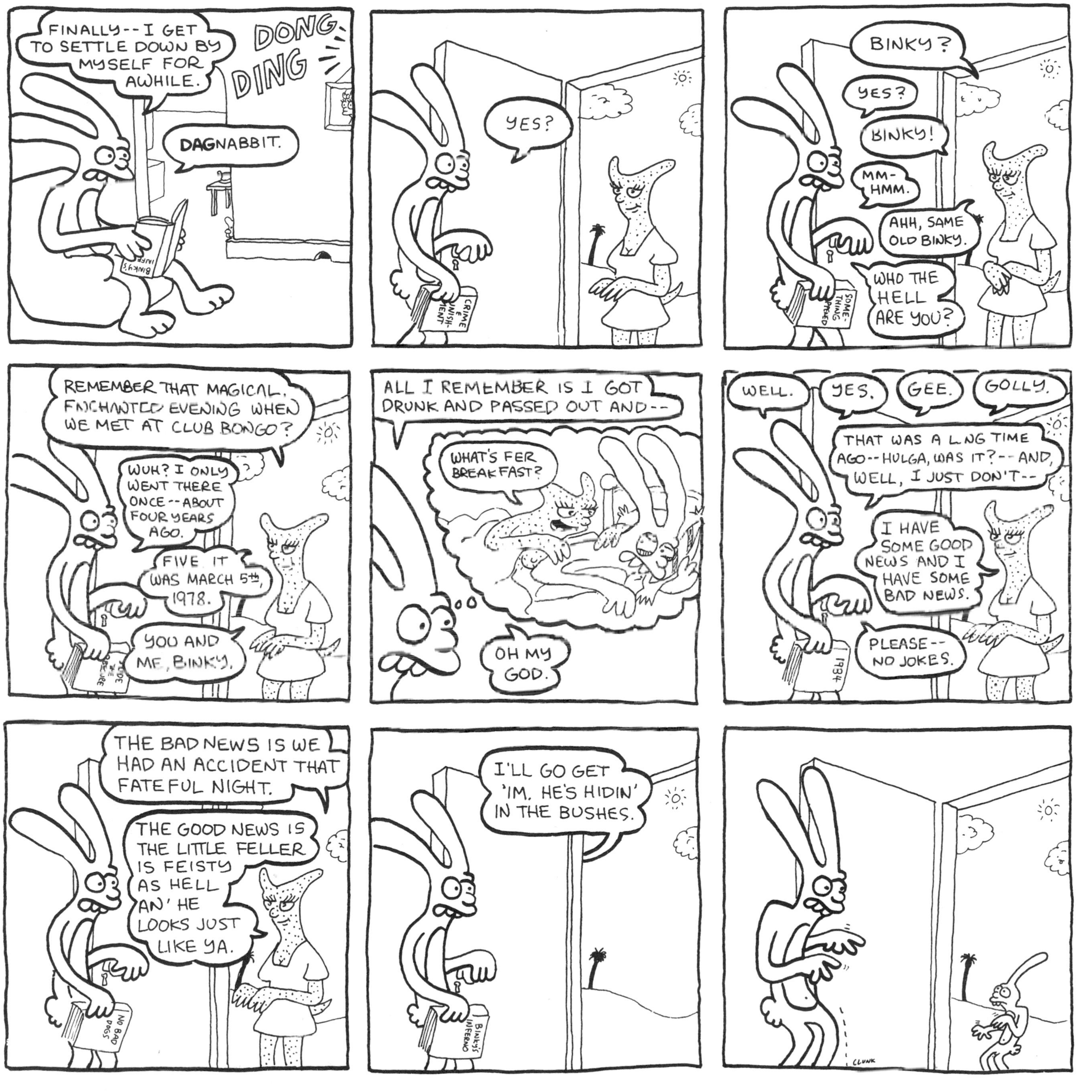

FINALLY--I GET TO SETTLE DOWN BY MYSELF FOR AWHILE.
DONG
DING
DAGNABBIT.
YES?
BINKY?
YES?
BINKY!
MM-HMM.
AHH, SAME OLD BINKY.
WHO THE HELL ARE YOU?
REMEMBER THAT MAGICAL, ENCHANTED EVENING WHEN WE MET AT CLUB BONGO?
WUH? I ONLY WENT THERE ONCE--ABOUT FOUR YEARS AGO.
FIVE. IT WAS MARCH 5th, 1978.
YOU AND ME, BINKY.
ALL I REMEMBER IS I GOT DRUNK AND PASSED OUT AND--
WHAT'S FER BREAKFAST?
OH MY GOD.
WELL.
YES.
GEE.
GOLLY.
THAT WAS A LONG TIME AGO--HULGA, WAS IT?--AND, WELL, I JUST DON'T--
I HAVE SOME GOOD NEWS AND I HAVE SOME BAD NEWS.
PLEASE--NO JOKES.
1984
THE BAD NEWS IS WE HAD AN ACCIDENT THAT FATEFUL NIGHT.
THE GOOD NEWS IS THE LITTLE FELLER IS FEISTY AS HELL AN' HE LOOKS JUST LIKE YA.
NO BAD DOGS
I'LL GO GET 'IM. HE'S HIDIN' IN THE BUSHES.
BINKY'S INFERNO
CLUNK

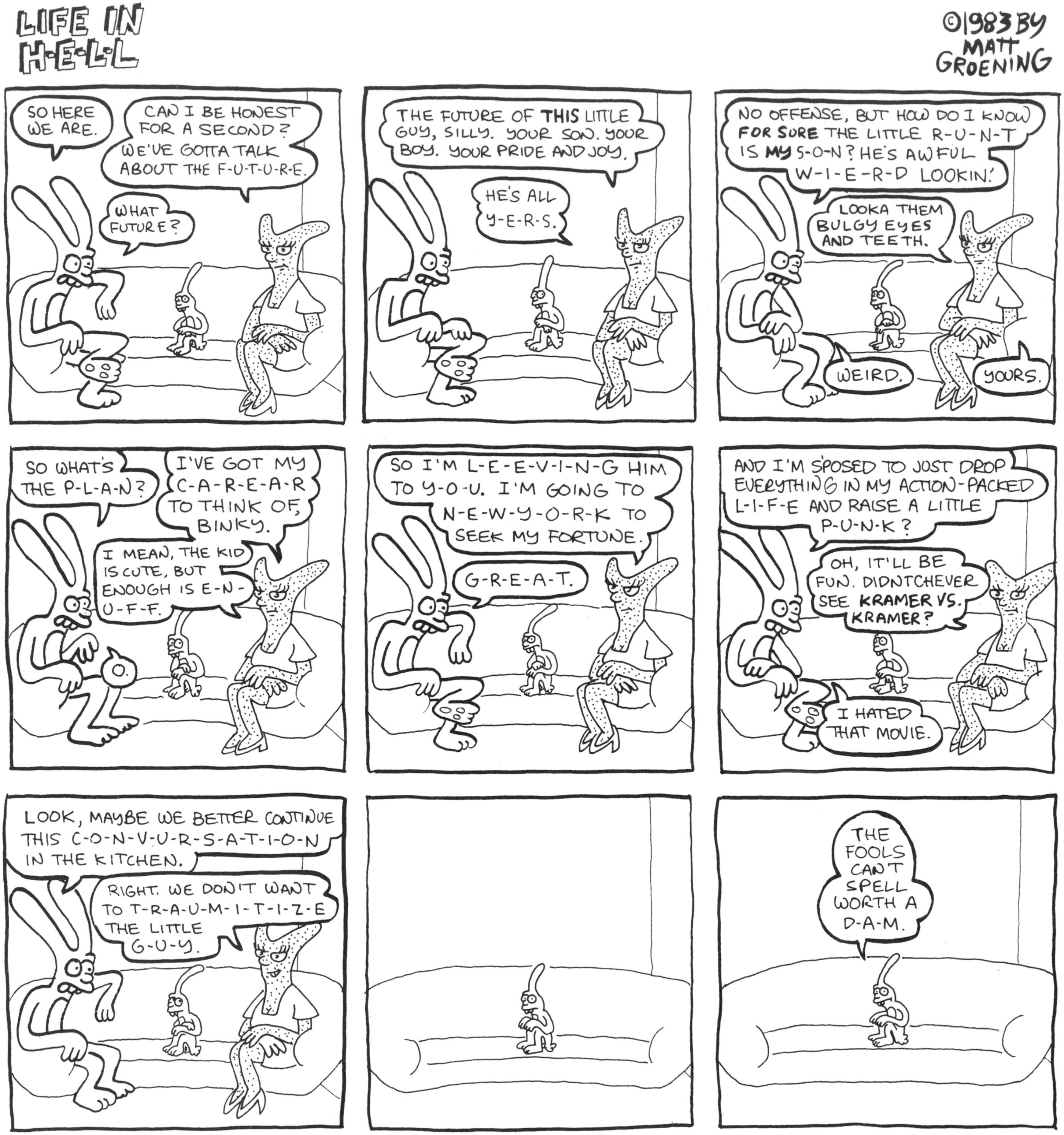
LIFE IN H·E·L·L
©1983 BY MATT GROENING
SO HERE WE ARE.
CAN I BE HONEST FOR A SECOND? WE'VE GOTTA TALK ABOUT THE F-U-T-U-R-E.
WHAT FUTURE?
THE FUTURE OF THIS LITTLE GUY, SILLY. YOUR SON. YOUR BOY. YOUR PRIDE AND JOY.
HE'S ALL Y-E-R-S.
NO OFFENSE, BUT HOW DO I KNOW FOR SURE THE LITTLE R-U-N-T IS MY S-O-N? HE'S AWFUL W-I-E-R-D LOOKIN'.
LOOKA THEM BULGY EYES AND TEETH.
WEIRD.
YOURS.
SO WHAT'S THE P-L-A-N?
I'VE GOT MY C-A-R-E-A-R TO THINK OF, BINKY.
I MEAN, THE KID IS CUTE, BUT ENOUGH IS E-N-U-F-F.
SO I'M L-E-E-V-I-N-G HIM TO Y-O-U. I'M GOING TO N-E-W-Y-O-R-K TO SEEK MY FORTUNE.
G-R-E-A-T.
AND I'M S'POSED TO JUST DROP EVERYTHING IN MY ACTION-PACKED L-I-F-E AND RAISE A LITTLE P-U-N-K?
OH, IT'LL BE FUN. DIDNTCHEVER SEE KRAMER VS. KRAMER?
I HATED THAT MOVIE.
LOOK, MAYBE WE BETTER CONTINUE THIS C-O-N-V-U-R-S-A-T-I-O-N IN THE KITCHEN.
RIGHT. WE DON'T WANT TO T-R-A-U-M-I-T-I-Z-E THE LITTLE G-U-Y.
THE FOOLS CAN'T SPELL WORTH A D-A-M.

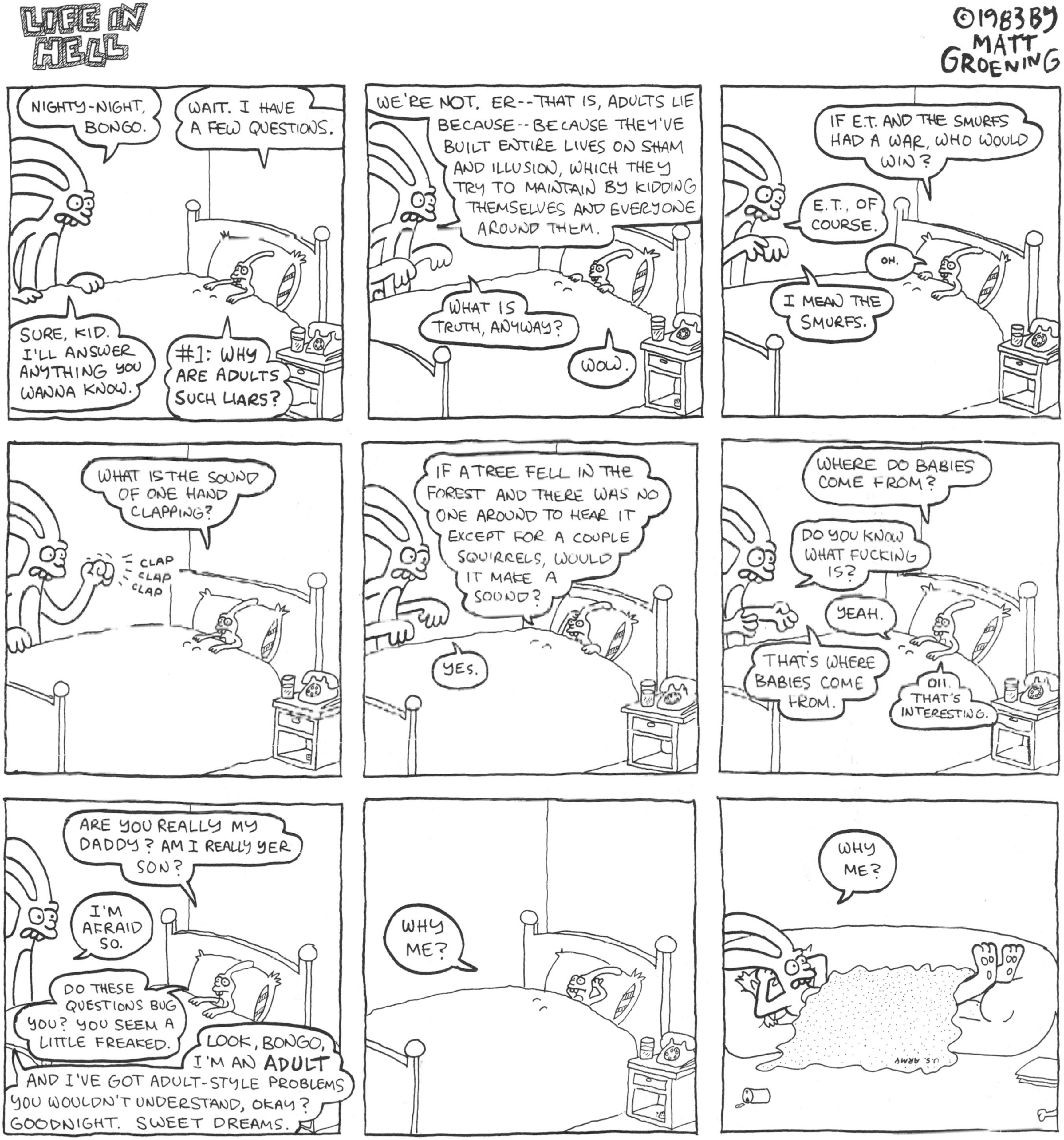
LIFE IN HELL
©1983 BY MATT GROENING
NIGHTY-NIGHT, BONGO.
WAIT. I HAVE A FEW QUESTIONS.
SURE, KID. I'LL ANSWER ANYTHING YOU WANNA KNOW.
#1: WHY ARE ADULTS SUCH LIARS?
WE'RE NOT. ER--THAT IS, ADULTS LIE BECAUSE--BECAUSE THEY'VE BUILT ENTIRE LIVES ON SHAM AND ILLUSION, WHICH THEY TRY TO MAINTAIN BY KIDDING THEMSELVES AND EVERYONE AROUND THEM.
WHAT IS TRUTH, ANYWAY?
WOW.
IF E.T. AND THE SMURFS HAD A WAR, WHO WOULD WIN?
E.T., OF COURSE.
OH.
I MEAN THE SMURFS.
WHAT IS THE SOUND OF ONE HAND CLAPPING?
CLAP CLAP CLAP
IF A TREE FELL IN THE FOREST AND THERE WAS NO ONE AROUND TO HEAR IT EXCEPT FOR A COUPLE SQUIRRELS, WOULD IT MAKE A SOUND?
YES.
WHERE DO BABIES COME FROM?
DO YOU KNOW WHAT FUCKING IS?
YEAH.
THAT'S WHERE BABIES COME FROM.
OH. THAT'S INTERESTING.
ARE YOU REALLY MY DADDY? AM I REALLY YER SON?
I'M AFRAID SO.
DO THESE QUESTIONS BUG YOU? YOU SEEM A LITTLE FREAKED.
LOOK, BONGO, I'M AN ADULT AND I'VE GOT ADULT-STYLE PROBLEMS YOU WOULDN'T UNDERSTAND, OKAY? GOODNIGHT. SWEET DREAMS.
WHY ME?
WHY ME?
U.S. ARMY

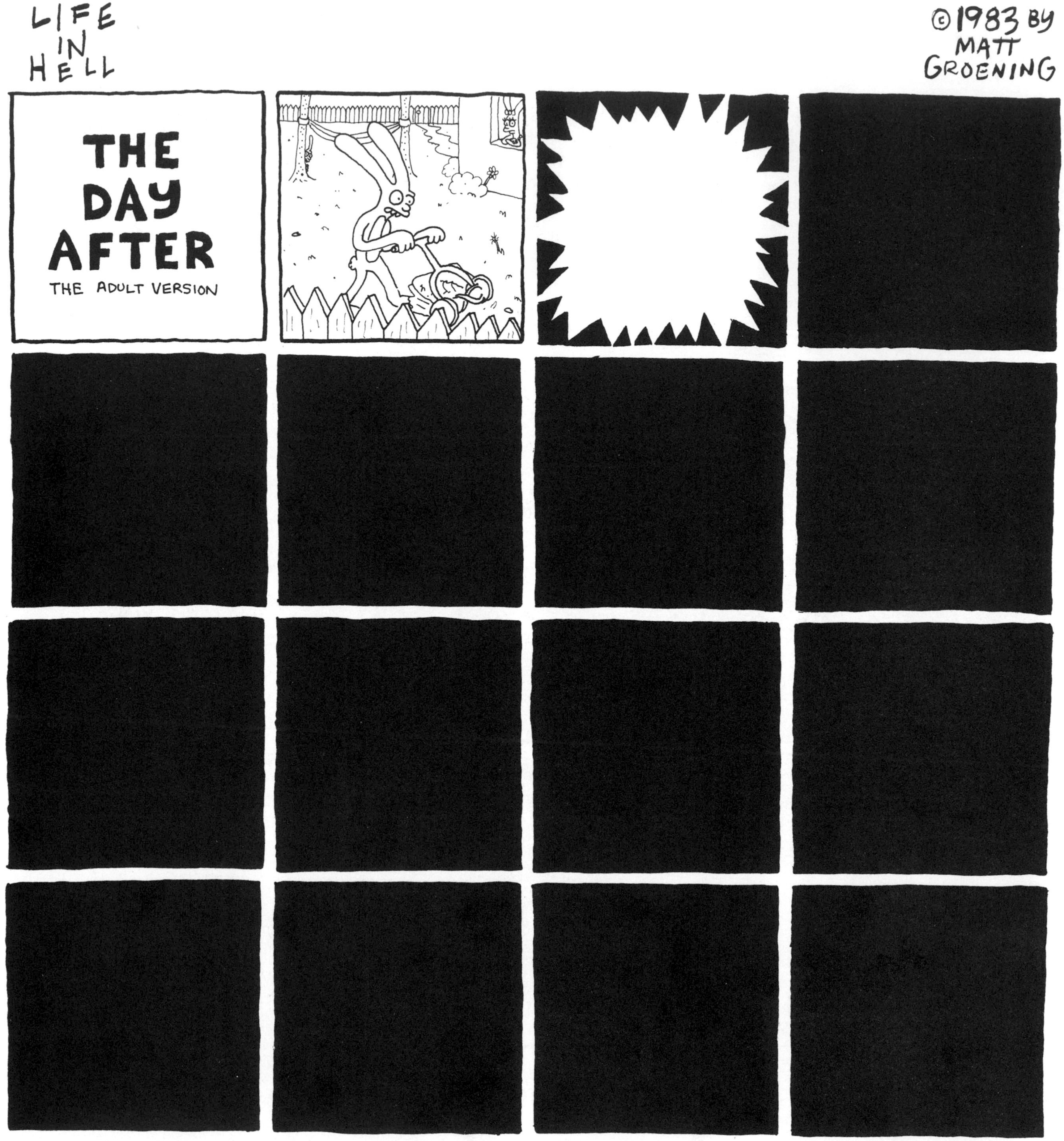

LIFE IN HELL
©1983 BY MATT GROENING
THE DAY AFTER
THE ADULT VERSION

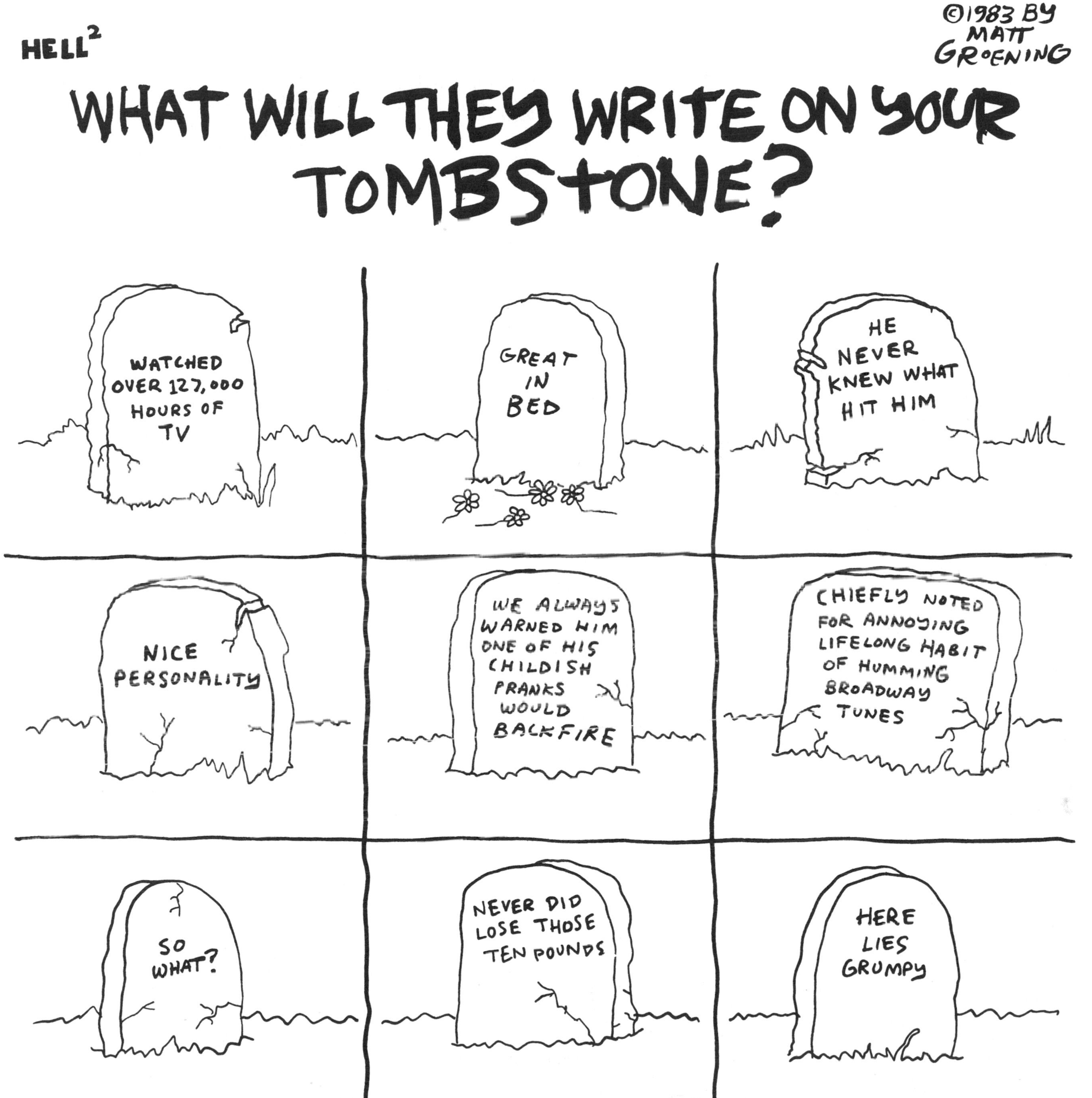
HELL²
©1983 BY MATT GROENING
WHAT WILL THEY WRITE ON YOUR TOMBSTONE?
WATCHED OVER 127,000 HOURS OF TV
GREAT IN BED
HE NEVER KNEW WHAT HIT HIM
NICE PERSONALITY
WE ALWAYS WARNED HIM ONE OF HIS CHILDISH PRANKS WOULD BACKFIRE
CHIEFLY NOTED FOR ANNOYING LIFELONG HABIT OF HUMMING BROADWAY TUNES
SO WHAT?
NEVER DID LOSE THOSE TEN POUNDS
HERE LIES GRUMPY

LAFFS IN HELL

©1983 BY MATT GROENING

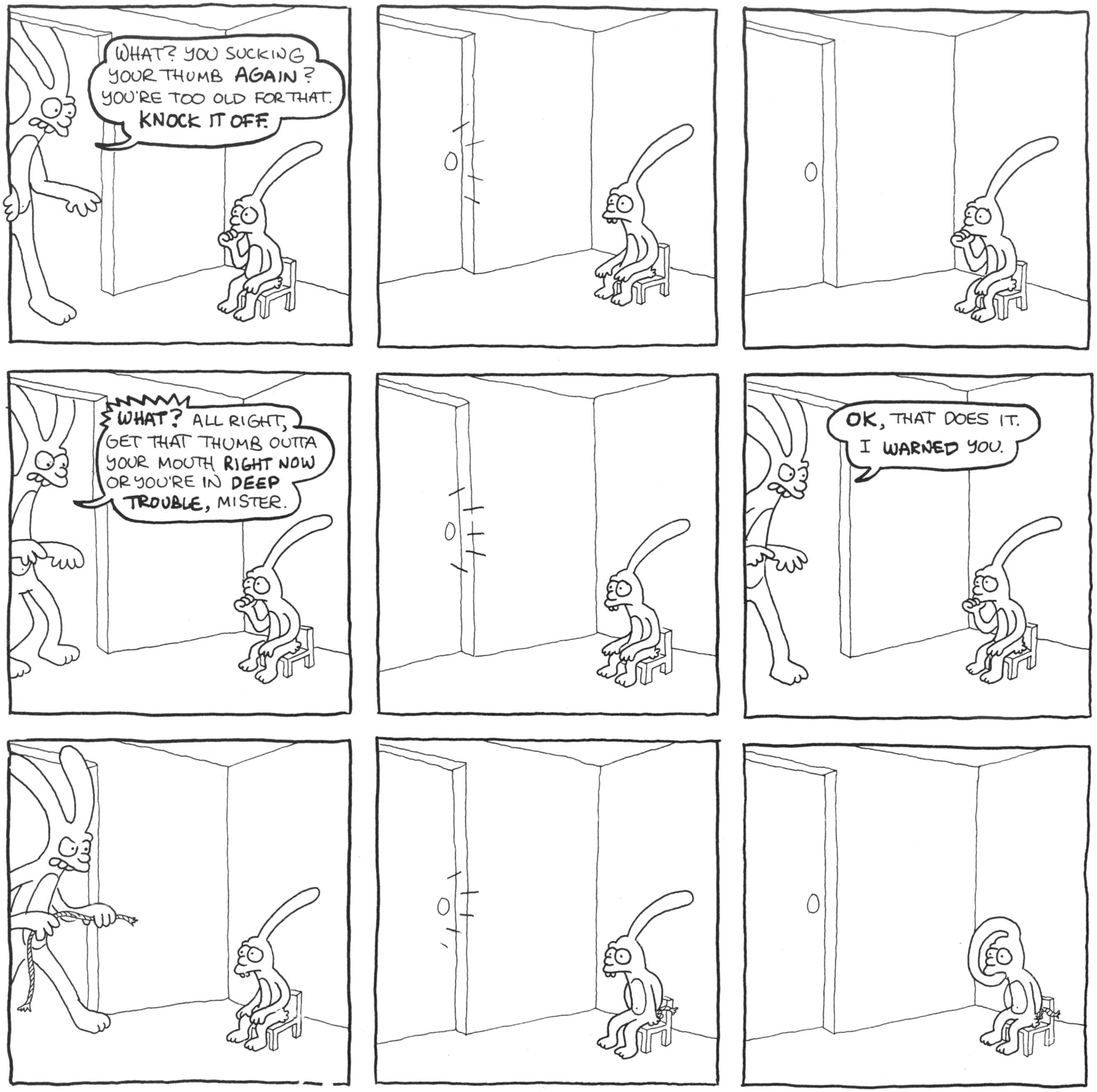
WHAT? YOU SUCKING YOUR THUMB AGAIN? YOU'RE TOO OLD FOR THAT. KNOCK IT OFF.
WHAT? ALL RIGHT, GET THAT THUMB OUTTA YOUR MOUTH RIGHT NOW OR YOU'RE IN DEEP TROUBLE, MISTER.
OK, THAT DOES IT. I WARNED YOU.

HELL, LIFE IN

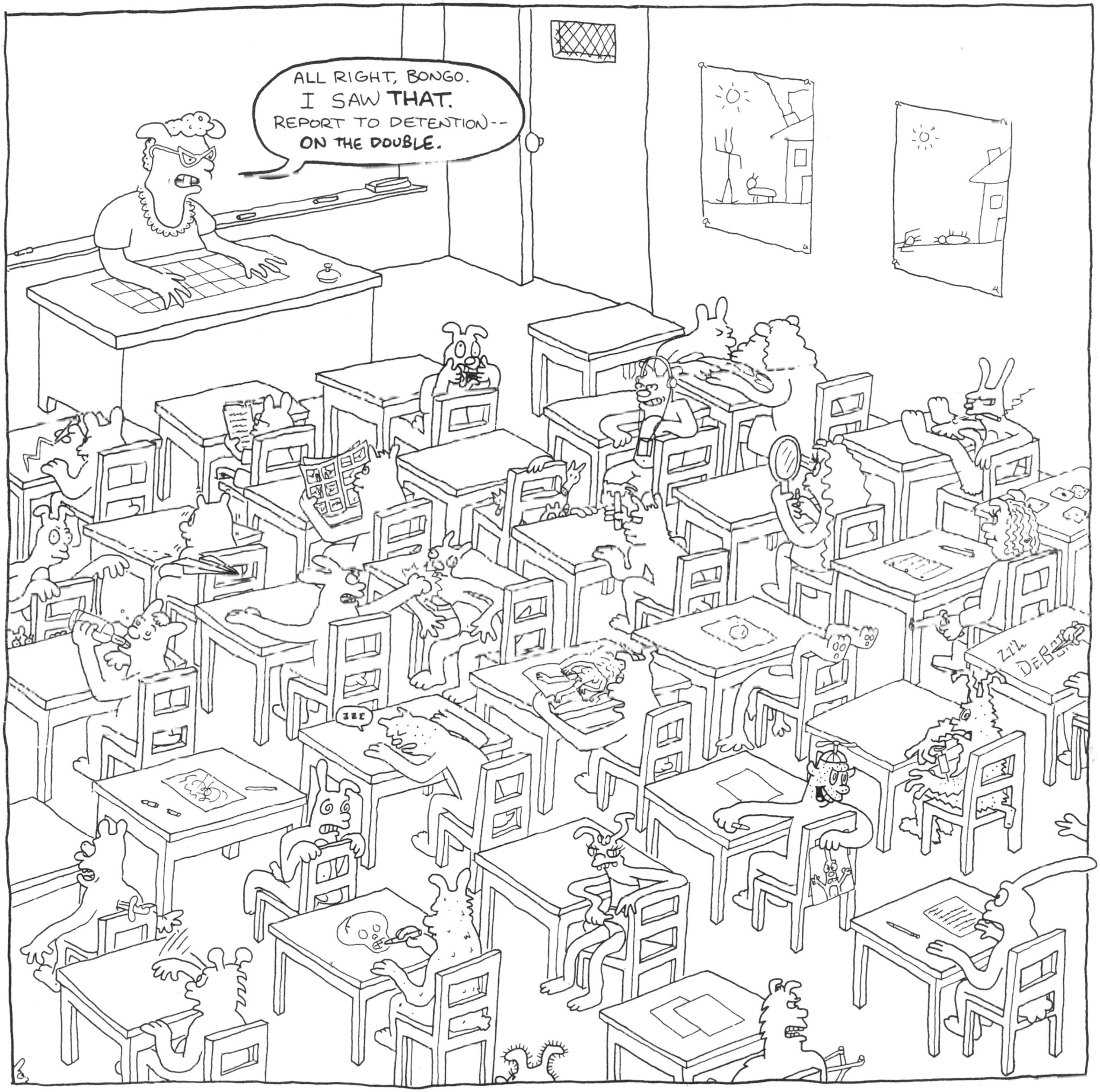
ALL RIGHT, BONGO. I SAW THAT. REPORT TO DETENTION-- ON THE DOUBLE.

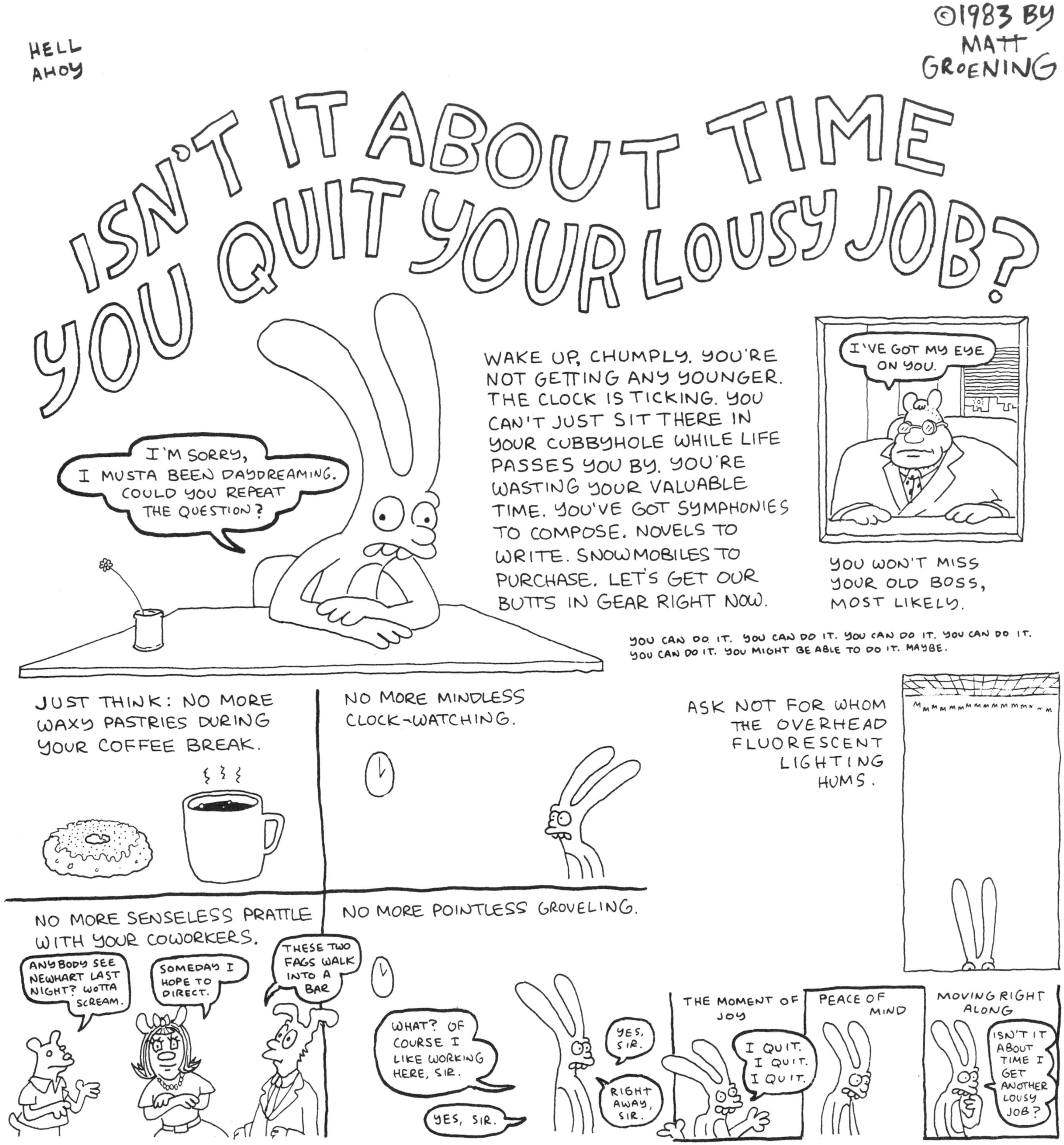
HELL AHOY
©1983 BY MATT GROENING
ISN'T IT ABOUT TIME YOU QUIT YOUR LOUSY JOB?
I'M SORRY, I MUSTA BEEN DAYDREAMING. COULD YOU REPEAT THE QUESTION?
WAKE UP, CHUMPLY. YOU'RE NOT GETTING ANY YOUNGER. THE CLOCK IS TICKING. YOU CAN'T JUST SIT THERE IN YOUR CUBBYHOLE WHILE LIFE PASSES YOU BY. YOU'RE WASTING YOUR VALUABLE TIME. YOU'VE GOT SYMPHONIES TO COMPOSE. NOVELS TO WRITE. SNOWMOBILES TO PURCHASE. LET'S GET OUR BUTTS IN GEAR RIGHT NOW.
I'VE GOT MY EYE ON YOU.
YOU WON'T MISS YOUR OLD BOSS, MOST LIKELY.
YOU CAN DO IT. YOU CAN DO IT. YOU CAN DO IT. YOU CAN DO IT. YOU CAN DO IT. YOU MIGHT BE ABLE TO DO IT. MAYBE.
JUST THINK: NO MORE WAXY PASTRIES DURING YOUR COFFEE BREAK.
NO MORE MINDLESS CLOCK-WATCHING.
ASK NOT FOR WHOM THE OVERHEAD FLUORESCENT LIGHTING HUMS.
MMMMMMMMMMMMMMMMM
NO MORE SENSELESS PRATTLE WITH YOUR COWORKERS.
ANYBODY SEE NEWHART LAST NIGHT? WOTTA SCREAM.
SOMEDAY I HOPE TO DIRECT.
THESE TWO FAGS WALK INTO A BAR
NO MORE POINTLESS GROVELING.
WHAT? OF COURSE I LIKE WORKING HERE, SIR.
YES, SIR.
YES, SIR.
RIGHT AWAY, SIR.
THE MOMENT OF JOY
I QUIT. I QUIT. I QUIT.
PEACE OF MIND
MOVING RIGHT ALONG
ISN'T IT ABOUT TIME I GET ANOTHER LOUSY JOB?

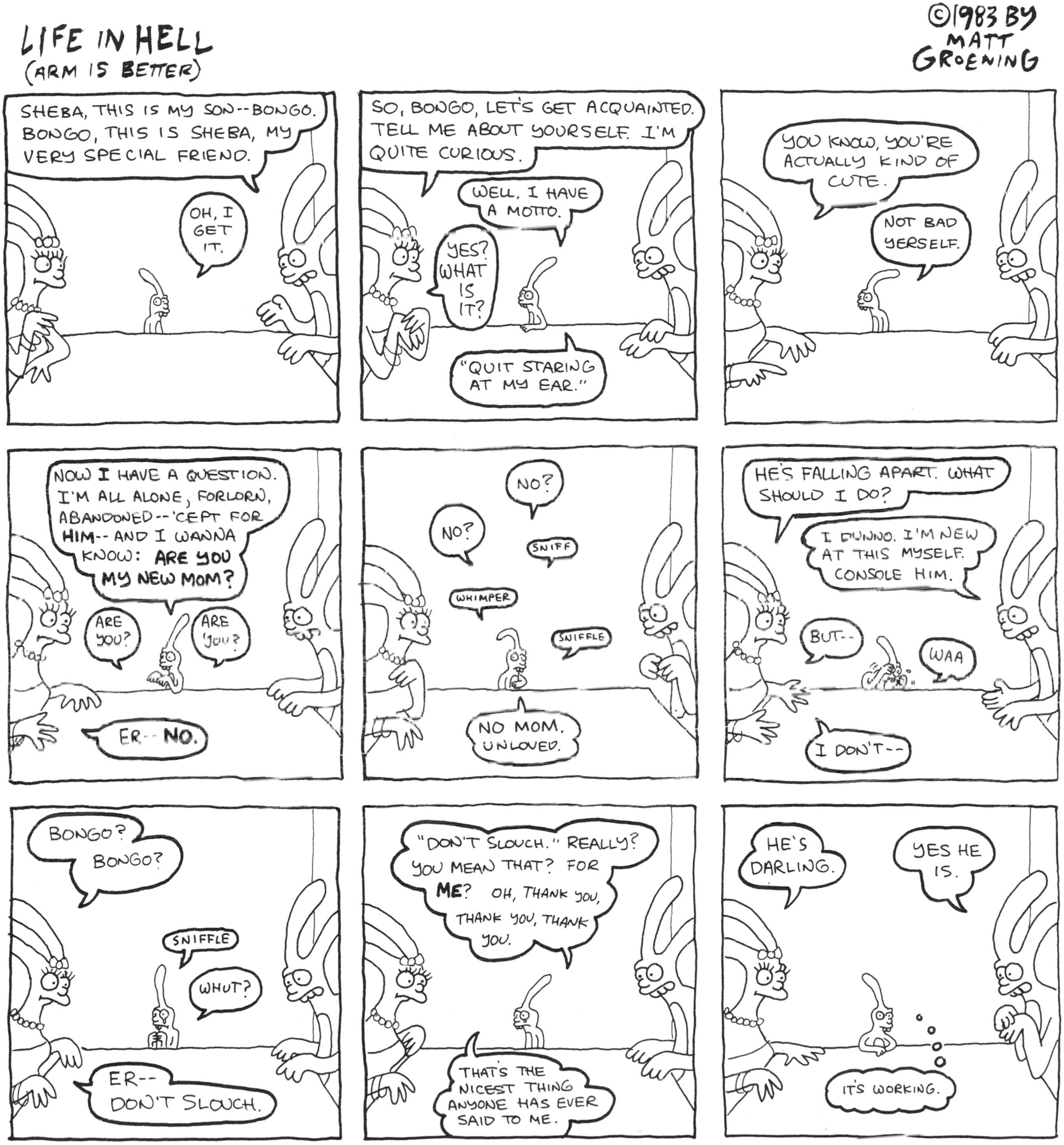
LIFE IN HELL
(ARM IS BETTER)
©1983 BY MATT GROENING
SHEBA, THIS IS MY SON--BONGO. BONGO, THIS IS SHEBA, MY VERY SPECIAL FRIEND.
OH, I GET IT.
SO, BONGO, LET'S GET ACQUAINTED. TELL ME ABOUT YOURSELF. I'M QUITE CURIOUS.
WELL, I HAVE A MOTTO.
YES? WHAT IS IT?
"QUIT STARING AT MY EAR."
YOU KNOW, YOU'RE ACTUALLY KIND OF CUTE.
NOT BAD YERSELF.
NOW I HAVE A QUESTION. I'M ALL ALONE, FORLORN, ABANDONED--'CEPT FOR HIM--AND I WANNA KNOW: ARE YOU MY NEW MOM?
ARE YOU?
ARE YOU?
ER--NO.
NO?
NO?
SNIFF
WHIMPER
SNIFFLE
NO MOM. UNLOVED.
HE'S FALLING APART. WHAT SHOULD I DO?
I DUNNO. I'M NEW AT THIS MYSELF. CONSOLE HIM.
BUT--
WAA
I DON'T--
BONGO? BONGO?
SNIFFLE
WHUT?
ER-- DON'T SLOUCH.
"DON'T SLOUCH." REALLY? YOU MEAN THAT? FOR ME? OH, THANK YOU, THANK YOU, THANK YOU.
THAT'S THE NICEST THING ANYONE HAS EVER SAID TO ME.
HE'S DARLING.
YES HE IS.
IT'S WORKING.

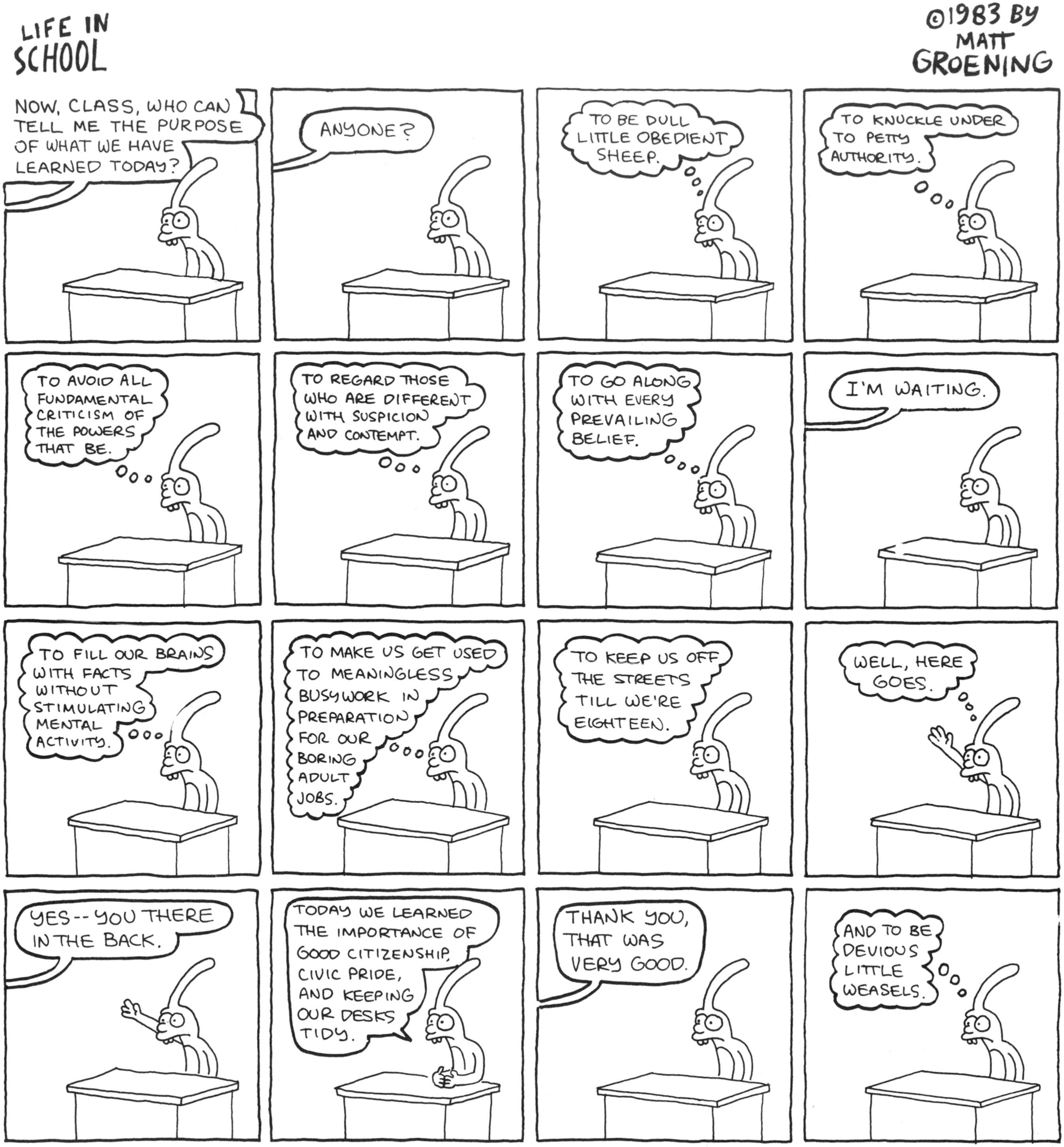
LIFE IN SCHOOL
©1983 BY MATT GROENING
NOW, CLASS, WHO CAN TELL ME THE PURPOSE OF WHAT WE HAVE LEARNED TODAY?
ANYONE?
TO BE DULL LITTLE OBEDIENT SHEEP.
TO KNUCKLE UNDER TO PETTY AUTHORITY.
TO AVOID ALL FUNDAMENTAL CRITICISM OF THE POWERS THAT BE.
TO REGARD THOSE WHO ARE DIFFERENT WITH SUSPICION AND CONTEMPT.
TO GO ALONG WITH EVERY PREVAILING BELIEF.
I'M WAITING.
TO FILL OUR BRAINS WITH FACTS WITHOUT STIMULATING MENTAL ACTIVITY.
TO MAKE US GET USED TO MEANINGLESS BUSYWORK IN PREPARATION FOR OUR BORING ADULT JOBS.
TO KEEP US OFF THE STREETS TILL WE'RE EIGHTEEN.
WELL, HERE GOES.
YES--YOU THERE IN THE BACK.
TODAY WE LEARNED THE IMPORTANCE OF GOOD CITIZENSHIP, CIVIC PRIDE, AND KEEPING OUR DESKS TIDY.
THANK YOU, THAT WAS VERY GOOD.
AND TO BE DEVIOUS LITTLE WEASELS.

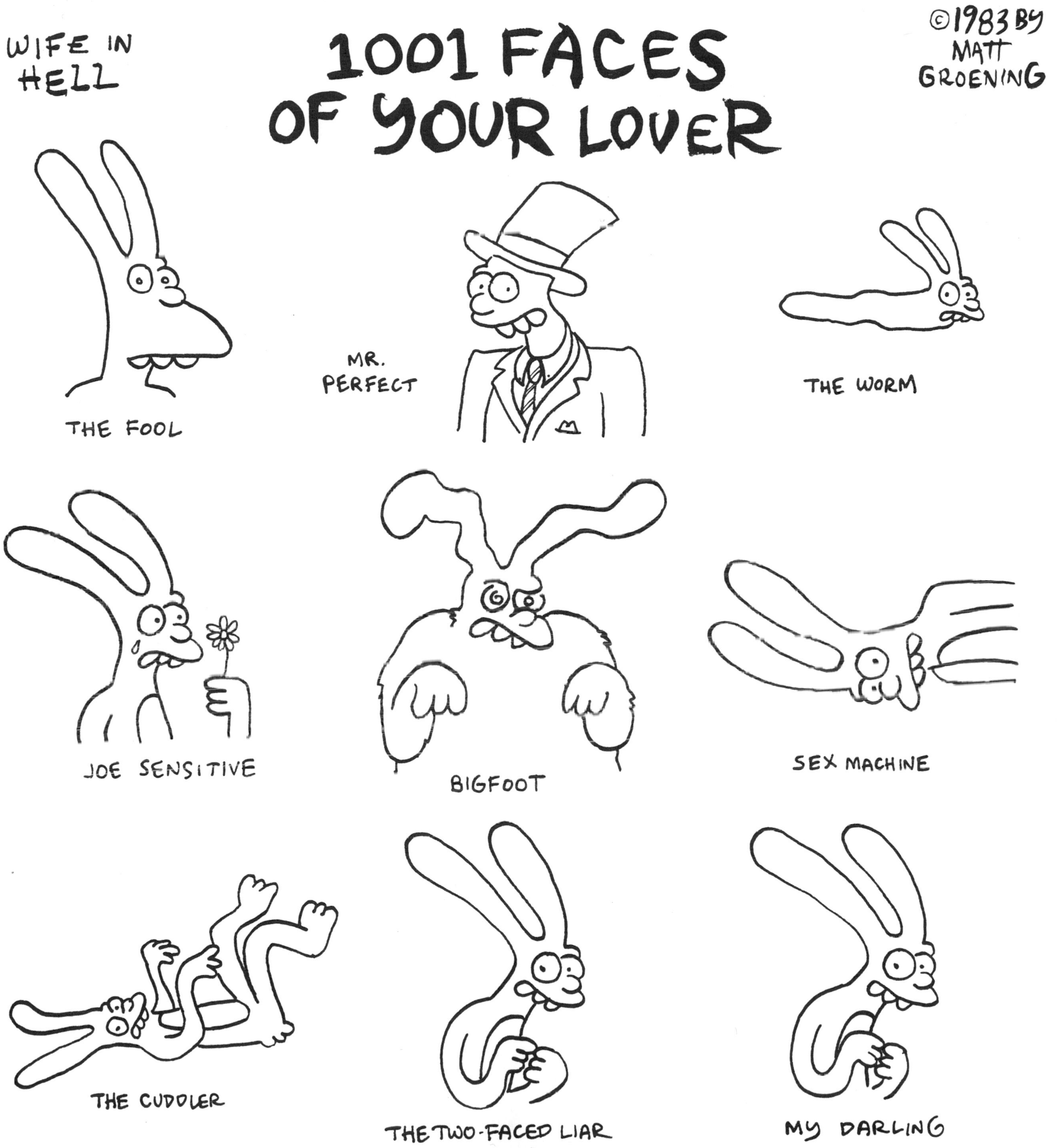
WIFE IN HELL
1001 FACES OF YOUR LOVER
©1983 BY MATT GROENING
THE FOOL
MR. PERFECT
THE WORM
JOE SENSITIVE
BIGFOOT
SEX MACHINE
THE CUDDLER
THE TWO-FACED LIAR
MY DARLING

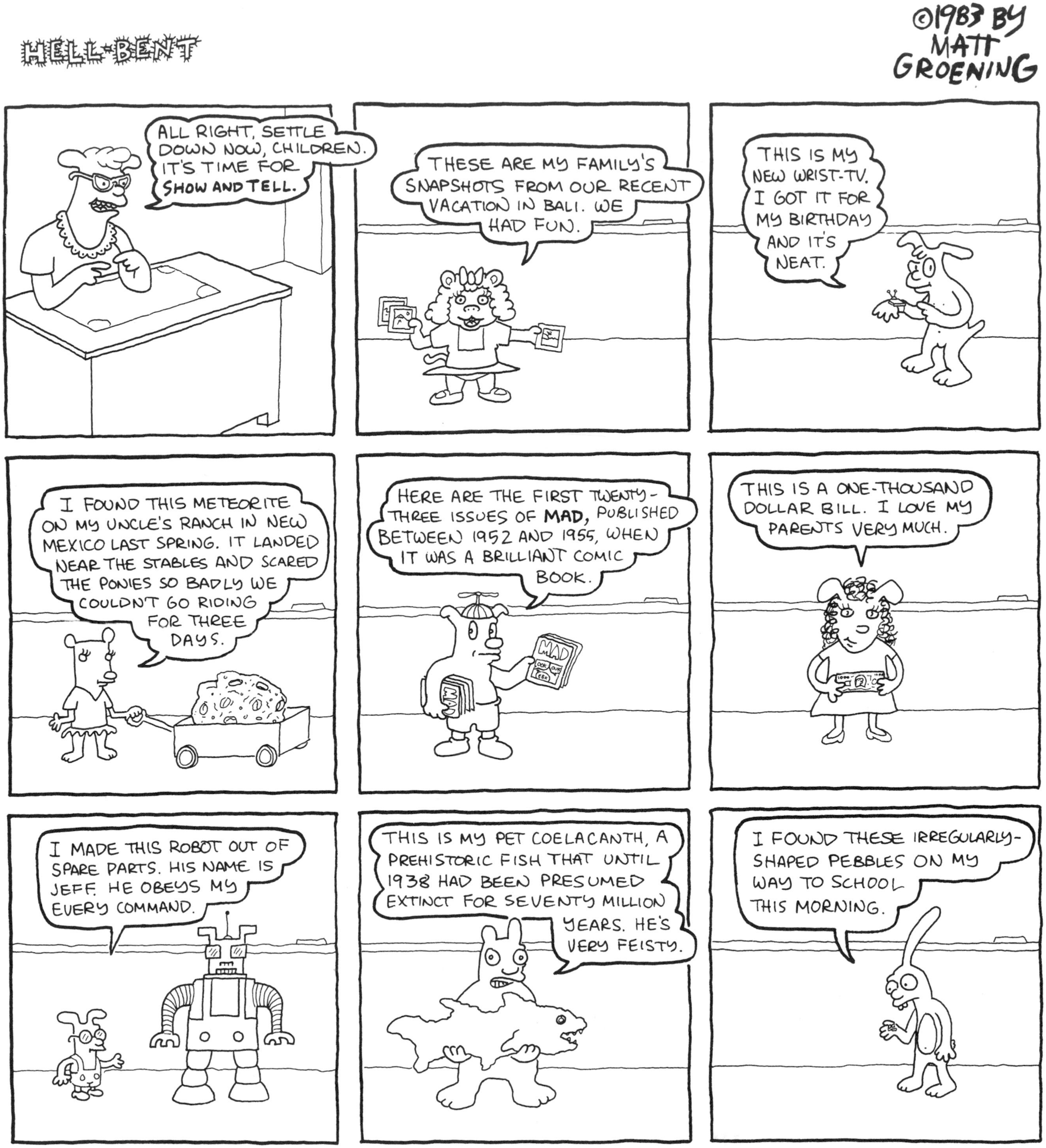
HELL-BENT
©1983 BY MATT GROENING
ALL RIGHT, SETTLE DOWN NOW, CHILDREN. IT'S TIME FOR SHOW AND TELL.
THESE ARE MY FAMILY'S SNAPSHOTS FROM OUR RECENT VACATION IN BALI. WE HAD FUN.
THIS IS MY NEW WRIST-TV. I GOT IT FOR MY BIRTHDAY AND IT'S NEAT.
I FOUND THIS METEORITE ON MY UNCLE'S RANCH IN NEW MEXICO LAST SPRING. IT LANDED NEAR THE STABLES AND SCARED THE PONIES SO BADLY WE COULDN'T GO RIDING FOR THREE DAYS.
HERE ARE THE FIRST TWENTY-THREE ISSUES OF MAD, PUBLISHED BETWEEN 1952 AND 1955, WHEN IT WAS A BRILLIANT COMIC BOOK.
MAD
THIS IS A ONE-THOUSAND DOLLAR BILL. I LOVE MY PARENTS VERY MUCH.
I MADE THIS ROBOT OUT OF SPARE PARTS. HIS NAME IS JEFF. HE OBEYS MY EVERY COMMAND.
THIS IS MY PET COELACANTH, A PREHISTORIC FISH THAT UNTIL 1938 HAD BEEN PRESUMED EXTINCT FOR SEVENTY MILLION YEARS. HE'S VERY FEISTY.
I FOUND THESE IRREGULARLY-SHAPED PEBBLES ON MY WAY TO SCHOOL THIS MORNING.

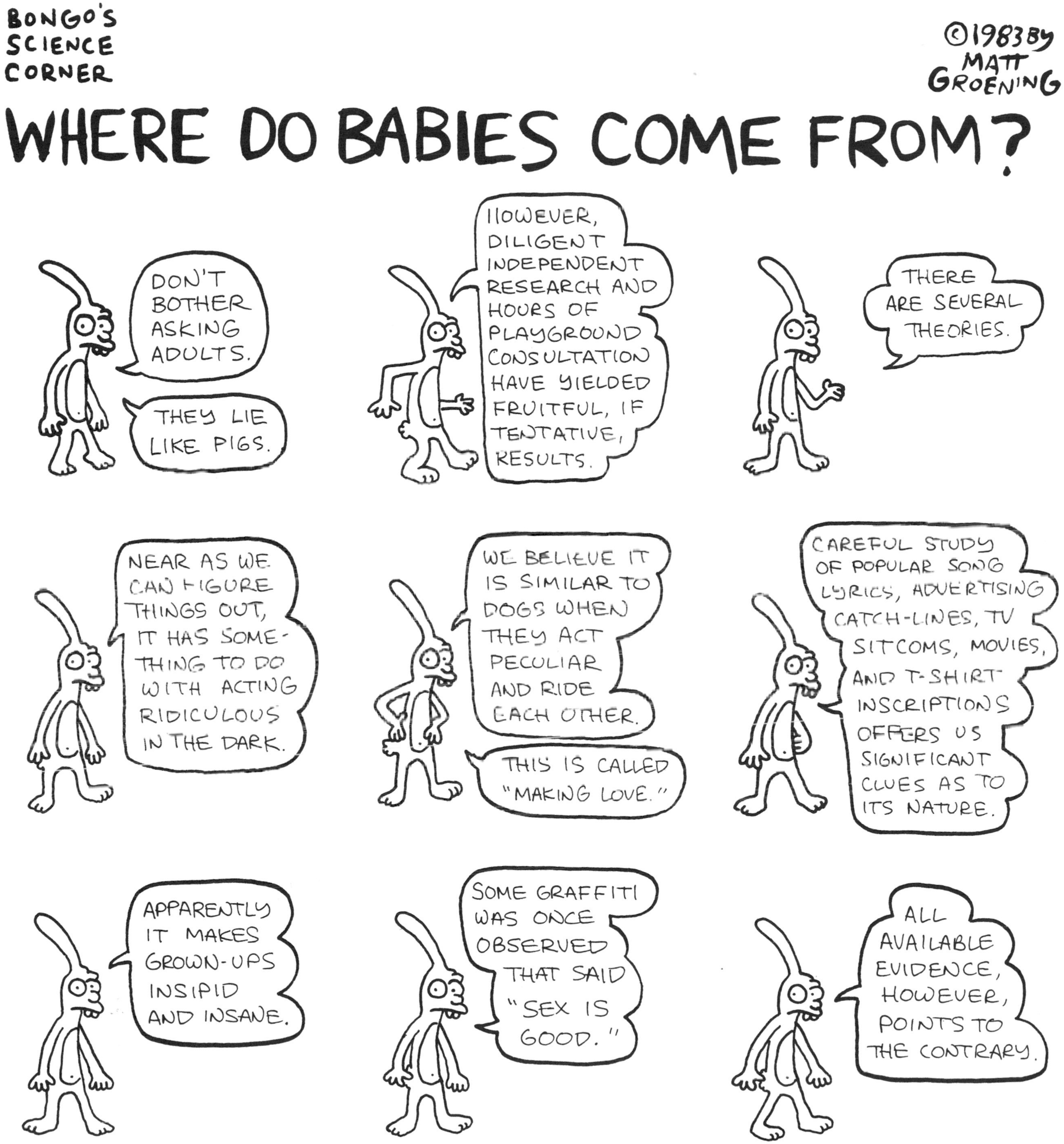
BONGO'S SCIENCE CORNER
©1983 BY MATT GROENING
WHERE DO BABIES COME FROM?
DON'T BOTHER ASKING ADULTS.
THEY LIE LIKE PIGS.
HOWEVER, DILIGENT INDEPENDENT RESEARCH AND HOURS OF PLAYGROUND CONSULTATION HAVE YIELDED FRUITFUL, IF TENTATIVE, RESULTS.
THERE ARE SEVERAL THEORIES.
NEAR AS WE CAN FIGURE THINGS OUT, IT HAS SOMETHING TO DO WITH ACTING RIDICULOUS IN THE DARK.
WE BELIEVE IT IS SIMILAR TO DOGS WHEN THEY ACT PECULIAR AND RIDE EACH OTHER.
THIS IS CALLED "MAKING LOVE."
CAREFUL STUDY OF POPULAR SONG LYRICS, ADVERTISING CATCH-LINES, TV SITCOMS, MOVIES, AND T-SHIRT INSCRIPTIONS OFFERS US SIGNIFICANT CLUES AS TO ITS NATURE.
APPARENTLY IT MAKES GROWN-UPS INSIPID AND INSANE.
SOME GRAFFITI WAS ONCE OBSERVED THAT SAID "SEX IS GOOD."
ALL AVAILABLE EVIDENCE, HOWEVER, POINTS TO THE CONTRARY.

LIFE IN HELL

PARENTS' GUIDE TO TEENAGE CRIME & PUNISHMENT

THE PROBLEM	THE CRIME	THE RESPONSE	THE PUNISHMENT	THE RESULT
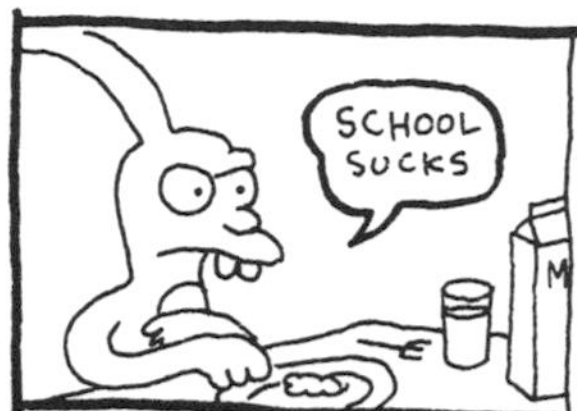 SCHOOL SUCKS	SOME SMARTASS REMARK AT DINNER	ICY STARE FORK POINTED IN KID'S DIRECTION "SHUT UP, YOU."	SILENT TREATMENT BARELY PERCEPTIBLE SHAKING OF HEAD WHENEVER KID SPEAKS	KID WILL MOVE OUT AT 18, GET A JOB IN COMPUTER PROGRAMMING, BE MARRIED, MISERABLE, AND DIVORCED BY 23
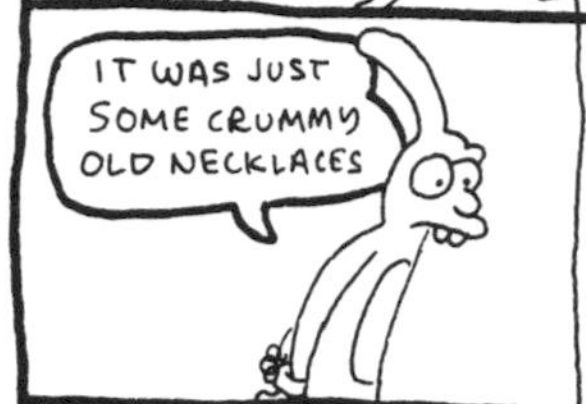 IT WAS JUST SOME CRUMMY OLD NECKLACES	CAUGHT SHOPLIFTING DOWN AT THE MALL	SLOW SHAKING OF HEAD IN DISGUST "SO YOU'RE A SLIMY LITTLE THIEF. I HOPE YOU'RE PROUD OF YOURSELF."	NO ALLOWANCE 2 MOS. GROUNDED 1 MO. REPROACHFUL LOOKS FROM NOW ON	KID WILL GO TO COMMUNITY COLLEGE, DROP OUT AFTER 2½ SEMESTERS, GO TO WORK FOR DAD'S BUSINESS
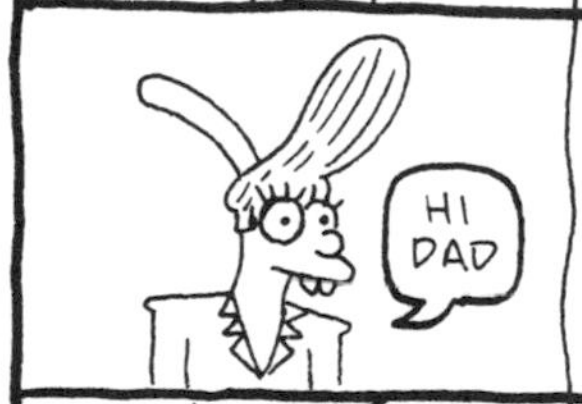 HI DAD	INSOLENT HAIR AND CLOTHING	SNORTS OF DISBELIEF "YOU'RE NOT LEAVING THIS HOUSE TILL YOU LOOK DECENT."	CONFISCATE CLOTHING CONTINUOUS BELITTLING SHIP KID OFF TO MILITARY SCHOOL	KID WILL SHAPE UP UPON GRADUATION, JOIN ARMY, WOUND SELF ON PATROL IN CENTRAL AMERICA
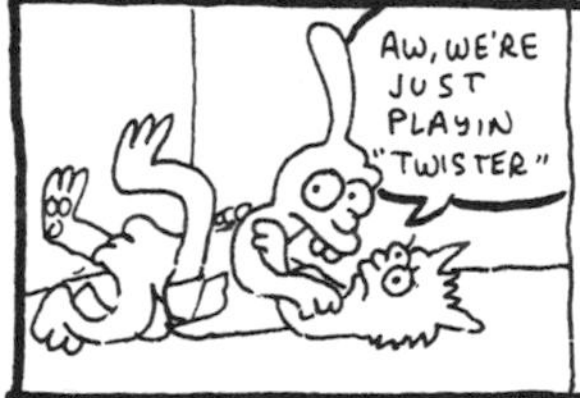 AW, WE'RE JUST PLAYIN "TWISTER"	HEAVY PETTING OR WORSE WITH SOME SQUINTY LITTLE CREEP IN THE BASEMENT REC ROOM	"JUST WHAT IN GOD'S NAME IS GOING ON AROUND HERE?"	KID'S DATE BANISHED EARLY CURFEW COMPULSORY CHURCH ATTENDANCE	KID WILL RUN AWAY AT 16, HITCHHIKE TO NEXT STATE, GET A JOB IN A TIRE WAREHOUSE, SETTLE DOWN BY 18
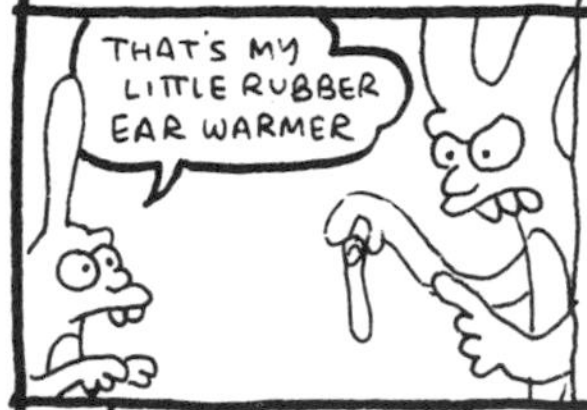 THAT'S MY LITTLE RUBBER EAR WARMER	SECRET INSPECTION OF BEDROOM REVEALS BIRTH CONTROL PILLS OR DEVICES	FLARING NOSTRILS HUFFING AND PUFFING SPUTTERING MAYBE KNOCK THE KID AROUND A BIT	EARLY CURFEW GROUNDED 1 MO. CONTINUED SECRET INSPECTIONS OF BEDROOM GLOWERING LOOKS	KID WILL BE MARRIED BY 19, 2 KIDS BY 21, 3 KIDS BY 23, COMPLETELY DEMORALIZED BY 25
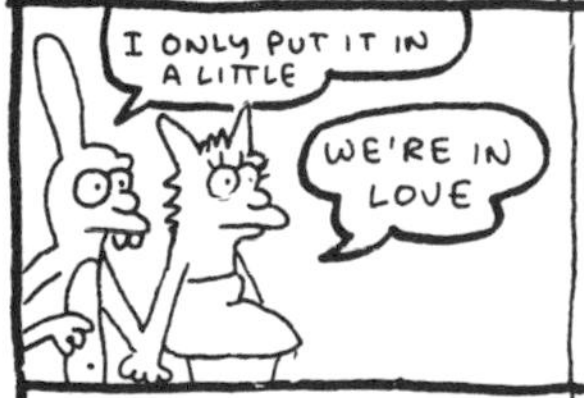 I ONLY PUT IT IN A LITTLE WE'RE IN LOVE	PREGNANT	"HOW THE **HELL** DID YOU GET PREGNANT?"	KICK KID OUT OF THE HOUSE	BABY WILL BE ABORTED OR GIVEN UP FOR ADOPTION, KID WILL MOVE ACROSS COUNTRY AND NEVER SPEAK TO YOU AGAIN
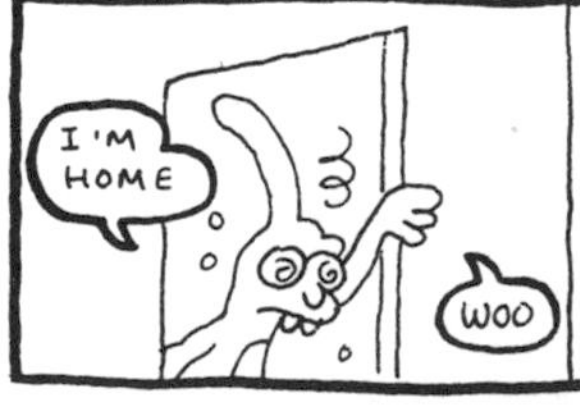 I'M HOME WOO	HOME AFTER CURFEW BEER ON BREATH	"IF THERE'S **ONE** SCRATCH ON MY CAR, YOU'RE GOING TO WISH YOU WERE NEVER BORN."	NO BORROWING DAD'S CAR 2 MOS. EARLY CURFEW BALEFUL LOOKS	KID WILL GO TO COLLEGE, JOIN FRATERNITY OR SORORITY, MEET FUTURE SPOUSE, GET MARRIED, END UP JUST LIKE YOU

THIS, BY THE WAY, IS
LIFE IN HELL
#200

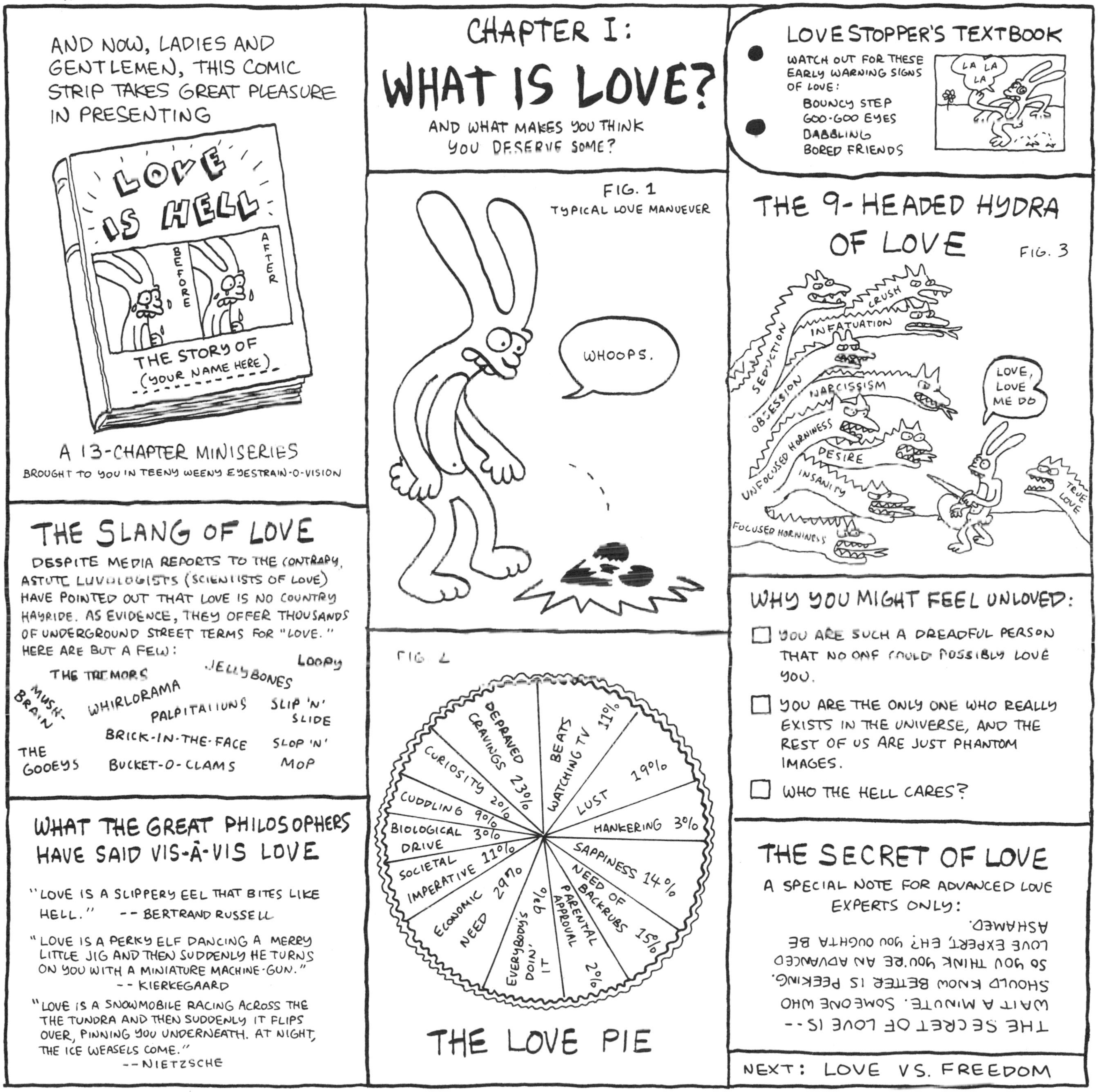
AND NOW, LADIES AND GENTLEMEN, THIS COMIC STRIP TAKES GREAT PLEASURE IN PRESENTING
LOVE IS HELL
BEFORE
AFTER
THE STORY OF (YOUR NAME HERE)
A 13-CHAPTER MINISERIES
BROUGHT TO YOU IN TEENY WEENY EYESTRAIN-O-VISION
CHAPTER I:
WHAT IS LOVE?
AND WHAT MAKES YOU THINK YOU DESERVE SOME?
LOVESTOPPER'S TEXTBOOK
WATCH OUT FOR THESE EARLY WARNING SIGNS OF LOVE:
BOUNCY STEP
GOO-GOO EYES
DABBLING
BORED FRIENDS
LA LA LA
FIG. 1
TYPICAL LOVE MANUEVER
WHOOPS.
THE 9-HEADED HYDRA OF LOVE
FIG. 3
CRUSH
INFATUATION
SEDUCTION
NARCISSISM
OBSESSION
UNFOCUSED HORNINESS
DESIRE
INSANITY
FOCUSED HORNINESS
LOVE, LOVE ME DO
TRUE LOVE
THE SLANG OF LOVE
DESPITE MEDIA REPORTS TO THE CONTRARY, ASTUTE LUVOLOGISTS (SCIENTISTS OF LOVE) HAVE POINTED OUT THAT LOVE IS NO COUNTRY HAYRIDE. AS EVIDENCE, THEY OFFER THOUSANDS OF UNDERGROUND STREET TERMS FOR "LOVE." HERE ARE BUT A FEW:
THE TREMORS
JELLYBONES
LOOPY
MUSH-BRAIN
WHIRLORAMA
PALPITATIONS
SLIP 'N' SLIDE
BRICK-IN-THE-FACE
SLOP 'N' MOP
THE GOOEYS
BUCKET-O-CLAMS
FIG. 2
DEPRAVED CRAVINGS 23%
BEATS WATCHING TV 11%
LUST 19%
HANKERING 3%
SAPPINESS 14%
NEED OF BACKRUBS 15%
PARENTAL APPROVAL 2%
EVERYBODY'S DOIN' IT 9%
ECONOMIC NEED 29%
SOCIETAL IMPERATIVE 11%
BIOLOGICAL DRIVE 3%
CUDDLING 9%
CURIOSITY 2%
THE LOVE PIE
WHY YOU MIGHT FEEL UNLOVED:
YOU ARE SUCH A DREADFUL PERSON THAT NO ONE COULD POSSIBLY LOVE YOU.
YOU ARE THE ONLY ONE WHO REALLY EXISTS IN THE UNIVERSE, AND THE REST OF US ARE JUST PHANTOM IMAGES.
WHO THE HELL CARES?
WHAT THE GREAT PHILOSOPHERS HAVE SAID VIS-À-VIS LOVE
"LOVE IS A SLIPPERY EEL THAT BITES LIKE HELL." --BERTRAND RUSSELL
"LOVE IS A PERKY ELF DANCING A MERRY LITTLE JIG AND THEN SUDDENLY HE TURNS ON YOU WITH A MINIATURE MACHINE-GUN." --KIERKEGAARD
"LOVE IS A SNOWMOBILE RACING ACROSS THE THE TUNDRA AND THEN SUDDENLY IT FLIPS OVER, PINNING YOU UNDERNEATH. AT NIGHT, THE ICE WEASELS COME." --NIETZSCHE
THE SECRET OF LOVE
A SPECIAL NOTE FOR ADVANCED LOVE EXPERTS ONLY:
THE SECRET OF LOVE IS-- WAIT A MINUTE. SOMEONE WHO SHOULD KNOW BETTER IS PEEKING. SO YOU THINK YOU'RE AN ADVANCED LOVE EXPERT, EH? YOU OUGHTA BE ASHAMED.
NEXT: LOVE VS. FREEDOM

© 1984 BY MATT GROENING

A SPECIAL 13-CHAPTER BONUS FUN SERIES! COLLECT 'EM ALL! YOU FORGOT TO CLIP LAST WEEK'S STRIP, IN WHICH CASE FORGET IT. (NOT RESPONSIBLE FOR ADVICE TAKEN.)

LOVE IS HELL

CHAPTER II: THE 57 VARIETIES OF LOVE

LOVEMONGER'S TEXTBOOK
○ AVOID SHARING AFFECTION WITH PEOPLE WEARING DESPERATE T-SHIRTS.
○ [t-shirt: WILL YOU BE MY FRIEND?]

IN WESTERN TRADITION, THERE HAVE BEEN APPROXIMATELY FOUR KINDS, OR FLAVORS, OF LOVE. THESE INCLUDE:

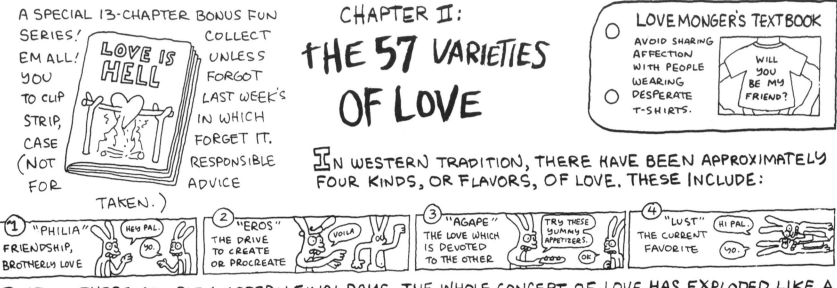

1 "PHILIA" FRIENDSHIP, BROTHERLY LOVE — HEY PAL. YO.

2 "EROS" THE DRIVE TO CREATE OR PROCREATE — VOILA

3 "AGAPE" THE LOVE WHICH IS DEVOTED TO THE OTHER — TRY THESE YUMMY APPETIZERS. OK

4 "LUST" THE CURRENT FAVORITE — HI PAL. YO.

BUT IN THESE COMPLEX MODERN FINAL DAYS, THE WHOLE CONCEPT OF LOVE HAS EXPLODED LIKE A CORNUCOPIA WITH A STICK OF DYNAMITE STUCK IN IT. THE MESS IS EVERYWHERE. IN FACT, YOU PROBABLY GOT SOME FLICKED ON YOU RIGHT NOW AND YOU DON'T EVEN KNOW IT.

SCIENTISTS WORKING LATE INTO THE NIGHT HAVE NOW ISOLATED SOME 57 VARIETIES OF LOVE. WHAT IS PECULIAR, THEY NOTE, IS THAT MANY OF THESE LOVE-VARIETIES INTERACT SIMULTANEOUSLY, CAUSING MUCH JOY, ECSTASY, CONFUSION, AND FUCK-UPS.

THIS IS CALLED THE "LOVE BLENDER EFFECT"; HENCE THE POPULAR STREET CRY:

I'VE JUST BEEN THROUGH THE LOVE BLENDER!!!

I CAN DIG IT.

WILL YOU BE MY FRIEND.

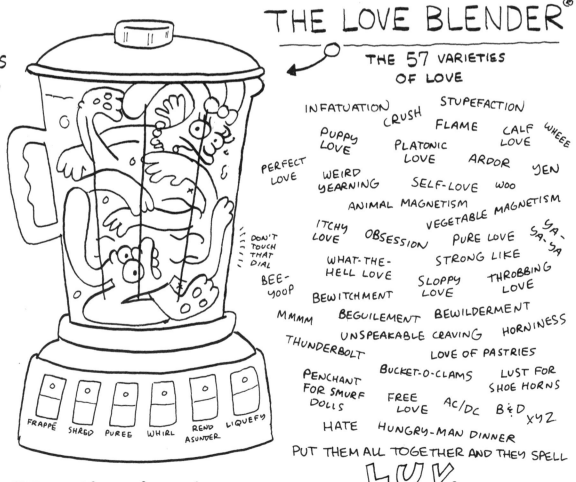

THE LOVE BLENDER®

FRAPPE SHRED PUREE WHIRL REND ASUNDER LIQUEFY

DON'T TOUCH THAT DIAL

THE 57 VARIETIES OF LOVE

INFATUATION STUPEFACTION
CRUSH FLAME CALF LOVE WHEEE
PUPPY LOVE PLATONIC LOVE ARDOR YEN
PERFECT LOVE WEIRD YEARNING SELF-LOVE WOO
ANIMAL MAGNETISM VEGETABLE MAGNETISM
ITCHY LOVE OBSESSION PURE LOVE SA-SA-SA
WHAT-THE-HELL LOVE STRONG LIKE
BEE-YOOP SLOPPY LOVE THROBBING LOVE
BEWITCHMENT
MMMM BEGUILEMENT BEWILDERMENT
UNSPEAKABLE CRAVING HORNINESS
THUNDERBOLT LOVE OF PASTRIES
PENCHANT FOR SMURF DOLLS BUCKET-O-CLAMS LUST FOR SHOE HORNS
FREE LOVE AC/DC B&D XYZ
HATE HUNGRY-MAN DINNER

PUT THEM ALL TOGETHER AND THEY SPELL LUV.

NEXT: DATING & MATING & HATING & BERATING

LIFE IN HELL

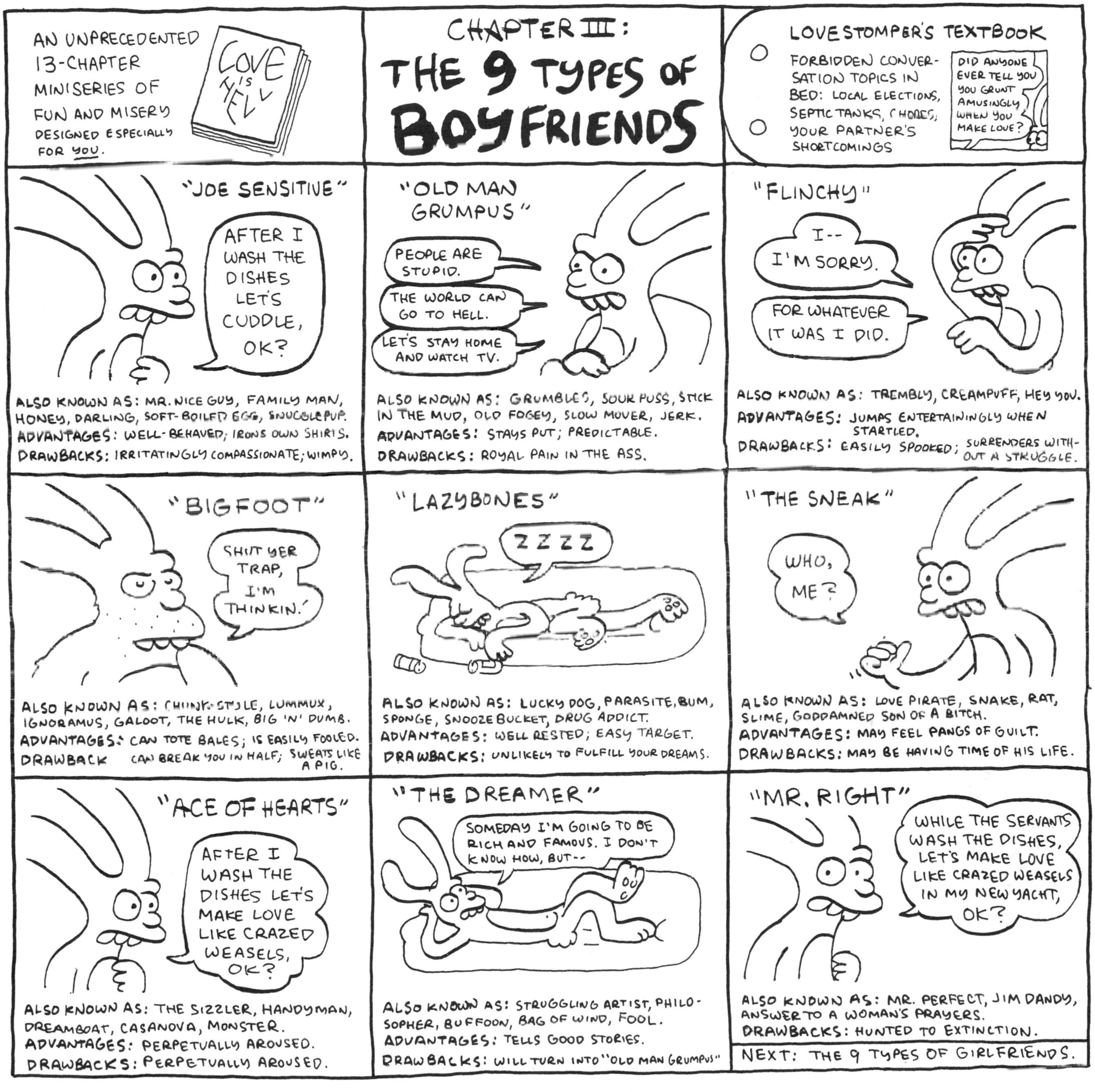
AN UNPRECEDENTED 13-CHAPTER MINISERIES OF FUN AND MISERY DESIGNED ESPECIALLY FOR YOU.
LOVE IS HELL
CHAPTER III: THE 9 TYPES OF BOYFRIENDS
LOVESTOMPER'S TEXTBOOK
FORBIDDEN CONVERSATION TOPICS IN BED: LOCAL ELECTIONS, SEPTIC TANKS, CHORES, YOUR PARTNER'S SHORTCOMINGS
DID ANYONE EVER TELL YOU YOU GRUNT AMUSINGLY WHEN YOU MAKE LOVE?
"JOE SENSITIVE"
AFTER I WASH THE DISHES LET'S CUDDLE, OK?
ALSO KNOWN AS: MR. NICE GUY, FAMILY MAN, HONEY, DARLING, SOFT-BOILED EGG, SNUGGLEPUP.
ADVANTAGES: WELL-BEHAVED; IRONS OWN SHIRTS.
DRAWBACKS: IRRITATINGLY COMPASSIONATE; WIMPY.
"OLD MAN GRUMPUS"
PEOPLE ARE STUPID.
THE WORLD CAN GO TO HELL.
LET'S STAY HOME AND WATCH TV.
ALSO KNOWN AS: GRUMBLES, SOUR PUSS, STICK IN THE MUD, OLD FOGEY, SLOW MOVER, JERK.
ADVANTAGES: STAYS PUT; PREDICTABLE.
DRAWBACKS: ROYAL PAIN IN THE ASS.
"FLINCHY"
I-- I'M SORRY.
FOR WHATEVER IT WAS I DID.
ALSO KNOWN AS: TREMBLY, CREAMPUFF, HEY YOU.
ADVANTAGES: JUMPS ENTERTAININGLY WHEN STARTLED.
DRAWBACKS: EASILY SPOOKED; SURRENDERS WITHOUT A STRUGGLE.
"BIGFOOT"
SHUT YER TRAP, I'M THINKIN.'
ALSO KNOWN AS: CHUNK-STYLE, LUMMOX, IGNORAMUS, GALOOT, THE HULK, BIG 'N' DUMB.
ADVANTAGES: CAN TOTE BALES; IS EASILY FOOLED.
DRAWBACK CAN BREAK YOU IN HALF; SWEATS LIKE A PIG.
"LAZYBONES"
Z Z Z Z
ALSO KNOWN AS: LUCKY DOG, PARASITE, BUM, SPONGE, SNOOZE BUCKET, DRUG ADDICT.
ADVANTAGES: WELL RESTED; EASY TARGET.
DRAWBACKS: UNLIKELY TO FULFILL YOUR DREAMS.
"THE SNEAK"
WHO, ME?
ALSO KNOWN AS: LOVE PIRATE, SNAKE, RAT, SLIME, GODDAMNED SON OF A BITCH.
ADVANTAGES: MAY FEEL PANGS OF GUILT.
DRAWBACKS: MAY BE HAVING TIME OF HIS LIFE.
"ACE OF HEARTS"
AFTER I WASH THE DISHES LET'S MAKE LOVE LIKE CRAZED WEASELS, OK?
ALSO KNOWN AS: THE SIZZLER, HANDYMAN, DREAMBOAT, CASANOVA, MONSTER.
ADVANTAGES: PERPETUALLY AROUSED.
DRAWBACKS: PERPETUALLY AROUSED.
"THE DREAMER"
SOMEDAY I'M GOING TO BE RICH AND FAMOUS. I DON'T KNOW HOW, BUT--
ALSO KNOWN AS: STRUGGLING ARTIST, PHILOSOPHER, BUFFOON, BAG OF WIND, FOOL.
ADVANTAGES: TELLS GOOD STORIES.
DRAWBACKS: WILL TURN INTO "OLD MAN GRUMPUS"
"MR. RIGHT"
WHILE THE SERVANTS WASH THE DISHES, LET'S MAKE LOVE LIKE CRAZED WEASELS IN MY NEW YACHT, OK?
ALSO KNOWN AS: MR. PERFECT, JIM DANDY, ANSWER TO A WOMAN'S PRAYERS.
DRAWBACKS: HUNTED TO EXTINCTION.
NEXT: THE 9 TYPES OF GIRLFRIENDS.

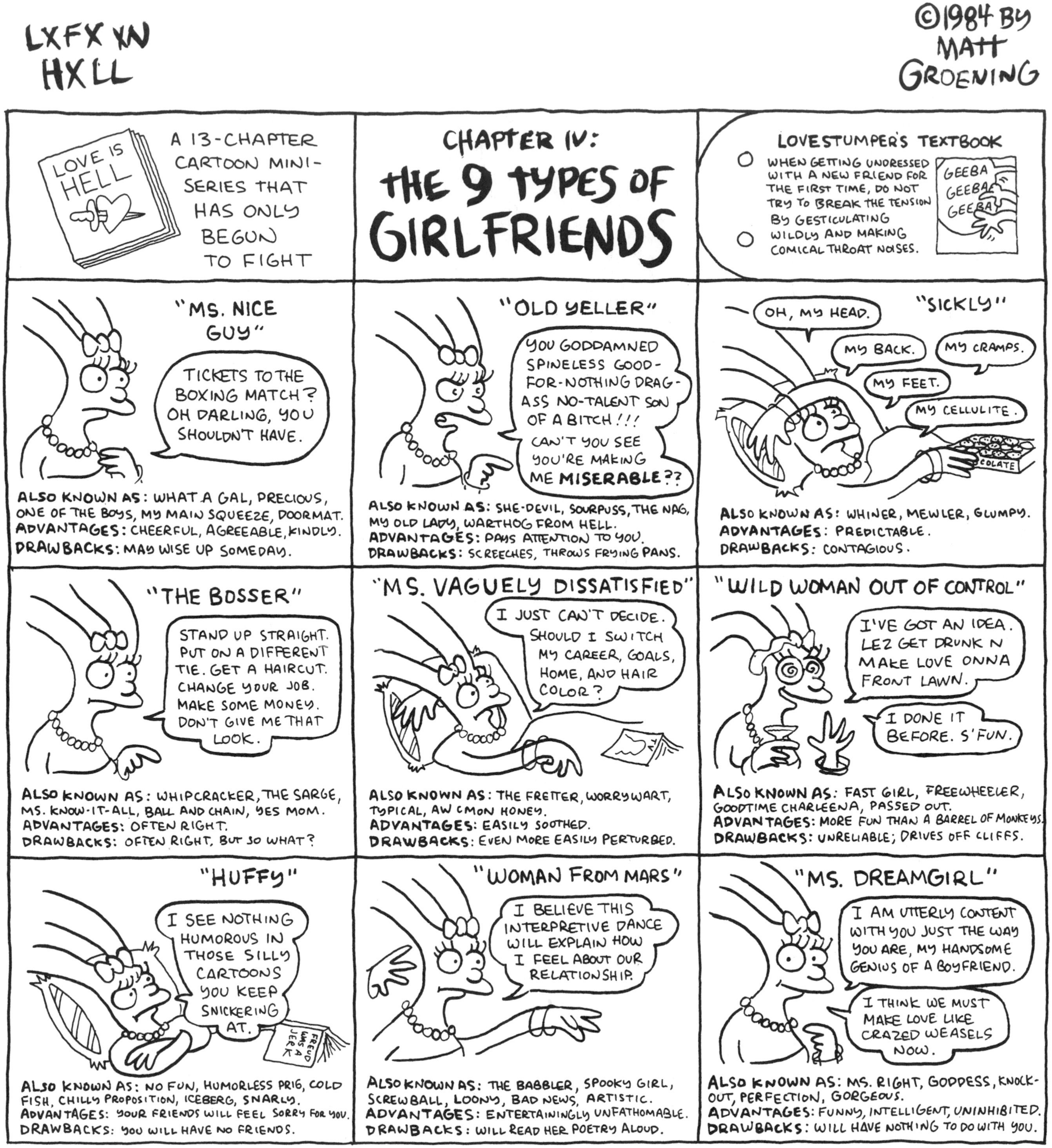
LXFX XN HXLL
©1984 BY MATT GROENING
LOVE IS HELL
A 13-CHAPTER CARTOON MINI-SERIES THAT HAS ONLY BEGUN TO FIGHT
CHAPTER IV:
THE 9 TYPES OF GIRLFRIENDS
LOVESTUMPER'S TEXTBOOK
WHEN GETTING UNDRESSED WITH A NEW FRIEND FOR THE FIRST TIME, DO NOT TRY TO BREAK THE TENSION BY GESTICULATING WILDLY AND MAKING COMICAL THROAT NOISES.
GEEBA GEEBA GEEBA
"MS. NICE GUY"
TICKETS TO THE BOXING MATCH? OH DARLING, YOU SHOULDN'T HAVE.
ALSO KNOWN AS: WHAT A GAL, PRECIOUS, ONE OF THE BOYS, MY MAIN SQUEEZE, DOORMAT.
ADVANTAGES: CHEERFUL, AGREEABLE, KINDLY.
DRAWBACKS: MAY WISE UP SOMEDAY.
"OLD YELLER"
YOU GODDAMNED SPINELESS GOOD-FOR-NOTHING DRAG-ASS NO-TALENT SON OF A BITCH!!! CAN'T YOU SEE YOU'RE MAKING ME MISERABLE??
ALSO KNOWN AS: SHE-DEVIL, SOURPUSS, THE NAG, MY OLD LADY, WARTHOG FROM HELL.
ADVANTAGES: PAYS ATTENTION TO YOU.
DRAWBACKS: SCREECHES, THROWS FRYING PANS.
"SICKLY"
OH, MY HEAD.
MY BACK.
MY CRAMPS.
MY FEET.
MY CELLULITE.
COLATE
ALSO KNOWN AS: WHINER, MEWLER, GLUMPY.
ADVANTAGES: PREDICTABLE.
DRAWBACKS: CONTAGIOUS.
"THE BOSSER"
STAND UP STRAIGHT. PUT ON A DIFFERENT TIE. GET A HAIRCUT. CHANGE YOUR JOB. MAKE SOME MONEY. DON'T GIVE ME THAT LOOK.
ALSO KNOWN AS: WHIPCRACKER, THE SARGE, MS. KNOW-IT-ALL, BALL AND CHAIN, YES MOM.
ADVANTAGES: OFTEN RIGHT.
DRAWBACKS: OFTEN RIGHT, BUT SO WHAT?
"MS. VAGUELY DISSATISFIED"
I JUST CAN'T DECIDE. SHOULD I SWITCH MY CAREER, GOALS, HOME, AND HAIR COLOR?
ALSO KNOWN AS: THE FRETTER, WORRYWART, TYPICAL, AW C'MON HONEY.
ADVANTAGES: EASILY SOOTHED.
DRAWBACKS: EVEN MORE EASILY PERTURBED.
"WILD WOMAN OUT OF CONTROL"
I'VE GOT AN IDEA. LEZ GET DRUNK N MAKE LOVE ONNA FRONT LAWN.
I DONE IT BEFORE. S'FUN.
ALSO KNOWN AS: FAST GIRL, FREEWHEELER, GOODTIME CHARLEENA, PASSED OUT.
ADVANTAGES: MORE FUN THAN A BARREL OF MONKEYS.
DRAWBACKS: UNRELIABLE; DRIVES OFF CLIFFS.
"HUFFY"
I SEE NOTHING HUMOROUS IN THOSE SILLY CARTOONS YOU KEEP SNICKERING AT.
FREUD WAS A JERK
ALSO KNOWN AS: NO FUN, HUMORLESS PRIG, COLD FISH, CHILLY PROPOSITION, ICEBERG, SNARLY.
ADVANTAGES: YOUR FRIENDS WILL FEEL SORRY FOR YOU.
DRAWBACKS: YOU WILL HAVE NO FRIENDS.
"WOMAN FROM MARS"
I BELIEVE THIS INTERPRETIVE DANCE WILL EXPLAIN HOW I FEEL ABOUT OUR RELATIONSHIP.
ALSO KNOWN AS: THE BABBLER, SPOOKY GIRL, SCREWBALL, LOONY, BAD NEWS, ARTISTIC.
ADVANTAGES: ENTERTAININGLY UNFATHOMABLE.
DRAWBACKS: WILL READ HER POETRY ALOUD.
"MS. DREAMGIRL"
I AM UTTERLY CONTENT WITH YOU JUST THE WAY YOU ARE, MY HANDSOME GENIUS OF A BOYFRIEND.
I THINK WE MUST MAKE LOVE LIKE CRAZED WEASELS NOW.
ALSO KNOWN AS: MS. RIGHT, GODDESS, KNOCK-OUT, PERFECTION, GORGEOUS.
ADVANTAGES: FUNNY, INTELLIGENT, UNINHIBITED.
DRAWBACKS: WILL HAVE NOTHING TO DO WITH YOU.

YOUR LITTLE OWN LIFE IN HELL

©1984 BY MATT GROENING

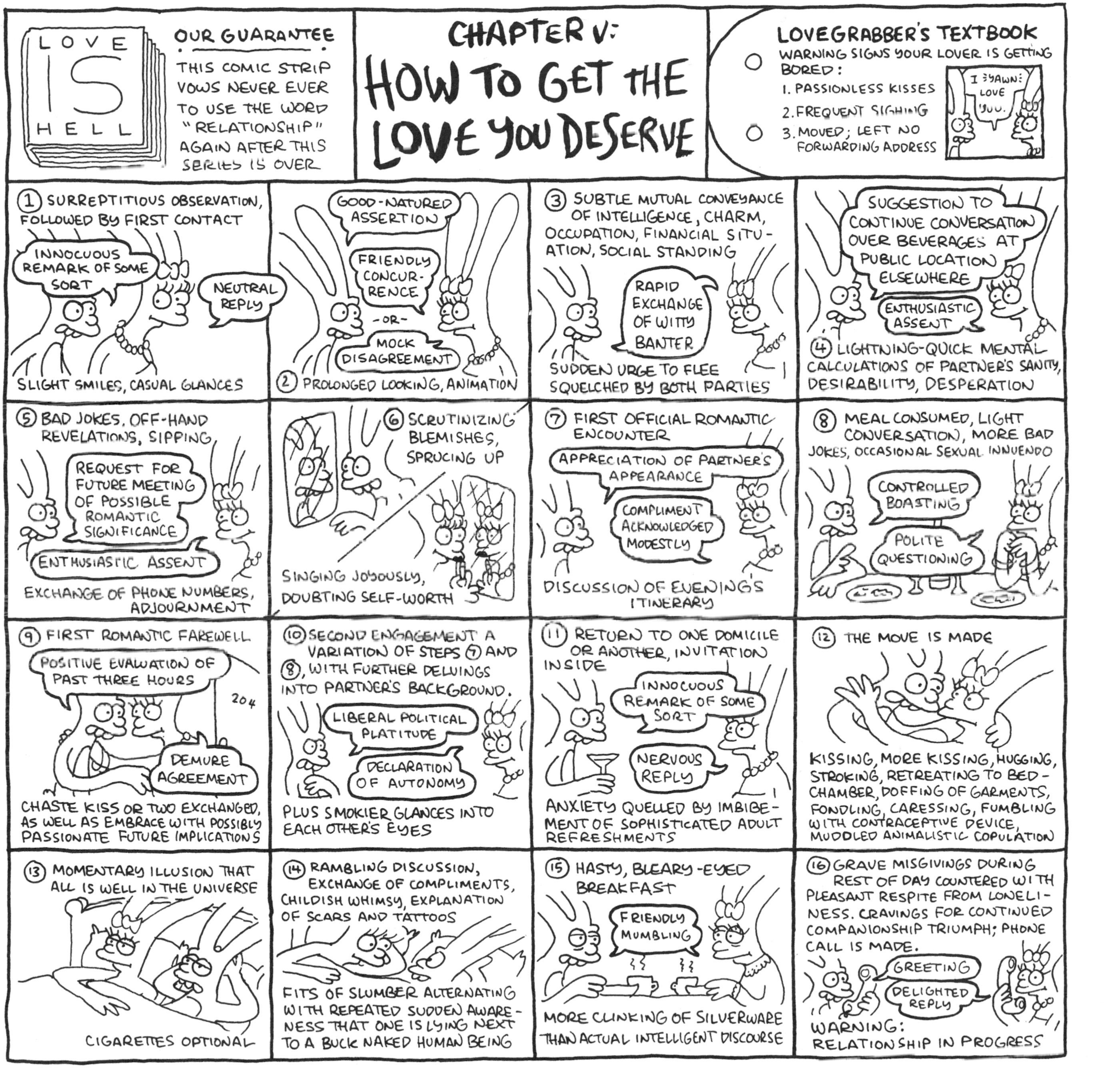
LOVE IS HELL
OUR GUARANTEE
THIS COMIC STRIP VOWS NEVER EVER TO USE THE WORD "RELATIONSHIP" AGAIN AFTER THIS SERIES IS OVER
CHAPTER V:
HOW TO GET THE LOVE YOU DESERVE
LOVEGRABBER'S TEXTBOOK
WARNING SIGNS YOUR LOVER IS GETTING BORED:
1. PASSIONLESS KISSES
2. FREQUENT SIGHING
3. MOVED; LEFT NO FORWARDING ADDRESS
I :YAWN: LOVE YOU.
1 SURREPTITIOUS OBSERVATION, FOLLOWED BY FIRST CONTACT
INNOCUOUS REMARK OF SOME SORT
NEUTRAL REPLY
SLIGHT SMILES, CASUAL GLANCES
GOOD-NATURED ASSERTION
FRIENDLY CONCURRENCE
-OR-
MOCK DISAGREEMENT
2 PROLONGED LOOKING, ANIMATION
3 SUBTLE MUTUAL CONVEYANCE OF INTELLIGENCE, CHARM, OCCUPATION, FINANCIAL SITUATION, SOCIAL STANDING
RAPID EXCHANGE OF WITTY BANTER
SUDDEN URGE TO FLEE SQUELCHED BY BOTH PARTIES
SUGGESTION TO CONTINUE CONVERSATION OVER BEVERAGES AT PUBLIC LOCATION ELSEWHERE
ENTHUSIASTIC ASSENT
4 LIGHTNING-QUICK MENTAL CALCULATIONS OF PARTNER'S SANITY, DESIRABILITY, DESPERATION
5 BAD JOKES, OFF-HAND REVELATIONS, SIPPING
REQUEST FOR FUTURE MEETING OF POSSIBLE ROMANTIC SIGNIFICANCE
ENTHUSIASTIC ASSENT
EXCHANGE OF PHONE NUMBERS, ADJOURNMENT
6 SCRUTINIZING BLEMISHES, SPRUCING UP
SINGING JOYOUSLY, DOUBTING SELF-WORTH
7 FIRST OFFICIAL ROMANTIC ENCOUNTER
APPRECIATION OF PARTNER'S APPEARANCE
COMPLIMENT ACKNOWLEDGED MODESTLY
DISCUSSION OF EVENING'S ITINERARY
8 MEAL CONSUMED, LIGHT CONVERSATION, MORE BAD JOKES, OCCASIONAL SEXUAL INNUENDO
CONTROLLED BOASTING
POLITE QUESTIONING
9 FIRST ROMANTIC FAREWELL
POSITIVE EVALUATION OF PAST THREE HOURS
204
DEMURE AGREEMENT
CHASTE KISS OR TWO EXCHANGED, AS WELL AS EMBRACE WITH POSSIBLY PASSIONATE FUTURE IMPLICATIONS
10 SECOND ENGAGEMENT A VARIATION OF STEPS 7 AND 8, WITH FURTHER DELVINGS INTO PARTNER'S BACKGROUND.
LIBERAL POLITICAL PLATITUDE
DECLARATION OF AUTONOMY
PLUS SMOKIER GLANCES INTO EACH OTHER'S EYES
11 RETURN TO ONE DOMICILE OR ANOTHER, INVITATION INSIDE
INNOCUOUS REMARK OF SOME SORT
NERVOUS REPLY
ANXIETY QUELLED BY IMBIBEMENT OF SOPHISTICATED ADULT REFRESHMENTS
12 THE MOVE IS MADE
KISSING, MORE KISSING, HUGGING, STROKING, RETREATING TO BEDCHAMBER, DOFFING OF GARMENTS, FONDLING, CARESSING, FUMBLING WITH CONTRACEPTIVE DEVICE, MUDDLED ANIMALISTIC COPULATION
13 MOMENTARY ILLUSION THAT ALL IS WELL IN THE UNIVERSE
CIGARETTES OPTIONAL
14 RAMBLING DISCUSSION, EXCHANGE OF COMPLIMENTS, CHILDISH WHIMSY, EXPLANATION OF SCARS AND TATTOOS
FITS OF SLUMBER ALTERNATING WITH REPEATED SUDDEN AWARENESS THAT ONE IS LYING NEXT TO A BUCK NAKED HUMAN BEING
15 HASTY, BLEARY-EYED BREAKFAST
FRIENDLY MUMBLING
MORE CLINKING OF SILVERWARE THAN ACTUAL INTELLIGENT DISCOURSE
16 GRAVE MISGIVINGS DURING REST OF DAY COUNTERED WITH PLEASANT RESPITE FROM LONELINESS. CRAVINGS FOR CONTINUED COMPANIONSHIP TRIUMPH; PHONE CALL IS MADE.
GREETING
DELIGHTED REPLY
WARNING: RELATIONSHIP IN PROGRESS

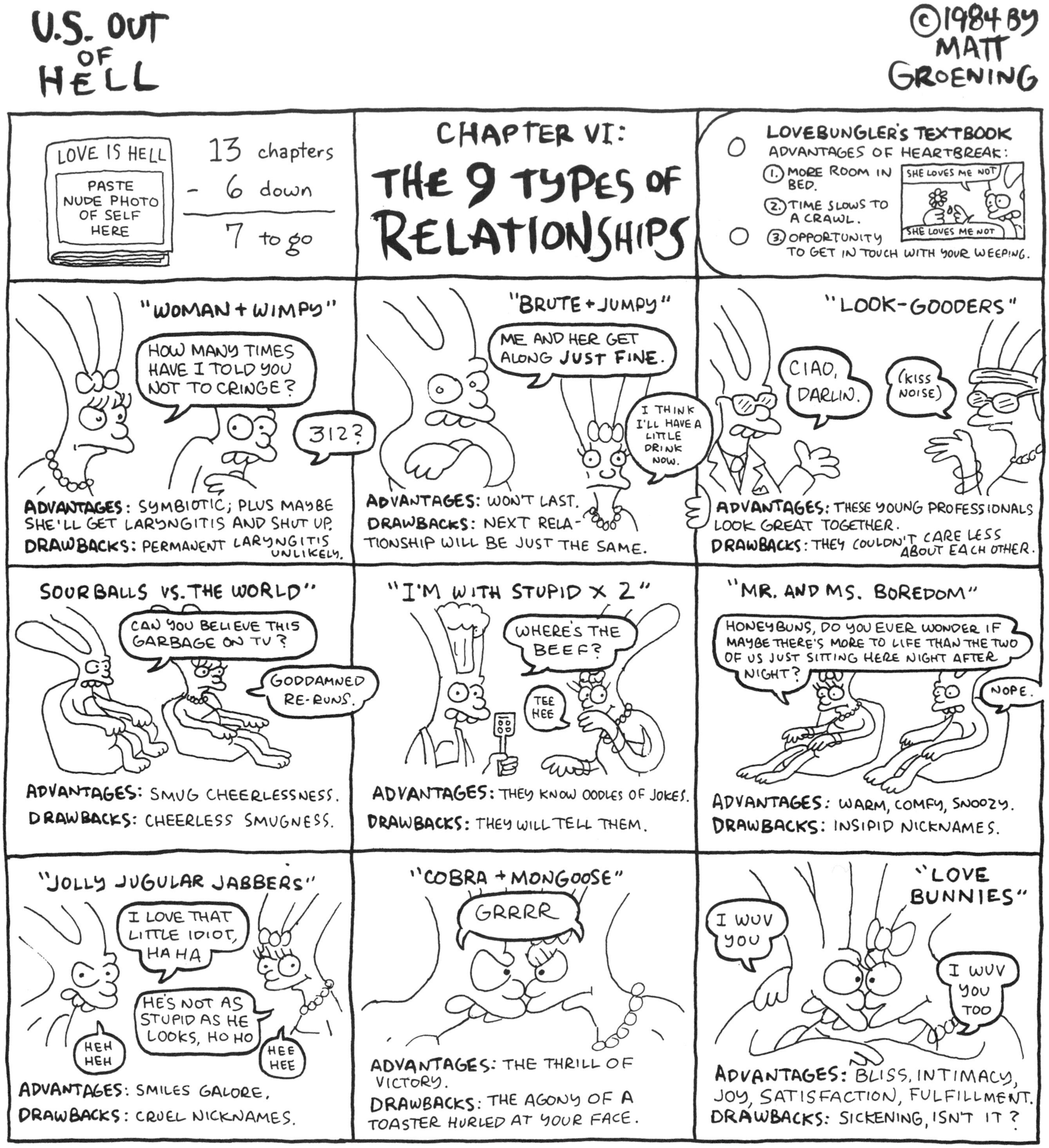

U.S. OUT OF HELL
©1984 BY MATT GROENING
LOVE IS HELL
PASTE NUDE PHOTO OF SELF HERE
13 chapters
- 6 down
7 to go
CHAPTER VI:
THE 9 TYPES OF RELATIONSHIPS
LOVEBUNGLER'S TEXTBOOK
ADVANTAGES OF HEARTBREAK:
1. MORE ROOM IN BED.
2. TIME SLOWS TO A CRAWL.
3. OPPORTUNITY TO GET IN TOUCH WITH YOUR WEEPING.
SHE LOVES ME NOT
SHE LOVES ME NOT
"WOMAN + WIMPY"
HOW MANY TIMES HAVE I TOLD YOU NOT TO CRINGE?
312?
ADVANTAGES: SYMBIOTIC; PLUS MAYBE SHE'LL GET LARYNGITIS AND SHUT UP.
DRAWBACKS: PERMANENT LARYNGITIS UNLIKELY.
"BRUTE + JUMPY"
ME AND HER GET ALONG JUST FINE.
I THINK I'LL HAVE A LITTLE DRINK NOW.
ADVANTAGES: WON'T LAST.
DRAWBACKS: NEXT RELATIONSHIP WILL BE JUST THE SAME.
"LOOK-GOODERS"
CIAO, DARLIN.
(KISS NOISE)
ADVANTAGES: THESE YOUNG PROFESSIONALS LOOK GREAT TOGETHER.
DRAWBACKS: THEY COULDN'T CARE LESS ABOUT EACH OTHER.
SOURBALLS VS. THE WORLD"
CAN YOU BELIEVE THIS GARBAGE ON TV?
GODDAMNED RE-RUNS.
ADVANTAGES: SMUG CHEERLESSNESS.
DRAWBACKS: CHEERLESS SMUGNESS.
"I'M WITH STUPID X 2"
WHERE'S THE BEEF?
TEE HEE
ADVANTAGES: THEY KNOW OODLES OF JOKES.
DRAWBACKS: THEY WILL TELL THEM.
"MR. AND MS. BOREDOM"
HONEYBUNS, DO YOU EVER WONDER IF MAYBE THERE'S MORE TO LIFE THAN THE TWO OF US JUST SITTING HERE NIGHT AFTER NIGHT?
NOPE.
ADVANTAGES: WARM, COMFY, SNOOZY.
DRAWBACKS: INSIPID NICKNAMES.
"JOLLY JUGULAR JABBERS"
I LOVE THAT LITTLE IDIOT, HA HA
HE'S NOT AS STUPID AS HE LOOKS, HO HO
HEH HEH
HEE HEE
ADVANTAGES: SMILES GALORE.
DRAWBACKS: CRUEL NICKNAMES.
"COBRA + MONGOOSE"
GRRRR
ADVANTAGES: THE THRILL OF VICTORY.
DRAWBACKS: THE AGONY OF A TOASTER HURLED AT YOUR FACE.
"LOVE BUNNIES"
I WUV YOU
I WUV YOU TOO
ADVANTAGES: BLISS, INTIMACY, JOY, SATISFACTION, FULFILLMENT.
DRAWBACKS: SICKENING, ISN'T IT?

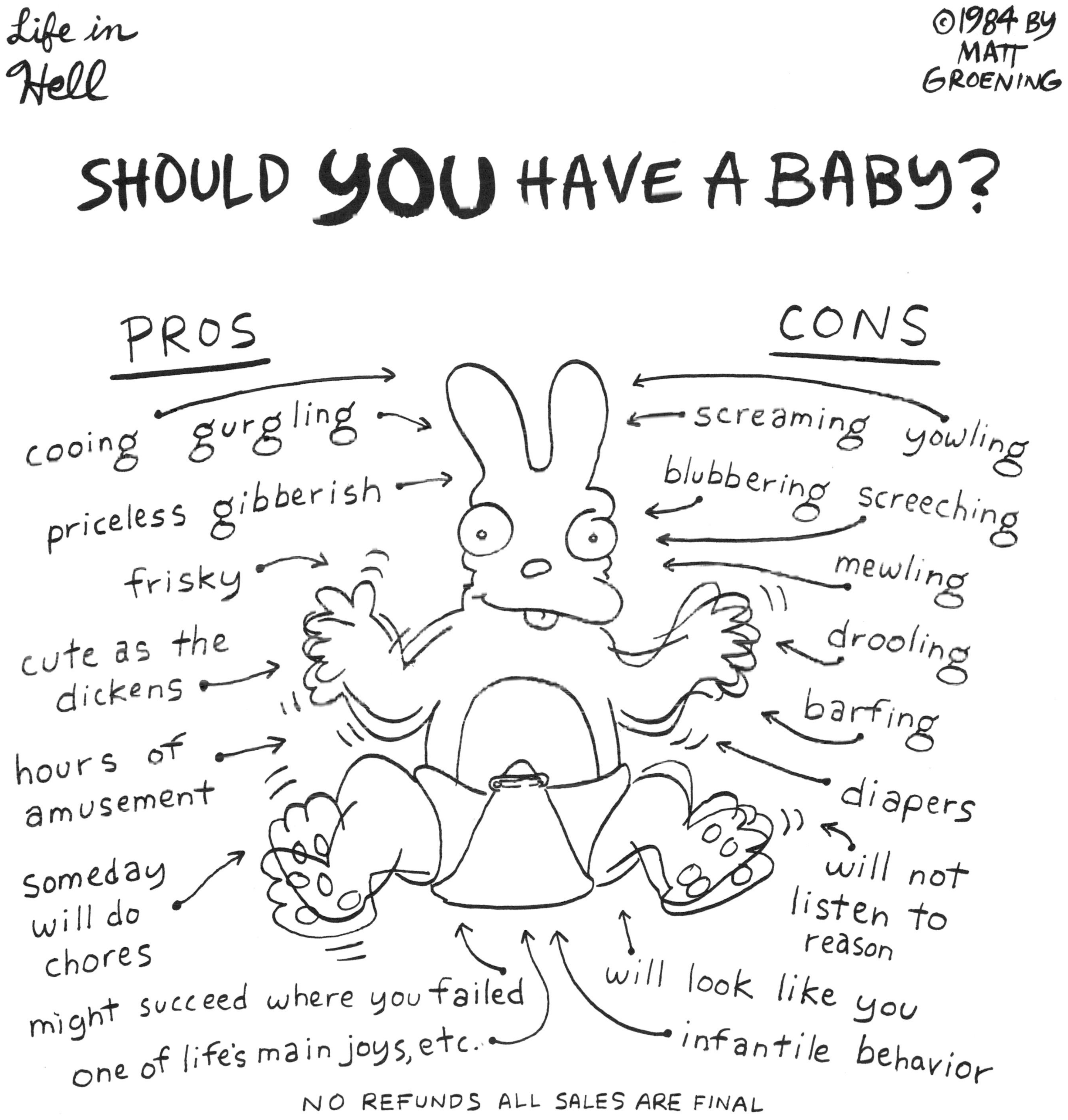
Life in Hell
©1984 BY MATT GROENING
SHOULD YOU HAVE A BABY?
PROS
CONS
cooing
gurgling
priceless gibberish
frisky
cute as the dickens
hours of amusement
someday will do chores
might succeed where you failed
one of life's main joys, etc.
screaming
yowling
blubbering
screeching
mewling
drooling
barfing
diapers
will not listen to reason
will look like you
infantile behavior
NO REFUNDS ALL SALES ARE FINAL

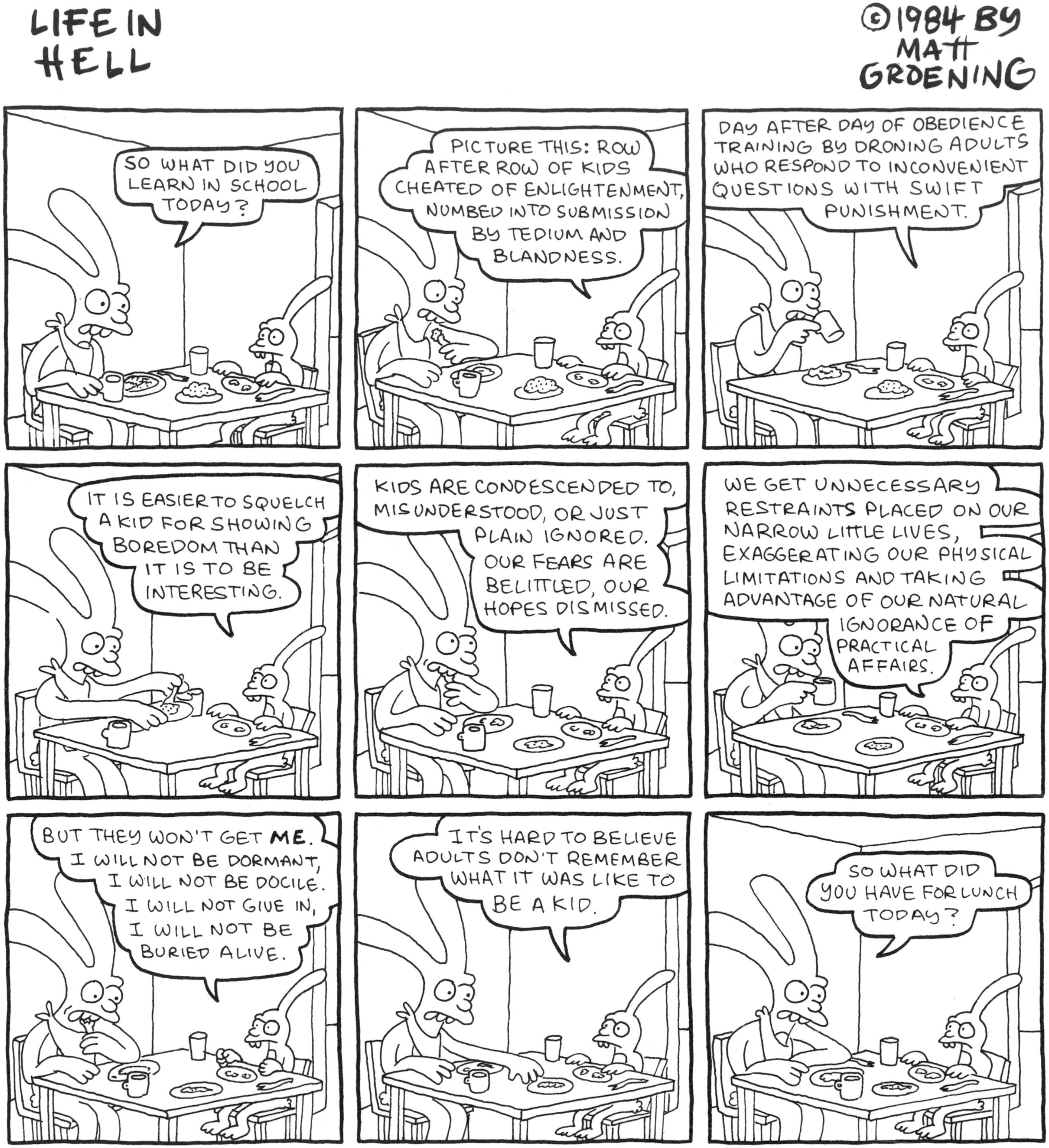
LIFE IN HELL
©1984 BY MATT GROENING
SO WHAT DID YOU LEARN IN SCHOOL TODAY?
PICTURE THIS: ROW AFTER ROW OF KIDS CHEATED OF ENLIGHTENMENT, NUMBED INTO SUBMISSION BY TEDIUM AND BLANDNESS.
DAY AFTER DAY OF OBEDIENCE TRAINING BY DRONING ADULTS WHO RESPOND TO INCONVENIENT QUESTIONS WITH SWIFT PUNISHMENT.
IT IS EASIER TO SQUELCH A KID FOR SHOWING BOREDOM THAN IT IS TO BE INTERESTING.
KIDS ARE CONDESCENDED TO, MISUNDERSTOOD, OR JUST PLAIN IGNORED. OUR FEARS ARE BELITTLED, OUR HOPES DISMISSED.
WE GET UNNECESSARY RESTRAINTS PLACED ON OUR NARROW LITTLE LIVES, EXAGGERATING OUR PHYSICAL LIMITATIONS AND TAKING ADVANTAGE OF OUR NATURAL IGNORANCE OF PRACTICAL AFFAIRS.
BUT THEY WON'T GET **ME**. I WILL NOT BE DORMANT, I WILL NOT BE DOCILE. I WILL NOT GIVE IN, I WILL NOT BE BURIED ALIVE.
IT'S HARD TO BELIEVE ADULTS DON'T REMEMBER WHAT IT WAS LIKE TO BE A KID.
SO WHAT DID YOU HAVE FOR LUNCH TODAY?

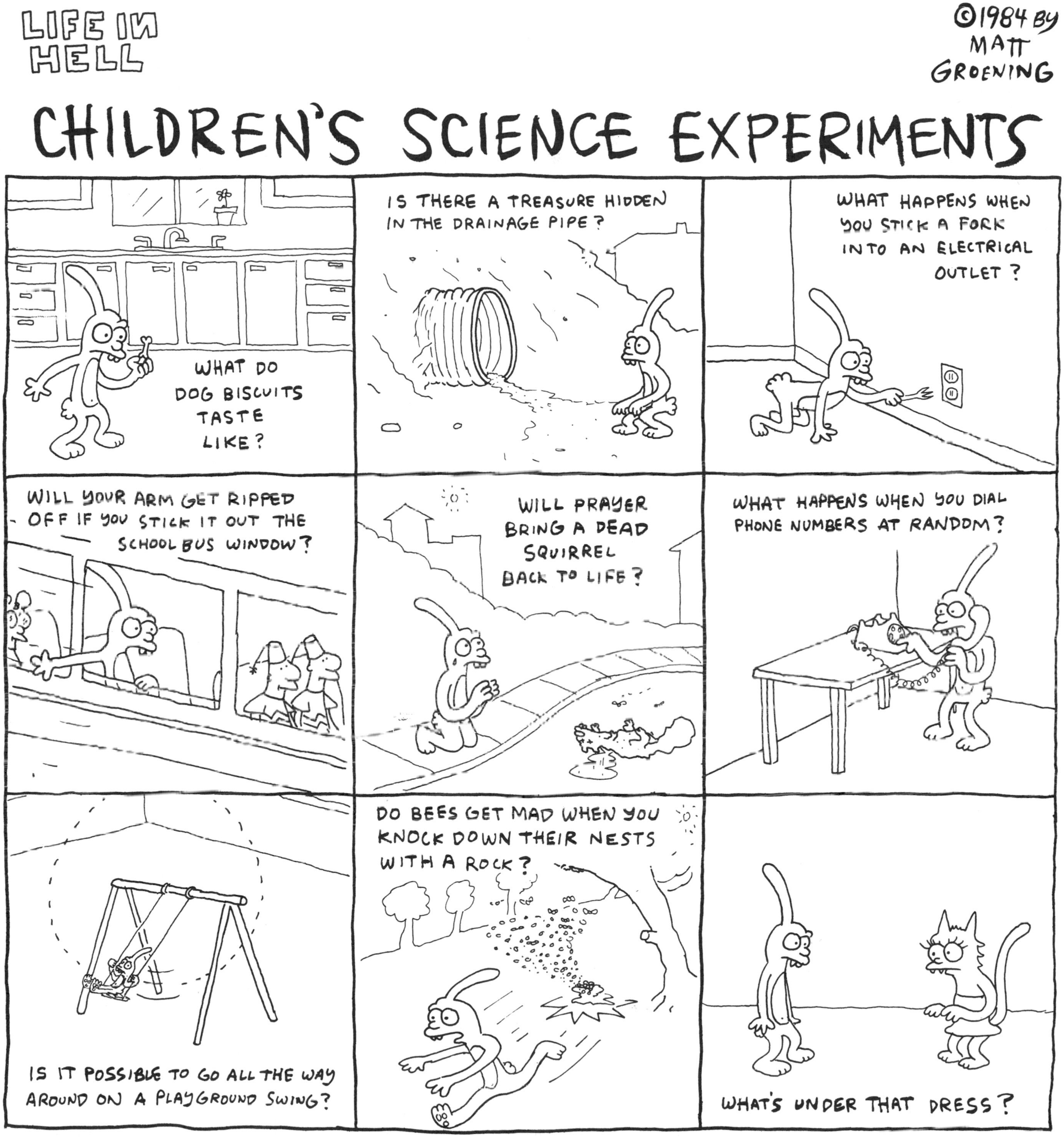
LIFE IN HELL
©1984 BY MATT GROENING
CHILDREN'S SCIENCE EXPERIMENTS
WHAT DO DOG BISCUITS TASTE LIKE?
IS THERE A TREASURE HIDDEN IN THE DRAINAGE PIPE?
WHAT HAPPENS WHEN YOU STICK A FORK INTO AN ELECTRICAL OUTLET?
WILL YOUR ARM GET RIPPED OFF IF YOU STICK IT OUT THE SCHOOL BUS WINDOW?
WILL PRAYER BRING A DEAD SQUIRREL BACK TO LIFE?
WHAT HAPPENS WHEN YOU DIAL PHONE NUMBERS AT RANDOM?
IS IT POSSIBLE TO GO ALL THE WAY AROUND ON A PLAYGROUND SWING?
DO BEES GET MAD WHEN YOU KNOCK DOWN THEIR NESTS WITH A ROCK?
WHAT'S UNDER THAT DRESS?

LIFE IN HELL

A BRIEF HISTORY OF THE LITTLE MORON JOKE

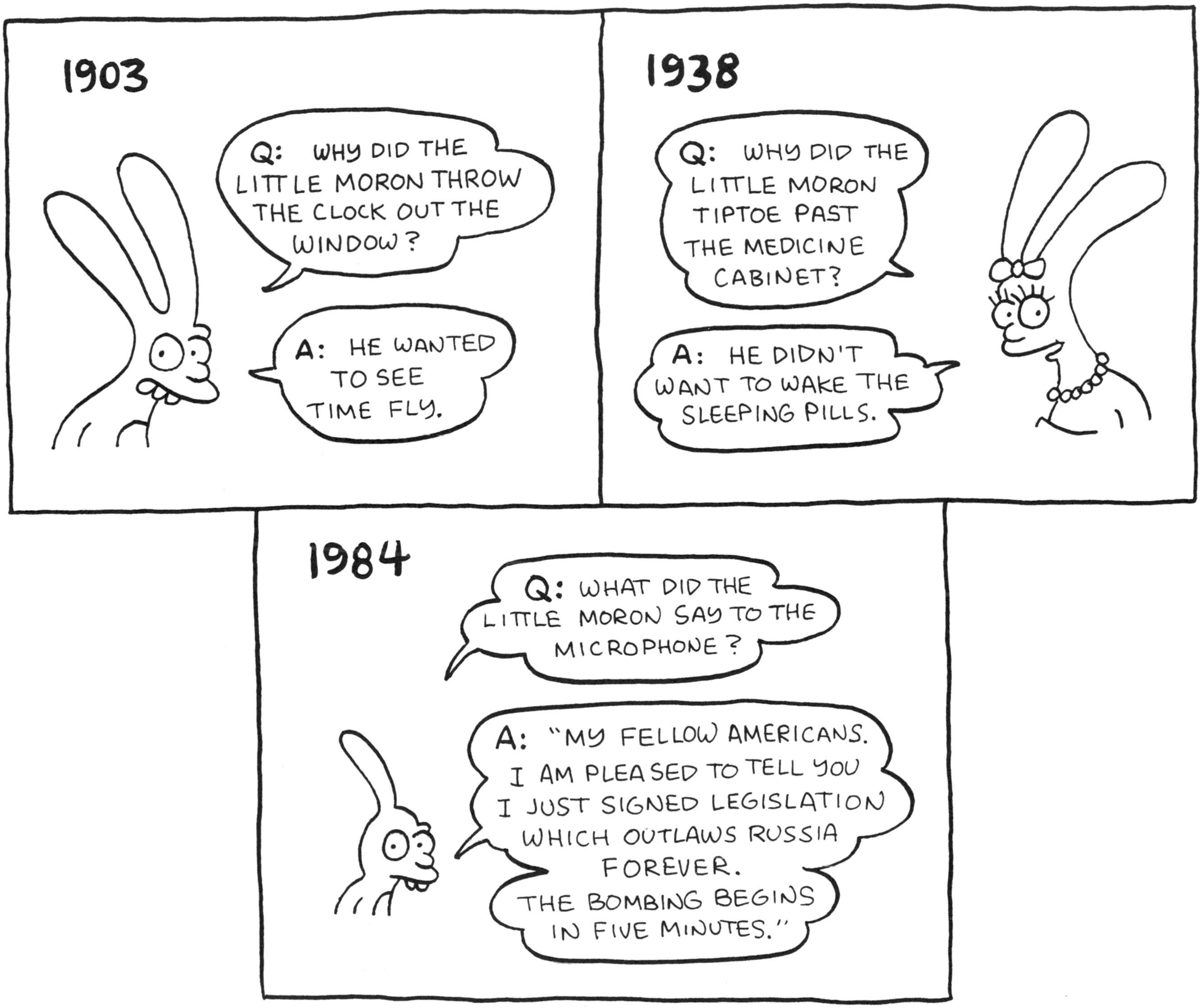
1903
Q: WHY DID THE LITTLE MORON THROW THE CLOCK OUT THE WINDOW?
A: HE WANTED TO SEE TIME FLY.
1938
Q: WHY DID THE LITTLE MORON TIPTOE PAST THE MEDICINE CABINET?
A: HE DIDN'T WANT TO WAKE THE SLEEPING PILLS.
1984
Q: WHAT DID THE LITTLE MORON SAY TO THE MICROPHONE?
A: "MY FELLOW AMERICANS. I AM PLEASED TO TELL YOU I JUST SIGNED LEGISLATION WHICH OUTLAWS RUSSIA FOREVER. THE BOMBING BEGINS IN FIVE MINUTES."

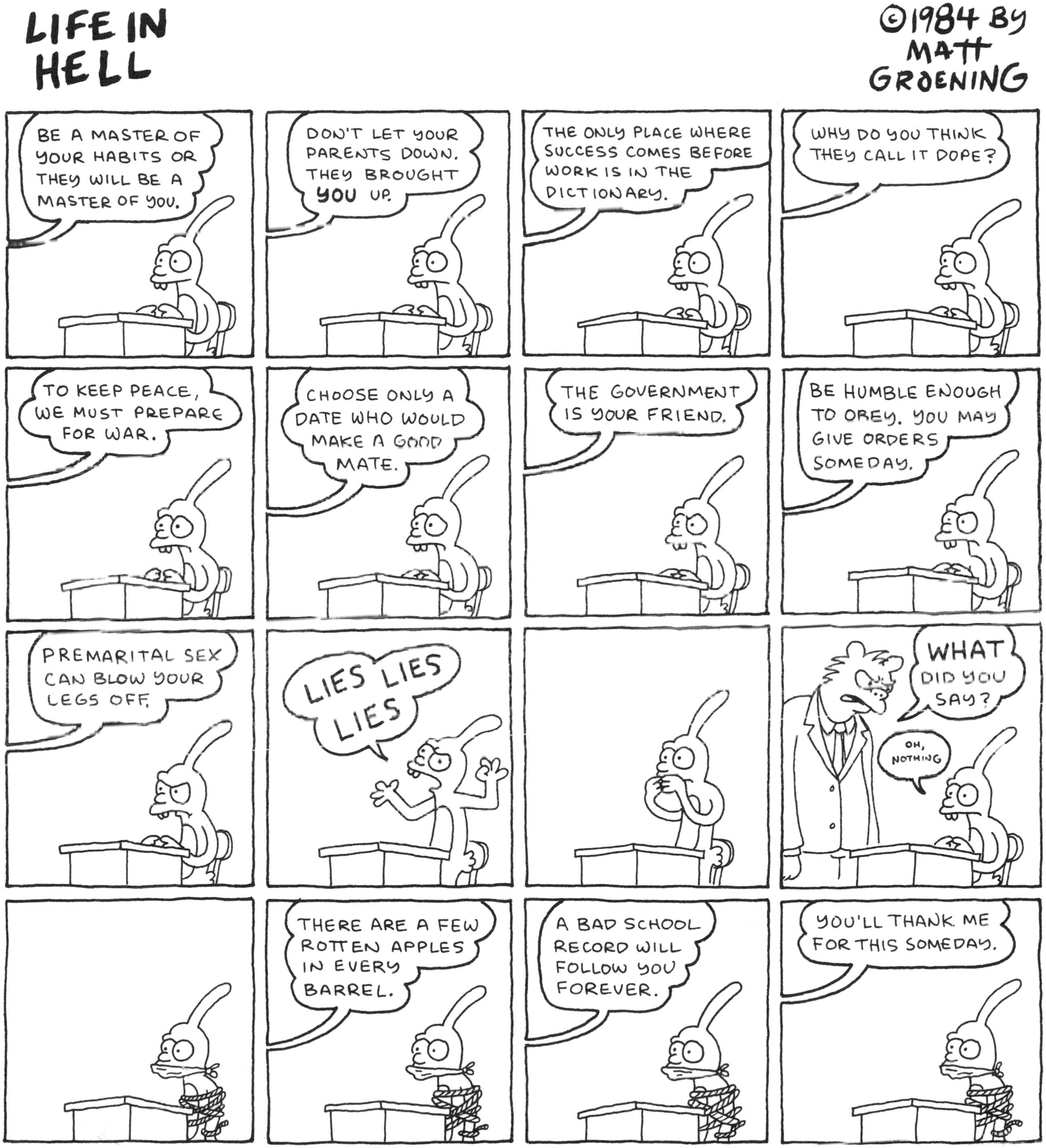
LIFE IN HELL
©1984 BY MATT GROENING
BE A MASTER OF YOUR HABITS OR THEY WILL BE A MASTER OF YOU.
DON'T LET YOUR PARENTS DOWN. THEY BROUGHT YOU UP.
THE ONLY PLACE WHERE SUCCESS COMES BEFORE WORK IS IN THE DICTIONARY.
WHY DO YOU THINK THEY CALL IT DOPE?
TO KEEP PEACE, WE MUST PREPARE FOR WAR.
CHOOSE ONLY A DATE WHO WOULD MAKE A GOOD MATE.
THE GOVERNMENT IS YOUR FRIEND.
BE HUMBLE ENOUGH TO OBEY. YOU MAY GIVE ORDERS SOMEDAY.
PREMARITAL SEX CAN BLOW YOUR LEGS OFF.
LIES LIES LIES
WHAT DID YOU SAY?
OH, NOTHING
THERE ARE A FEW ROTTEN APPLES IN EVERY BARREL.
A BAD SCHOOL RECORD WILL FOLLOW YOU FOREVER.
YOU'LL THANK ME FOR THIS SOMEDAY.

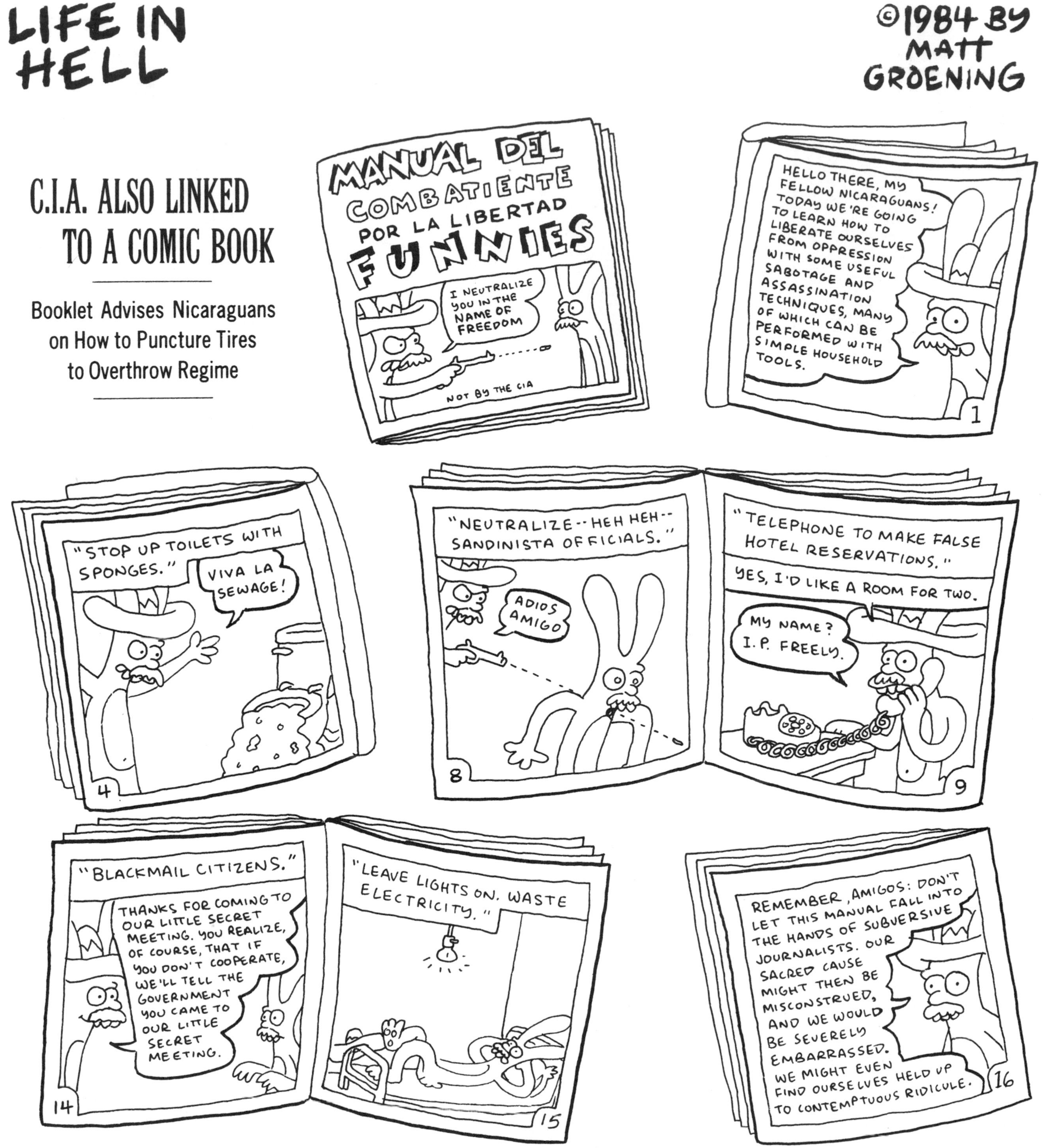
LIFE IN HELL
©1984 BY MATT GROENING
C.I.A. ALSO LINKED TO A COMIC BOOK
Booklet Advises Nicaraguans on How to Puncture Tires to Overthrow Regime
MANUAL DEL COMBATIENTE POR LA LIBERTAD FUNNIES
I NEUTRALIZE YOU IN THE NAME OF FREEDOM
NOT BY THE CIA
HELLO THERE, MY FELLOW NICARAGUANS! TODAY WE'RE GOING TO LEARN HOW TO LIBERATE OURSELVES FROM OPPRESSION WITH SOME USEFUL SABOTAGE AND ASSASSINATION TECHNIQUES, MANY OF WHICH CAN BE PERFORMED WITH SIMPLE HOUSEHOLD TOOLS.
1
"STOP UP TOILETS WITH SPONGES."
VIVA LA SEWAGE!
4
"NEUTRALIZE--HEH HEH--SANDINISTA OFFICIALS."
ADIOS AMIGO
8
"TELEPHONE TO MAKE FALSE HOTEL RESERVATIONS."
YES, I'D LIKE A ROOM FOR TWO.
MY NAME? I.P. FREELY.
9
"BLACKMAIL CITIZENS."
THANKS FOR COMING TO OUR LITTLE SECRET MEETING. YOU REALIZE, OF COURSE, THAT IF YOU DON'T COOPERATE, WE'LL TELL THE GOVERNMENT YOU CAME TO OUR LITTLE SECRET MEETING.
14
"LEAVE LIGHTS ON. WASTE ELECTRICITY."
15
REMEMBER, AMIGOS: DON'T LET THIS MANUAL FALL INTO THE HANDS OF SUBVERSIVE JOURNALISTS. OUR SACRED CAUSE MIGHT THEN BE MISCONSTRUED, AND WE WOULD BE SEVERELY EMBARRASSED. WE MIGHT EVEN FIND OURSELVES HELD UP TO CONTEMPTUOUS RIDICULE.
16

LIFE IN HELL

© 1984 BY MATT GROENING

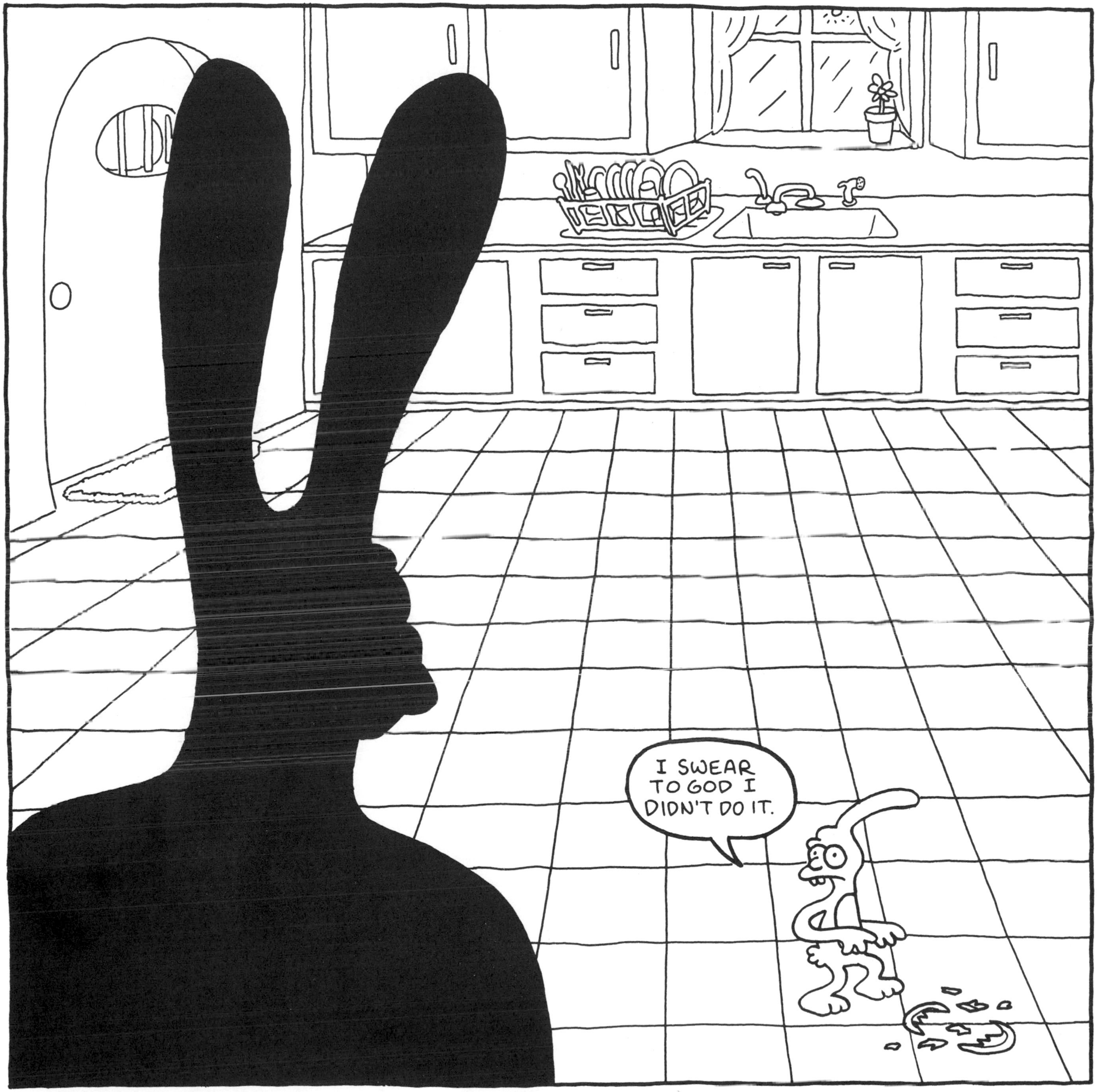
I SWEAR TO GOD I DIDN'T DO IT.

LIFE IN HELL

©1984 BY MATT GROENING

YOUR GUIDE TO THE MODERN CREATIVE ARTISTIC TYPES

CREATIVE ARTISTIC TYPE	DOMINANT PERSONALITY TRAIT	SECONDARY PERSONALITY TRAITS	DISTINGUISHING FEATURES	HAUNTING QUESTION	HOW TO ANNOY THEM
WRITER 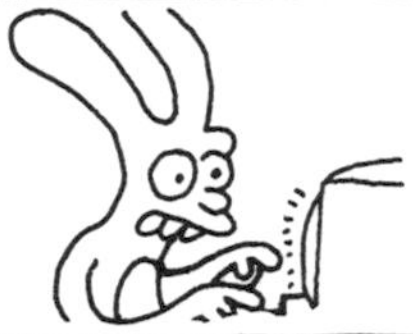	SELF-ABSORPTION	POMPOSITY IRRITABILITY WHINING	NERVOUS TWITCHING, BAD POSTURE	"AM I JUST A HACK?"	SAY: BUT HOW DO YOU MAKE A LIVING?
PAINTER 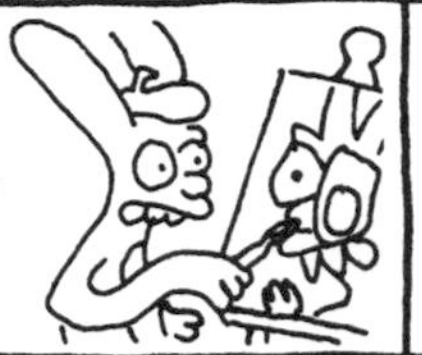	SELF-OBSESSION	DELUSIONS OF GRANDEUR	SPATTERED PANTS, INARTICULATE EXPLANATIONS	"SHOULD I MOVE TO NEW YORK?"	SAY: IT'S NOT FINISHED, IS IT?
POET 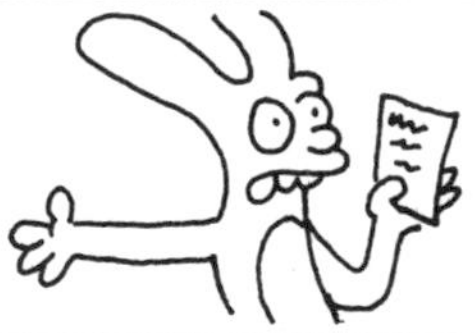	SELF-PITY	PARANOIA BITTERNESS BILE	WEIRD LIPS SNIVELING POVERTY	"WHY DOES EVERYONE AVOID ME?"	BE ANOTHER POET.
PERFORMANCE ARTIST 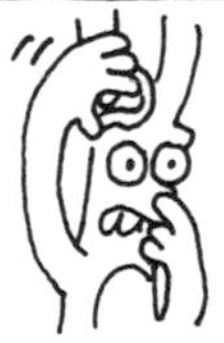	SELF-INDULGENCE	ALIENATION IRRATIONALITY SHAMELESSNESS	VAGUELY PUNKISH LOOK, ONLY WITH WRINKLED SKIN	"GIVEN THE INFINITE NUMBER OF THINGS I COULD DO WITH MY LIFE, WHY AM I STANDING HERE ONSTAGE SLAPPING MEAT ON MY HEAD?"	SAY: I SAW SOMETHING JUST LIKE THAT ONCE ON THE GONG SHOW.
ACTOR 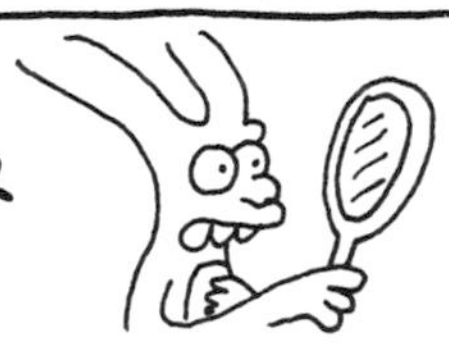	SELF-DEVOTION	SELF-DOUBT	AURA OF INSINCERITY	"DO I HAVE ANY TALENT?"	SAY: PUT ON A FEW POUNDS, HAVEN'T YOU?
ROCK & ROLL GUITARIST 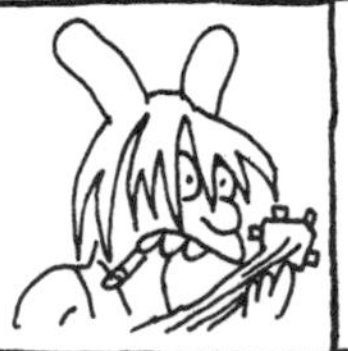	SELF-COMPLACENCY	SLEAZINESS SLIMINESS SMUGNESS	SALLOW COMPLEXION, VENEREAL SCABS	"WHERE AM I?"	THROW BEER BOTTLES AT THEIR HEADS DURING CONCERTS.
STREET MIME 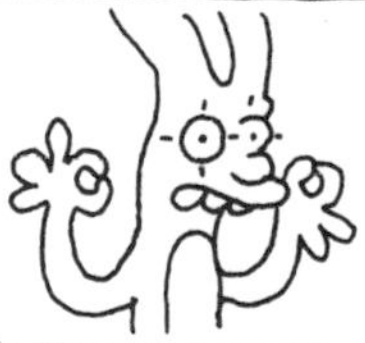	SELF-SATISFACTION	COMPULSION TO PESTER	SCRAWNY BOD TORN LEOTARDS IMPISH BEHAVIOR	"HAVE I NO SHAME?"	PUNCH 'EM IN THE MOUTH.
CARTOONIST 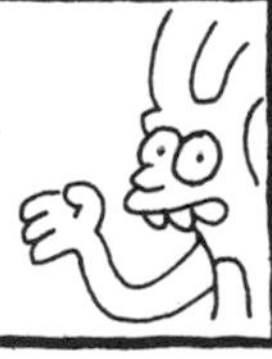	MALICIOUS FRIVOLITY	FRIVOLOUS MALICIOUSNESS	INKY FINGERS INKY SHIRTS INKY PANTS	"WILL I BE DRAWING GODDAMNED RABBITS FOR THE REST OF MY LIFE?"	IT IS UNWISE TO ANNOY CARTOONISTS.

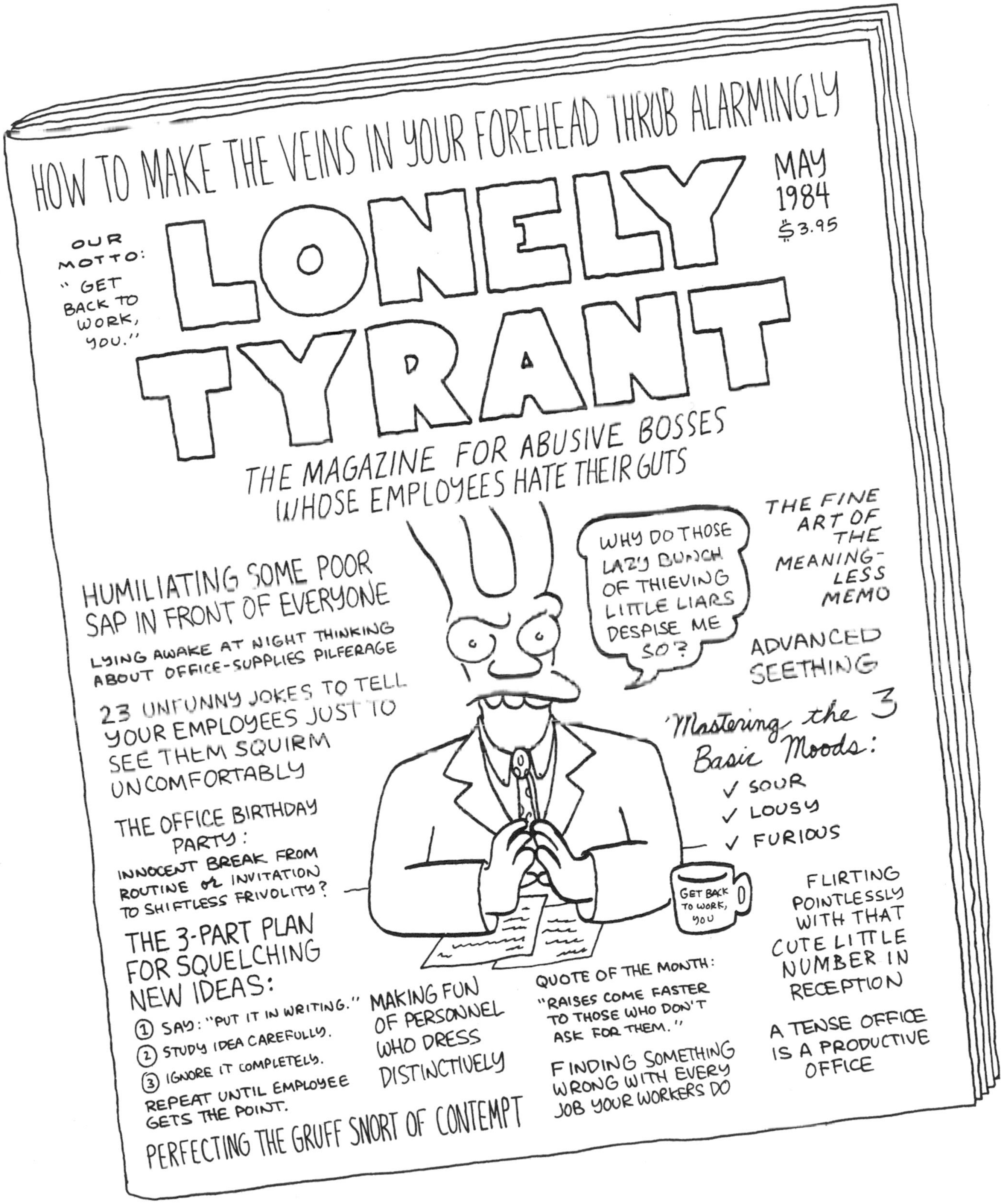

HOW TO MAKE THE VEINS IN YOUR FOREHEAD THROB ALARMINGLY
MAY 1984 $3.95
OUR MOTTO: "GET BACK TO WORK, YOU."
LONELY TYRANT
THE MAGAZINE FOR ABUSIVE BOSSES WHOSE EMPLOYEES HATE THEIR GUTS
WHY DO THOSE LAZY BUNCH OF THIEVING LITTLE LIARS DESPISE ME SO?
THE FINE ART OF THE MEANINGLESS MEMO
HUMILIATING SOME POOR SAP IN FRONT OF EVERYONE
LYING AWAKE AT NIGHT THINKING ABOUT OFFICE-SUPPLIES PILFERAGE
ADVANCED SEETHING
23 UNFUNNY JOKES TO TELL YOUR EMPLOYEES JUST TO SEE THEM SQUIRM UNCOMFORTABLY
Mastering the 3 Basic Moods:
✓ SOUR
✓ LOUSY
✓ FURIOUS
THE OFFICE BIRTHDAY PARTY: INNOCENT BREAK FROM ROUTINE OR INVITATION TO SHIFTLESS FRIVOLITY?
GET BACK TO WORK, YOU
FLIRTING POINTLESSLY WITH THAT CUTE LITTLE NUMBER IN RECEPTION
THE 3-PART PLAN FOR SQUELCHING NEW IDEAS:
① SAY: "PUT IT IN WRITING."
② STUDY IDEA CAREFULLY.
③ IGNORE IT COMPLETELY.
REPEAT UNTIL EMPLOYEE GETS THE POINT.
MAKING FUN OF PERSONNEL WHO DRESS DISTINCTIVELY
QUOTE OF THE MONTH: "RAISES COME FASTER TO THOSE WHO DON'T ASK FOR THEM."
FINDING SOMETHING WRONG WITH EVERY JOB YOUR WORKERS DO
A TENSE OFFICE IS A PRODUCTIVE OFFICE
PERFECTING THE GRUFF SNORT OF CONTEMPT

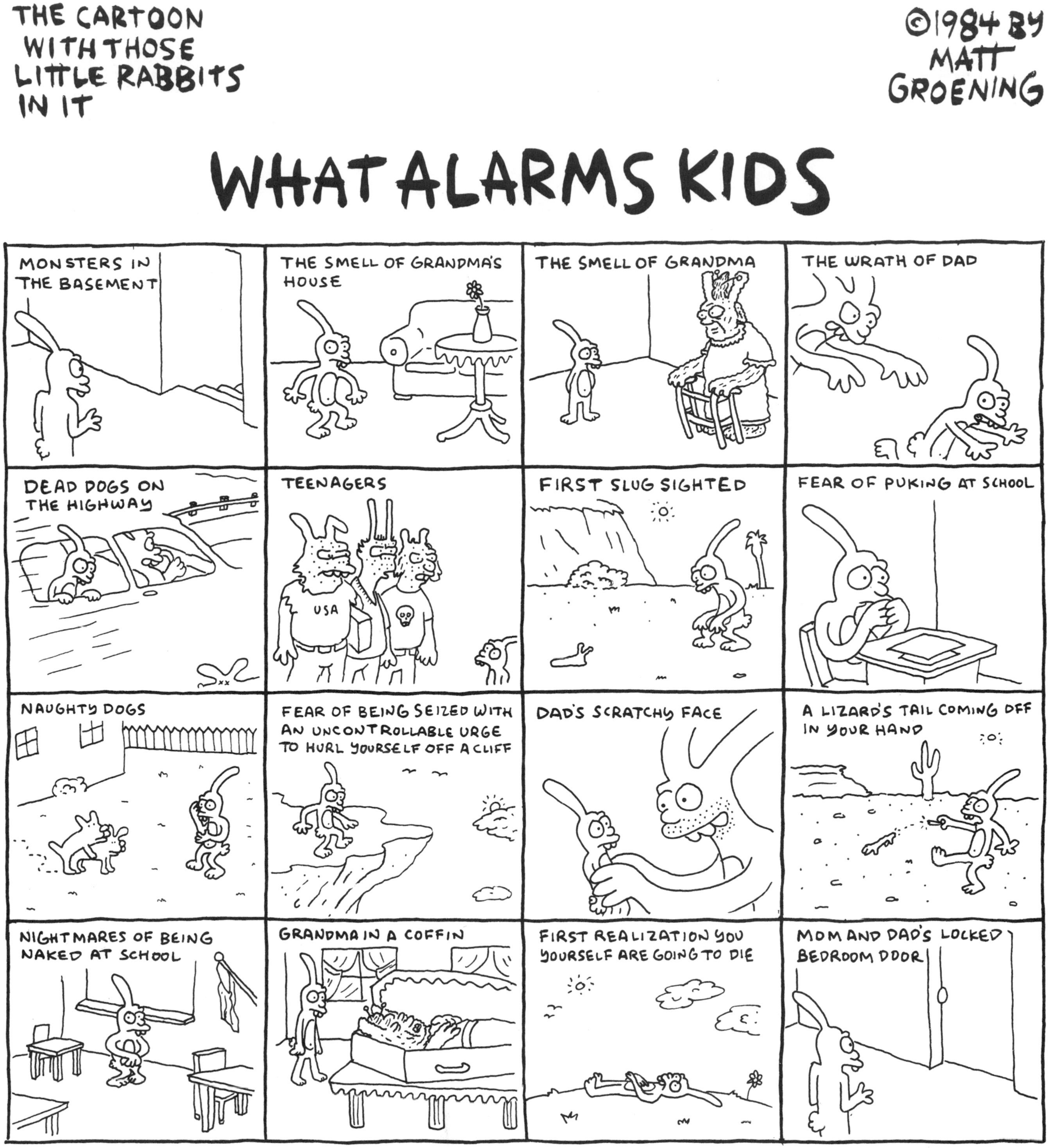
THE CARTOON WITH THOSE LITTLE RABBITS IN IT
©1984 BY MATT GROENING
WHAT ALARMS KIDS
MONSTERS IN THE BASEMENT
THE SMELL OF GRANDMA'S HOUSE
THE SMELL OF GRANDMA
THE WRATH OF DAD
DEAD DOGS ON THE HIGHWAY
TEENAGERS
USA
FIRST SLUG SIGHTED
FEAR OF PUKING AT SCHOOL
NAUGHTY DOGS
FEAR OF BEING SEIZED WITH AN UNCONTROLLABLE URGE TO HURL YOURSELF OFF A CLIFF
DAD'S SCRATCHY FACE
A LIZARD'S TAIL COMING OFF IN YOUR HAND
NIGHTMARES OF BEING NAKED AT SCHOOL
GRANDMA IN A COFFIN
FIRST REALIZATION YOU YOURSELF ARE GOING TO DIE
MOM AND DAD'S LOCKED BEDROOM DOOR

LIFE UNDER REAGAN

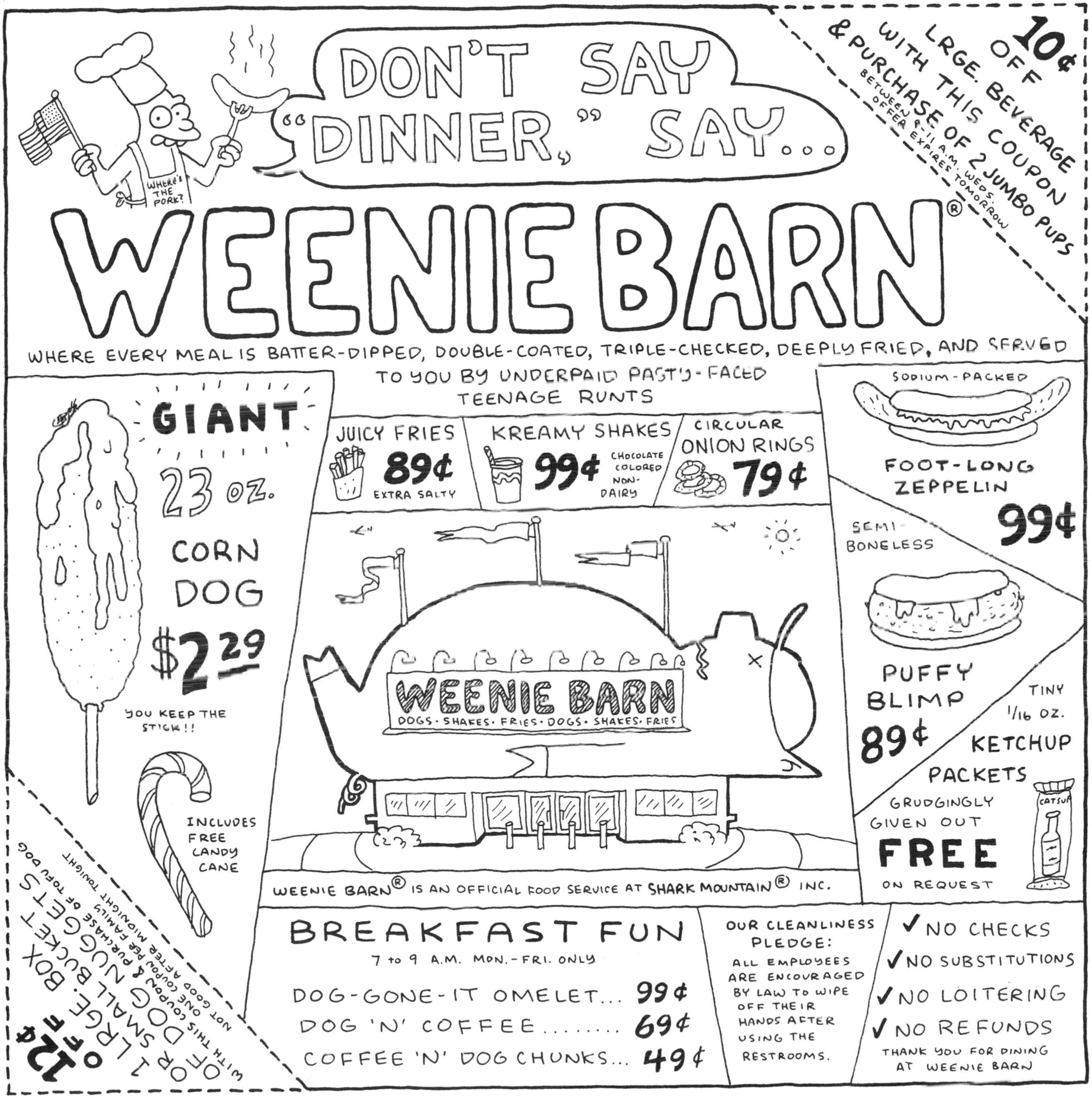
WHERE'S THE PORK?
DON'T SAY "DINNER," SAY...
10¢ OFF LRGE. BEVERAGE WITH THIS COUPON & PURCHASE OF 2 JUMBO PUPS
BETWEEN 8-11 A.M. WEDS.
OFFER EXPIRES TOMORROW
WEENIE BARN®
WHERE EVERY MEAL IS BATTER-DIPPED, DOUBLE-COATED, TRIPLE-CHECKED, DEEPLY FRIED, AND SERVED TO YOU BY UNDERPAID PASTY-FACED TEENAGE RUNTS
GIANT 23 OZ. CORN DOG $2.29
YOU KEEP THE STICK!!
INCLUDES FREE CANDY CANE
JUICY FRIES 89¢ EXTRA SALTY
KREAMY SHAKES 99¢ CHOCOLATE COLORED NON-DAIRY
CIRCULAR ONION RINGS 79¢
SODIUM-PACKED
FOOT-LONG ZEPPELIN 99¢
SEMI-BONELESS
PUFFY BLIMP 89¢
TINY 1/16 OZ. KETCHUP PACKETS GRUDGINGLY GIVEN OUT FREE ON REQUEST
CATSUP
WEENIE BARN
DOGS · SHAKES · FRIES · DOGS · SHAKES · FRIES
WEENIE BARN® IS AN OFFICIAL FOOD SERVICE AT SHARK MOUNTAIN® INC.
12¢ OFF 1 LRGE. BOX OR SMALL BUCKET OF DOG NUGGETS
WITH THIS COUPON & PURCHASE OF TOFU DOG
NOT ONE COUPON PER FAMILY
NOT GOOD AFTER MIDNIGHT TONIGHT
BREAKFAST FUN
7 to 9 A.M. MON.-FRI. ONLY
DOG-GONE-IT OMELET... 99¢
DOG 'N' COFFEE........ 69¢
COFFEE 'N' DOG CHUNKS... 49¢
OUR CLEANLINESS PLEDGE:
ALL EMPLOYEES ARE ENCOURAGED BY LAW TO WIPE OFF THEIR HANDS AFTER USING THE RESTROOMS.
✓NO CHECKS
✓NO SUBSTITUTIONS
✓NO LOITERING
✓NO REFUNDS
THANK YOU FOR DINING AT WEENIE BARN

LIFE IN HELL

CAN **YOU** HELP WEE LITTLE BONGO SAFELY FIND HIS WAY HOME?

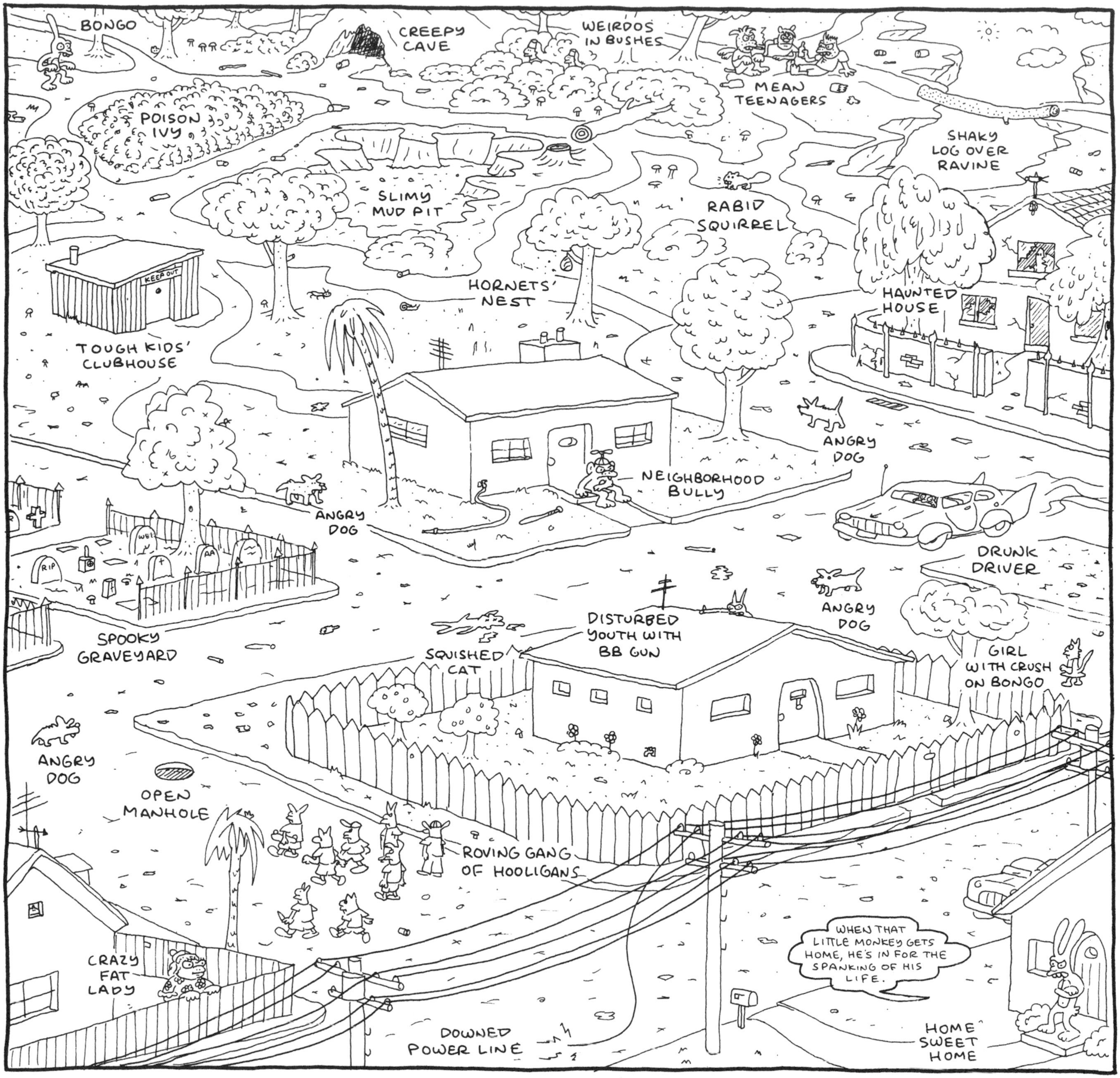
BONGO
CREEPY CAVE
WEIRDOS IN BUSHES
MEAN TEENAGERS
POISON IVY
SLIMY MUD PIT
SHAKY LOG OVER RAVINE
RABID SQUIRREL
KEEP OUT
HORNETS' NEST
HAUNTED HOUSE
TOUGH KIDS' CLUBHOUSE
ANGRY DOG
NEIGHBORHOOD BULLY
ANGRY DOG
RIP
DRUNK DRIVER
ANGRY DOG
DISTURBED YOUTH WITH BB GUN
SQUISHED CAT
SPOOKY GRAVEYARD
GIRL WITH CRUSH ON BONGO
ANGRY DOG
OPEN MANHOLE
ROVING GANG OF HOOLIGANS
CRAZY FAT LADY
WHEN THAT LITTLE MONKEY GETS HOME, HE'S IN FOR THE SPANKING OF HIS LIFE.
DOWNED POWER LINE
HOME SWEET HOME

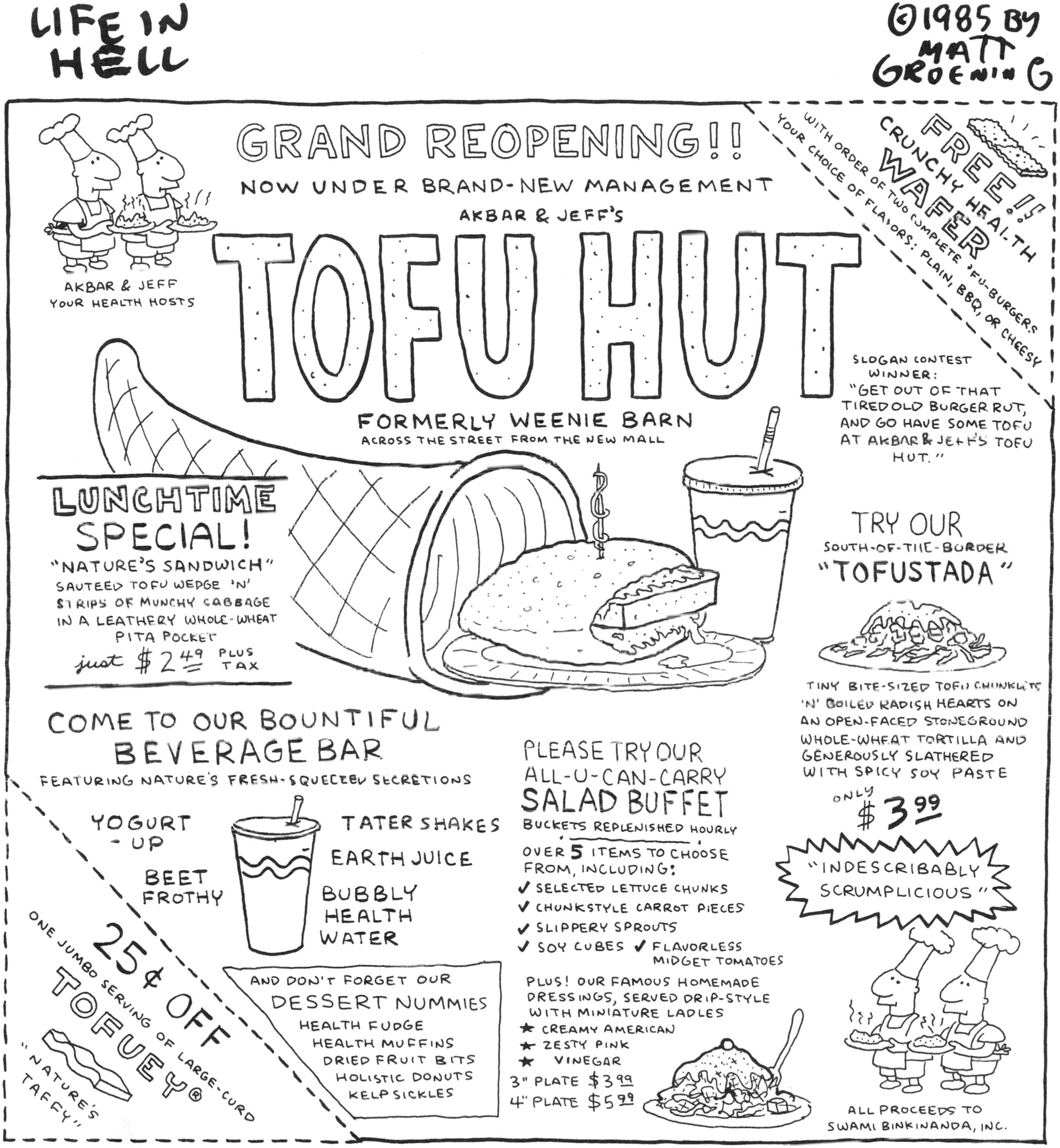
LIFE IN HELL
©1985 BY MATT GROENING
GRAND REOPENING!!
NOW UNDER BRAND-NEW MANAGEMENT
AKBAR & JEFF'S
TOFU HUT
FORMERLY WEENIE BARN
ACROSS THE STREET FROM THE NEW MALL
AKBAR & JEFF YOUR HEALTH HOSTS
FREE!! CRUNCHY HEALTH WAFER
WITH ORDER OF TWO COMPLETE TOFU-BURGERS
YOUR CHOICE OF FLAVORS: PLAIN, BBQ, OR CHEESY
SLOGAN CONTEST WINNER: "GET OUT OF THAT TIRED OLD BURGER RUT, AND GO HAVE SOME TOFU AT AKBAR & JEFF'S TOFU HUT."
LUNCHTIME SPECIAL!
"NATURE'S SANDWICH"
SAUTEED TOFU WEDGE 'N' STRIPS OF MUNCHY CABBAGE IN A LEATHERY WHOLE-WHEAT PITA POCKET
just $2.49 PLUS TAX
TRY OUR SOUTH-OF-THE-BORDER "TOFUSTADA"
TINY BITE-SIZED TOFU CHUNKLETS 'N' BOILED RADISH HEARTS ON AN OPEN-FACED STONEGROUND WHOLE-WHEAT TORTILLA AND GENEROUSLY SLATHERED WITH SPICY SOY PASTE
ONLY $3.99
"INDESCRIBABLY SCRUMPLICIOUS"
COME TO OUR BOUNTIFUL BEVERAGE BAR
FEATURING NATURE'S FRESH-SQUEEZED SECRETIONS
YOGURT-UP
BEET FROTHY
TATER SHAKES
EARTH JUICE
BUBBLY HEALTH WATER
PLEASE TRY OUR ALL-U-CAN-CARRY SALAD BUFFET
BUCKETS REPLENISHED HOURLY
OVER 5 ITEMS TO CHOOSE FROM, INCLUDING:
✓ SELECTED LETTUCE CHUNKS
✓ CHUNKSTYLE CARROT PIECES
✓ SLIPPERY SPROUTS
✓ SOY CUBES ✓ FLAVORLESS MIDGET TOMATOES
PLUS! OUR FAMOUS HOMEMADE DRESSINGS, SERVED DRIP-STYLE WITH MINIATURE LADLES
★ CREAMY AMERICAN
★ ZESTY PINK
★ VINEGAR
3" PLATE $3.99
4" PLATE $5.99
AND DON'T FORGET OUR DESSERT NUMMIES
HEALTH FUDGE
HEALTH MUFFINS
DRIED FRUIT BITS
HOLISTIC DONUTS
KELPSICKLES
25¢ OFF
ONE JUMBO SERVING OF LARGE-CURD TOFUEY®
"NATURE'S TAFFY"
ALL PROCEEDS TO SWAMI BINKINANDA, INC.

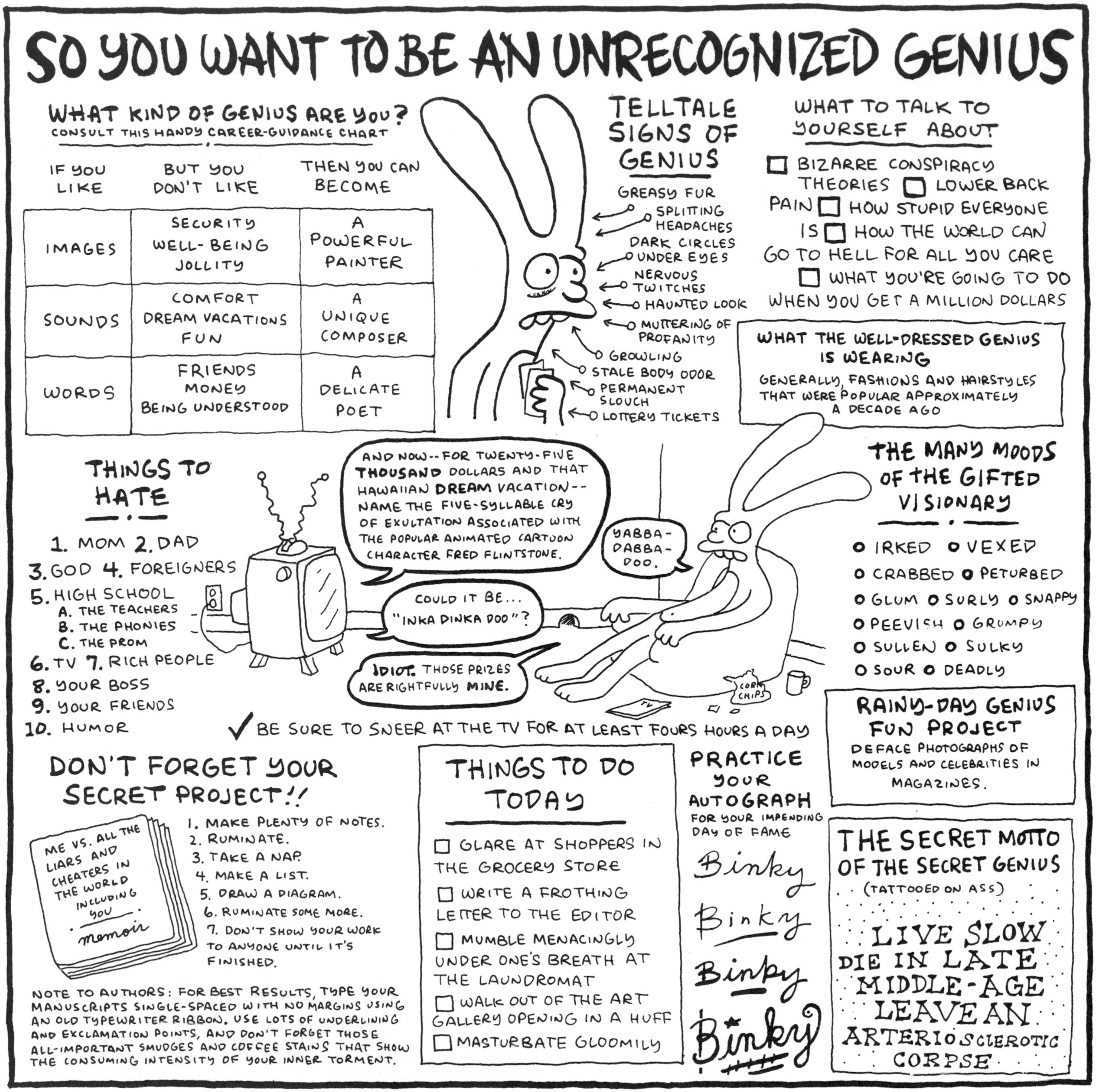
SO YOU WANT TO BE AN UNRECOGNIZED GENIUS
WHAT KIND OF GENIUS ARE YOU? CONSULT THIS HANDY CAREER-GUIDANCE CHART
IF YOU LIKE
BUT YOU DON'T LIKE
THEN YOU CAN BECOME
IMAGES
SECURITY WELL-BEING JOLLITY
A POWERFUL PAINTER
SOUNDS
COMFORT DREAM VACATIONS FUN
A UNIQUE COMPOSER
WORDS
FRIENDS MONEY BEING UNDERSTOOD
A DELICATE POET
TELLTALE SIGNS OF GENIUS
GREASY FUR
SPLITTING HEADACHES
DARK CIRCLES UNDER EYES
NERVOUS TWITCHES
HAUNTED LOOK
MUTTERING OF PROFANITY
GROWLING
STALE BODY ODOR
PERMANENT SLOUCH
LOTTERY TICKETS
WHAT TO TALK TO YOURSELF ABOUT
☐ BIZARRE CONSPIRACY THEORIES ☐ LOWER BACK PAIN ☐ HOW STUPID EVERYONE IS ☐ HOW THE WORLD CAN GO TO HELL FOR ALL YOU CARE ☐ WHAT YOU'RE GOING TO DO WHEN YOU GET A MILLION DOLLARS
WHAT THE WELL-DRESSED GENIUS IS WEARING
GENERALLY, FASHIONS AND HAIRSTYLES THAT WERE POPULAR APPROXIMATELY A DECADE AGO
THINGS TO HATE
1. MOM 2. DAD
3. GOD 4. FOREIGNERS
5. HIGH SCHOOL
A. THE TEACHERS
B. THE PHONIES
C. THE PROM
6. TV 7. RICH PEOPLE
8. YOUR BOSS
9. YOUR FRIENDS
10. HUMOR
AND NOW-- FOR TWENTY-FIVE THOUSAND DOLLARS AND THAT HAWAIIAN DREAM VACATION-- NAME THE FIVE-SYLLABLE CRY OF EXULTATION ASSOCIATED WITH THE POPULAR ANIMATED CARTOON CHARACTER FRED FLINTSTONE.
COULD IT BE... "INKA DINKA DOO"?
YABBA-DABBA-DOO.
IDIOT. THOSE PRIZES ARE RIGHTFULLY MINE.
CORN CHIPS
TV
THE MANY MOODS OF THE GIFTED VISIONARY
○ IRKED ○ VEXED
○ CRABBED ○ PETURBED
○ GLUM ○ SURLY ○ SNAPPY
○ PEEVISH ○ GRUMPY
○ SULLEN ○ SULKY
○ SOUR ○ DEADLY
✓ BE SURE TO SNEER AT THE TV FOR AT LEAST FOURS HOURS A DAY
RAINY-DAY GENIUS FUN PROJECT
DEFACE PHOTOGRAPHS OF MODELS AND CELEBRITIES IN MAGAZINES.
DON'T FORGET YOUR SECRET PROJECT!!
ME VS. ALL THE LIARS AND CHEATERS IN THE WORLD INCLUDING YOU
memoir
1. MAKE PLENTY OF NOTES.
2. RUMINATE.
3. TAKE A NAP.
4. MAKE A LIST.
5. DRAW A DIAGRAM.
6. RUMINATE SOME MORE.
7. DON'T SHOW YOUR WORK TO ANYONE UNTIL IT'S FINISHED.
NOTE TO AUTHORS: FOR BEST RESULTS, TYPE YOUR MANUSCRIPTS SINGLE-SPACED WITH NO MARGINS USING AN OLD TYPEWRITER RIBBON. USE LOTS OF UNDERLINING AND EXCLAMATION POINTS, AND DON'T FORGET THOSE ALL-IMPORTANT SMUDGES AND COFFEE STAINS THAT SHOW THE CONSUMING INTENSITY OF YOUR INNER TORMENT.
THINGS TO DO TODAY
☐ GLARE AT SHOPPERS IN THE GROCERY STORE
☐ WRITE A FROTHING LETTER TO THE EDITOR
☐ MUMBLE MENACINGLY UNDER ONE'S BREATH AT THE LAUNDROMAT
☐ WALK OUT OF THE ART GALLERY OPENING IN A HUFF
☐ MASTURBATE GLOOMILY
PRACTICE YOUR AUTOGRAPH FOR YOUR IMPENDING DAY OF FAME
Binky
Binky
Binky
Binky
THE SECRET MOTTO OF THE SECRET GENIUS
(TATTOOED ON ASS)
LIVE SLOW DIE IN LATE MIDDLE-AGE LEAVE AN ARTERIOSCLEROTIC CORPSE

LIFE IN HELL

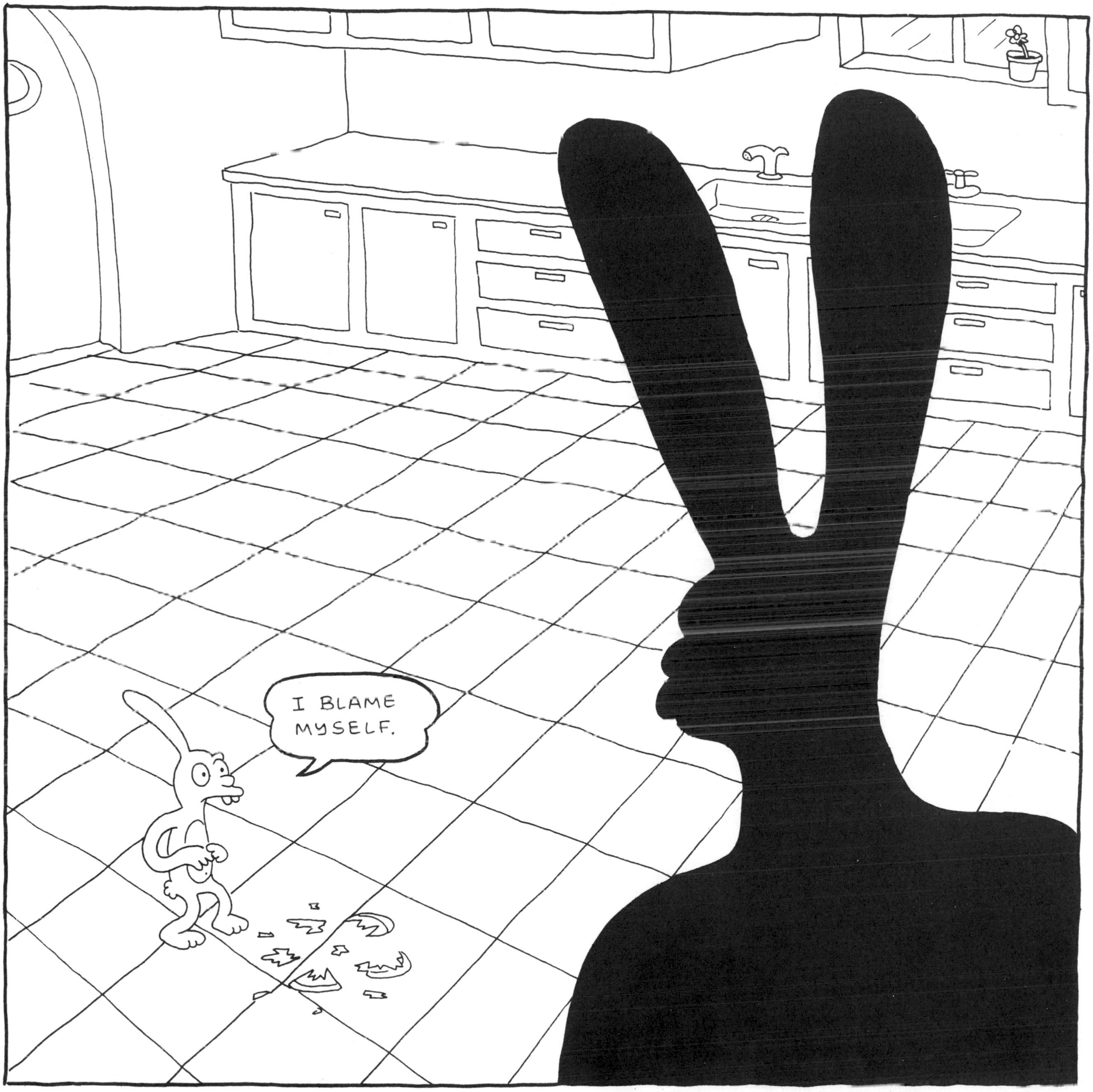
I BLAME MYSELF.

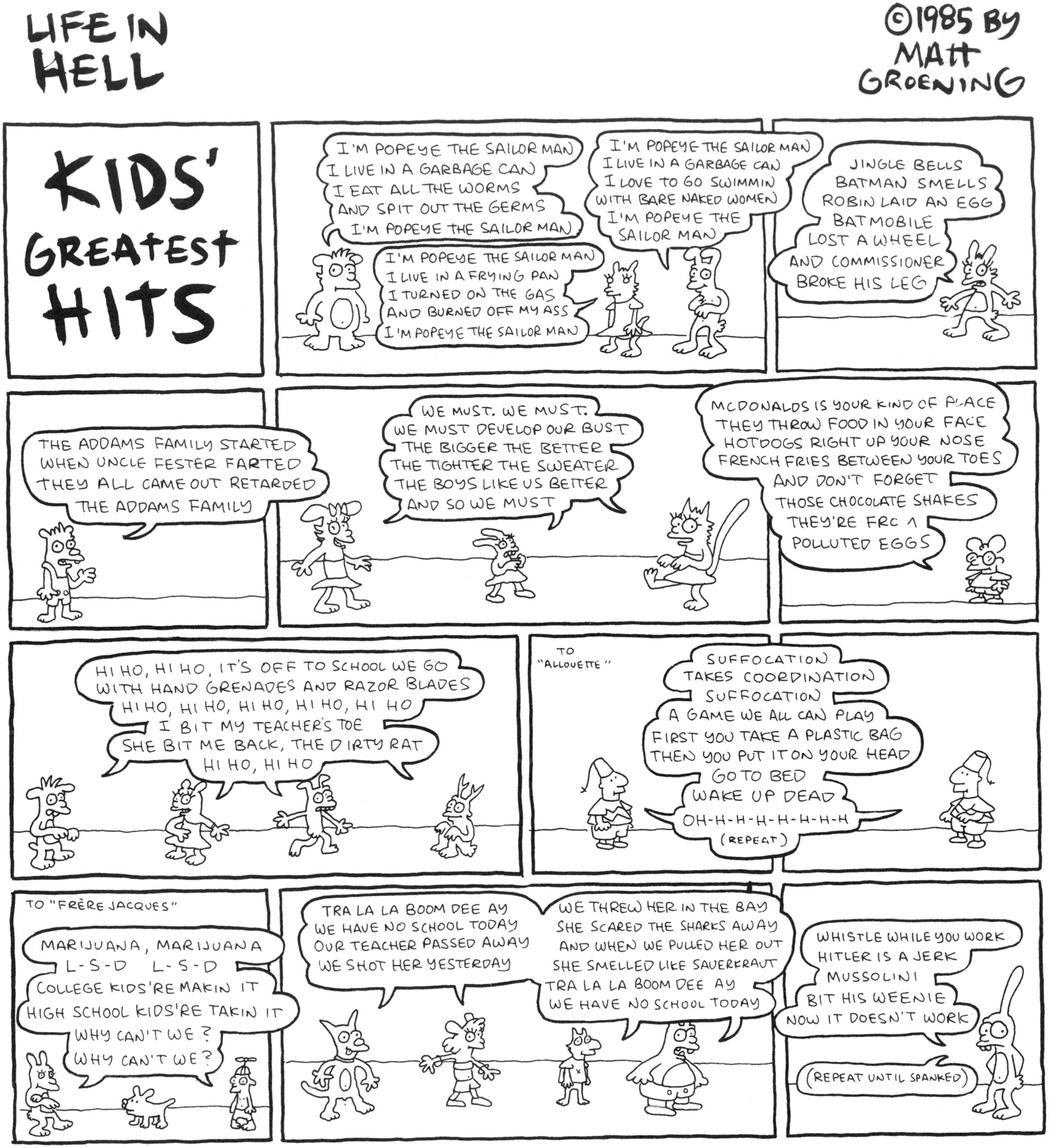
LIFE IN HELL
©1985 BY MATT GROENING
KIDS' GREATEST HITS
I'M POPEYE THE SAILOR MAN I LIVE IN A GARBAGE CAN I EAT ALL THE WORMS AND SPIT OUT THE GERMS I'M POPEYE THE SAILOR MAN
I'M POPEYE THE SAILOR MAN I LIVE IN A FRYING PAN I TURNED ON THE GAS AND BURNED OFF MY ASS I'M POPEYE THE SAILOR MAN
I'M POPEYE THE SAILOR MAN I LIVE IN A GARBAGE CAN I LOVE TO GO SWIMMIN WITH BARE NAKED WOMEN I'M POPEYE THE SAILOR MAN
JINGLE BELLS BATMAN SMELLS ROBIN LAID AN EGG BATMOBILE LOST A WHEEL AND COMMISSIONER BROKE HIS LEG
THE ADDAMS FAMILY STARTED WHEN UNCLE FESTER FARTED THEY ALL CAME OUT RETARDED THE ADDAMS FAMILY
WE MUST. WE MUST. WE MUST DEVELOP OUR BUST THE BIGGER THE BETTER THE TIGHTER THE SWEATER THE BOYS LIKE US BETTER AND SO WE MUST
MCDONALDS IS YOUR KIND OF PLACE THEY THROW FOOD IN YOUR FACE HOTDOGS RIGHT UP YOUR NOSE FRENCH FRIES BETWEEN YOUR TOES AND DON'T FORGET THOSE CHOCOLATE SHAKES THEY'RE FRC 1 POLLUTED EGGS
HI HO, HI HO, IT'S OFF TO SCHOOL WE GO WITH HAND GRENADES AND RAZOR BLADES HI HO, HI HO, HI HO, HI HO, HI HO I BIT MY TEACHER'S TOE SHE BIT ME BACK, THE DIRTY RAT HI HO, HI HO
TO "ALLOUETTE"
SUFFOCATION TAKES COORDINATION SUFFOCATION A GAME WE ALL CAN PLAY FIRST YOU TAKE A PLASTIC BAG THEN YOU PUT IT ON YOUR HEAD GO TO BED WAKE UP DEAD OH-H-H-H-H-H-H-H (REPEAT)
TO "FRÈRE JACQUES"
MARIJUANA, MARIJUANA L-S-D L-S-D COLLEGE KIDS'RE MAKIN IT HIGH SCHOOL KIDS'RE TAKIN IT WHY CAN'T WE? WHY CAN'T WE?
TRA LA LA BOOM DEE AY WE HAVE NO SCHOOL TODAY OUR TEACHER PASSED AWAY WE SHOT HER YESTERDAY
WE THREW HER IN THE BAY SHE SCARED THE SHARKS AWAY AND WHEN WE PULLED HER OUT SHE SMELLED LIKE SAUERKRAUT TRA LA LA BOOM DEE AY WE HAVE NO SCHOOL TODAY
WHISTLE WHILE YOU WORK HITLER IS A JERK MUSSOLINI BIT HIS WEENIE NOW IT DOESN'T WORK
(REPEAT UNTIL SPANKED)

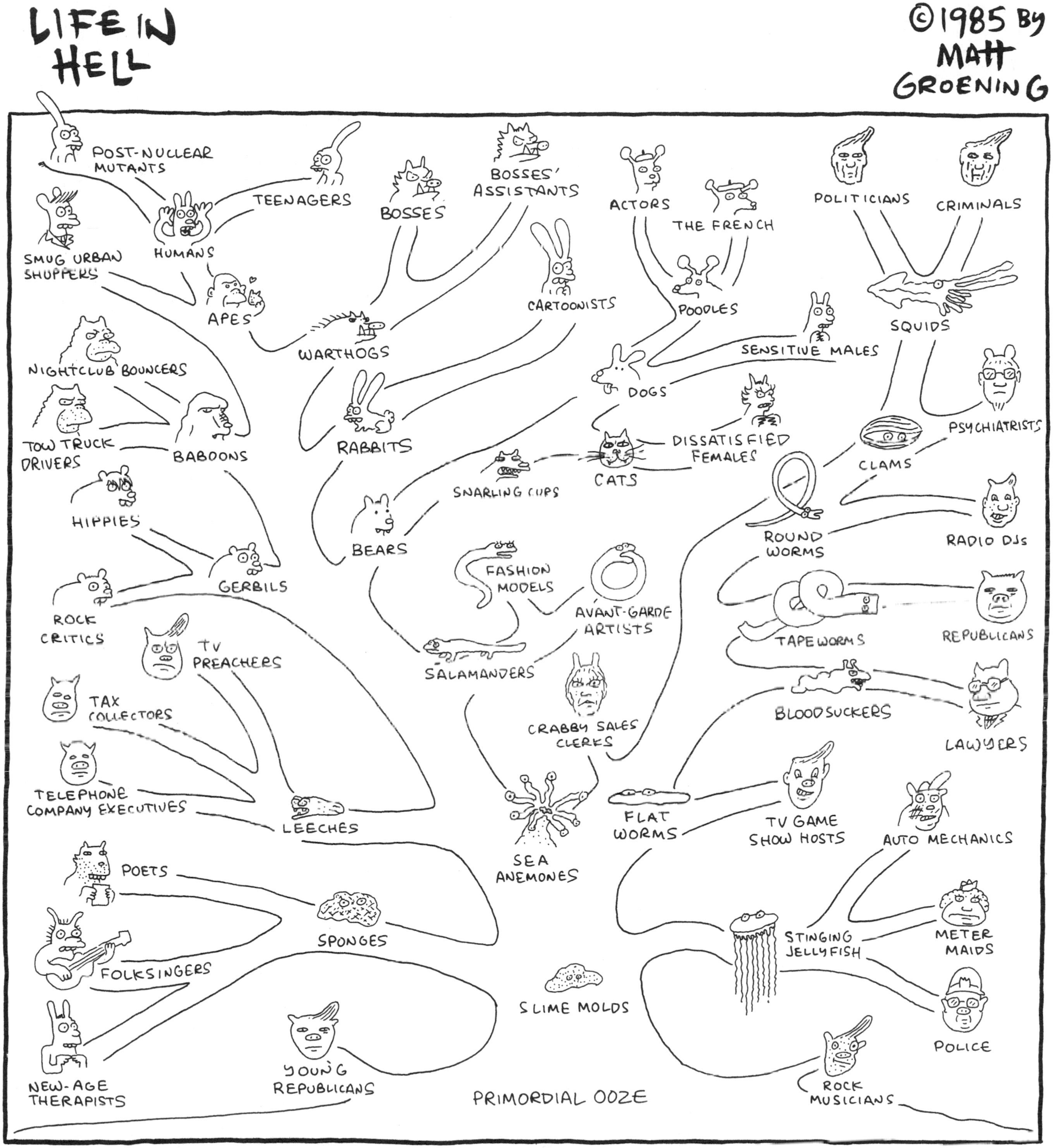

LIFE IN HELL
©1985 BY MATT GROENING
POST-NUCLEAR MUTANTS
TEENAGERS
HUMANS
SMUG URBAN SHOPPERS
APES
BOSSES
BOSSES' ASSISTANTS
WARTHOGS
CARTOONISTS
ACTORS
THE FRENCH
POODLES
POLITICIANS
CRIMINALS
SQUIDS
SENSITIVE MALES
DOGS
NIGHTCLUB BOUNCERS
TOW TRUCK DRIVERS
BABOONS
RABBITS
DISSATISFIED FEMALES
CATS
SNARLING CUPS
PSYCHIATRISTS
CLAMS
HIPPIES
GERBILS
BEARS
ROUND WORMS
RADIO DJs
FASHION MODELS
AVANT-GARDE ARTISTS
ROCK CRITICS
TV PREACHERS
SALAMANDERS
TAPEWORMS
REPUBLICANS
TAX COLLECTORS
BLOODSUCKERS
LAWYERS
CRABBY SALES CLERKS
TELEPHONE COMPANY EXECUTIVES
LEECHES
SEA ANEMONES
FLAT WORMS
TV GAME SHOW HOSTS
AUTO MECHANICS
POETS
SPONGES
STINGING JELLYFISH
METER MAIDS
FOLKSINGERS
SLIME MOLDS
POLICE
NEW-AGE THERAPISTS
YOUNG REPUBLICANS
PRIMORDIAL OOZE
ROCK MUSICIANS

© 1985 BY MATT GROENING

HOW TO BE A CLEVER FILM CRITIC

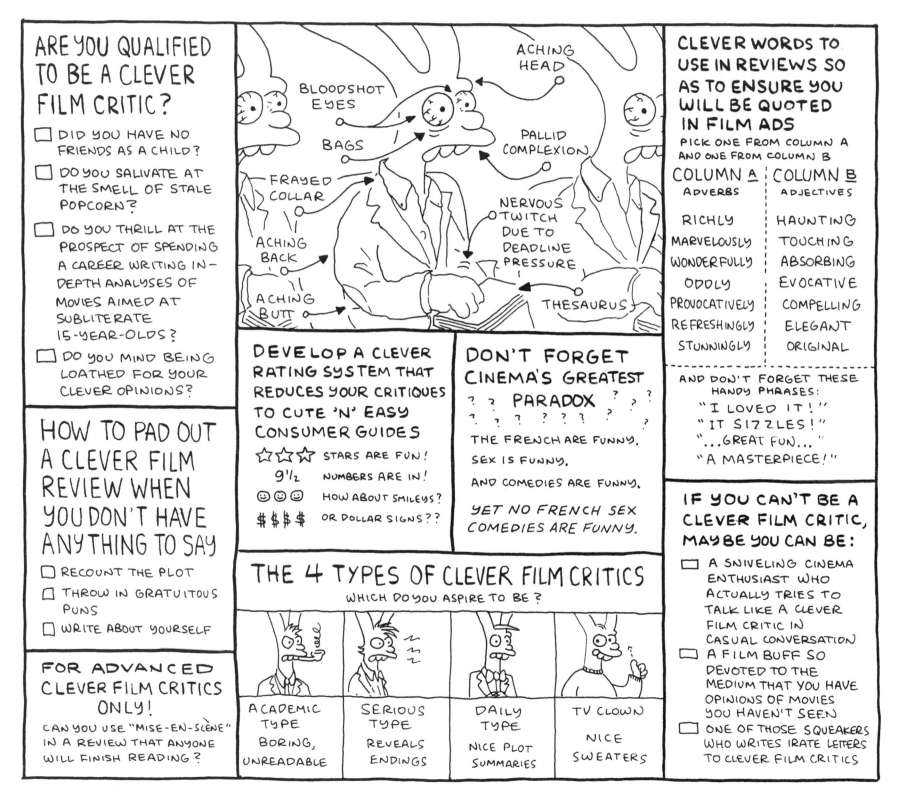

ARE YOU QUALIFIED TO BE A CLEVER FILM CRITIC?

☐ DID YOU HAVE NO FRIENDS AS A CHILD?

☐ DO YOU SALIVATE AT THE SMELL OF STALE POPCORN?

☐ DO YOU THRILL AT THE PROSPECT OF SPENDING A CAREER WRITING IN-DEPTH ANALYSES OF MOVIES AIMED AT SUBLITERATE 15-YEAR-OLDS?

☐ DO YOU MIND BEING LOATHED FOR YOUR CLEVER OPINIONS?

HOW TO PAD OUT A CLEVER FILM REVIEW WHEN YOU DON'T HAVE ANYTHING TO SAY

☐ RECOUNT THE PLOT

☐ THROW IN GRATUITOUS PUNS

☐ WRITE ABOUT YOURSELF

FOR ADVANCED CLEVER FILM CRITICS ONLY!

CAN YOU USE "MISE-EN-SCÈNE" IN A REVIEW THAT ANYONE WILL FINISH READING?

(Labels on central figure: ACHING HEAD, BLOODSHOT EYES, BAGS, PALLID COMPLEXION, FRAYED COLLAR, NERVOUS TWITCH DUE TO DEADLINE PRESSURE, ACHING BACK, ACHING BUTT, THESAURUS)

DEVELOP A CLEVER RATING SYSTEM THAT REDUCES YOUR CRITIQUES TO CUTE 'N' EASY CONSUMER GUIDES

☆☆☆ STARS ARE FUN!

9½ NUMBERS ARE IN!

☺☺☺ HOW ABOUT SMILEYS?

$$$ OR DOLLAR SIGNS??

DON'T FORGET CINEMA'S GREATEST PARADOX ??? ?? ?? ??? ? ?

THE FRENCH ARE FUNNY.

SEX IS FUNNY.

AND COMEDIES ARE FUNNY.

YET NO FRENCH SEX COMEDIES ARE FUNNY.

THE 4 TYPES OF CLEVER FILM CRITICS

WHICH DO YOU ASPIRE TO BE?

ACADEMIC TYPE BORING, UNREADABLE	SERIOUS TYPE REVEALS ENDINGS	DAILY TYPE NICE PLOT SUMMARIES	TV CLOWN NICE SWEATERS

CLEVER WORDS TO USE IN REVIEWS SO AS TO ENSURE YOU WILL BE QUOTED IN FILM ADS

PICK ONE FROM COLUMN A AND ONE FROM COLUMN B

COLUMN A ADVERBS	COLUMN B ADJECTIVES
RICHLY	HAUNTING
MARVELOUSLY	TOUCHING
WONDERFULLY	ABSORBING
ODDLY	EVOCATIVE
PROVOCATIVELY	COMPELLING
REFRESHINGLY	ELEGANT
STUNNINGLY	ORIGINAL

AND DON'T FORGET THESE HANDY PHRASES:

"I LOVED IT!"

"IT SIZZLES!"

"...GREAT FUN..."

"A MASTERPIECE!"

IF YOU CAN'T BE A CLEVER FILM CRITIC, MAYBE YOU CAN BE:

☐ A SNIVELING CINEMA ENTHUSIAST WHO ACTUALLY TRIES TO TALK LIKE A CLEVER FILM CRITIC IN CASUAL CONVERSATION

☐ A FILM BUFF SO DEVOTED TO THE MEDIUM THAT YOU HAVE OPINIONS OF MOVIES YOU HAVEN'T SEEN

☐ ONE OF THOSE SQUEAKERS WHO WRITES IRATE LETTERS TO CLEVER FILM CRITICS

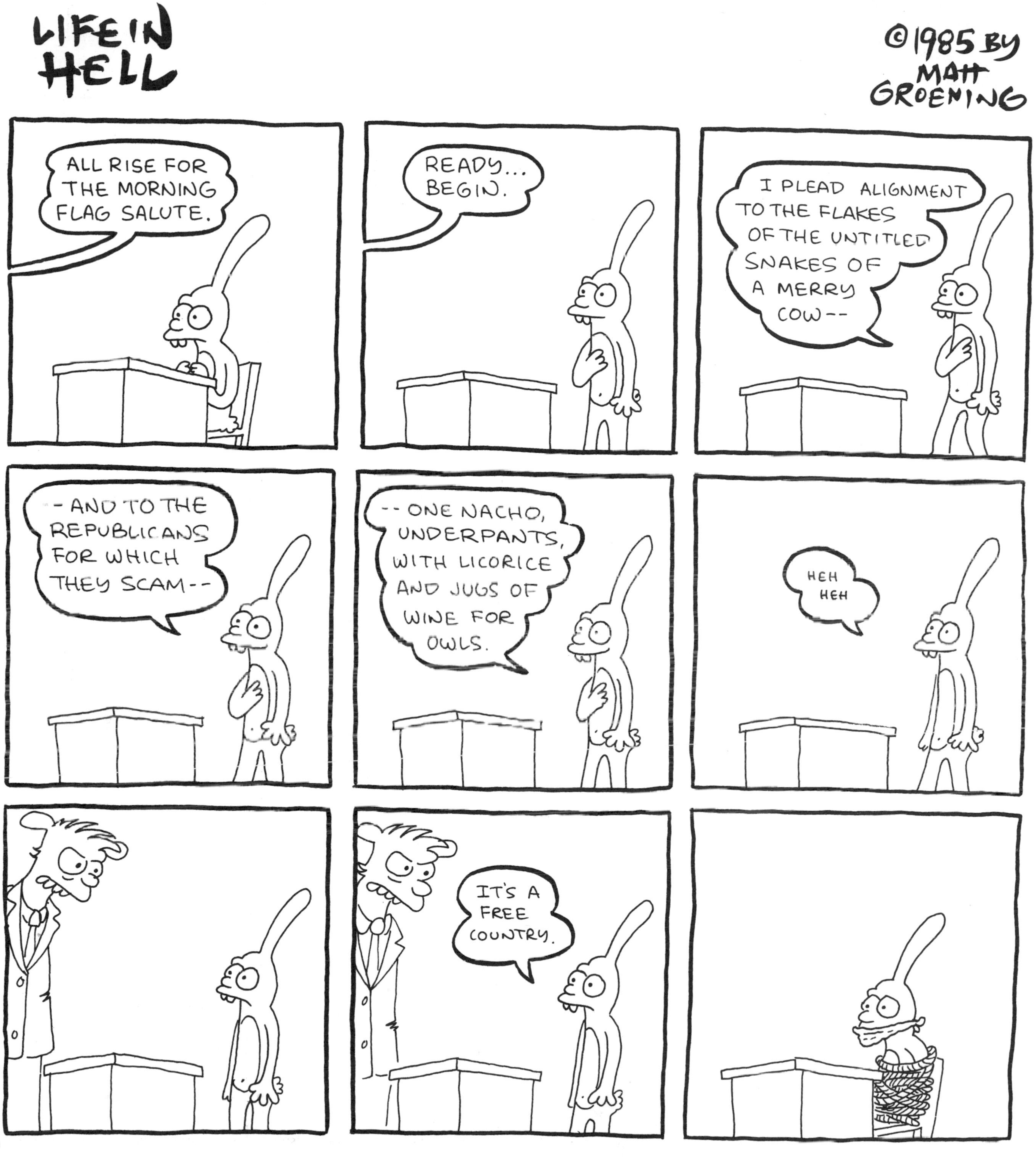
LIFE IN HELL
©1985 BY MATT GROENING
ALL RISE FOR THE MORNING FLAG SALUTE.
READY... BEGIN.
I PLEAD ALIGNMENT TO THE FLAKES OF THE UNTITLED SNAKES OF A MERRY COW--
-AND TO THE REPUBLICANS FOR WHICH THEY SCAM--
--ONE NACHO, UNDERPANTS, WITH LICORICE AND JUGS OF WINE FOR OWLS.
HEH HEH
IT'S A FREE COUNTRY.

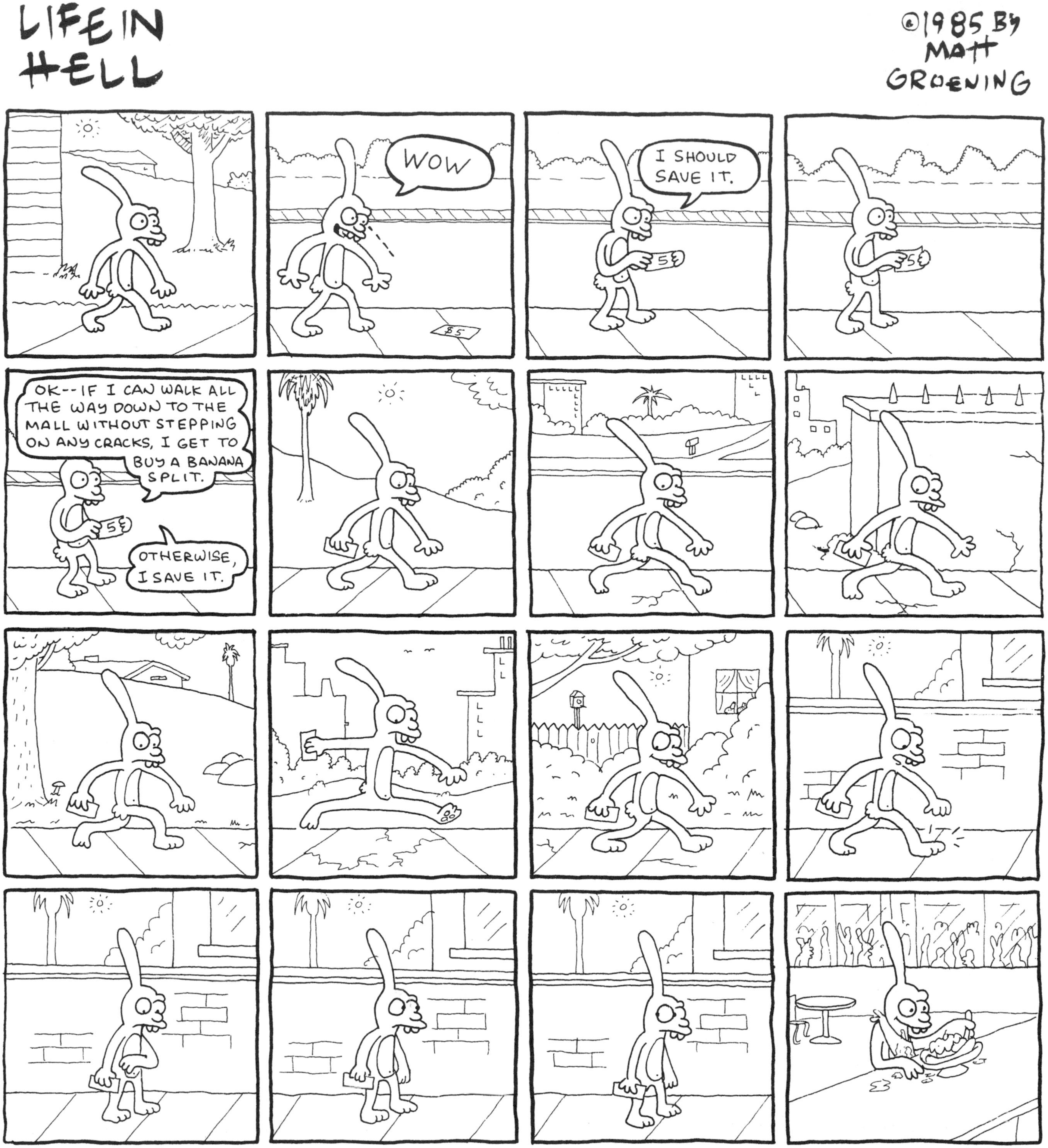
LIFE IN HELL
©1985 BY MATT GROENING
WOW
$5
I SHOULD SAVE IT.
5
OK--IF I CAN WALK ALL THE WAY DOWN TO THE MALL WITHOUT STEPPING ON ANY CRACKS, I GET TO BUY A BANANA SPLIT.
OTHERWISE, I SAVE IT.

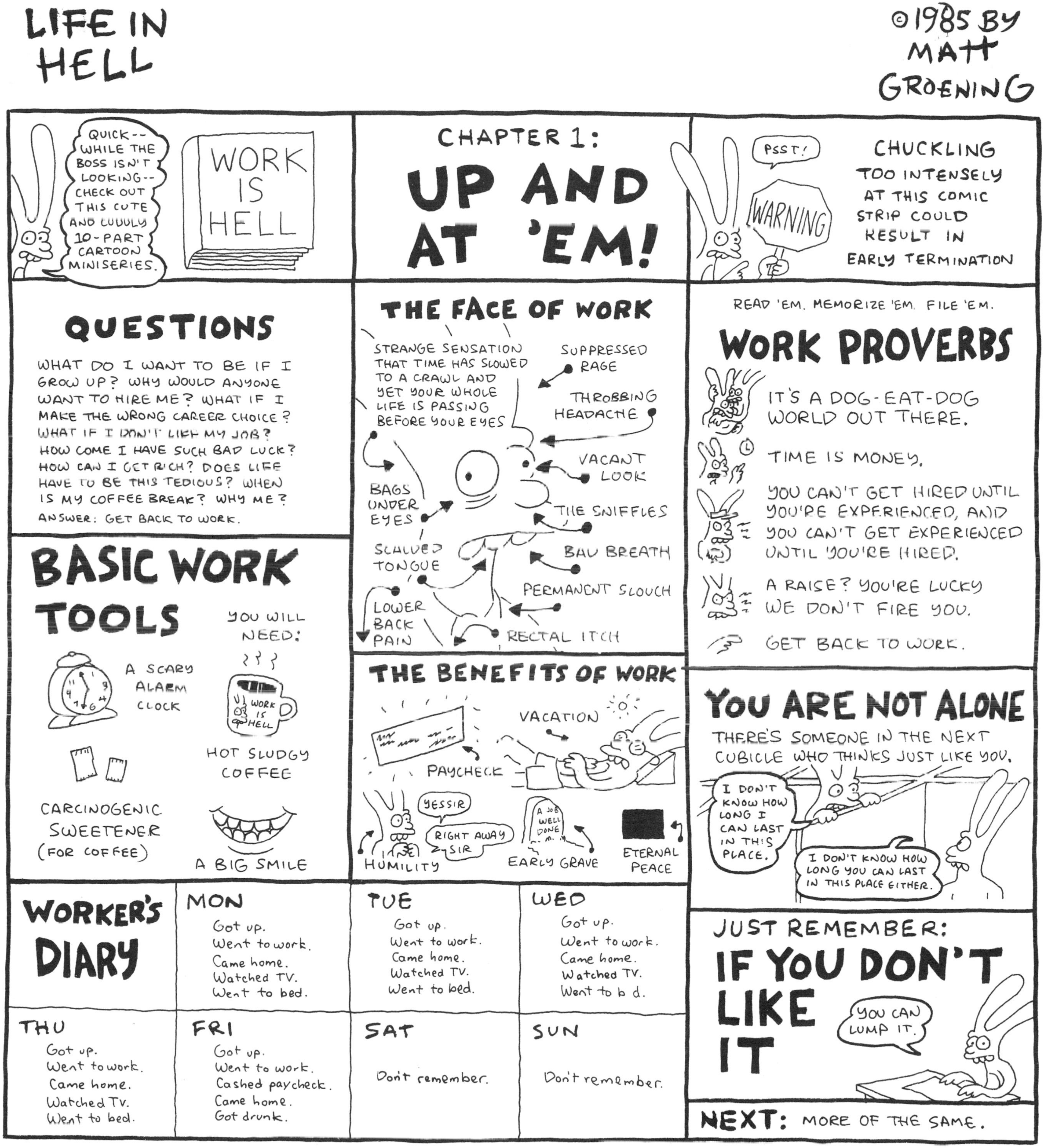
LIFE IN HELL
©1985 BY MATT GROENING
QUICK -- WHILE THE BOSS ISN'T LOOKING -- CHECK OUT THIS CUTE AND CUDDLY 10-PART CARTOON MINISERIES.
WORK IS HELL
CHAPTER 1:
UP AND AT 'EM!
PSST!
WARNING
CHUCKLING TOO INTENSELY AT THIS COMIC STRIP COULD RESULT IN EARLY TERMINATION
QUESTIONS
WHAT DO I WANT TO BE IF I GROW UP? WHY WOULD ANYONE WANT TO HIRE ME? WHAT IF I MAKE THE WRONG CAREER CHOICE? WHAT IF I DON'T LIKE MY JOB? HOW COME I HAVE SUCH BAD LUCK? HOW CAN I GET RICH? DOES LIFE HAVE TO BE THIS TEDIOUS? WHEN IS MY COFFEE BREAK? WHY ME?
ANSWER: GET BACK TO WORK.
THE FACE OF WORK
STRANGE SENSATION THAT TIME HAS SLOWED TO A CRAWL AND YET YOUR WHOLE LIFE IS PASSING BEFORE YOUR EYES
SUPPRESSED RAGE
THROBBING HEADACHE
VACANT LOOK
BAGS UNDER EYES
THE SNIFFLES
SCALDED TONGUE
BAD BREATH
PERMANENT SLOUCH
LOWER BACK PAIN
RECTAL ITCH
READ 'EM. MEMORIZE 'EM. FILE 'EM.
WORK PROVERBS
IT'S A DOG-EAT-DOG WORLD OUT THERE.
TIME IS MONEY.
YOU CAN'T GET HIRED UNTIL YOU'RE EXPERIENCED, AND YOU CAN'T GET EXPERIENCED UNTIL YOU'RE HIRED.
A RAISE? YOU'RE LUCKY WE DON'T FIRE YOU.
GET BACK TO WORK.
BASIC WORK TOOLS
YOU WILL NEED:
A SCARY ALARM CLOCK
WORK IS HELL
HOT SLUDGY COFFEE
CARCINOGENIC SWEETENER (FOR COFFEE)
A BIG SMILE
THE BENEFITS OF WORK
VACATION
PAYCHECK
YESSIR
RIGHT AWAY SIR
HUMILITY
A JOB WELL DONE
EARLY GRAVE
ETERNAL PEACE
YOU ARE NOT ALONE
THERE'S SOMEONE IN THE NEXT CUBICLE WHO THINKS JUST LIKE YOU.
I DON'T KNOW HOW LONG I CAN LAST IN THIS PLACE.
I DON'T KNOW HOW LONG YOU CAN LAST IN THIS PLACE EITHER.
WORKER'S DIARY
MON
Got up.
Went to work.
Came home.
Watched TV.
Went to bed.
TUE
Got up.
Went to work.
Came home.
Watched TV.
Went to bed.
WED
Got up.
Went to work.
Came home.
Watched TV.
Went to b d.
THU
Got up.
Went to work.
Came home.
Watched TV.
Went to bed.
FRI
Got up.
Went to work.
Cashed paycheck.
Came home.
Got drunk.
SAT
Don't remember.
SUN
Don't remember.
JUST REMEMBER:
IF YOU DON'T LIKE IT
YOU CAN LUMP IT.
NEXT: MORE OF THE SAME.

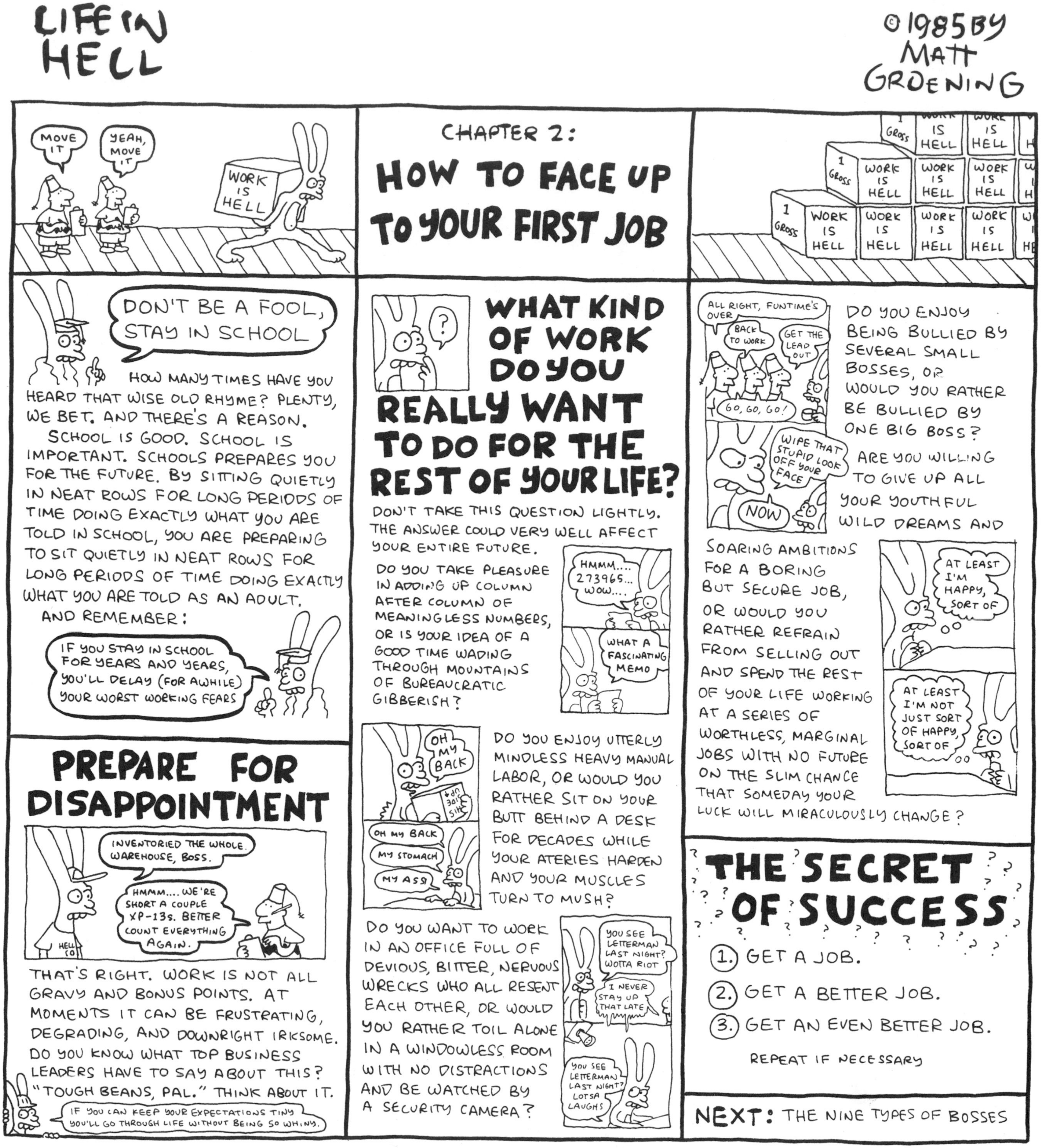
LIFE IN HELL
©1985 BY MATT GROENING
MOVE IT
YEAH, MOVE IT
WORK IS HELL
CHAPTER 2:
HOW TO FACE UP TO YOUR FIRST JOB
1 GROSS
WORK IS HELL
DON'T BE A FOOL, STAY IN SCHOOL
HOW MANY TIMES HAVE YOU HEARD THAT WISE OLD RHYME? PLENTY, WE BET. AND THERE'S A REASON.
SCHOOL IS GOOD. SCHOOL IS IMPORTANT. SCHOOLS PREPARES YOU FOR THE FUTURE. BY SITTING QUIETLY IN NEAT ROWS FOR LONG PERIODS OF TIME DOING EXACTLY WHAT YOU ARE TOLD IN SCHOOL, YOU ARE PREPARING TO SIT QUIETLY IN NEAT ROWS FOR LONG PERIODS OF TIME DOING EXACTLY WHAT YOU ARE TOLD AS AN ADULT.
AND REMEMBER:
IF YOU STAY IN SCHOOL FOR YEARS AND YEARS, YOU'LL DELAY (FOR AWHILE) YOUR WORST WORKING FEARS
PREPARE FOR DISAPPOINTMENT
INVENTORIED THE WHOLE WAREHOUSE, BOSS.
HMMM.... WE'RE SHORT A COUPLE XP-13s. BETTER COUNT EVERYTHING AGAIN.
THAT'S RIGHT. WORK IS NOT ALL GRAVY AND BONUS POINTS. AT MOMENTS IT CAN BE FRUSTRATING, DEGRADING, AND DOWNRIGHT IRKSOME. DO YOU KNOW WHAT TOP BUSINESS LEADERS HAVE TO SAY ABOUT THIS? "TOUGH BEANS, PAL." THINK ABOUT IT.
IF YOU CAN KEEP YOUR EXPECTATIONS TINY YOU'LL GO THROUGH LIFE WITHOUT BEING SO WHINY.
?
WHAT KIND OF WORK DO YOU REALLY WANT TO DO FOR THE REST OF YOUR LIFE?
DON'T TAKE THIS QUESTION LIGHTLY. THE ANSWER COULD VERY WELL AFFECT YOUR ENTIRE FUTURE.
DO YOU TAKE PLEASURE IN ADDING UP COLUMN AFTER COLUMN OF MEANINGLESS NUMBERS, OR IS YOUR IDEA OF A GOOD TIME WADING THROUGH MOUNTAINS OF BUREAUCRATIC GIBBERISH?
HMMM.... 273965... WOW....
WHAT A FASCINATING MEMO
OH MY BACK
DO YOU ENJOY UTTERLY MINDLESS HEAVY MANUAL LABOR, OR WOULD YOU RATHER SIT ON YOUR BUTT BEHIND A DESK FOR DECADES WHILE YOUR ATERIES HARDEN AND YOUR MUSCLES TURN TO MUSH?
OH MY BACK
MY STOMACH
MY ASS
DO YOU WANT TO WORK IN AN OFFICE FULL OF DEVIOUS, BITTER, NERVOUS WRECKS WHO ALL RESENT EACH OTHER, OR WOULD YOU RATHER TOIL ALONE IN A WINDOWLESS ROOM WITH NO DISTRACTIONS AND BE WATCHED BY A SECURITY CAMERA?
YOU SEE LETTERMAN LAST NIGHT? WOTTA RIOT
I NEVER STAY UP THAT LATE
YOU SEE LETTERMAN LAST NIGHT? LOTSA LAUGHS
ALL RIGHT, FUNTIME'S OVER
BACK TO WORK
GET THE LEAD OUT
GO, GO, GO!
WIPE THAT STUPID LOOK OFF YOUR FACE
NOW
DO YOU ENJOY BEING BULLIED BY SEVERAL SMALL BOSSES, OR WOULD YOU RATHER BE BULLIED BY ONE BIG BOSS?
ARE YOU WILLING TO GIVE UP ALL YOUR YOUTHFUL WILD DREAMS AND SOARING AMBITIONS FOR A BORING BUT SECURE JOB, OR WOULD YOU RATHER REFRAIN FROM SELLING OUT AND SPEND THE REST OF YOUR LIFE WORKING AT A SERIES OF WORTHLESS, MARGINAL JOBS WITH NO FUTURE ON THE SLIM CHANCE THAT SOMEDAY YOUR LUCK WILL MIRACULOUSLY CHANGE?
AT LEAST I'M HAPPY, SORT OF
AT LEAST I'M NOT JUST SORT OF HAPPY, SORT OF
THE SECRET OF SUCCESS
1. GET A JOB.
2. GET A BETTER JOB.
3. GET AN EVEN BETTER JOB.
REPEAT IF NECESSARY
NEXT: THE NINE TYPES OF BOSSES

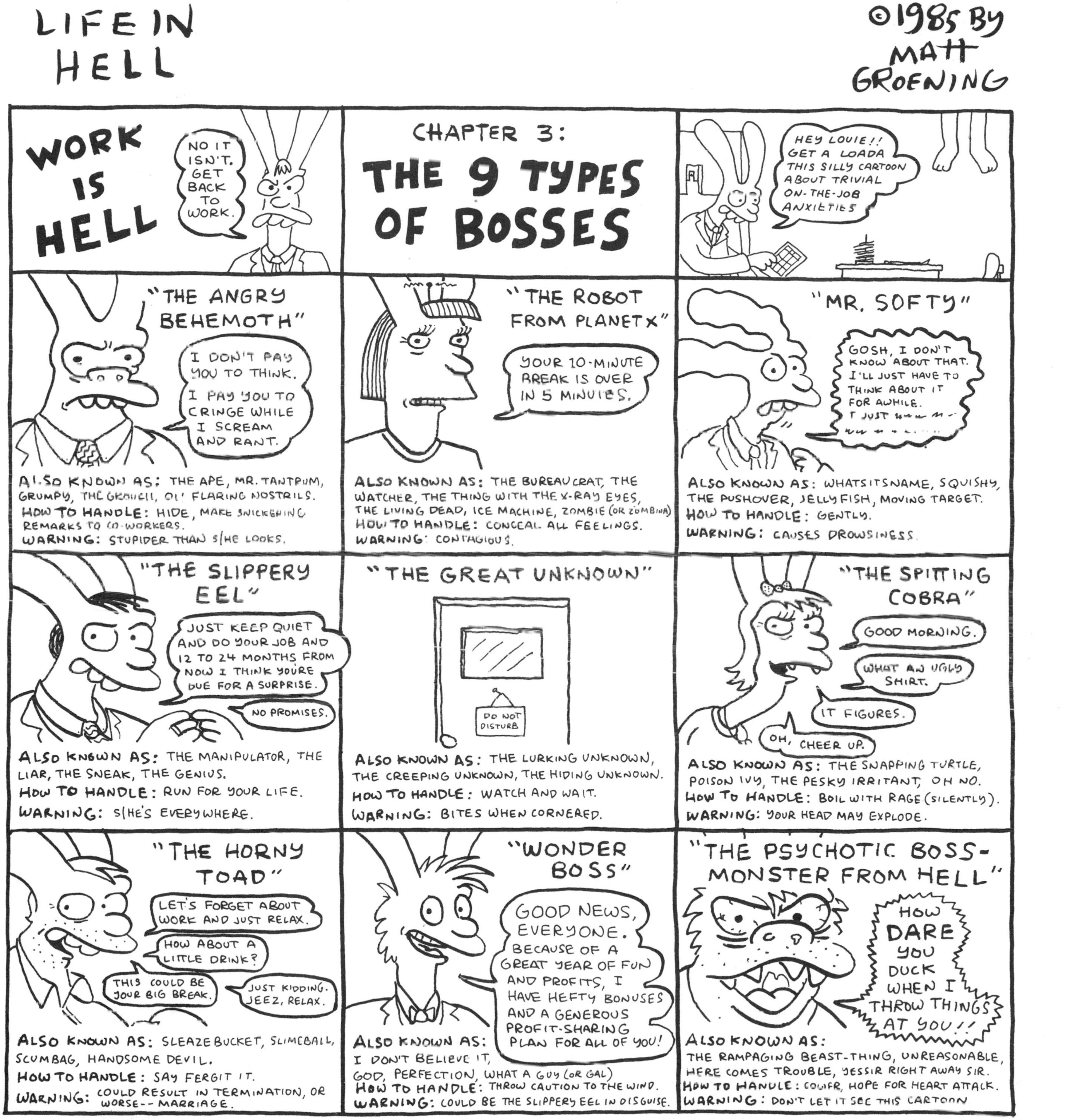
LIFE IN HELL
©1985 BY MATT GROENING
WORK IS HELL
NO IT ISN'T. GET BACK TO WORK.
CHAPTER 3:
THE 9 TYPES OF BOSSES
HEY LOUIE!! GET A LOADA THIS SILLY CARTOON ABOUT TRIVIAL ON-THE-JOB ANXIETIES
"THE ANGRY BEHEMOTH"
I DON'T PAY YOU TO THINK.
I PAY YOU TO CRINGE WHILE I SCREAM AND RANT.
ALSO KNOWN AS: THE APE, MR. TANTRUM, GRUMPY, THE GROUCH, OL' FLARING NOSTRILS.
HOW TO HANDLE: HIDE, MAKE SNICKERING REMARKS TO CO-WORKERS.
WARNING: STUPIDER THAN S/HE LOOKS.
"THE ROBOT FROM PLANET X"
YOUR 10-MINUTE BREAK IS OVER IN 5 MINUTES.
ALSO KNOWN AS: THE BUREAUCRAT, THE WATCHER, THE THING WITH THE X-RAY EYES, THE LIVING DEAD, ICE MACHINE, ZOMBIE (OR ZOMBINA)
HOW TO HANDLE: CONCEAL ALL FEELINGS.
WARNING: CONTAGIOUS.
"MR. SOFTY"
GOSH, I DON'T KNOW ABOUT THAT. I'LL JUST HAVE TO THINK ABOUT IT FOR AWHILE. I JUST
ALSO KNOWN AS: WHATSITSNAME, SQUISHY, THE PUSHOVER, JELLYFISH, MOVING TARGET.
HOW TO HANDLE: GENTLY.
WARNING: CAUSES DROWSINESS.
"THE SLIPPERY EEL"
JUST KEEP QUIET AND DO YOUR JOB AND 12 TO 24 MONTHS FROM NOW I THINK YOU'RE DUE FOR A SURPRISE.
NO PROMISES.
ALSO KNOWN AS: THE MANIPULATOR, THE LIAR, THE SNEAK, THE GENIUS.
HOW TO HANDLE: RUN FOR YOUR LIFE.
WARNING: S/HE'S EVERYWHERE.
"THE GREAT UNKNOWN"
DO NOT DISTURB
ALSO KNOWN AS: THE LURKING UNKNOWN, THE CREEPING UNKNOWN, THE HIDING UNKNOWN.
HOW TO HANDLE: WATCH AND WAIT.
WARNING: BITES WHEN CORNERED.
"THE SPITTING COBRA"
GOOD MORNING.
WHAT AN UGLY SHIRT.
IT FIGURES.
OH, CHEER UP.
ALSO KNOWN AS: THE SNAPPING TURTLE, POISON IVY, THE PESKY IRRITANT, OH NO.
HOW TO HANDLE: BOIL WITH RAGE (SILENTLY).
WARNING: YOUR HEAD MAY EXPLODE.
"THE HORNY TOAD"
LET'S FORGET ABOUT WORK AND JUST RELAX.
HOW ABOUT A LITTLE DRINK?
THIS COULD BE YOUR BIG BREAK.
JUST KIDDING. JEEZ, RELAX.
ALSO KNOWN AS: SLEAZEBUCKET, SLIMEBALL, SCUMBAG, HANDSOME DEVIL.
HOW TO HANDLE: SAY FERGIT IT.
WARNING: COULD RESULT IN TERMINATION, OR WORSE-- MARRIAGE.
"WONDER BOSS"
GOOD NEWS, EVERYONE. BECAUSE OF A GREAT YEAR OF FUN AND PROFITS, I HAVE HEFTY BONUSES AND A GENEROUS PROFIT-SHARING PLAN FOR ALL OF YOU!
ALSO KNOWN AS: I DON'T BELIEVE IT, GOD, PERFECTION, WHAT A GUY (OR GAL)
HOW TO HANDLE: THROW CAUTION TO THE WIND.
WARNING: COULD BE THE SLIPPERY EEL IN DISGUISE.
"THE PSYCHOTIC BOSS-MONSTER FROM HELL"
HOW DARE YOU DUCK WHEN I THROW THINGS AT YOU!!
ALSO KNOWN AS: THE RAMPAGING BEAST-THING, UNREASONABLE, HERE COMES TROUBLE, YESSIR RIGHT AWAY SIR.
HOW TO HANDLE: COWER, HOPE FOR HEART ATTACK.
WARNING: DON'T LET IT SEE THIS CARTOON

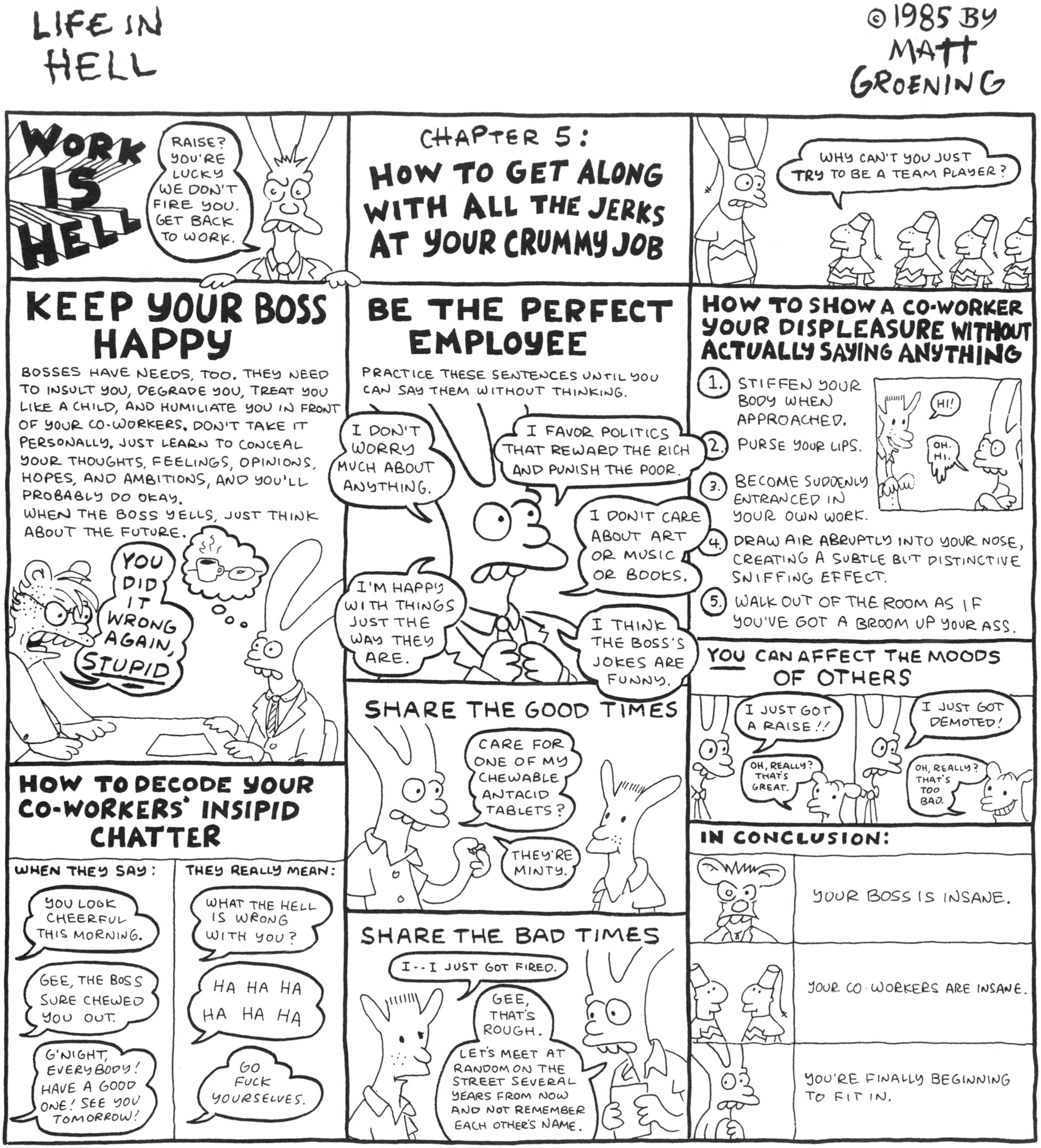
LIFE IN HELL
©1985 BY MATT GROENING
WORK IS HELL
RAISE? YOU'RE LUCKY WE DON'T FIRE YOU. GET BACK TO WORK.
CHAPTER 5:
HOW TO GET ALONG WITH ALL THE JERKS AT YOUR CRUMMY JOB
WHY CAN'T YOU JUST TRY TO BE A TEAM PLAYER?
KEEP YOUR BOSS HAPPY
BOSSES HAVE NEEDS, TOO. THEY NEED TO INSULT YOU, DEGRADE YOU, TREAT YOU LIKE A CHILD, AND HUMILIATE YOU IN FRONT OF YOUR CO-WORKERS. DON'T TAKE IT PERSONALLY. JUST LEARN TO CONCEAL YOUR THOUGHTS, FEELINGS, OPINIONS, HOPES, AND AMBITIONS, AND YOU'LL PROBABLY DO OKAY.
WHEN THE BOSS YELLS, JUST THINK ABOUT THE FUTURE.
YOU DID IT WRONG AGAIN, STUPID
BE THE PERFECT EMPLOYEE
PRACTICE THESE SENTENCES UNTIL YOU CAN SAY THEM WITHOUT THINKING.
I DON'T WORRY MUCH ABOUT ANYTHING.
I FAVOR POLITICS THAT REWARD THE RICH AND PUNISH THE POOR.
I DON'T CARE ABOUT ART OR MUSIC OR BOOKS.
I'M HAPPY WITH THINGS JUST THE WAY THEY ARE.
I THINK THE BOSS'S JOKES ARE FUNNY.
HOW TO SHOW A CO-WORKER YOUR DISPLEASURE WITHOUT ACTUALLY SAYING ANYTHING
1. STIFFEN YOUR BODY WHEN APPROACHED.
2. PURSE YOUR LIPS.
3. BECOME SUDDENLY ENTRANCED IN YOUR OWN WORK.
4. DRAW AIR ABRUPTLY INTO YOUR NOSE, CREATING A SUBTLE BUT DISTINCTIVE SNIFFING EFFECT.
5. WALK OUT OF THE ROOM AS IF YOU'VE GOT A BROOM UP YOUR ASS.
HI!
OH. HI.
SHARE THE GOOD TIMES
CARE FOR ONE OF MY CHEWABLE ANTACID TABLETS?
THEY'RE MINTY.
YOU CAN AFFECT THE MOODS OF OTHERS
I JUST GOT A RAISE!!
OH, REALLY? THAT'S GREAT.
I JUST GOT DEMOTED!
OH, REALLY? THAT'S TOO BAD.
HOW TO DECODE YOUR CO-WORKERS' INSIPID CHATTER
WHEN THEY SAY:
THEY REALLY MEAN:
YOU LOOK CHEERFUL THIS MORNING.
WHAT THE HELL IS WRONG WITH YOU?
GEE, THE BOSS SURE CHEWED YOU OUT.
HA HA HA HA HA HA
G'NIGHT, EVERYBODY! HAVE A GOOD ONE! SEE YOU TOMORROW!
GO FUCK YOURSELVES.
SHARE THE BAD TIMES
I--I JUST GOT FIRED.
GEE, THAT'S ROUGH.
LET'S MEET AT RANDOM ON THE STREET SEVERAL YEARS FROM NOW AND NOT REMEMBER EACH OTHER'S NAME.
IN CONCLUSION:
YOUR BOSS IS INSANE.
YOUR CO-WORKERS ARE INSANE.
YOU'RE FINALLY BEGINNING TO FIT IN.

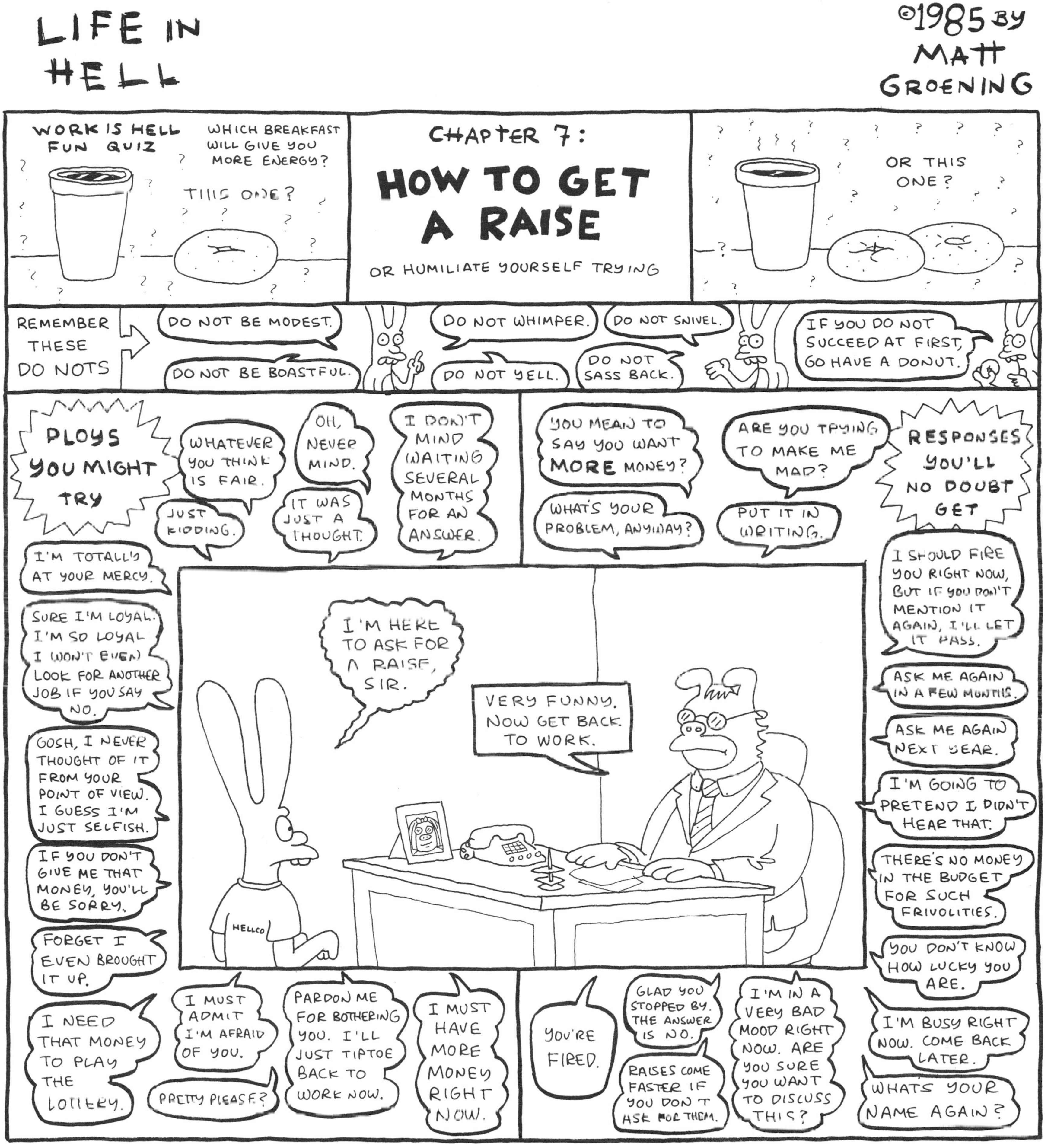
LIFE IN HELL
©1985 BY MATT GROENING
WORK IS HELL FUN QUIZ
WHICH BREAKFAST WILL GIVE YOU MORE ENERGY?
THIS ONE?
CHAPTER 7:
HOW TO GET A RAISE
OR HUMILIATE YOURSELF TRYING
OR THIS ONE?
REMEMBER THESE DO NOTS
DO NOT BE MODEST.
DO NOT BE BOASTFUL.
DO NOT WHIMPER.
DO NOT YELL.
DO NOT SNIVEL.
DO NOT SASS BACK.
IF YOU DO NOT SUCCEED AT FIRST, GO HAVE A DONUT.
PLOYS YOU MIGHT TRY
WHATEVER YOU THINK IS FAIR.
JUST KIDDING.
OH, NEVER MIND.
IT WAS JUST A THOUGHT.
I DON'T MIND WAITING SEVERAL MONTHS FOR AN ANSWER.
I'M TOTALLY AT YOUR MERCY.
SURE I'M LOYAL. I'M SO LOYAL I WON'T EVEN LOOK FOR ANOTHER JOB IF YOU SAY NO.
GOSH, I NEVER THOUGHT OF IT FROM YOUR POINT OF VIEW. I GUESS I'M JUST SELFISH.
IF YOU DON'T GIVE ME THAT MONEY, YOU'LL BE SORRY.
FORGET I EVEN BROUGHT IT UP.
I NEED THAT MONEY TO PLAY THE LOTTERY.
I MUST ADMIT I'M AFRAID OF YOU.
PRETTY PLEASE?
PARDON ME FOR BOTHERING YOU. I'LL JUST TIPTOE BACK TO WORK NOW.
I MUST HAVE MORE MONEY RIGHT NOW.
I'M HERE TO ASK FOR A RAISE, SIR.
VERY FUNNY. NOW GET BACK TO WORK.
HELLCO
RESPONSES YOU'LL NO DOUBT GET
YOU MEAN TO SAY YOU WANT MORE MONEY?
WHAT'S YOUR PROBLEM, ANYWAY?
ARE YOU TRYING TO MAKE ME MAD?
PUT IT IN WRITING.
I SHOULD FIRE YOU RIGHT NOW, BUT IF YOU DON'T MENTION IT AGAIN, I'LL LET IT PASS.
ASK ME AGAIN IN A FEW MONTHS.
ASK ME AGAIN NEXT YEAR.
I'M GOING TO PRETEND I DIDN'T HEAR THAT.
THERE'S NO MONEY IN THE BUDGET FOR SUCH FRIVOLITIES.
YOU DON'T KNOW HOW LUCKY YOU ARE.
I'M BUSY RIGHT NOW. COME BACK LATER.
WHAT'S YOUR NAME AGAIN?
YOU'RE FIRED.
GLAD YOU STOPPED BY. THE ANSWER IS NO.
RAISES COME FASTER IF YOU DON'T ASK FOR THEM.
I'M IN A VERY BAD MOOD RIGHT NOW. ARE YOU SURE YOU WANT TO DISCUSS THIS?

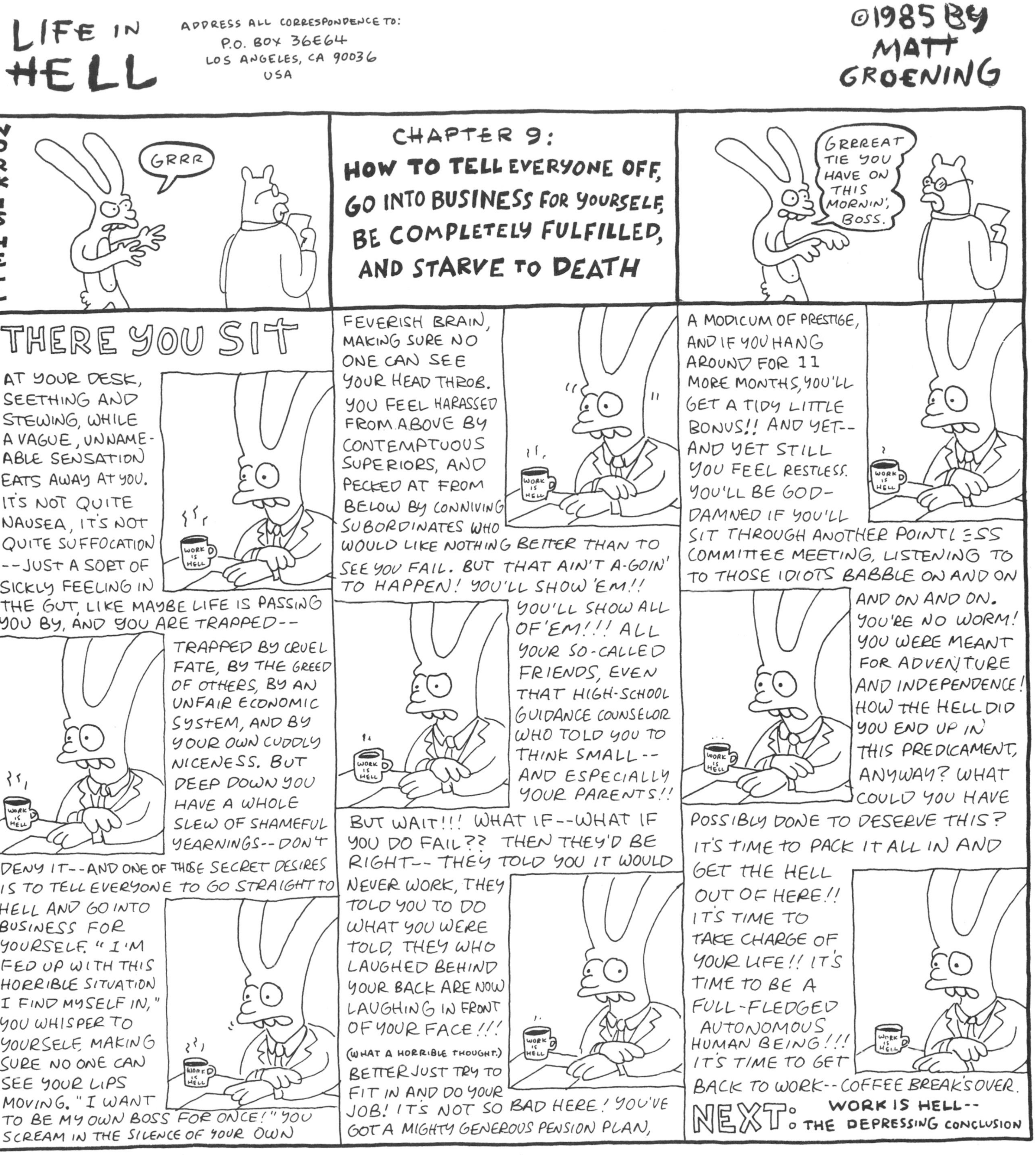
LIFE IN HELL
ADDRESS ALL CORRESPONDENCE TO: P.O. BOX 36E64 LOS ANGELES, CA 90036 USA
©1985 BY MATT GROENING
WORK IS HELL
GRRR
CHAPTER 9: HOW TO TELL EVERYONE OFF, GO INTO BUSINESS FOR YOURSELF, BE COMPLETELY FULFILLED, AND STARVE TO DEATH
GRRREAT TIE YOU HAVE ON THIS MORNIN', BOSS.
THERE YOU SIT
AT YOUR DESK, SEETHING AND STEWING, WHILE A VAGUE, UNNAME-ABLE SENSATION EATS AWAY AT YOU. IT'S NOT QUITE NAUSEA, IT'S NOT QUITE SUFFOCATION --JUST A SORT OF SICKLY FEELING IN THE GUT, LIKE MAYBE LIFE IS PASSING YOU BY, AND YOU ARE TRAPPED--
TRAPPED BY CRUEL FATE, BY THE GREED OF OTHERS, BY AN UNFAIR ECONOMIC SYSTEM, AND BY YOUR OWN CUDDLY NICENESS. BUT DEEP DOWN YOU HAVE A WHOLE SLEW OF SHAMEFUL YEARNINGS--DON'T DENY IT--AND ONE OF THOSE SECRET DESIRES IS TO TELL EVERYONE TO GO STRAIGHT TO HELL AND GO INTO BUSINESS FOR YOURSELF. "I'M FED UP WITH THIS HORRIBLE SITUATION I FIND MYSELF IN," YOU WHISPER TO YOURSELF, MAKING SURE NO ONE CAN SEE YOUR LIPS MOVING. "I WANT TO BE MY OWN BOSS FOR ONCE!" YOU SCREAM IN THE SILENCE OF YOUR OWN
FEVERISH BRAIN, MAKING SURE NO ONE CAN SEE YOUR HEAD THROB. YOU FEEL HARASSED FROM ABOVE BY CONTEMPTUOUS SUPERIORS, AND PECKED AT FROM BELOW BY CONNIVING SUBORDINATES WHO WOULD LIKE NOTHING BETTER THAN TO SEE YOU FAIL. BUT THAT AIN'T A-GOIN' TO HAPPEN! YOU'LL SHOW 'EM!!
YOU'LL SHOW ALL OF 'EM!!! ALL YOUR SO-CALLED FRIENDS, EVEN THAT HIGH-SCHOOL GUIDANCE COUNSELOR WHO TOLD YOU TO THINK SMALL-- AND ESPECIALLY YOUR PARENTS!!
BUT WAIT!!! WHAT IF--WHAT IF YOU DO FAIL?? THEN THEY'D BE RIGHT-- THEY TOLD YOU IT WOULD NEVER WORK, THEY TOLD YOU TO DO WHAT YOU WERE TOLD, THEY WHO LAUGHED BEHIND YOUR BACK ARE NOW LAUGHING IN FRONT OF YOUR FACE!!!
(WHAT A HORRIBLE THOUGHT.)
BETTER JUST TRY TO FIT IN AND DO YOUR JOB! IT'S NOT SO BAD HERE! YOU'VE GOT A MIGHTY GENEROUS PENSION PLAN,
A MODICUM OF PRESTIGE, AND IF YOU HANG AROUND FOR 11 MORE MONTHS, YOU'LL GET A TIDY LITTLE BONUS!! AND YET-- AND YET STILL YOU FEEL RESTLESS. YOU'LL BE GOD-DAMNED IF YOU'LL SIT THROUGH ANOTHER POINTLESS COMMITTEE MEETING, LISTENING TO TO THOSE IDIOTS BABBLE ON AND ON AND ON AND ON.
YOU'RE NO WORM! YOU WERE MEANT FOR ADVENTURE AND INDEPENDENCE! HOW THE HELL DID YOU END UP IN THIS PREDICAMENT, ANYWAY? WHAT COULD YOU HAVE POSSIBLY DONE TO DESERVE THIS?
IT'S TIME TO PACK IT ALL IN AND GET THE HELL OUT OF HERE!! IT'S TIME TO TAKE CHARGE OF YOUR LIFE!! IT'S TIME TO BE A FULL-FLEDGED AUTONOMOUS HUMAN BEING!!! IT'S TIME TO GET BACK TO WORK--COFFEE BREAK'S OVER.
WORK IS HELL
NEXT: WORK IS HELL-- THE DEPRESSING CONCLUSION

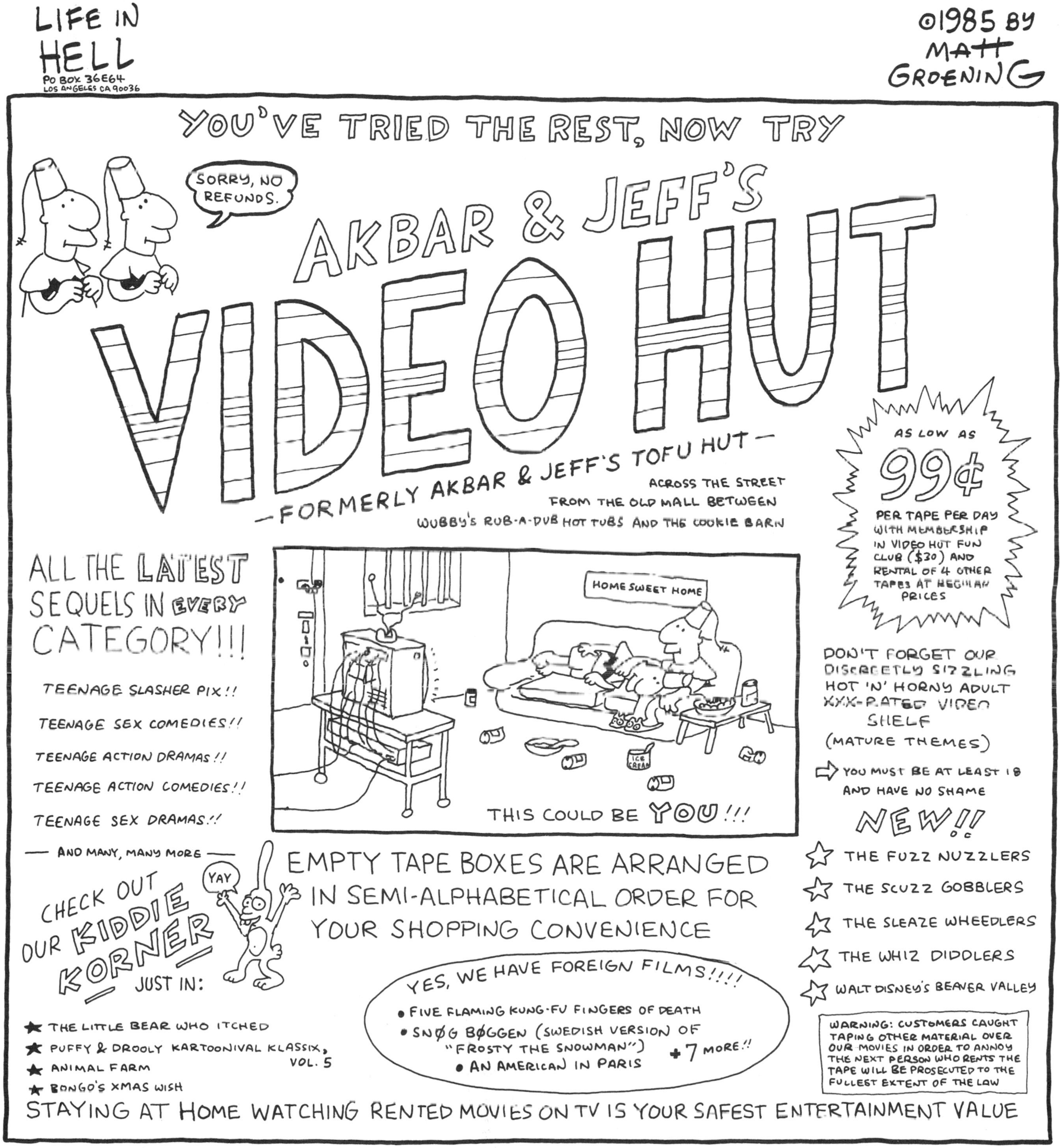

LIFE IN HELL
PO BOX 36E64 LOS ANGELES CA 90036
©1985 BY MATT GROENING
YOU'VE TRIED THE REST, NOW TRY
SORRY, NO REFUNDS.
AKBAR & JEFF'S VIDEO HUT
—FORMERLY AKBAR & JEFF'S TOFU HUT—
ACROSS THE STREET FROM THE OLD MALL BETWEEN WUBBY'S RUB-A-DUB HOT TUBS AND THE COOKIE BARN
AS LOW AS 99¢ PER TAPE PER DAY WITH MEMBERSHIP IN VIDEO HUT FUN CLUB ($30) AND RENTAL OF 4 OTHER TAPES AT REGULAR PRICES
ALL THE LATEST SEQUELS IN EVERY CATEGORY!!!
TEENAGE SLASHER PIX!!
TEENAGE SEX COMEDIES!!
TEENAGE ACTION DRAMAS!!
TEENAGE ACTION COMEDIES!!
TEENAGE SEX DRAMAS!!
— AND MANY, MANY MORE —
HOME SWEET HOME
ICE CREAM
THIS COULD BE YOU!!!
DON'T FORGET OUR DISCREETLY SIZZLING HOT 'N' HORNY ADULT XXX-RATED VIDEO SHELF
(MATURE THEMES)
YOU MUST BE AT LEAST 18 AND HAVE NO SHAME
NEW!!
THE FUZZ NUZZLERS
THE SCUZZ GOBBLERS
THE SLEAZE WHEEDLERS
THE WHIZ DIDDLERS
WALT DISNEY'S BEAVER VALLEY
CHECK OUT OUR KIDDIE KORNER
YAY
JUST IN:
THE LITTLE BEAR WHO ITCHED
PUFFY & DROOLY KARTOONIVAL KLASSIX, VOL. 5
ANIMAL FARM
BONGO'S XMAS WISH
EMPTY TAPE BOXES ARE ARRANGED IN SEMI-ALPHABETICAL ORDER FOR YOUR SHOPPING CONVENIENCE
YES, WE HAVE FOREIGN FILMS!!!!
FIVE FLAMING KUNG-FU FINGERS OF DEATH
SNØG BØGGEN (SWEDISH VERSION OF "FROSTY THE SNOWMAN")
AN AMERICAN IN PARIS
+7 MORE!!
WARNING: CUSTOMERS CAUGHT TAPING OTHER MATERIAL OVER OUR MOVIES IN ORDER TO ANNOY THE NEXT PERSON WHO RENTS THE TAPE WILL BE PROSECUTED TO THE FULLEST EXTENT OF THE LAW
STAYING AT HOME WATCHING RENTED MOVIES ON TV IS YOUR SAFEST ENTERTAINMENT VALUE

LIFE IN HELL

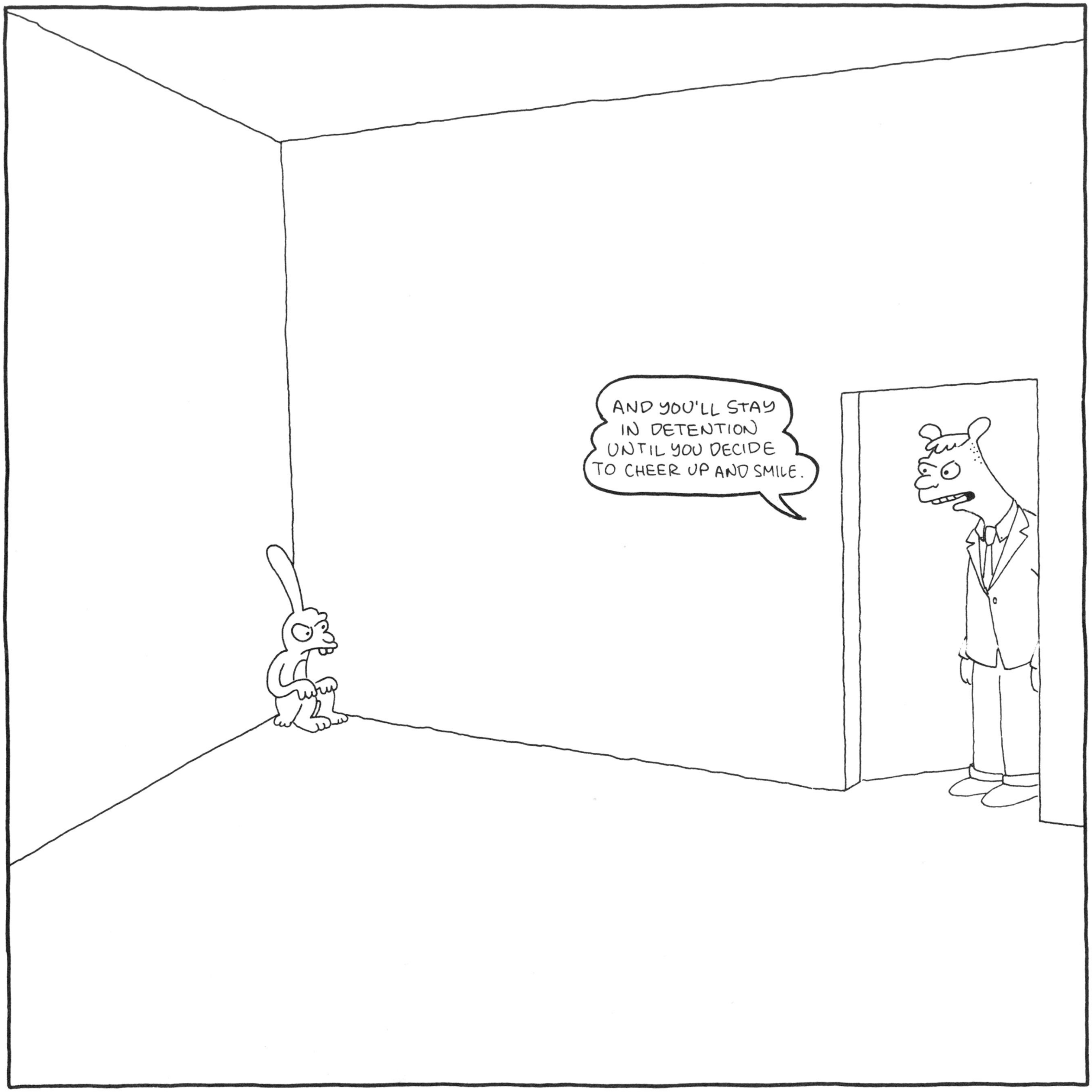
AND YOU'LL STAY IN DETENTION UNTIL YOU DECIDE TO CHEER UP AND SMILE.

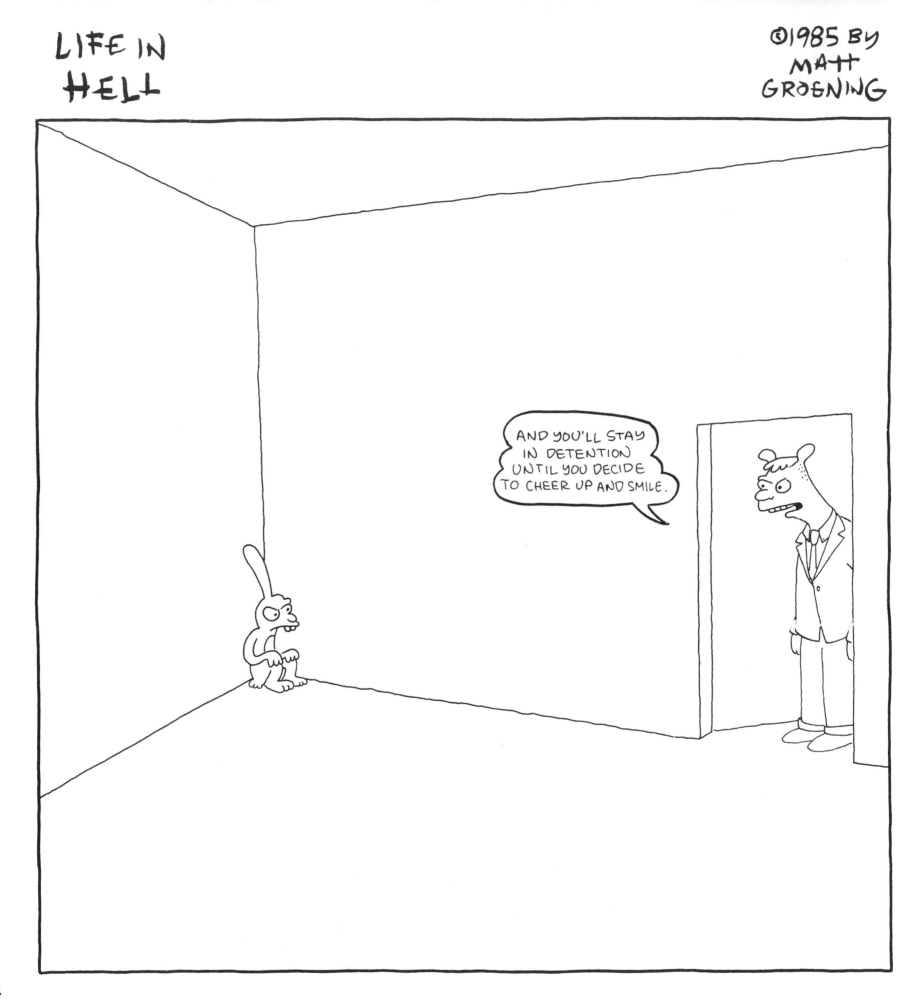

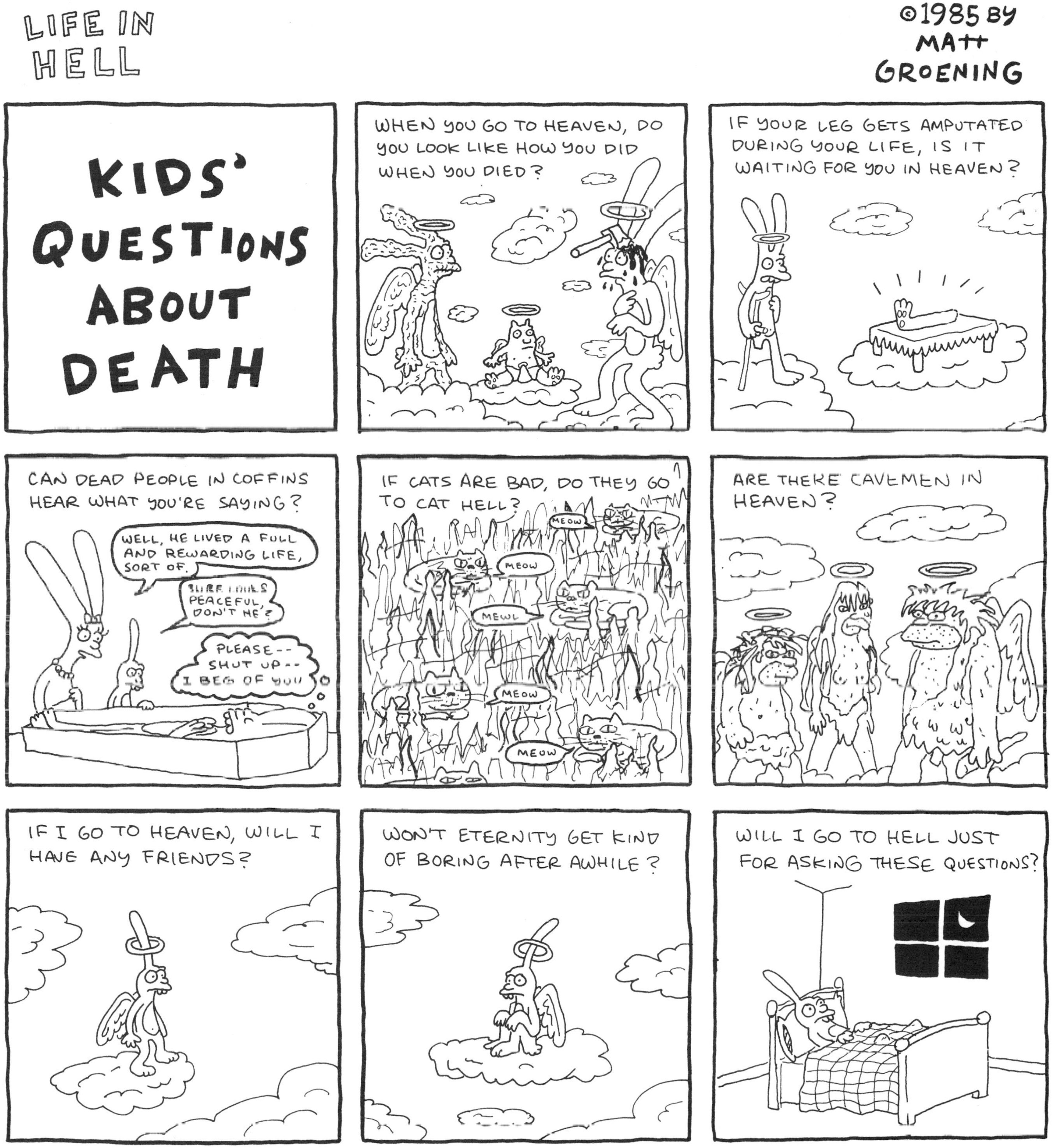
LIFE IN HELL
©1985 BY MATT GROENING
KIDS' QUESTIONS ABOUT DEATH
WHEN YOU GO TO HEAVEN, DO YOU LOOK LIKE HOW YOU DID WHEN YOU DIED?
IF YOUR LEG GETS AMPUTATED DURING YOUR LIFE, IS IT WAITING FOR YOU IN HEAVEN?
CAN DEAD PEOPLE IN COFFINS HEAR WHAT YOU'RE SAYING?
WELL, HE LIVED A FULL AND REWARDING LIFE, SORT OF.
SURE LOOKS PEACEFUL, DON'T HE?
PLEASE-- SHUT UP-- I BEG OF YOU
IF CATS ARE BAD, DO THEY GO TO CAT HELL?
MEOW
MEOW
MEWL
MEOW
MEOW
ARE THERE CAVEMEN IN HEAVEN?
IF I GO TO HEAVEN, WILL I HAVE ANY FRIENDS?
WON'T ETERNITY GET KIND OF BORING AFTER AWHILE?
WILL I GO TO HELL JUST FOR ASKING THESE QUESTIONS?

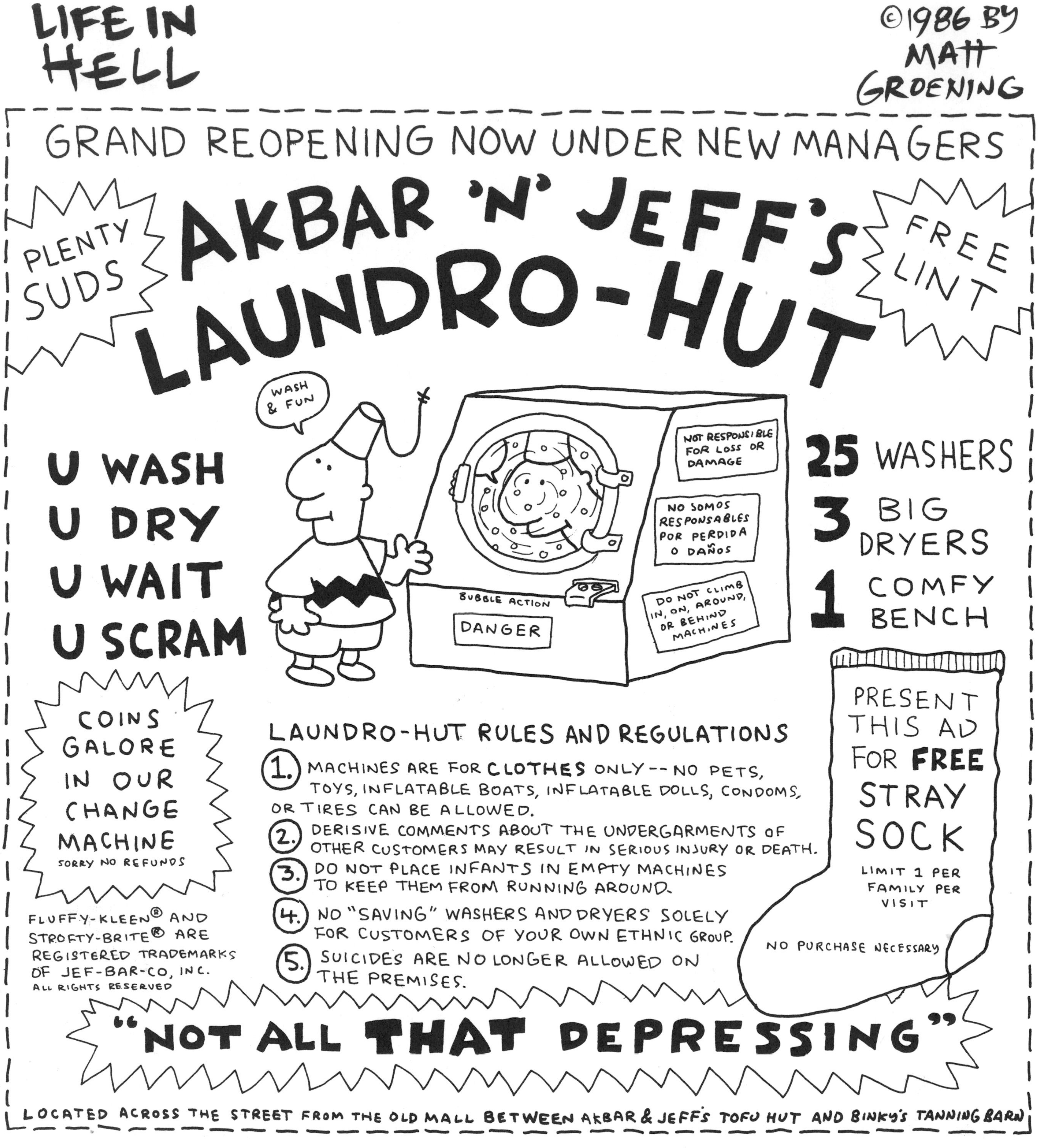
LIFE IN HELL
©1986 BY MATT GROENING
GRAND REOPENING NOW UNDER NEW MANAGERS
PLENTY SUDS
AKBAR 'N' JEFF'S LAUNDRO-HUT
FREE LINT
WASH & FUN
U WASH
U DRY
U WAIT
U SCRAM
NOT RESPONSIBLE FOR LOSS OR DAMAGE
NO SOMOS RESPONSABLES POR PERDIDA O DAÑOS
DO NOT CLIMB IN, ON, AROUND, OR BEHIND MACHINES
BUBBLE ACTION
DANGER
25 WASHERS
3 BIG DRYERS
1 COMFY BENCH
COINS GALORE IN OUR CHANGE MACHINE
SORRY NO REFUNDS
LAUNDRO-HUT RULES AND REGULATIONS
1. MACHINES ARE FOR CLOTHES ONLY -- NO PETS, TOYS, INFLATABLE BOATS, INFLATABLE DOLLS, CONDOMS, OR TIRES CAN BE ALLOWED.
2. DERISIVE COMMENTS ABOUT THE UNDERGARMENTS OF OTHER CUSTOMERS MAY RESULT IN SERIOUS INJURY OR DEATH.
3. DO NOT PLACE INFANTS IN EMPTY MACHINES TO KEEP THEM FROM RUNNING AROUND.
4. NO "SAVING" WASHERS AND DRYERS SOLELY FOR CUSTOMERS OF YOUR OWN ETHNIC GROUP.
5. SUICIDES ARE NO LONGER ALLOWED ON THE PREMISES.
PRESENT THIS AD FOR FREE STRAY SOCK
LIMIT 1 PER FAMILY PER VISIT
NO PURCHASE NECESSARY
FLUFFY-KLEEN® AND STROFTY-BRITE® ARE REGISTERED TRADEMARKS OF JEF-BAR-CO, INC.
ALL RIGHTS RESERVED
"NOT ALL THAT DEPRESSING"
LOCATED ACROSS THE STREET FROM THE OLD MALL BETWEEN AKBAR & JEFF'S TOFU HUT AND BINKY'S TANNING BARN

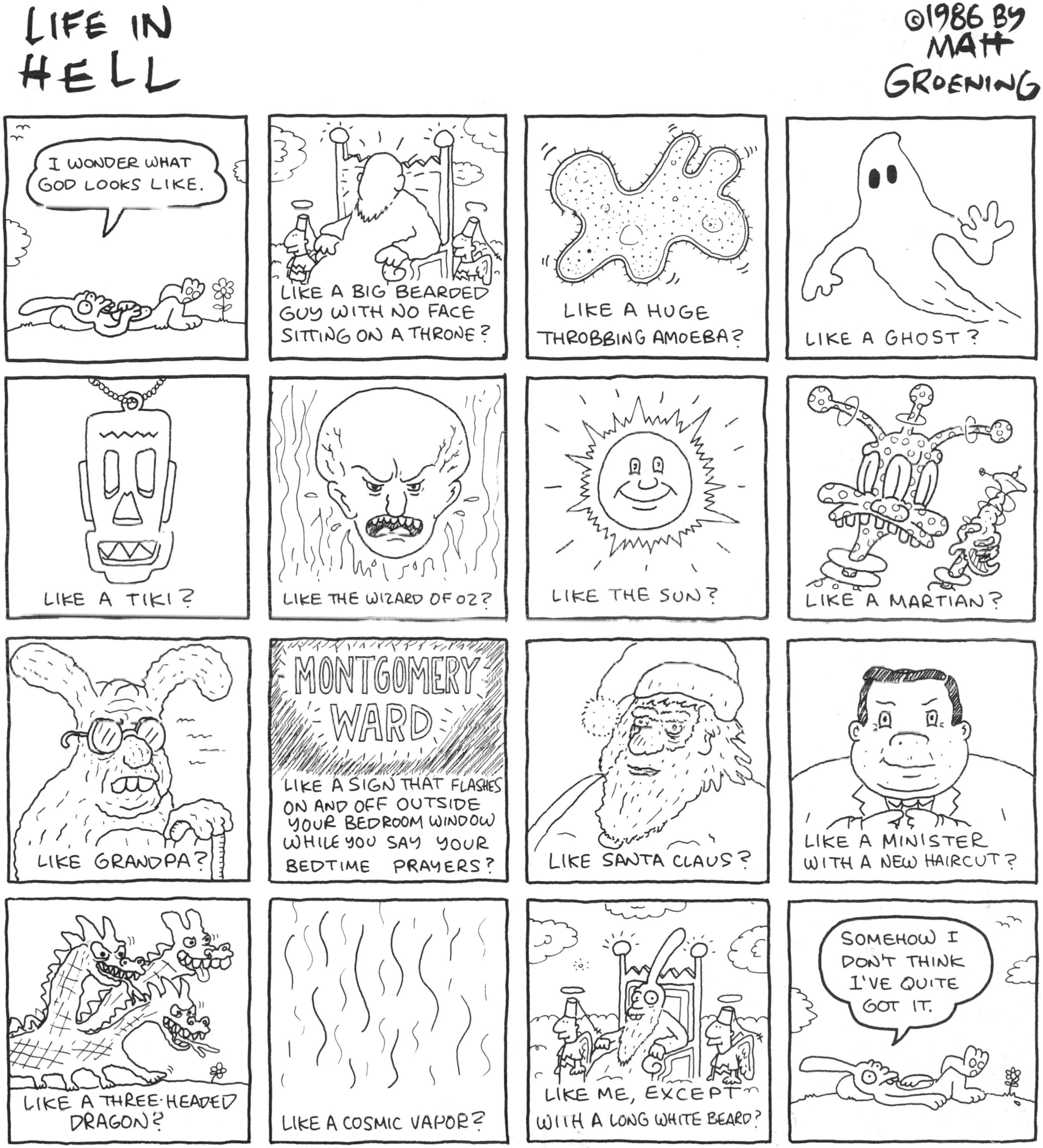
LIFE IN HELL
©1986 BY MATT GROENING
I WONDER WHAT GOD LOOKS LIKE.
LIKE A BIG BEARDED GUY WITH NO FACE SITTING ON A THRONE?
LIKE A HUGE THROBBING AMOEBA?
LIKE A GHOST?
LIKE A TIKI?
LIKE THE WIZARD OF OZ?
LIKE THE SUN?
LIKE A MARTIAN?
LIKE GRANDPA?
MONTGOMERY WARD
LIKE A SIGN THAT FLASHES ON AND OFF OUTSIDE YOUR BEDROOM WINDOW WHILE YOU SAY YOUR BEDTIME PRAYERS?
LIKE SANTA CLAUS?
LIKE A MINISTER WITH A NEW HAIRCUT?
LIKE A THREE-HEADED DRAGON?
LIKE A COSMIC VAPOR?
LIKE ME, EXCEPT WITH A LONG WHITE BEARD?
SOMEHOW I DON'T THINK I'VE QUITE GOT IT.

LIKE HELL I WILL

©1986 BY MATT GROENING

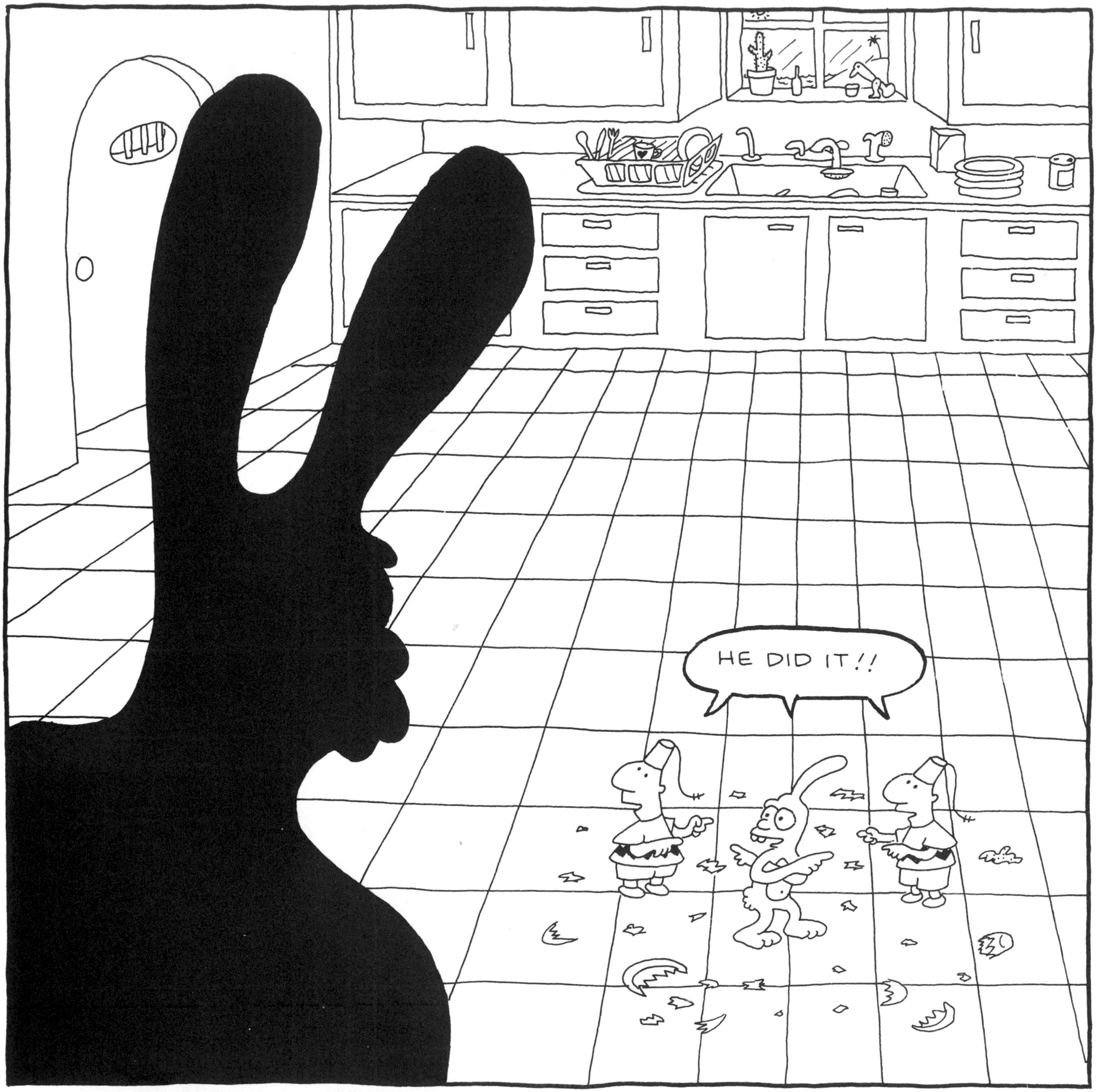

HE DID IT!!

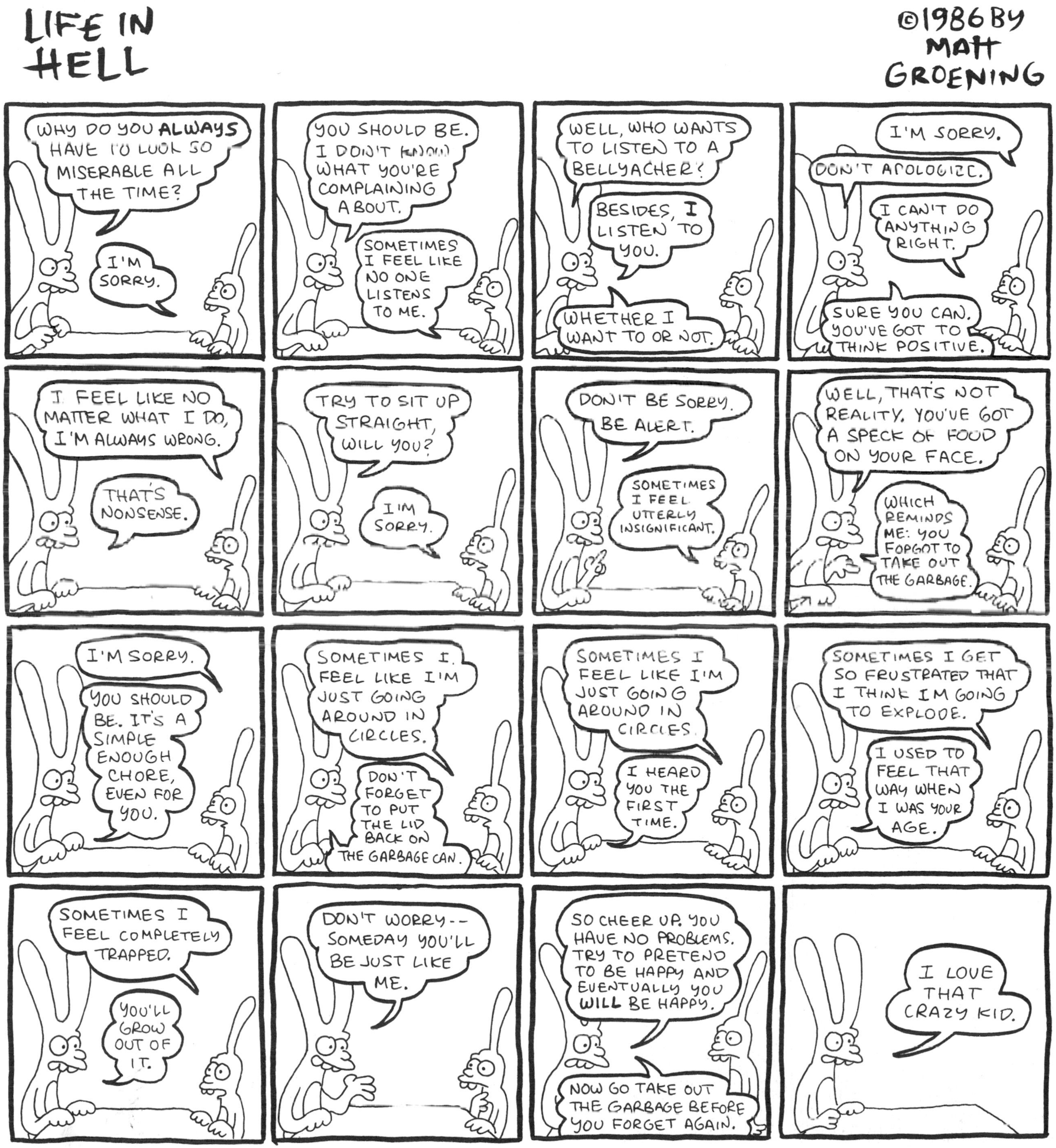
LIFE IN HELL
©1986 BY MATT GROENING
WHY DO YOU ALWAYS HAVE TO LOOK SO MISERABLE ALL THE TIME?
I'M SORRY.
YOU SHOULD BE. I DON'T KNOW WHAT YOU'RE COMPLAINING ABOUT.
SOMETIMES I FEEL LIKE NO ONE LISTENS TO ME.
WELL, WHO WANTS TO LISTEN TO A BELLYACHER?
BESIDES, I LISTEN TO YOU.
WHETHER I WANT TO OR NOT.
I'M SORRY.
DON'T APOLOGIZE.
I CAN'T DO ANYTHING RIGHT.
SURE YOU CAN. YOU'VE GOT TO THINK POSITIVE.
I FEEL LIKE NO MATTER WHAT I DO, I'M ALWAYS WRONG.
THAT'S NONSENSE.
TRY TO SIT UP STRAIGHT, WILL YOU?
I'M SORRY.
DON'T BE SORRY. BE ALERT.
SOMETIMES I FEEL UTTERLY INSIGNIFICANT.
WELL, THAT'S NOT REALITY. YOU'VE GOT A SPECK OF FOOD ON YOUR FACE.
WHICH REMINDS ME: YOU FORGOT TO TAKE OUT THE GARBAGE.
I'M SORRY.
YOU SHOULD BE. IT'S A SIMPLE ENOUGH CHORE, EVEN FOR YOU.
SOMETIMES I FEEL LIKE I'M JUST GOING AROUND IN CIRCLES.
DON'T FORGET TO PUT THE LID BACK ON THE GARBAGE CAN.
SOMETIMES I FEEL LIKE I'M JUST GOING AROUND IN CIRCLES.
I HEARD YOU THE FIRST TIME.
SOMETIMES I GET SO FRUSTRATED THAT I THINK I'M GOING TO EXPLODE.
I USED TO FEEL THAT WAY WHEN I WAS YOUR AGE.
SOMETIMES I FEEL COMPLETELY TRAPPED.
YOU'LL GROW OUT OF IT.
DON'T WORRY-- SOMEDAY YOU'LL BE JUST LIKE ME.
SO CHEER UP. YOU HAVE NO PROBLEMS. TRY TO PRETEND TO BE HAPPY AND EVENTUALLY YOU WILL BE HAPPY.
NOW GO TAKE OUT THE GARBAGE BEFORE YOU FORGET AGAIN.
I LOVE THAT CRAZY KID.

LIFE IN HELL

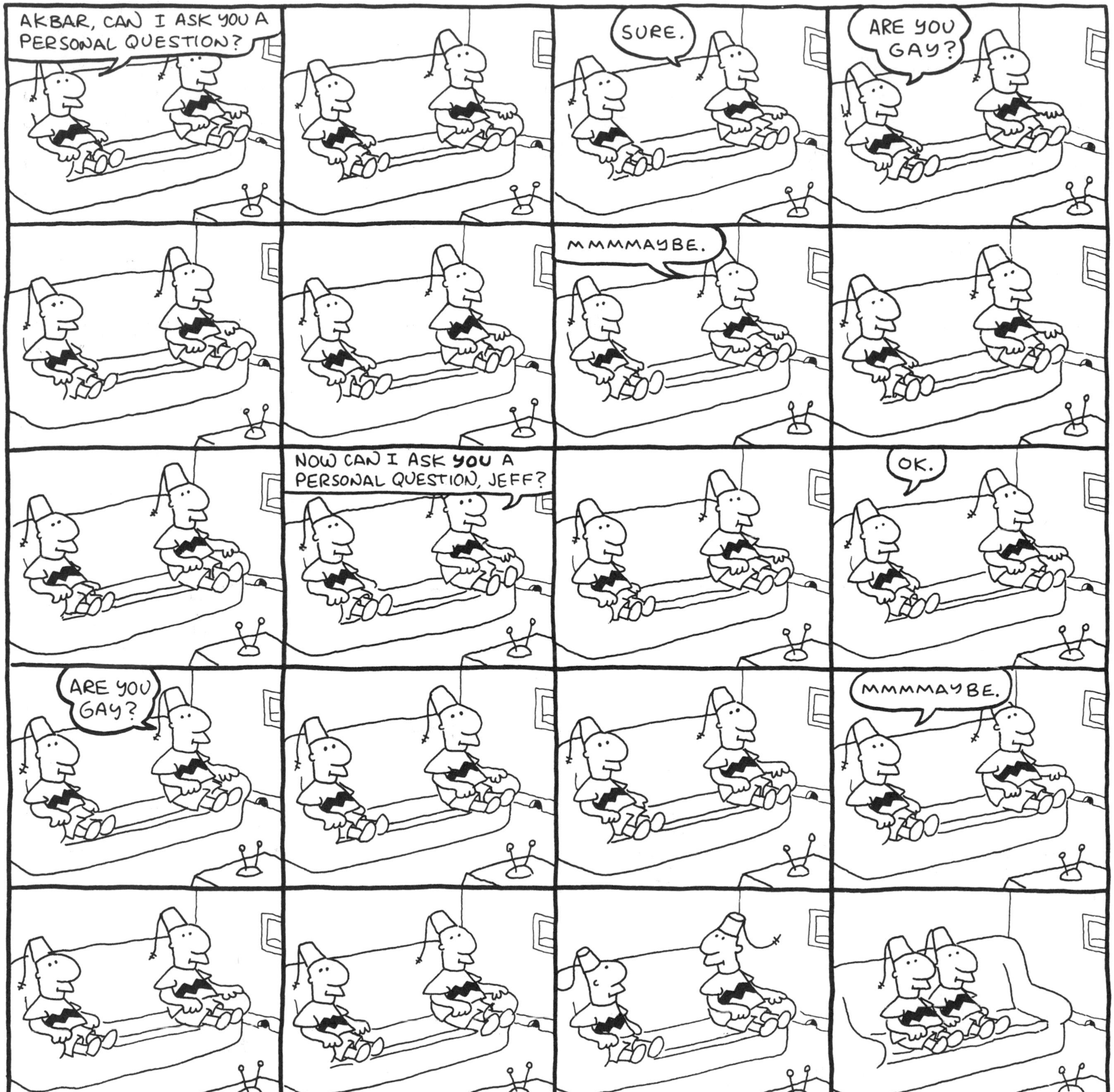
AKBAR, CAN I ASK YOU A PERSONAL QUESTION?
SURE.
ARE YOU GAY?
MMMMAYBE.
NOW CAN I ASK YOU A PERSONAL QUESTION, JEFF?
OK.
ARE YOU GAY?
MMMMAYBE.

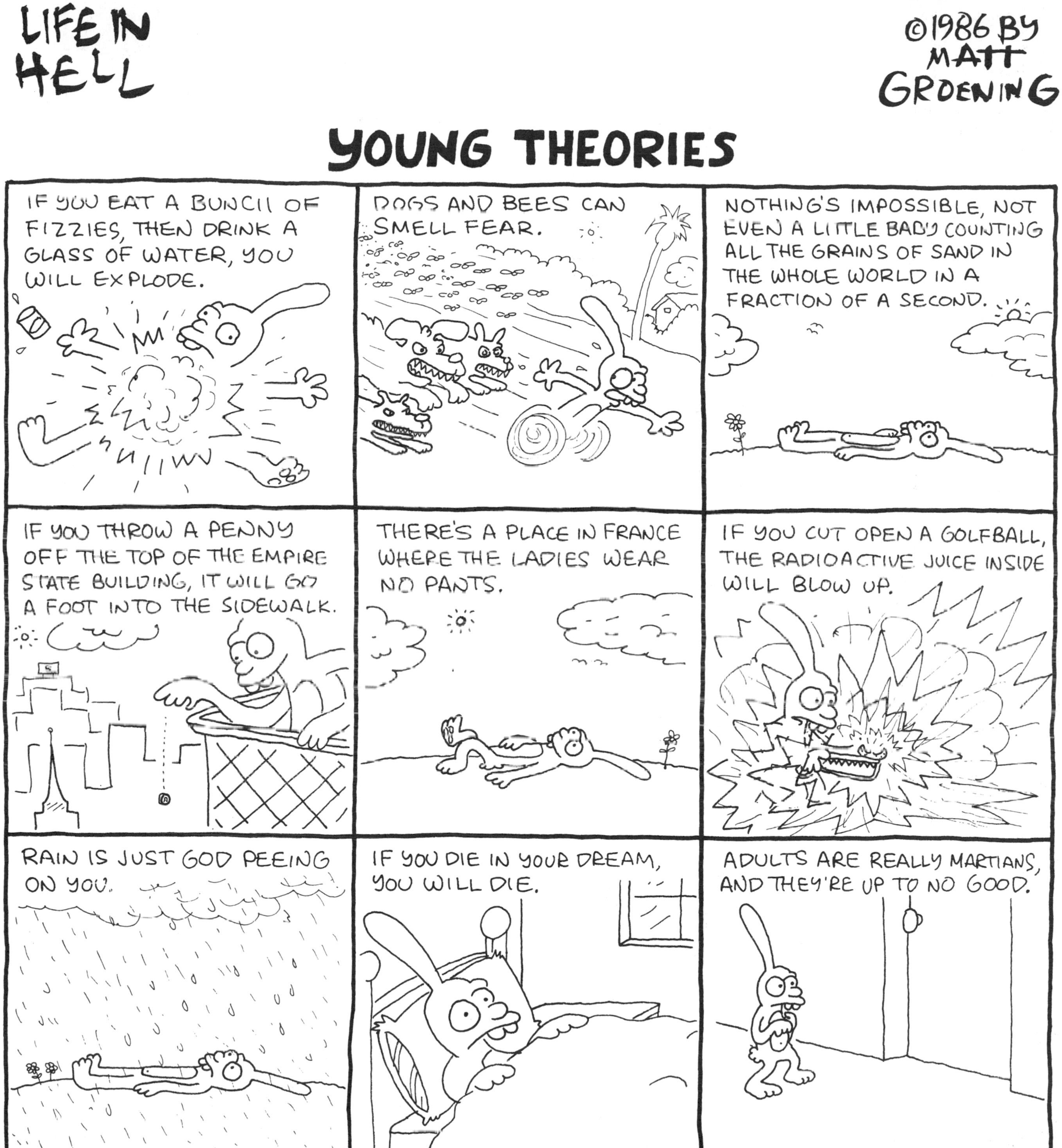
LIFE IN HELL
©1986 BY MATT GROENING
YOUNG THEORIES
IF YOU EAT A BUNCH OF FIZZIES, THEN DRINK A GLASS OF WATER, YOU WILL EXPLODE.
DOGS AND BEES CAN SMELL FEAR.
NOTHING'S IMPOSSIBLE, NOT EVEN A LITTLE BABY COUNTING ALL THE GRAINS OF SAND IN THE WHOLE WORLD IN A FRACTION OF A SECOND.
IF YOU THROW A PENNY OFF THE TOP OF THE EMPIRE STATE BUILDING, IT WILL GO A FOOT INTO THE SIDEWALK.
THERE'S A PLACE IN FRANCE WHERE THE LADIES WEAR NO PANTS.
IF YOU CUT OPEN A GOLFBALL, THE RADIOACTIVE JUICE INSIDE WILL BLOW UP.
RAIN IS JUST GOD PEEING ON YOU.
IF YOU DIE IN YOUR DREAM, YOU WILL DIE.
ADULTS ARE REALLY MARTIANS, AND THEY'RE UP TO NO GOOD.

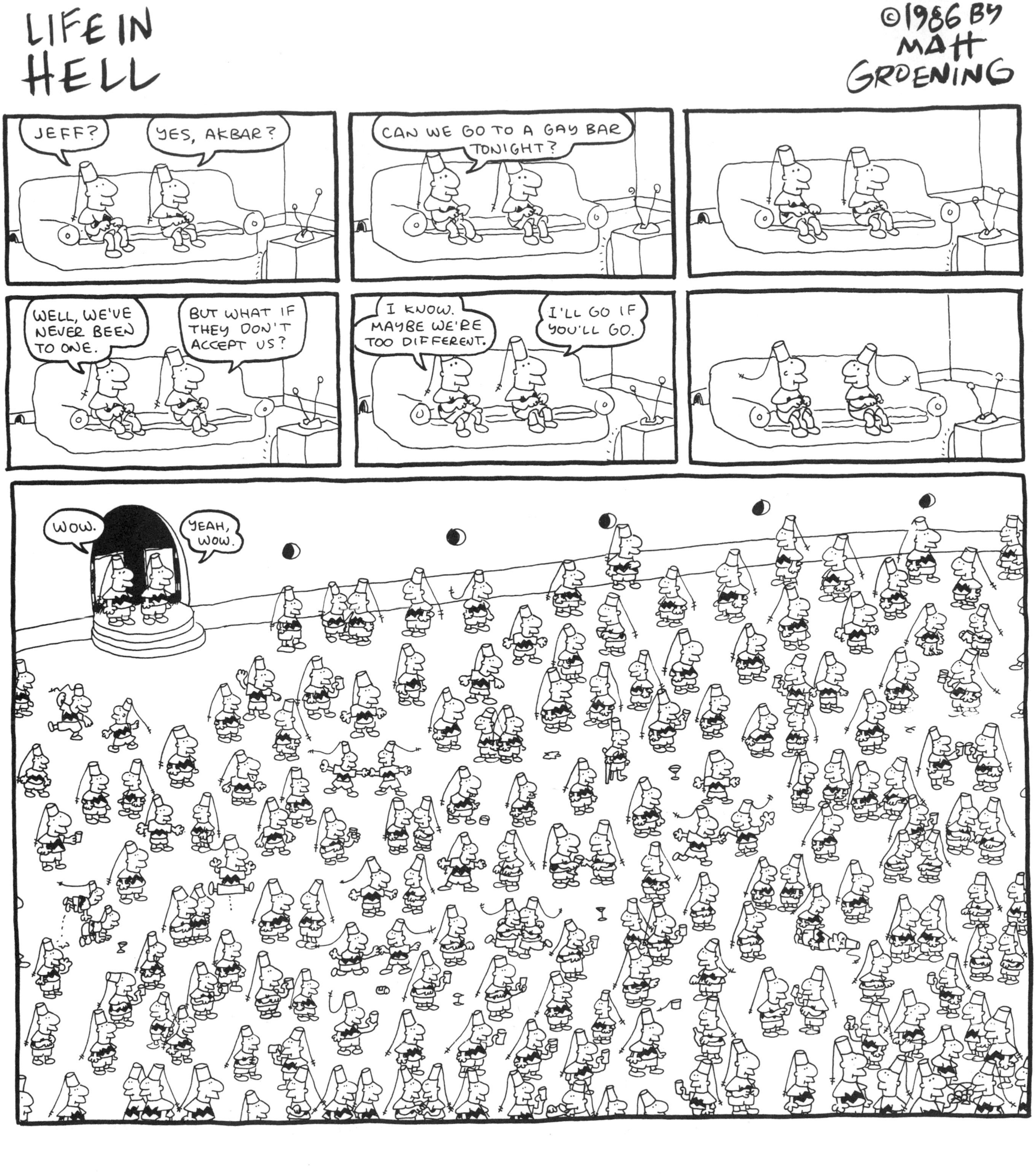
LIFE IN HELL
©1986 BY MATT GROENING
JEFF?
YES, AKBAR?
CAN WE GO TO A GAY BAR TONIGHT?
WELL, WE'VE NEVER BEEN TO ONE.
BUT WHAT IF THEY DON'T ACCEPT US?
I KNOW. MAYBE WE'RE TOO DIFFERENT.
I'LL GO IF YOU'LL GO.
WOW.
YEAH, WOW.

LIFE IN HELL

©1986 BY MATT GROENING

HOW TO BE A FEISTY ROCK CRITIC

HOW TO TELL IF YOU HAVE WHAT IT TAKES

☐ DID YOU PLAY "AIR GUITAR" AS A CHILD?

☐ DID YOU PLAY "AIR GUITAR" AS A TEEN?

☐ DO YOU DENY YOU PLAY "AIR GUITAR" AS AN ADULT?

WHEN YOU HEAR SOME ROCK 'N' ROLL, DO YOU FEEL THE URGE TO:

☐ TAP YOUR FOOT?

☐ SHUT YOUR EYES TIGHTLY, BITE YOUR LOWER LIP, AND NOD YOUR HEAD RHYTHMICALLY?

☐ STAND THERE WITH YOUR ARMS FOLDED, THEN GO HOME AND WRITE AN IN-DEPTH ANALYSIS OF THE EXPERIENCE?

WOULD YOU CHARACTERIZE YOUR EMOTIONAL STATE AS:

☐ PRE-ADOLESCENT?

☐ ADOLESCENT?

☐ SEMI-POST-ADOLESCENT?

CONGRATULATIONS! IF YOU CHECKED ANY BOX ABOVE, YOU ARE QUALIFIED TO BE A FEISTY ROCK CRITIC. AND IF YOU CHECKED NO BOXES, DON'T FEEL BAD. YOU ARE QUALIFIED TO BE A VERY FEISTY ROCK CRITIC.

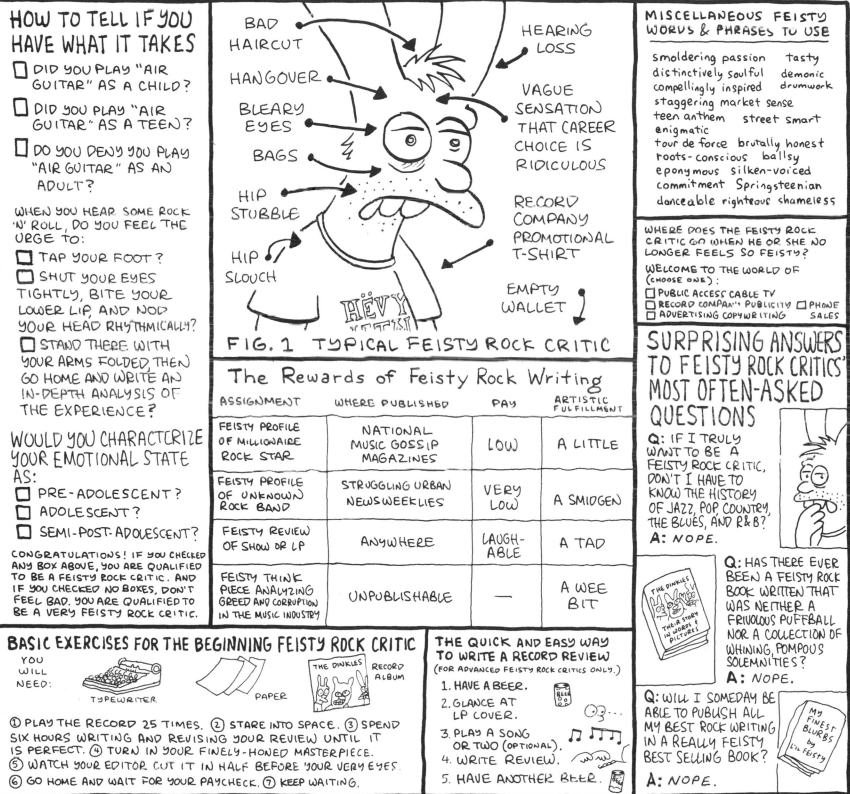

FIG. 1 TYPICAL FEISTY ROCK CRITIC

(labels: BAD HAIRCUT · HANGOVER · BLEARY EYES · BAGS · HIP STUBBLE · HIP SLOUCH · HEARING LOSS · VAGUE SENSATION THAT CAREER CHOICE IS RIDICULOUS · RECORD COMPANY PROMOTIONAL T-SHIRT · EMPTY WALLET · HËVY)

The Rewards of Feisty Rock Writing

ASSIGNMENT	WHERE PUBLISHED	PAY	ARTISTIC FULFILLMENT
FEISTY PROFILE OF MILLIONAIRE ROCK STAR	NATIONAL MUSIC GOSSIP MAGAZINES	LOW	A LITTLE
FEISTY PROFILE OF UNKNOWN ROCK BAND	STRUGGLING URBAN NEWSWEEKLIES	VERY LOW	A SMIDGEN
FEISTY REVIEW OF SHOW OR LP	ANYWHERE	LAUGH-ABLE	A TAD
FEISTY THINK PIECE ANALYZING GREED AND CORRUPTION IN THE MUSIC INDUSTRY	UNPUBLISHABLE	—	A WEE BIT

MISCELLANEOUS FEISTY WORDS & PHRASES TO USE

smoldering passion · tasty · distinctively soulful · demonic · compellingly inspired · drumwork · staggering market sense · teen anthem · street smart · enigmatic · tour de force · brutally honest · roots-conscious · ballsy · eponymous · silken-voiced · commitment · Springsteenian · danceable · righteous · shameless

WHERE DOES THE FEISTY ROCK CRITIC GO WHEN HE OR SHE NO LONGER FEELS SO FEISTY?

WELCOME TO THE WORLD OF (CHOOSE ONE):

☐ PUBLIC ACCESS CABLE TV

☐ RECORD COMPANY PUBLICITY ☐ PHONE SALES

☐ ADVERTISING COPYWRITING

SURPRISING ANSWERS TO FEISTY ROCK CRITICS' MOST OFTEN-ASKED QUESTIONS

Q: IF I TRULY WANT TO BE A FEISTY ROCK CRITIC, DON'T I HAVE TO KNOW THE HISTORY OF JAZZ, POP, COUNTRY, THE BLUES, AND R&B?

A: NOPE.

Q: HAS THERE EVER BEEN A FEISTY ROCK BOOK WRITTEN THAT WAS NEITHER A FRIVOLOUS PUFFBALL NOR A COLLECTION OF WHINING, POMPOUS SOLEMNITIES? (THE DINKLES: THEIR STORY IN WORDS & PICTURES)

A: NOPE.

Q: WILL I SOMEDAY BE ABLE TO PUBLISH ALL MY BEST ROCK WRITING IN A REALLY FEISTY BEST SELLING BOOK? (MY FINEST BLURBS by L'IL FEISTY)

A: NOPE.

BASIC EXERCISES FOR THE BEGINNING FEISTY ROCK CRITIC

YOU WILL NEED: (TYPEWRITER · PAPER · THE DINKLES RECORD ALBUM)

① PLAY THE RECORD 25 TIMES. ② STARE INTO SPACE. ③ SPEND SIX HOURS WRITING AND REVISING YOUR REVIEW UNTIL IT IS PERFECT. ④ TURN IN YOUR FINELY-HONED MASTERPIECE. ⑤ WATCH YOUR EDITOR CUT IT IN HALF BEFORE YOUR VERY EYES. ⑥ GO HOME AND WAIT FOR YOUR PAYCHECK. ⑦ KEEP WAITING.

THE QUICK AND EASY WAY TO WRITE A RECORD REVIEW
(FOR ADVANCED FEISTY ROCK CRITICS ONLY.)

1. HAVE A BEER.
2. GLANCE AT LP COVER.
3. PLAY A SONG OR TWO (OPTIONAL).
4. WRITE REVIEW.
5. HAVE ANOTHER BEER.

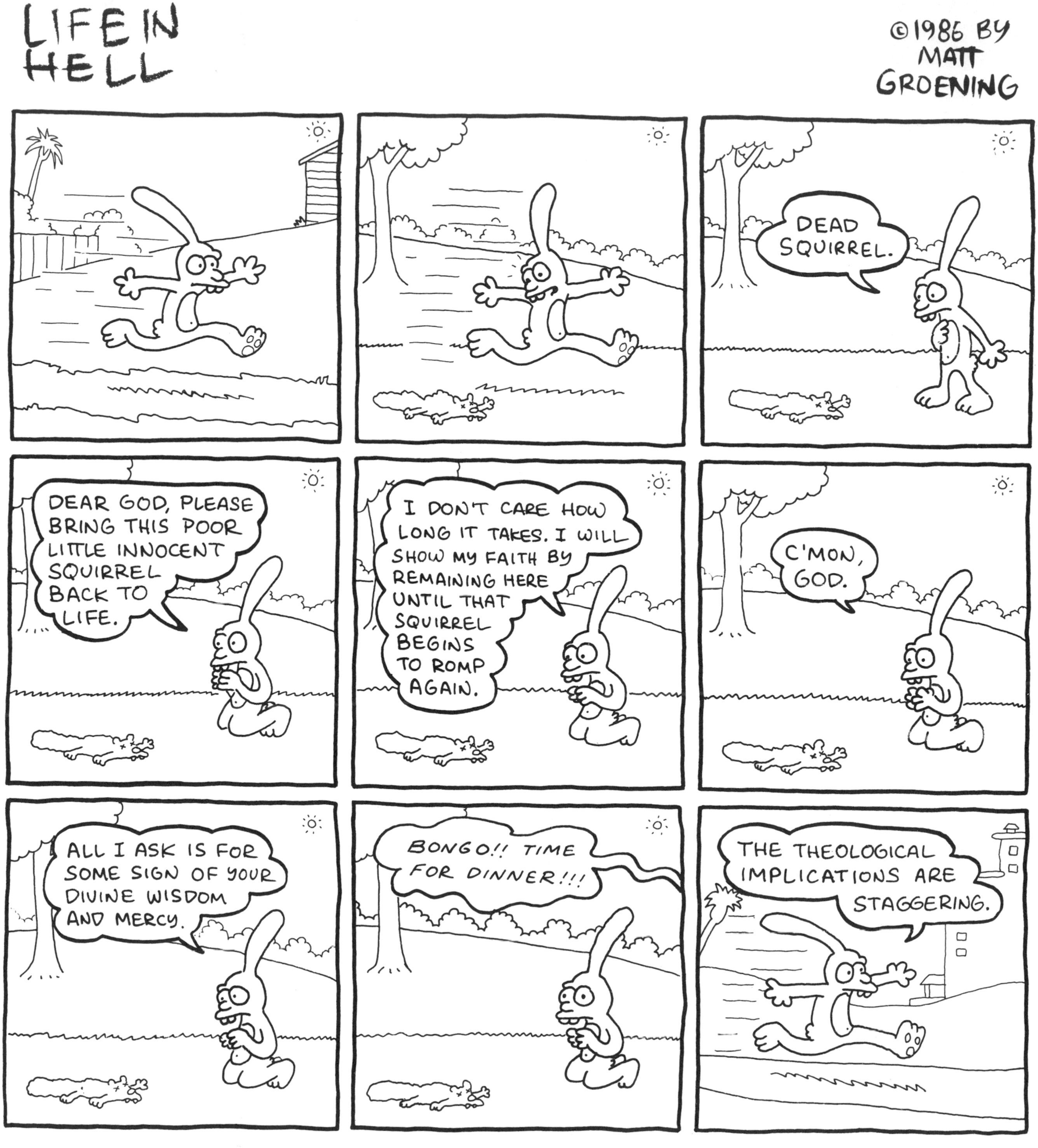
LIFE IN HELL
©1986 BY MATT GROENING
DEAD SQUIRREL.
DEAR GOD, PLEASE BRING THIS POOR LITTLE INNOCENT SQUIRREL BACK TO LIFE.
I DON'T CARE HOW LONG IT TAKES. I WILL SHOW MY FAITH BY REMAINING HERE UNTIL THAT SQUIRREL BEGINS TO ROMP AGAIN.
C'MON, GOD.
ALL I ASK IS FOR SOME SIGN OF YOUR DIVINE WISDOM AND MERCY.
BONGO!! TIME FOR DINNER!!!
THE THEOLOGICAL IMPLICATIONS ARE STAGGERING.

LIFE IN HELL

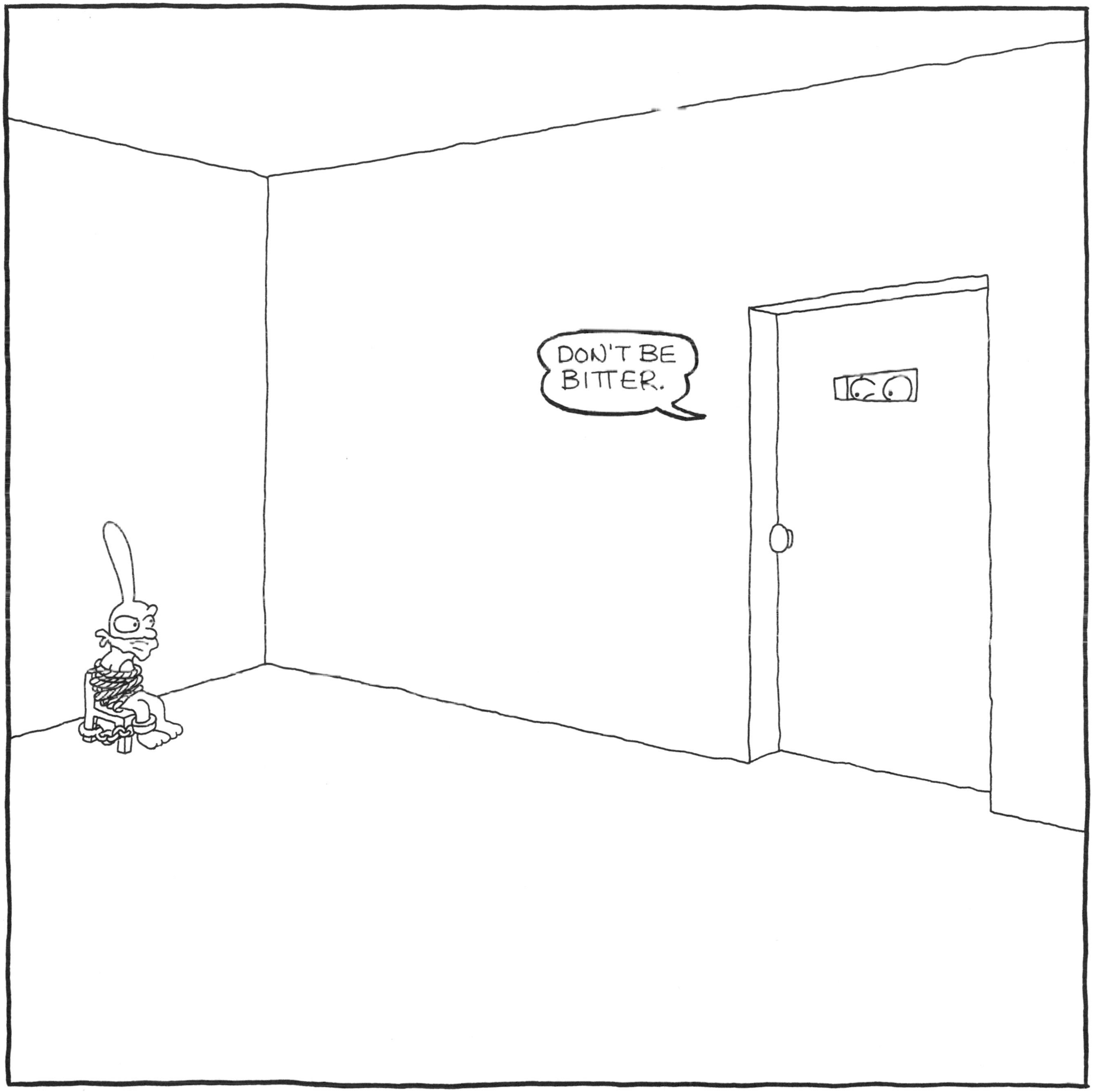
DON'T BE BITTER.

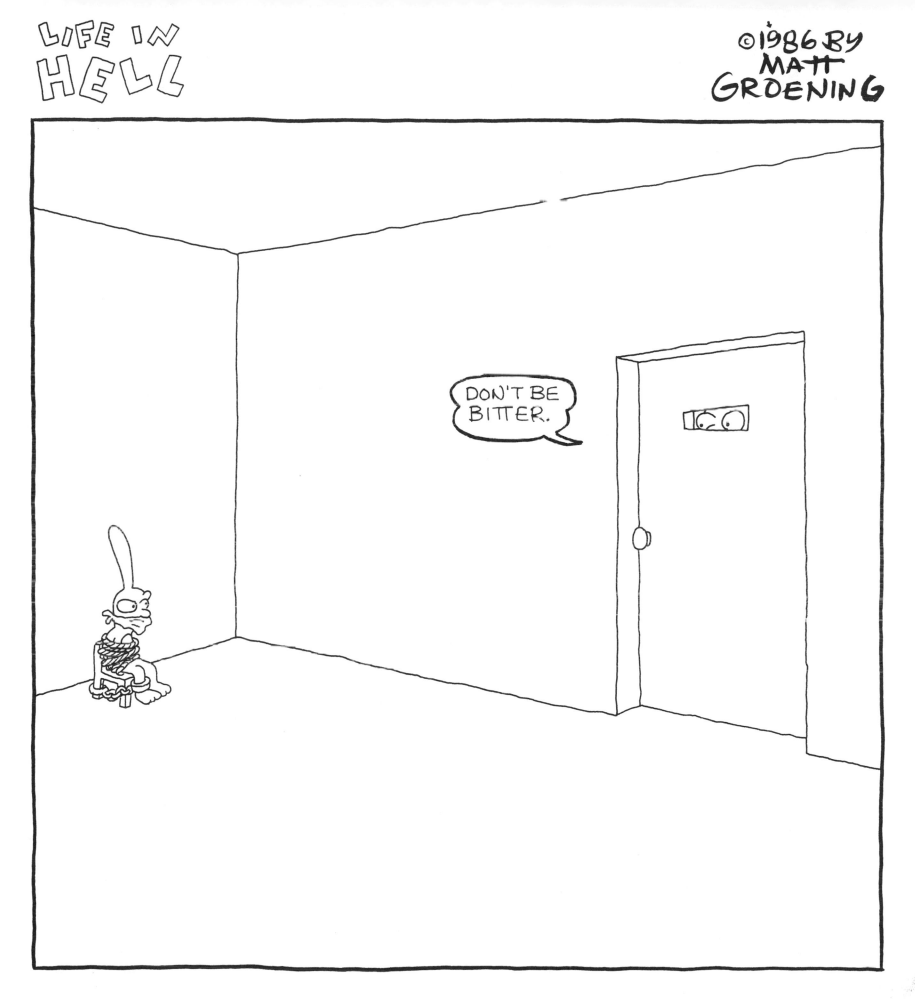

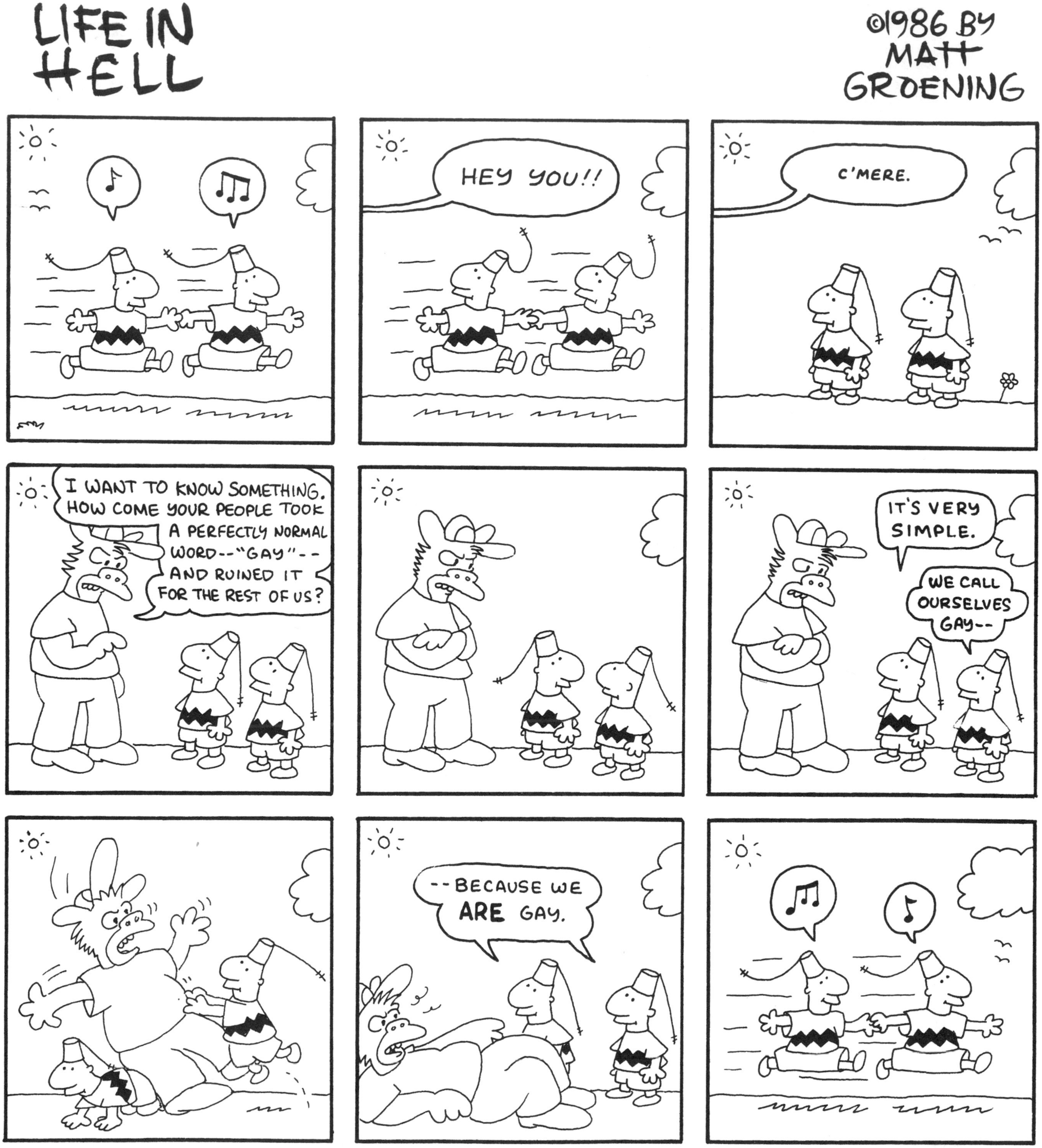
LIFE IN HELL
©1986 BY MATT GROENING
HEY YOU!!
C'MERE.
I WANT TO KNOW SOMETHING. HOW COME YOUR PEOPLE TOOK A PERFECTLY NORMAL WORD--"GAY"--AND RUINED IT FOR THE REST OF US?
IT'S VERY SIMPLE.
WE CALL OURSELVES GAY--
--BECAUSE WE ARE GAY.

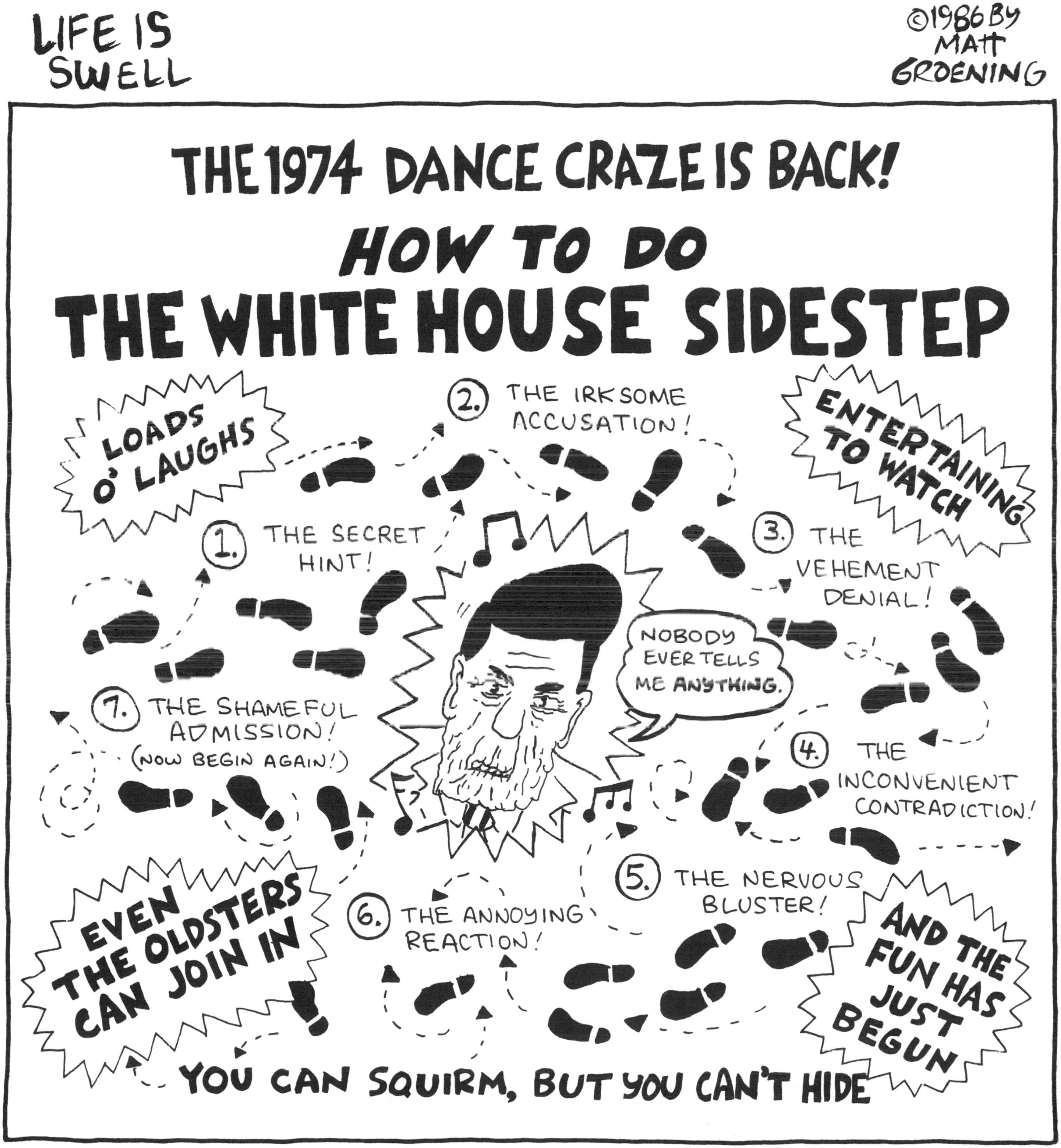
LIFE IS SWELL
©1986 BY MATT GROENING
THE 1974 DANCE CRAZE IS BACK!
HOW TO DO
THE WHITE HOUSE SIDESTEP
LOADS O' LAUGHS
ENTERTAINING TO WATCH
1. THE SECRET HINT!
2. THE IRKSOME ACCUSATION!
3. THE VEHEMENT DENIAL!
NOBODY EVER TELLS ME ANYTHING.
4. THE INCONVENIENT CONTRADICTION!
5. THE NERVOUS BLUSTER!
6. THE ANNOYING REACTION!
7. THE SHAMEFUL ADMISSION! (NOW BEGIN AGAIN!)
EVEN THE OLDSTERS CAN JOIN IN
AND THE FUN HAS JUST BEGUN
YOU CAN SQUIRM, BUT YOU CAN'T HIDE

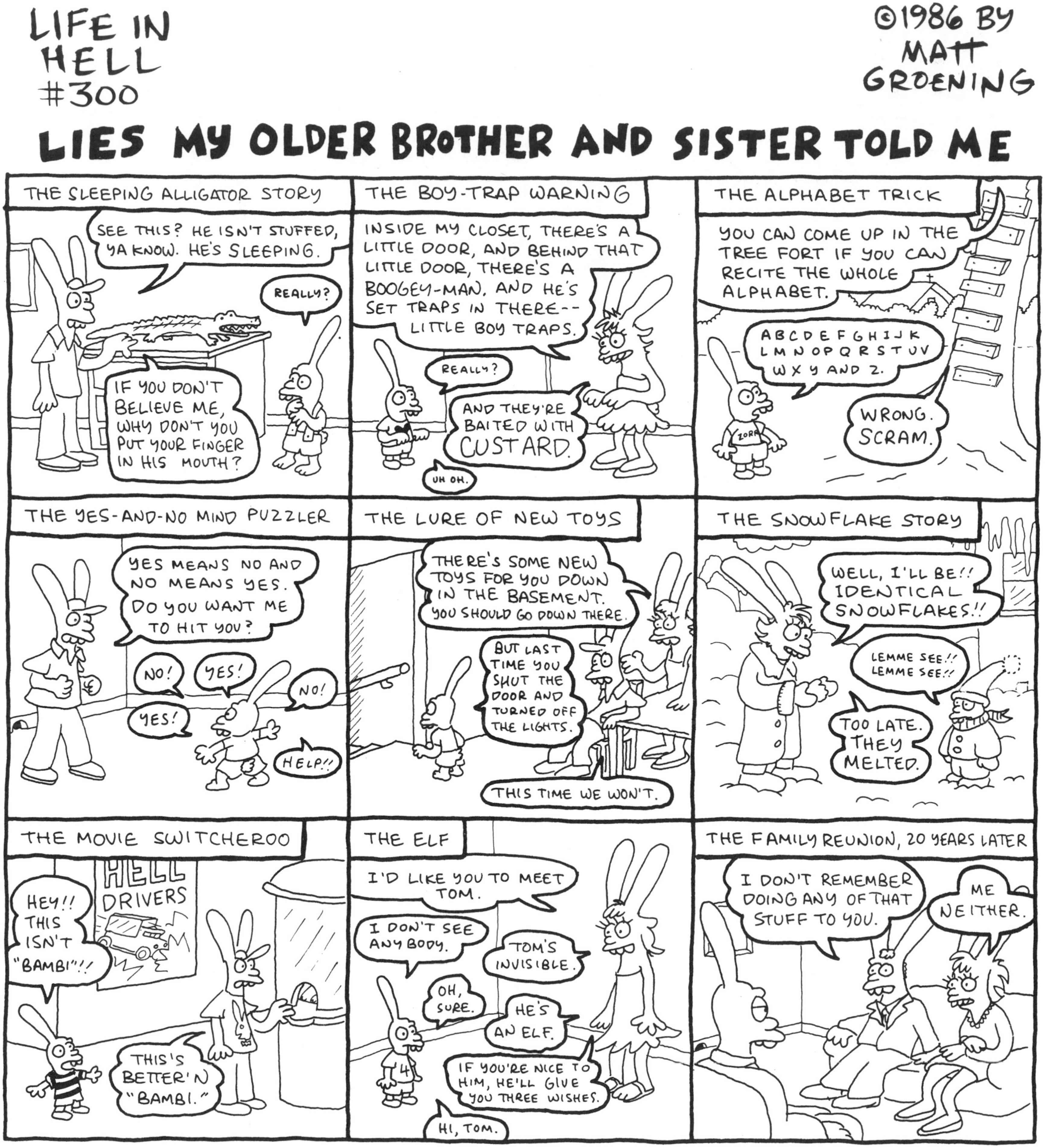
LIFE IN HELL #300
©1986 BY MATT GROENING
LIES MY OLDER BROTHER AND SISTER TOLD ME
THE SLEEPING ALLIGATOR STORY
SEE THIS? HE ISN'T STUFFED, YA KNOW. HE'S SLEEPING.
REALLY?
IF YOU DON'T BELIEVE ME, WHY DON'T YOU PUT YOUR FINGER IN HIS MOUTH?
THE BOY-TRAP WARNING
INSIDE MY CLOSET, THERE'S A LITTLE DOOR, AND BEHIND THAT LITTLE DOOR, THERE'S A BOOGEY-MAN, AND HE'S SET TRAPS IN THERE-- LITTLE BOY TRAPS.
REALLY?
AND THEY'RE BAITED WITH CUSTARD.
UH OH.
THE ALPHABET TRICK
YOU CAN COME UP IN THE TREE FORT IF YOU CAN RECITE THE WHOLE ALPHABET.
A B C D E F G H I J K L M N O P Q R S T U V W X Y AND Z.
WRONG. SCRAM.
ZORRO
THE YES-AND-NO MIND PUZZLER
YES MEANS NO AND NO MEANS YES. DO YOU WANT ME TO HIT YOU?
NO!
YES!
NO!
YES!
HELP!!
THE LURE OF NEW TOYS
THERE'S SOME NEW TOYS FOR YOU DOWN IN THE BASEMENT. YOU SHOULD GO DOWN THERE.
BUT LAST TIME YOU SHUT THE DOOR AND TURNED OFF THE LIGHTS.
THIS TIME WE WON'T.
THE SNOWFLAKE STORY
WELL, I'LL BE!! IDENTICAL SNOWFLAKES!!
LEMME SEE!! LEMME SEE!!
TOO LATE. THEY MELTED.
THE MOVIE SWITCHEROO
HELL DRIVERS
HEY!! THIS ISN'T "BAMBI"!!
THIS'S BETTER'N "BAMBI."
THE ELF
I'D LIKE YOU TO MEET TOM.
I DON'T SEE ANYBODY.
TOM'S INVISIBLE.
OH, SURE.
HE'S AN ELF.
IF YOU'RE NICE TO HIM, HE'LL GIVE YOU THREE WISHES.
HI, TOM.
THE FAMILY REUNION, 20 YEARS LATER
I DON'T REMEMBER DOING ANY OF THAT STUFF TO YOU.
ME NEITHER.

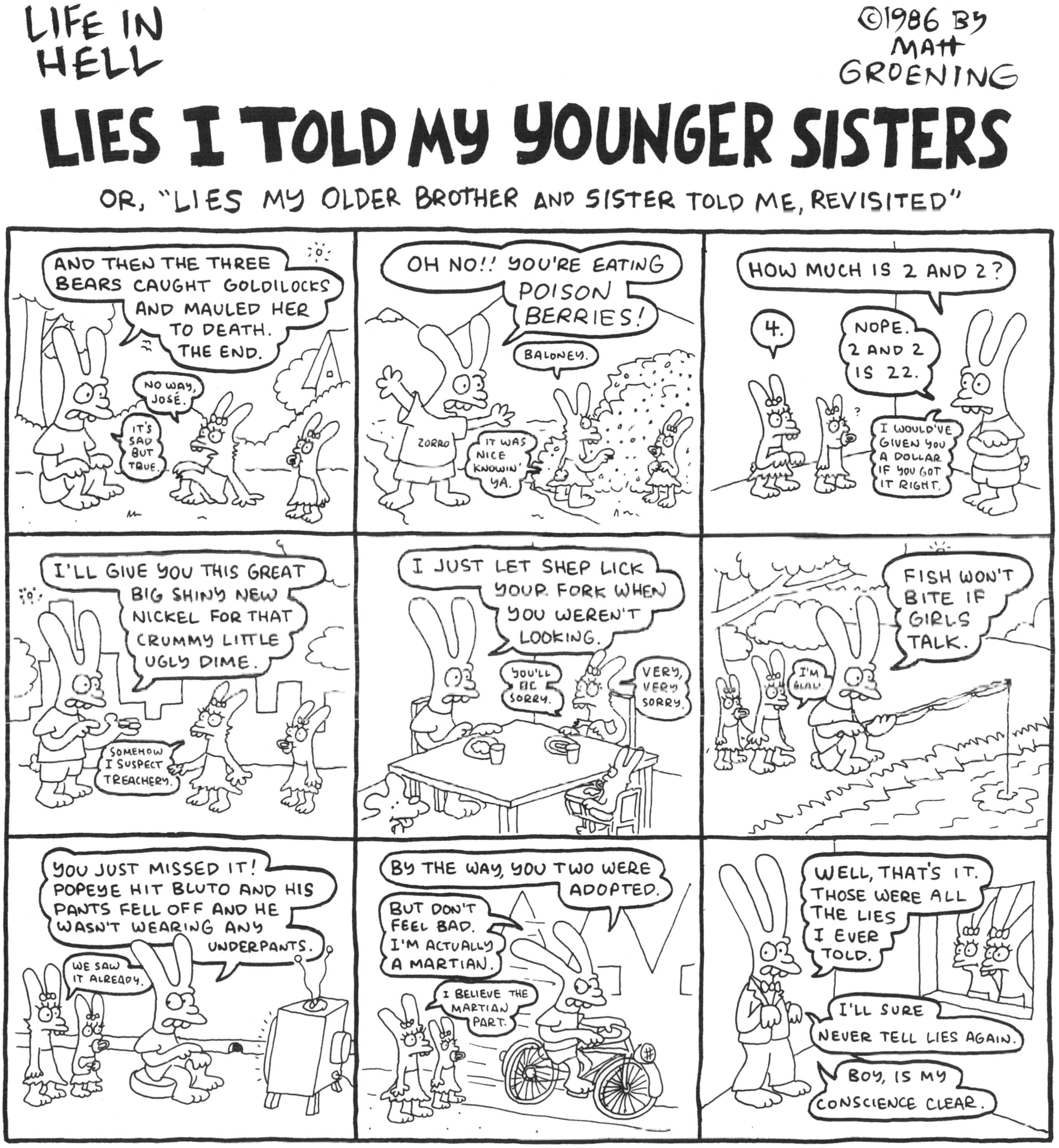
LIFE IN HELL
©1986 BY MATT GROENING
LIES I TOLD MY YOUNGER SISTERS
OR, "LIES MY OLDER BROTHER AND SISTER TOLD ME, REVISITED"
AND THEN THE THREE BEARS CAUGHT GOLDILOCKS AND MAULED HER TO DEATH. THE END.
NO WAY, JOSÉ.
IT'S SAD BUT TRUE.
OH NO!! YOU'RE EATING POISON BERRIES!
BALONEY.
ZORRO
IT WAS NICE KNOWIN' YA.
HOW MUCH IS 2 AND 2?
4.
NOPE. 2 AND 2 IS 22.
I WOULD'VE GIVEN YOU A DOLLAR IF YOU GOT IT RIGHT.
I'LL GIVE YOU THIS GREAT BIG SHINY NEW NICKEL FOR THAT CRUMMY LITTLE UGLY DIME.
SOMEHOW I SUSPECT TREACHERY.
I JUST LET SHEP LICK YOUR FORK WHEN YOU WEREN'T LOOKING.
YOU'LL BE SORRY.
VERY, VERY SORRY.
FISH WON'T BITE IF GIRLS TALK.
I'M
YOU JUST MISSED IT! POPEYE HIT BLUTO AND HIS PANTS FELL OFF AND HE WASN'T WEARING ANY UNDERPANTS.
WE SAW IT ALREADY.
BY THE WAY, YOU TWO WERE ADOPTED.
BUT DON'T FEEL BAD. I'M ACTUALLY A MARTIAN.
I BELIEVE THE MARTIAN PART.
WELL, THAT'S IT. THOSE WERE ALL THE LIES I EVER TOLD.
I'LL SURE NEVER TELL LIES AGAIN.
BOY, IS MY CONSCIENCE CLEAR.

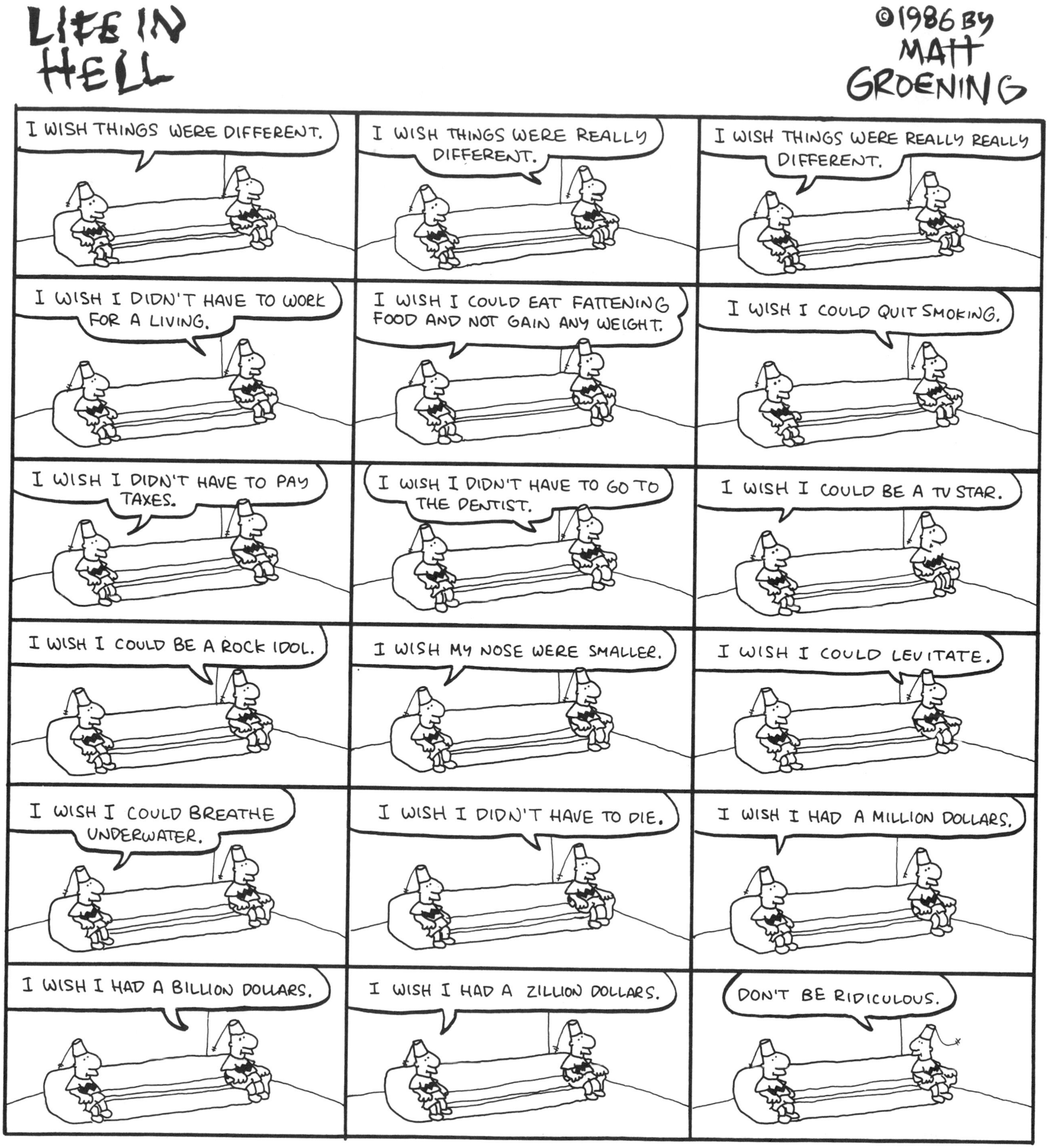
LIFE IN HELL
©1986 BY MATT GROENING
I WISH THINGS WERE DIFFERENT.
I WISH THINGS WERE REALLY DIFFERENT.
I WISH THINGS WERE REALLY REALLY DIFFERENT.
I WISH I DIDN'T HAVE TO WORK FOR A LIVING.
I WISH I COULD EAT FATTENING FOOD AND NOT GAIN ANY WEIGHT.
I WISH I COULD QUIT SMOKING.
I WISH I DIDN'T HAVE TO PAY TAXES.
I WISH I DIDN'T HAVE TO GO TO THE DENTIST.
I WISH I COULD BE A TV STAR.
I WISH I COULD BE A ROCK IDOL.
I WISH MY NOSE WERE SMALLER.
I WISH I COULD LEVITATE.
I WISH I COULD BREATHE UNDERWATER.
I WISH I DIDN'T HAVE TO DIE.
I WISH I HAD A MILLION DOLLARS.
I WISH I HAD A BILLION DOLLARS.
I WISH I HAD A ZILLION DOLLARS.
DON'T BE RIDICULOUS.

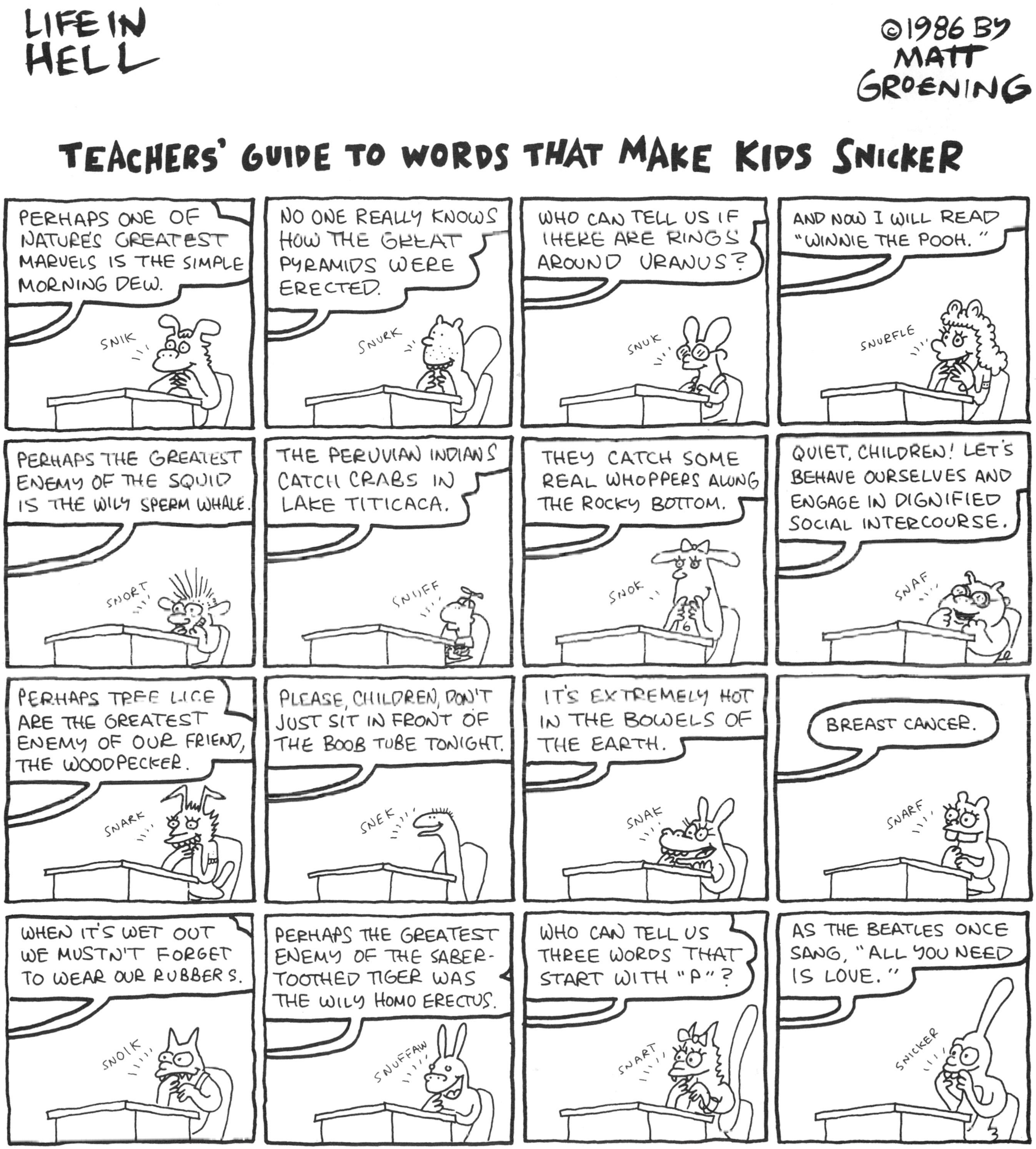
LIFE IN HELL
©1986 BY MATT GROENING
TEACHERS' GUIDE TO WORDS THAT MAKE KIDS SNICKER
PERHAPS ONE OF NATURE'S GREATEST MARVELS IS THE SIMPLE MORNING DEW.
SNIK
NO ONE REALLY KNOWS HOW THE GREAT PYRAMIDS WERE ERECTED.
SNURK
WHO CAN TELL US IF THERE ARE RINGS AROUND URANUS?
SNUK
AND NOW I WILL READ "WINNIE THE POOH."
SNURFLE
PERHAPS THE GREATEST ENEMY OF THE SQUID IS THE WILY SPERM WHALE.
SNORT
THE PERUVIAN INDIANS CATCH CRABS IN LAKE TITICACA.
SNUFF
THEY CATCH SOME REAL WHOPPERS ALONG THE ROCKY BOTTOM.
SNOK
QUIET, CHILDREN! LET'S BEHAVE OURSELVES AND ENGAGE IN DIGNIFIED SOCIAL INTERCOURSE.
SNAF
PERHAPS TREE LICE ARE THE GREATEST ENEMY OF OUR FRIEND, THE WOODPECKER.
SNARK
PLEASE, CHILDREN, DON'T JUST SIT IN FRONT OF THE BOOB TUBE TONIGHT.
SNEK
IT'S EXTREMELY HOT IN THE BOWELS OF THE EARTH.
SNAK
BREAST CANCER.
SNARF
WHEN IT'S WET OUT WE MUSTN'T FORGET TO WEAR OUR RUBBERS.
SNOIK
PERHAPS THE GREATEST ENEMY OF THE SABER-TOOTHED TIGER WAS THE WILY HOMO ERECTUS.
SNUFFAW
WHO CAN TELL US THREE WORDS THAT START WITH "P"?
SNART
AS THE BEATLES ONCE SANG, "ALL YOU NEED IS LOVE."
SNICKER

LIFE IN HELL

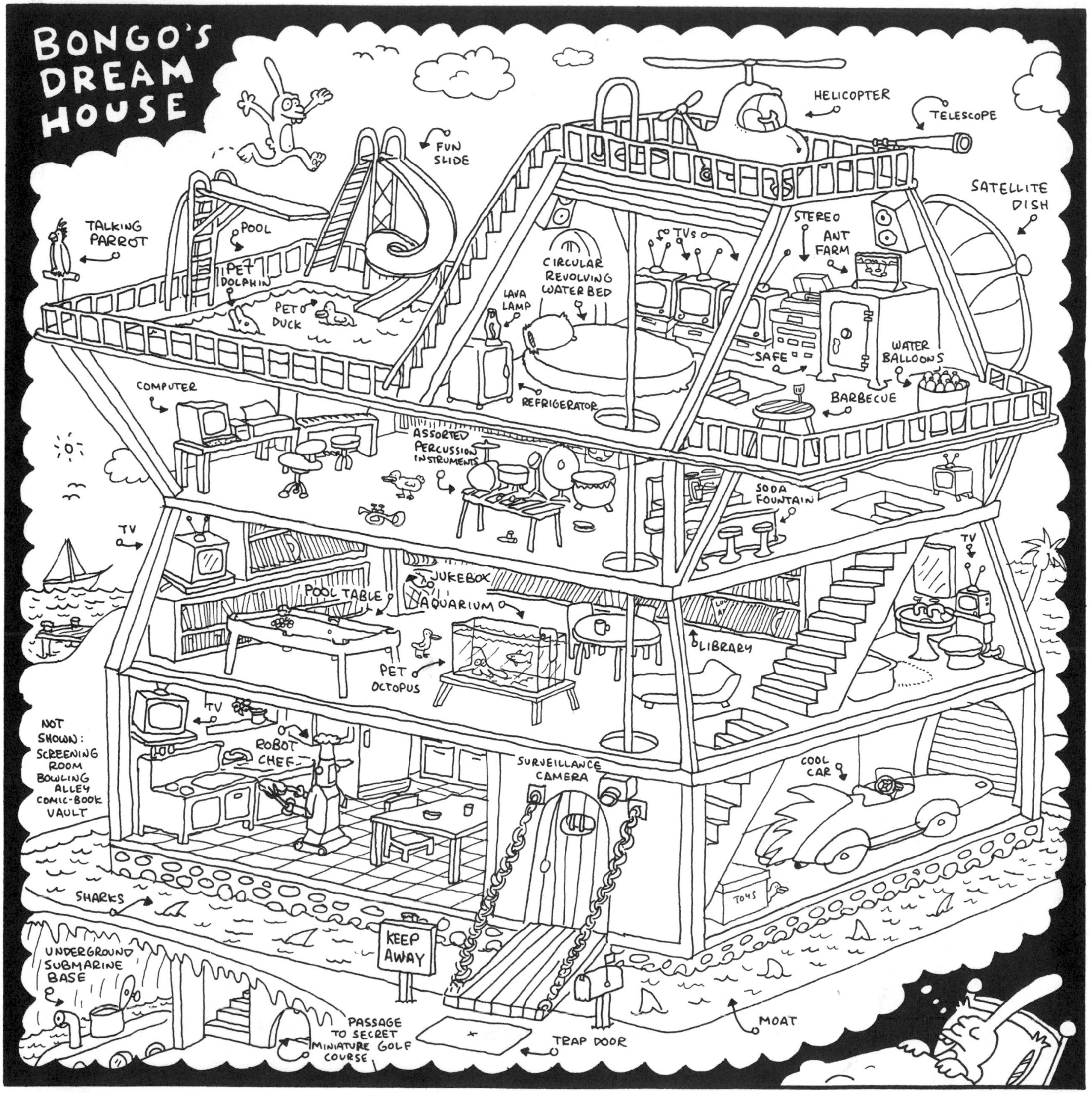
BONGO'S DREAM HOUSE
FUN SLIDE
HELICOPTER
TELESCOPE
SATELLITE DISH
TALKING PARROT
POOL
PET DOLPHIN
PET DUCK
TVs
STEREO
ANT FARM
CIRCULAR REVOLVING WATER BED
LAVA LAMP
SAFE
WATER BALLOONS
BARBECUE
REFRIGERATOR
COMPUTER
ASSORTED PERCUSSION INSTRUMENTS
SODA FOUNTAIN
TV
TV
JUKEBOX
POOL TABLE
AQUARIUM
LIBRARY
PET OCTOPUS
TV
ROBOT CHEF
NOT SHOWN: SCREENING ROOM BOWLING ALLEY COMIC-BOOK VAULT
SURVEILLANCE CAMERA
COOL CAR
TOYS
SHARKS
KEEP AWAY
UNDERGROUND SUBMARINE BASE
PASSAGE TO SECRET MINIATURE GOLF COURSE
TRAP DOOR
MOAT

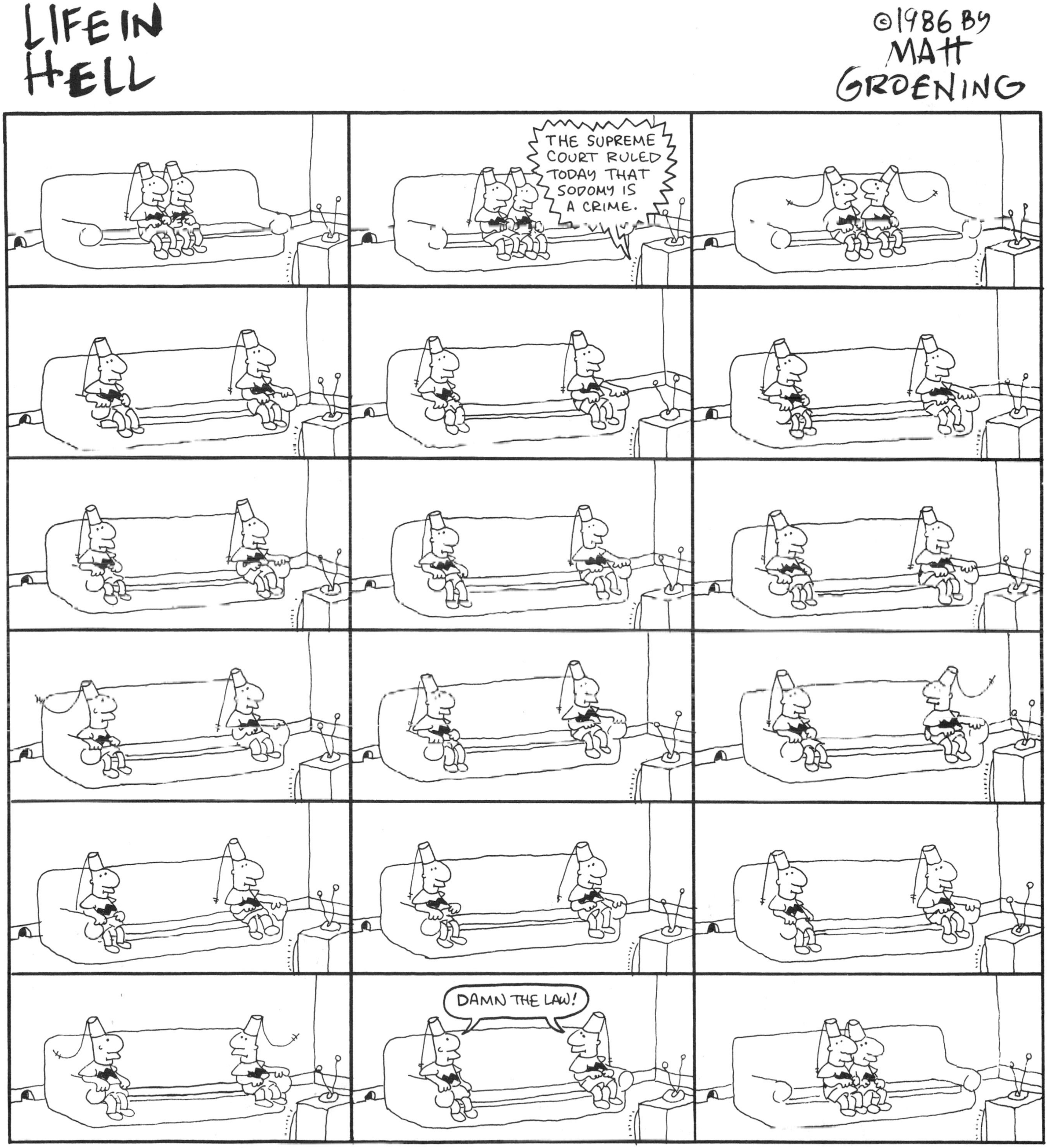
LIFE IN HELL
©1986 BY MATT GROENING
THE SUPREME COURT RULED TODAY THAT SODOMY IS A CRIME.
DAMN THE LAW!

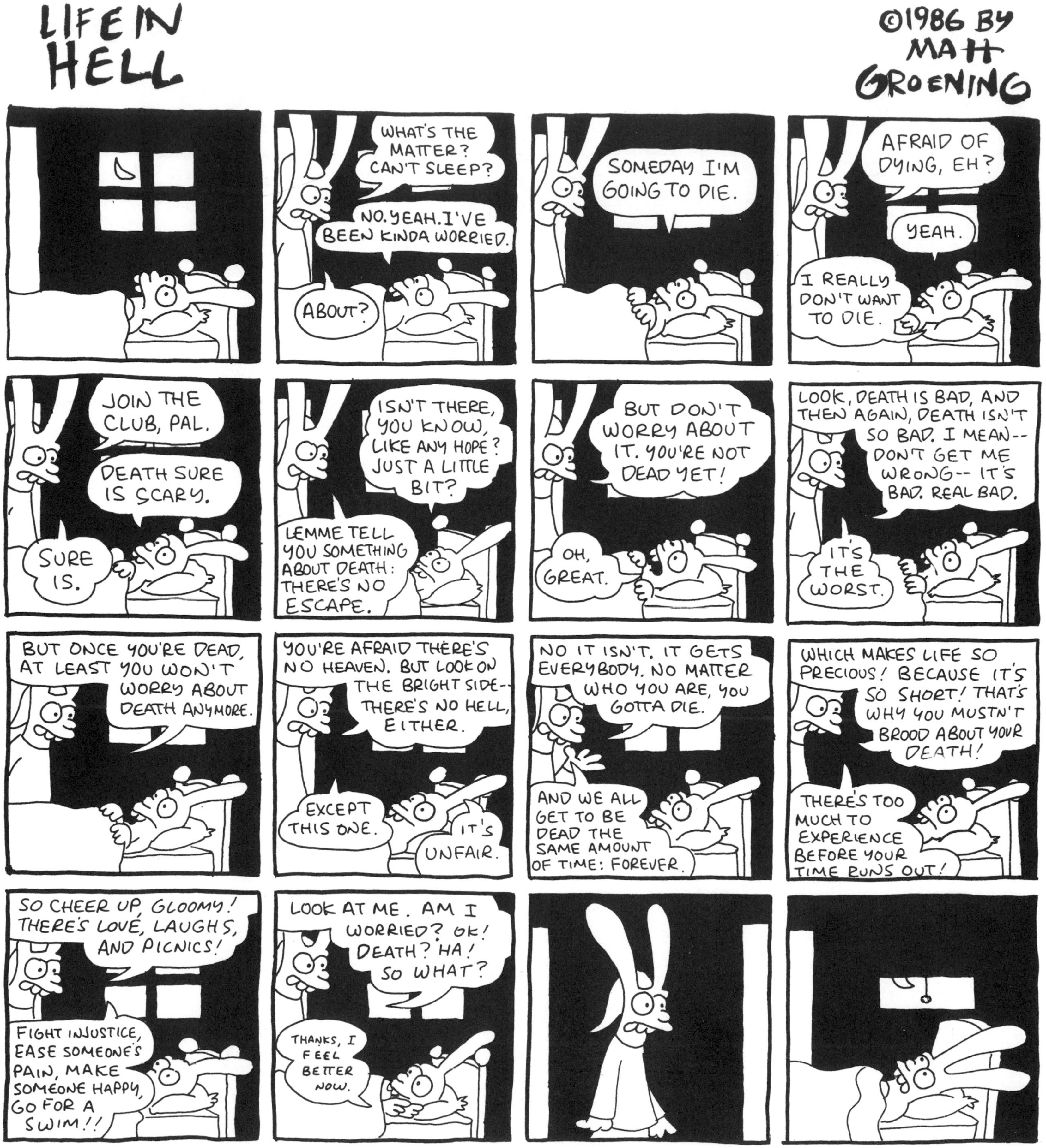
LIFE IN HELL
©1986 BY MATT GROENING
WHAT'S THE MATTER? CAN'T SLEEP?
NO. YEAH. I'VE BEEN KINDA WORRIED.
ABOUT?
SOMEDAY I'M GOING TO DIE.
AFRAID OF DYING, EH?
YEAH.
I REALLY DON'T WANT TO DIE.
JOIN THE CLUB, PAL.
DEATH SURE IS SCARY.
SURE IS.
ISN'T THERE, YOU KNOW, LIKE ANY HOPE? JUST A LITTLE BIT?
LEMME TELL YOU SOMETHING ABOUT DEATH: THERE'S NO ESCAPE.
BUT DON'T WORRY ABOUT IT. YOU'RE NOT DEAD YET!
OH, GREAT.
LOOK, DEATH IS BAD, AND THEN AGAIN, DEATH ISN'T SO BAD. I MEAN-- DON'T GET ME WRONG-- IT'S BAD. REAL BAD.
IT'S THE WORST.
BUT ONCE YOU'RE DEAD, AT LEAST YOU WON'T WORRY ABOUT DEATH ANYMORE.
YOU'RE AFRAID THERE'S NO HEAVEN. BUT LOOK ON THE BRIGHT SIDE-- THERE'S NO HELL, EITHER.
EXCEPT THIS ONE.
IT'S UNFAIR.
NO IT ISN'T. IT GETS EVERYBODY. NO MATTER WHO YOU ARE, YOU GOTTA DIE.
AND WE ALL GET TO BE DEAD THE SAME AMOUNT OF TIME: FOREVER.
WHICH MAKES LIFE SO PRECIOUS! BECAUSE IT'S SO SHORT! THAT'S WHY YOU MUSTN'T BROOD ABOUT YOUR DEATH!
THERE'S TOO MUCH TO EXPERIENCE BEFORE YOUR TIME RUNS OUT!
SO CHEER UP, GLOOMY! THERE'S LOVE, LAUGHS, AND PICNICS!
FIGHT INJUSTICE, EASE SOMEONE'S PAIN, MAKE SOMEONE HAPPY, GO FOR A SWIM!!
LOOK AT ME. AM I WORRIED? OK! DEATH? HA! SO WHAT?
THANKS, I FEEL BETTER NOW.

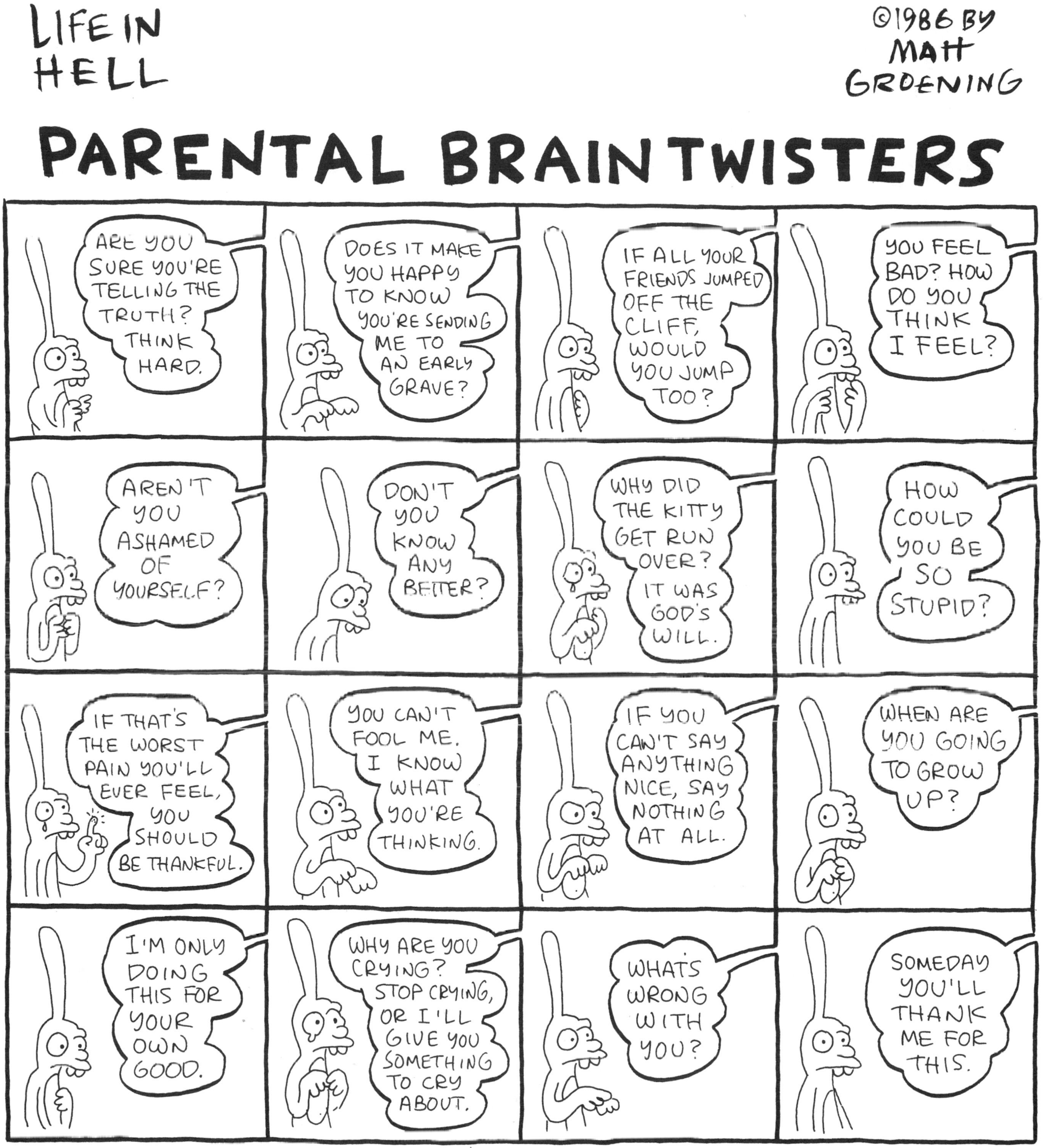
LIFE IN HELL
©1986 BY MATT GROENING
PARENTAL BRAINTWISTERS
ARE YOU SURE YOU'RE TELLING THE TRUTH? THINK HARD.
DOES IT MAKE YOU HAPPY TO KNOW YOU'RE SENDING ME TO AN EARLY GRAVE?
IF ALL YOUR FRIENDS JUMPED OFF THE CLIFF, WOULD YOU JUMP TOO?
YOU FEEL BAD? HOW DO YOU THINK I FEEL?
AREN'T YOU ASHAMED OF YOURSELF?
DON'T YOU KNOW ANY BETTER?
WHY DID THE KITTY GET RUN OVER? IT WAS GOD'S WILL.
HOW COULD YOU BE SO STUPID?
IF THAT'S THE WORST PAIN YOU'LL EVER FEEL, YOU SHOULD BE THANKFUL.
YOU CAN'T FOOL ME. I KNOW WHAT YOU'RE THINKING.
IF YOU CAN'T SAY ANYTHING NICE, SAY NOTHING AT ALL.
WHEN ARE YOU GOING TO GROW UP?
I'M ONLY DOING THIS FOR YOUR OWN GOOD.
WHY ARE YOU CRYING? STOP CRYING, OR I'LL GIVE YOU SOMETHING TO CRY ABOUT.
WHAT'S WRONG WITH YOU?
SOMEDAY YOU'LL THANK ME FOR THIS.

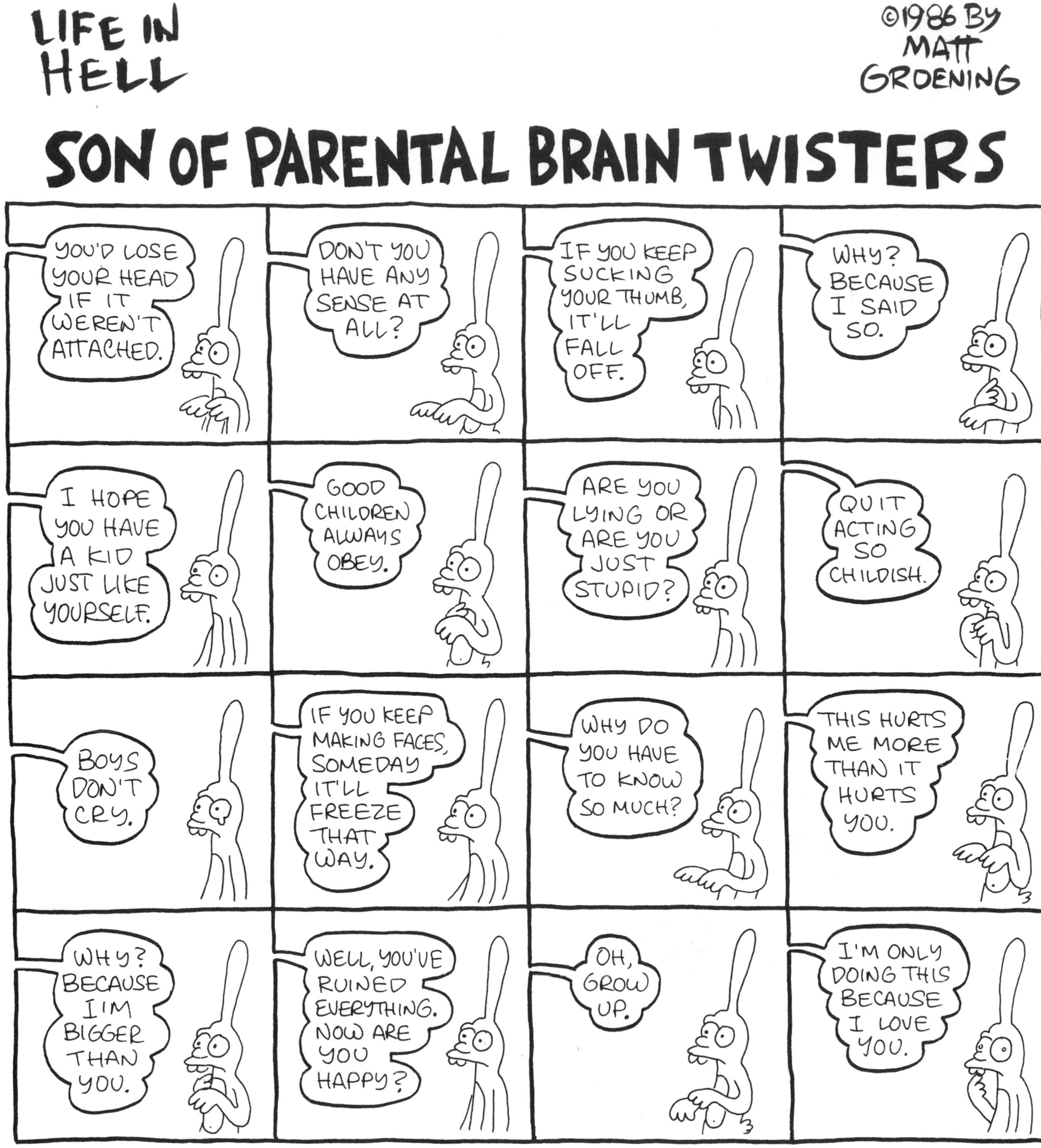
LIFE IN HELL
©1986 BY MATT GROENING
SON OF PARENTAL BRAIN TWISTERS
YOU'D LOSE YOUR HEAD IF IT WEREN'T ATTACHED.
DON'T YOU HAVE ANY SENSE AT ALL?
IF YOU KEEP SUCKING YOUR THUMB, IT'LL FALL OFF.
WHY? BECAUSE I SAID SO.
I HOPE YOU HAVE A KID JUST LIKE YOURSELF.
GOOD CHILDREN ALWAYS OBEY.
ARE YOU LYING OR ARE YOU JUST STUPID?
QUIT ACTING SO CHILDISH.
BOYS DON'T CRY.
IF YOU KEEP MAKING FACES, SOMEDAY IT'LL FREEZE THAT WAY.
WHY DO YOU HAVE TO KNOW SO MUCH?
THIS HURTS ME MORE THAN IT HURTS YOU.
WHY? BECAUSE I'M BIGGER THAN YOU.
WELL, YOU'VE RUINED EVERYTHING. NOW ARE YOU HAPPY?
OH, GROW UP.
I'M ONLY DOING THIS BECAUSE I LOVE YOU.

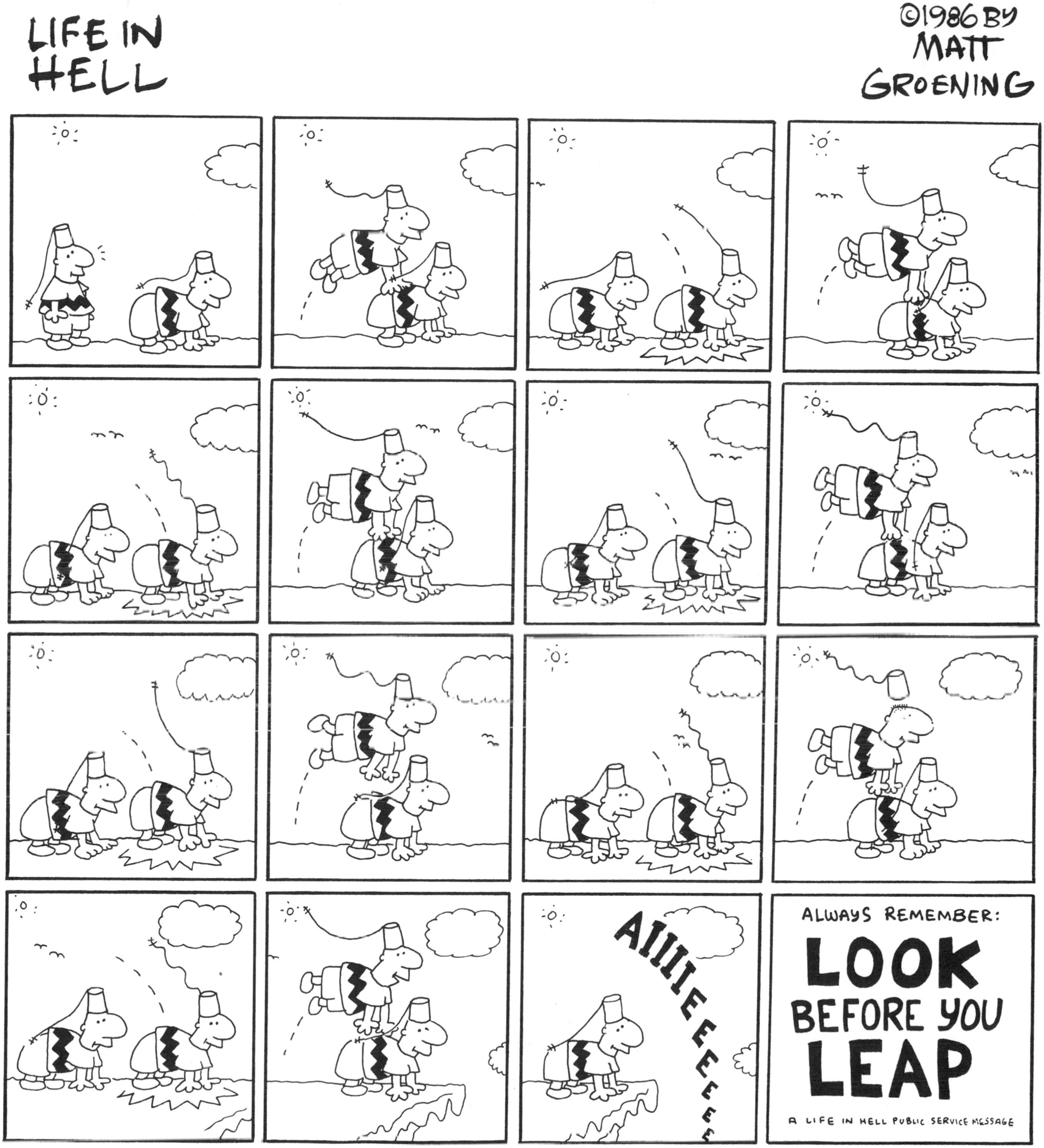

LIFE IN HELL
©1986 BY MATT GROENING
AIIIIEEEEEE
ALWAYS REMEMBER:
LOOK BEFORE YOU LEAP
A LIFE IN HELL PUBLIC SERVICE MESSAGE

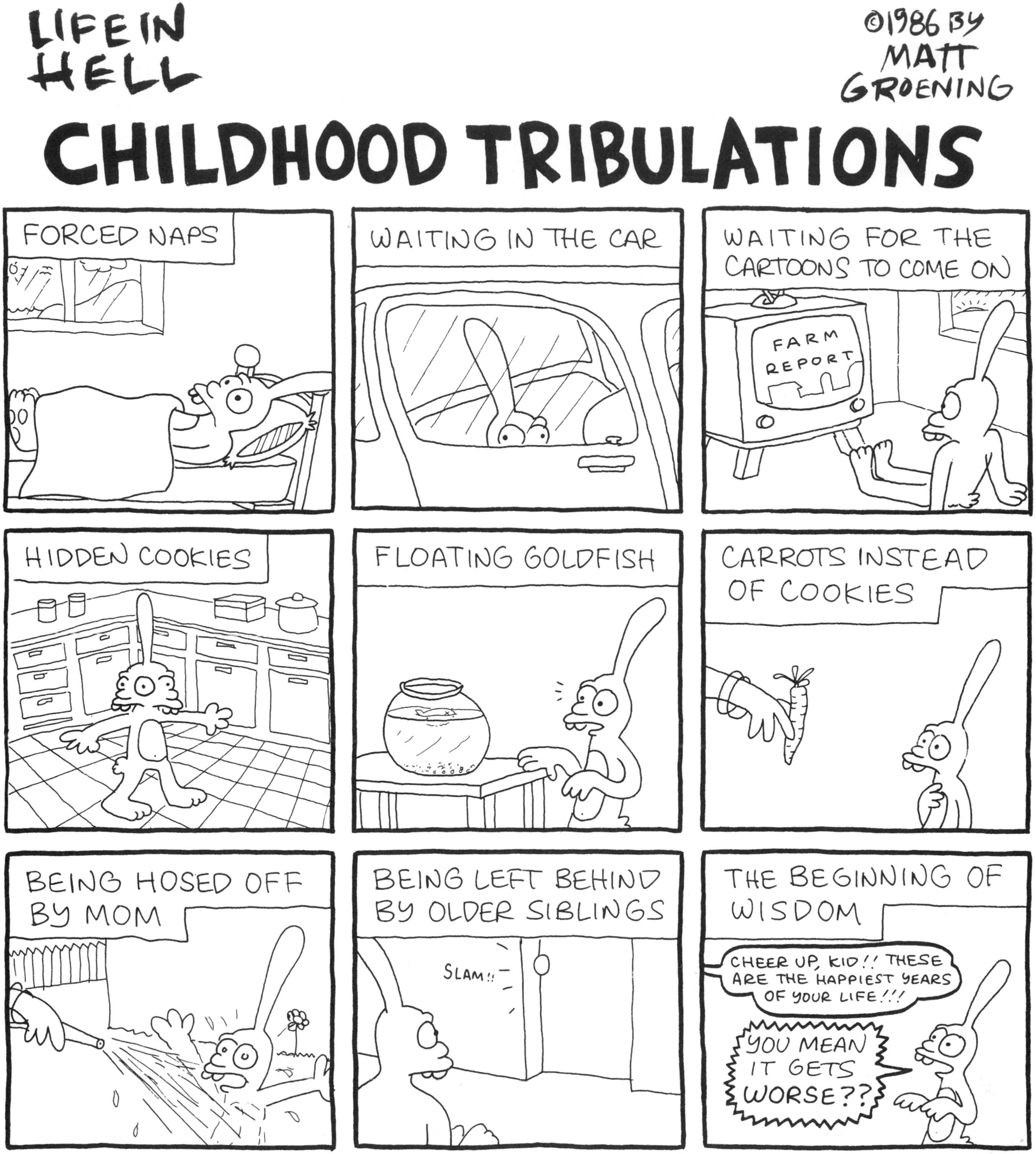
LIFE IN HELL
©1986 BY MATT GROENING
CHILDHOOD TRIBULATIONS
FORCED NAPS
WAITING IN THE CAR
WAITING FOR THE CARTOONS TO COME ON
FARM REPORT
HIDDEN COOKIES
FLOATING GOLDFISH
CARROTS INSTEAD OF COOKIES
BEING HOSED OFF BY MOM
BEING LEFT BEHIND BY OLDER SIBLINGS
SLAM!!
THE BEGINNING OF WISDOM
CHEER UP, KID!! THESE ARE THE HAPPIEST YEARS OF YOUR LIFE!!!
YOU MEAN IT GETS WORSE??

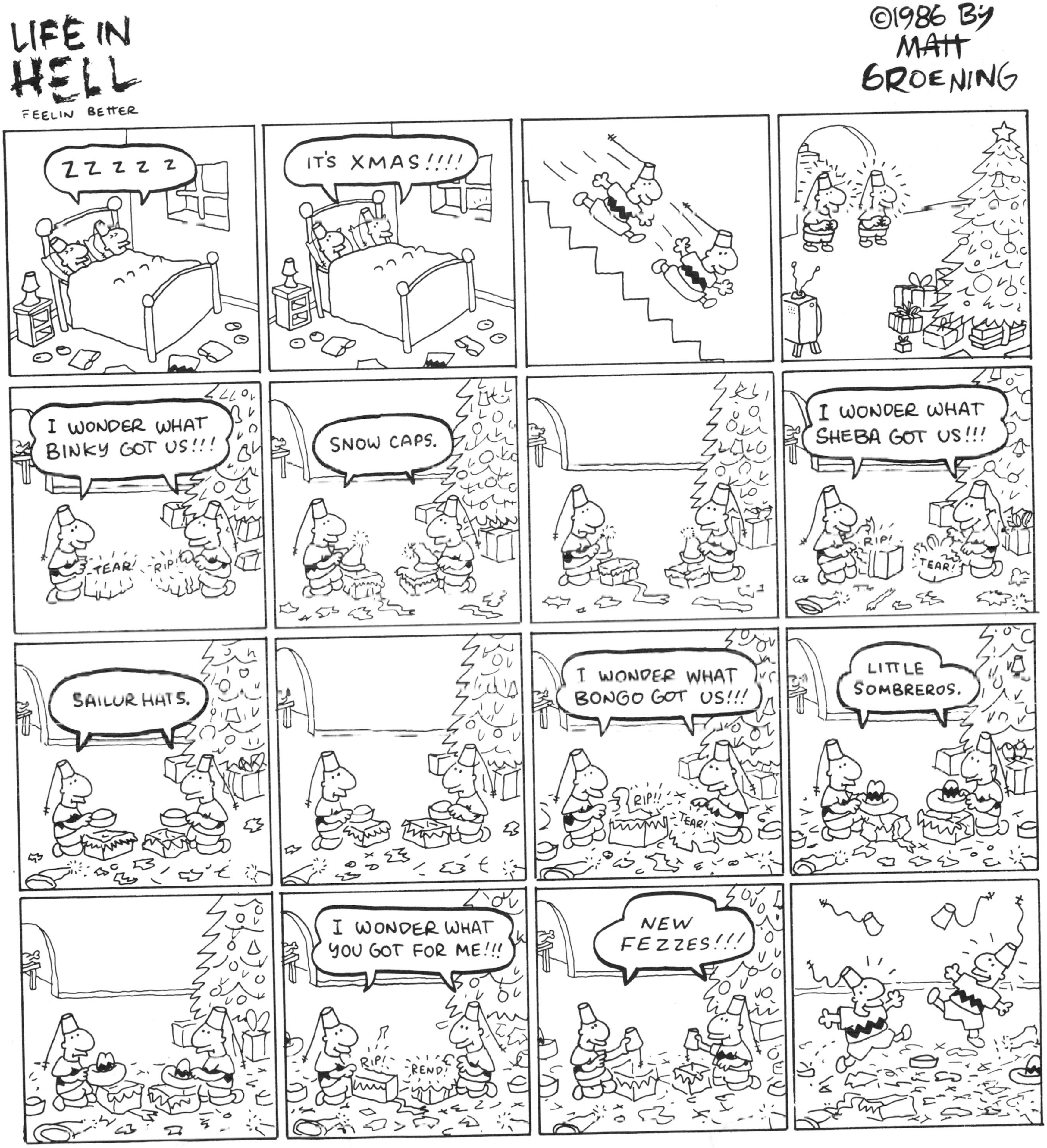
LIFE IN HELL
FEELIN BETTER
©1986 BY MATT GROENING
ZZZZZ
IT'S XMAS!!!!
I WONDER WHAT BINKY GOT US!!!
TEAR!
RIP!
SNOW CAPS.
I WONDER WHAT SHEBA GOT US!!!
RIP!
TEAR!
SAILOR HATS.
I WONDER WHAT BONGO GOT US!!!
RIP!!
TEAR!
LITTLE SOMBREROS.
I WONDER WHAT YOU GOT FOR ME!!!
RIP!
REND!
NEW FEZZES!!!

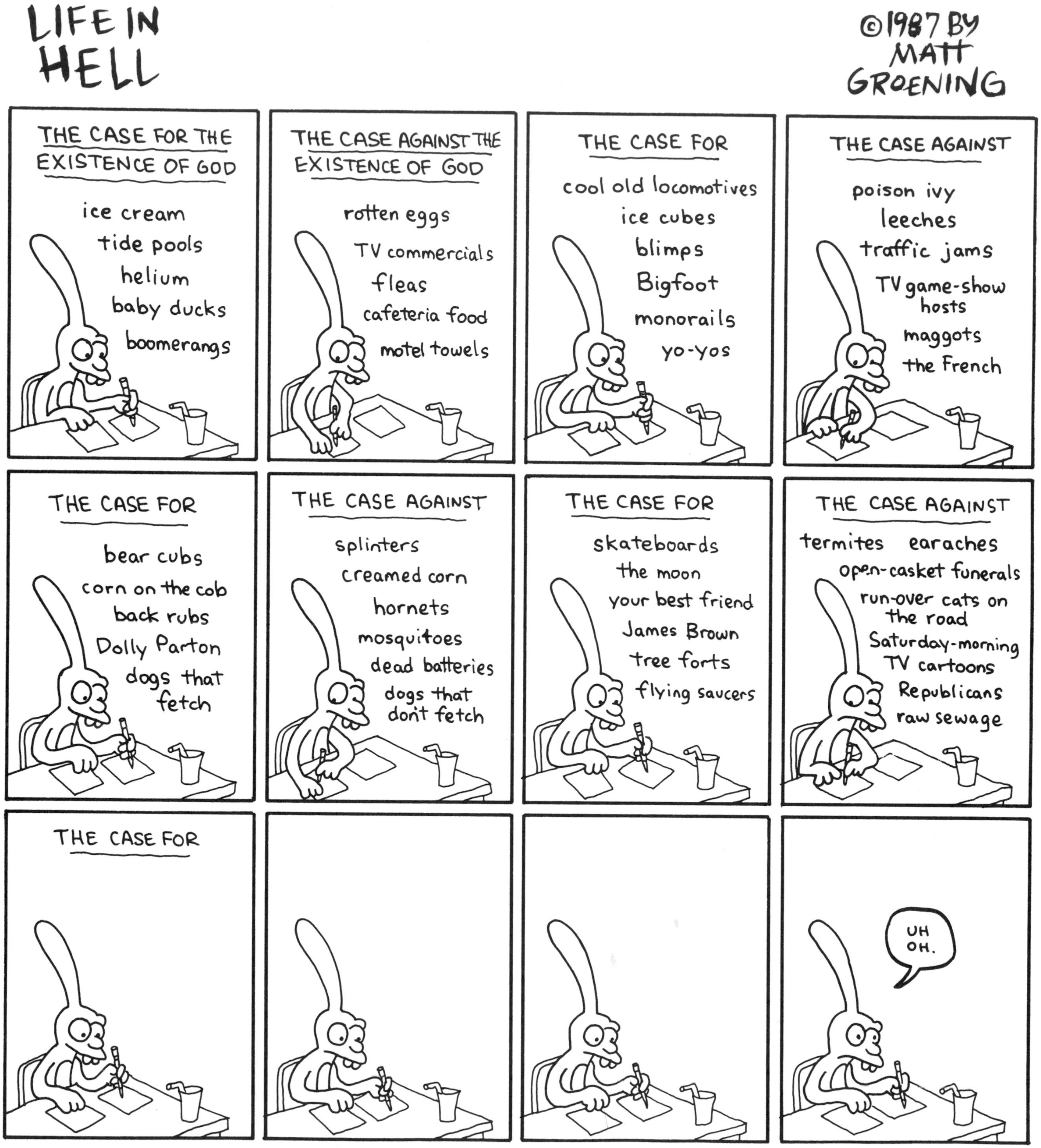
LIFE IN HELL
©1987 BY MATT GROENING
THE CASE FOR THE EXISTENCE OF GOD
ice cream
tide pools
helium
baby ducks
boomerangs
THE CASE AGAINST THE EXISTENCE OF GOD
rotten eggs
TV commercials
fleas
cafeteria food
motel towels
THE CASE FOR
cool old locomotives
ice cubes
blimps
Bigfoot
monorails
yo-yos
THE CASE AGAINST
poison ivy
leeches
traffic jams
TV game-show hosts
maggots
the French
THE CASE FOR
bear cubs
corn on the cob
back rubs
Dolly Parton
dogs that fetch
THE CASE AGAINST
splinters
creamed corn
hornets
mosquitoes
dead batteries
dogs that don't fetch
THE CASE FOR
skateboards
the moon
your best friend
James Brown
tree forts
flying saucers
THE CASE AGAINST
termites
earaches
open-casket funerals
run-over cats on the road
Saturday-morning TV cartoons
Republicans
raw sewage
THE CASE FOR
UH OH.

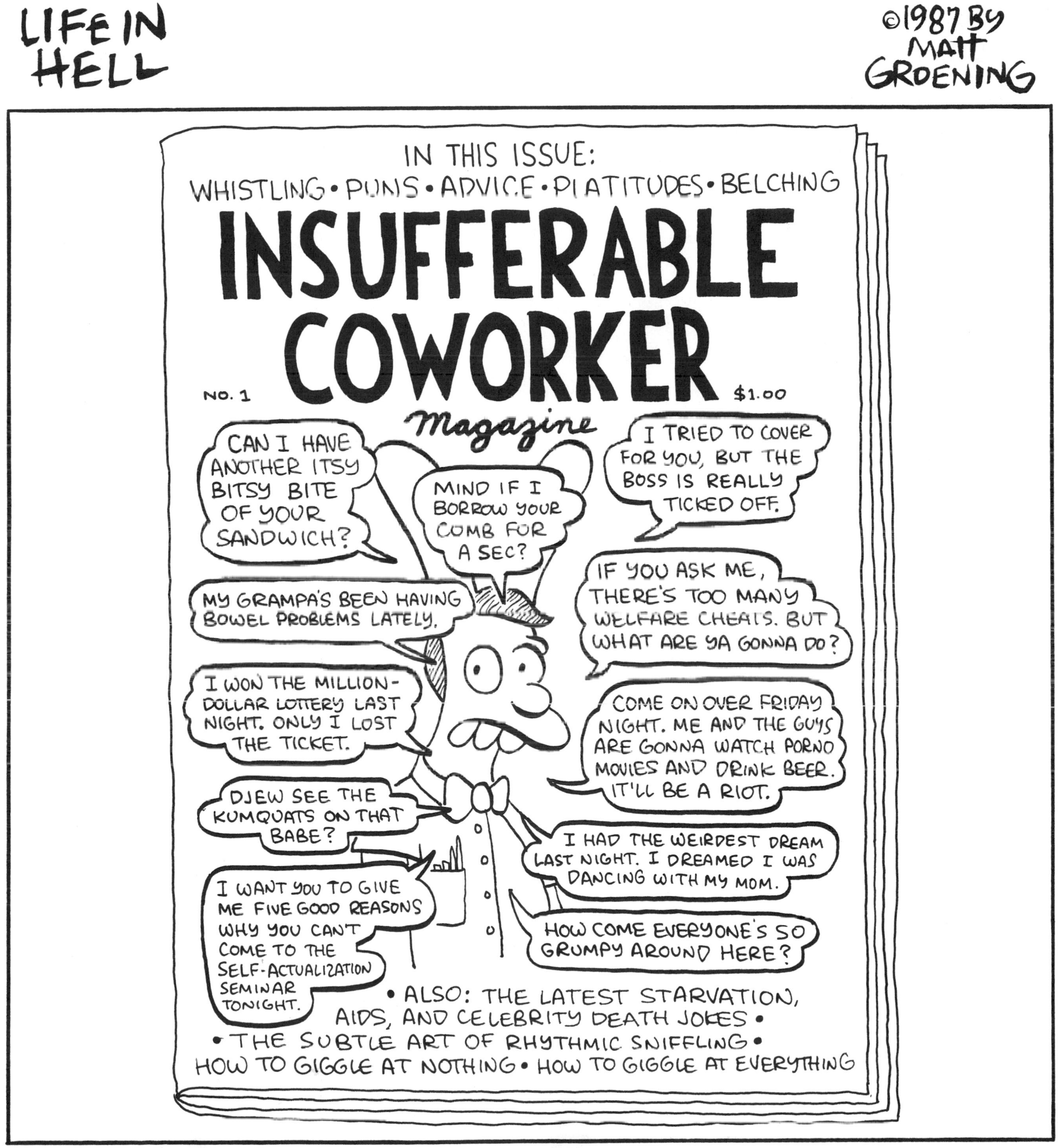
LIFE IN HELL
©1987 BY MATT GROENING
IN THIS ISSUE:
WHISTLING • PUNS • ADVICE • PLATITUDES • BELCHING
INSUFFERABLE COWORKER
NO. 1
$1.00
Magazine
CAN I HAVE ANOTHER ITSY BITSY BITE OF YOUR SANDWICH?
MIND IF I BORROW YOUR COMB FOR A SEC?
I TRIED TO COVER FOR YOU, BUT THE BOSS IS REALLY TICKED OFF.
MY GRAMPA'S BEEN HAVING BOWEL PROBLEMS LATELY.
IF YOU ASK ME, THERE'S TOO MANY WELFARE CHEATS. BUT WHAT ARE YA GONNA DO?
I WON THE MILLION-DOLLAR LOTTERY LAST NIGHT. ONLY I LOST THE TICKET.
COME ON OVER FRIDAY NIGHT. ME AND THE GUYS ARE GONNA WATCH PORNO MOVIES AND DRINK BEER. IT'LL BE A RIOT.
DJEW SEE THE KUMQUATS ON THAT BABE?
I HAD THE WEIRDEST DREAM LAST NIGHT. I DREAMED I WAS DANCING WITH MY MOM.
I WANT YOU TO GIVE ME FIVE GOOD REASONS WHY YOU CAN'T COME TO THE SELF-ACTUALIZATION SEMINAR TONIGHT.
HOW COME EVERYONE'S SO GRUMPY AROUND HERE?
• ALSO: THE LATEST STARVATION, AIDS, AND CELEBRITY DEATH JOKES •
• THE SUBTLE ART OF RHYTHMIC SNIFFLING •
HOW TO GIGGLE AT NOTHING • HOW TO GIGGLE AT EVERYTHING

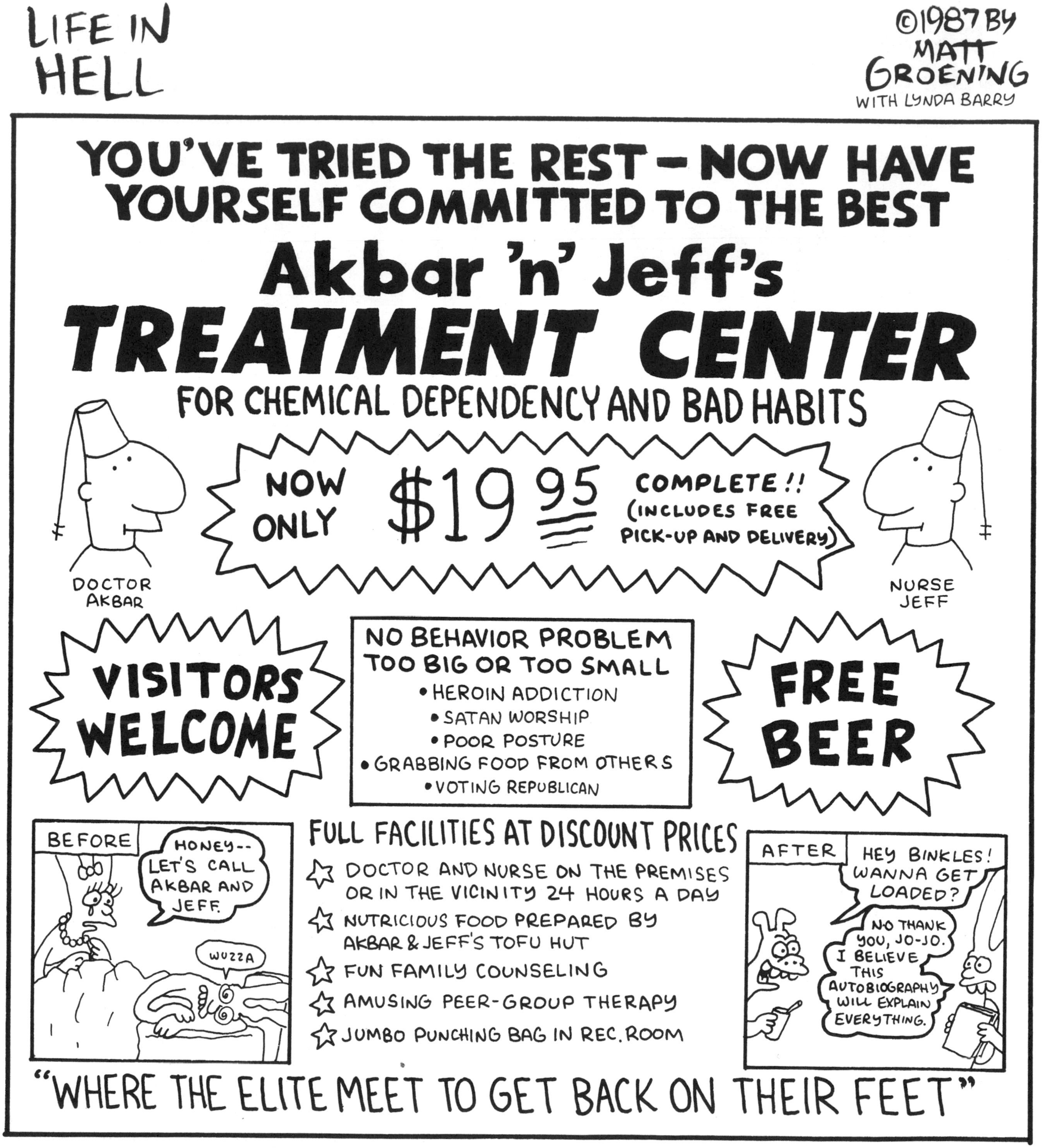

LIFE IN HELL
©1987 BY MATT GROENING
WITH LYNDA BARRY
YOU'VE TRIED THE REST – NOW HAVE YOURSELF COMMITTED TO THE BEST
Akbar 'n' Jeff's
TREATMENT CENTER
FOR CHEMICAL DEPENDENCY AND BAD HABITS
NOW ONLY $19.95 COMPLETE!!
(INCLUDES FREE PICK-UP AND DELIVERY)
DOCTOR AKBAR
NURSE JEFF
VISITORS WELCOME
NO BEHAVIOR PROBLEM TOO BIG OR TOO SMALL
• HEROIN ADDICTION
• SATAN WORSHIP
• POOR POSTURE
• GRABBING FOOD FROM OTHERS
• VOTING REPUBLICAN
FREE BEER
BEFORE
HONEY-- LET'S CALL AKBAR AND JEFF.
WUZZA
FULL FACILITIES AT DISCOUNT PRICES
DOCTOR AND NURSE ON THE PREMISES OR IN THE VICINITY 24 HOURS A DAY
NUTRICIOUS FOOD PREPARED BY AKBAR & JEFF'S TOFU HUT
FUN FAMILY COUNSELING
AMUSING PEER-GROUP THERAPY
JUMBO PUNCHING BAG IN REC. ROOM
AFTER
HEY BINKLES! WANNA GET LOADED?
NO THANK YOU, JO-JO. I BELIEVE THIS AUTOBIOGRAPHY WILL EXPLAIN EVERYTHING.
"WHERE THE ELITE MEET TO GET BACK ON THEIR FEET"

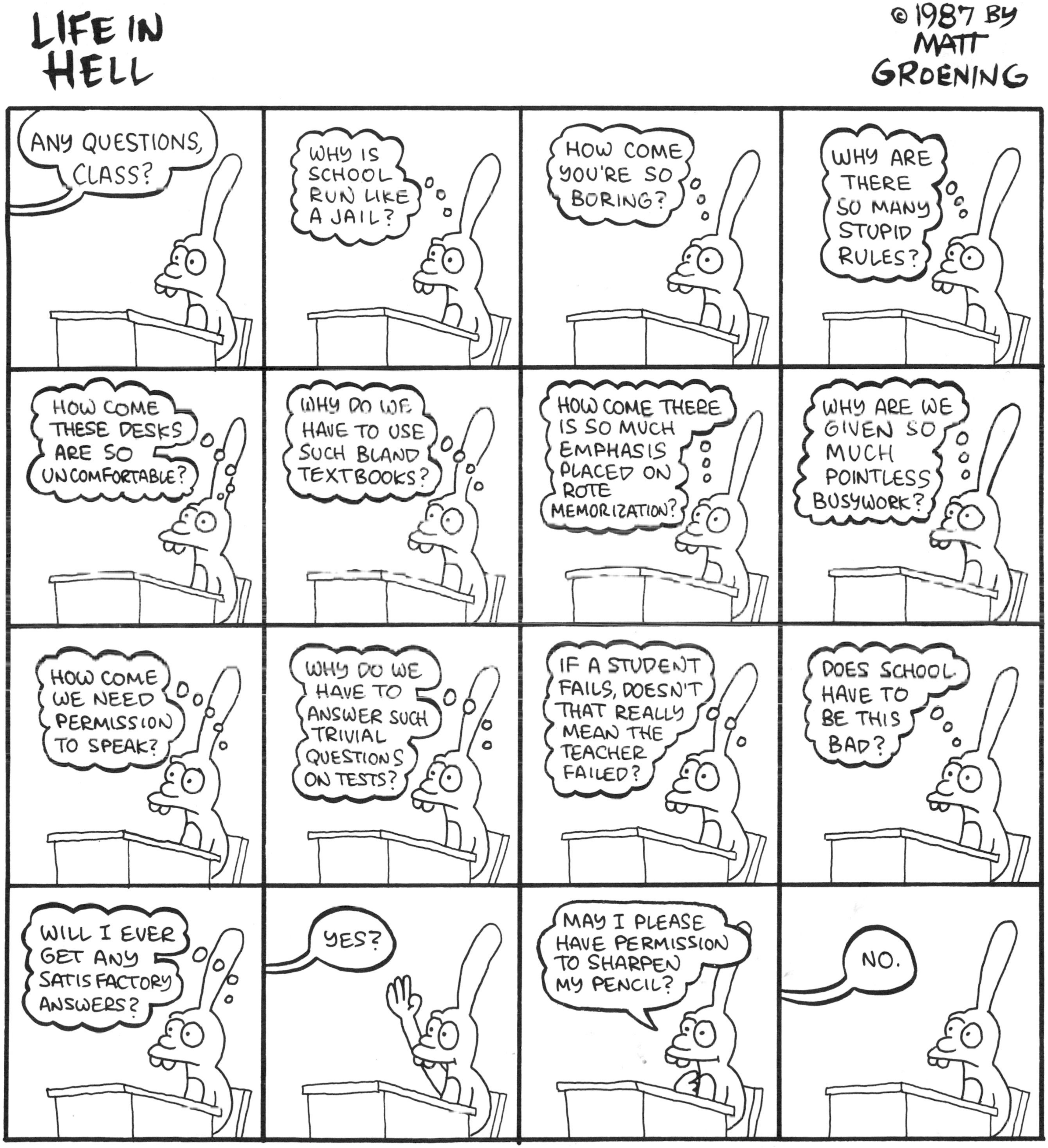
LIFE IN HELL
© 1987 BY MATT GROENING
ANY QUESTIONS, CLASS?
WHY IS SCHOOL RUN LIKE A JAIL?
HOW COME YOU'RE SO BORING?
WHY ARE THERE SO MANY STUPID RULES?
HOW COME THESE DESKS ARE SO UNCOMFORTABLE?
WHY DO WE HAVE TO USE SUCH BLAND TEXTBOOKS?
HOW COME THERE IS SO MUCH EMPHASIS PLACED ON ROTE MEMORIZATION?
WHY ARE WE GIVEN SO MUCH POINTLESS BUSYWORK?
HOW COME WE NEED PERMISSION TO SPEAK?
WHY DO WE HAVE TO ANSWER SUCH TRIVIAL QUESTIONS ON TESTS?
IF A STUDENT FAILS, DOESN'T THAT REALLY MEAN THE TEACHER FAILED?
DOES SCHOOL HAVE TO BE THIS BAD?
WILL I EVER GET ANY SATISFACTORY ANSWERS?
YES?
MAY I PLEASE HAVE PERMISSION TO SHARPEN MY PENCIL?
NO.

LIFE IN HELL

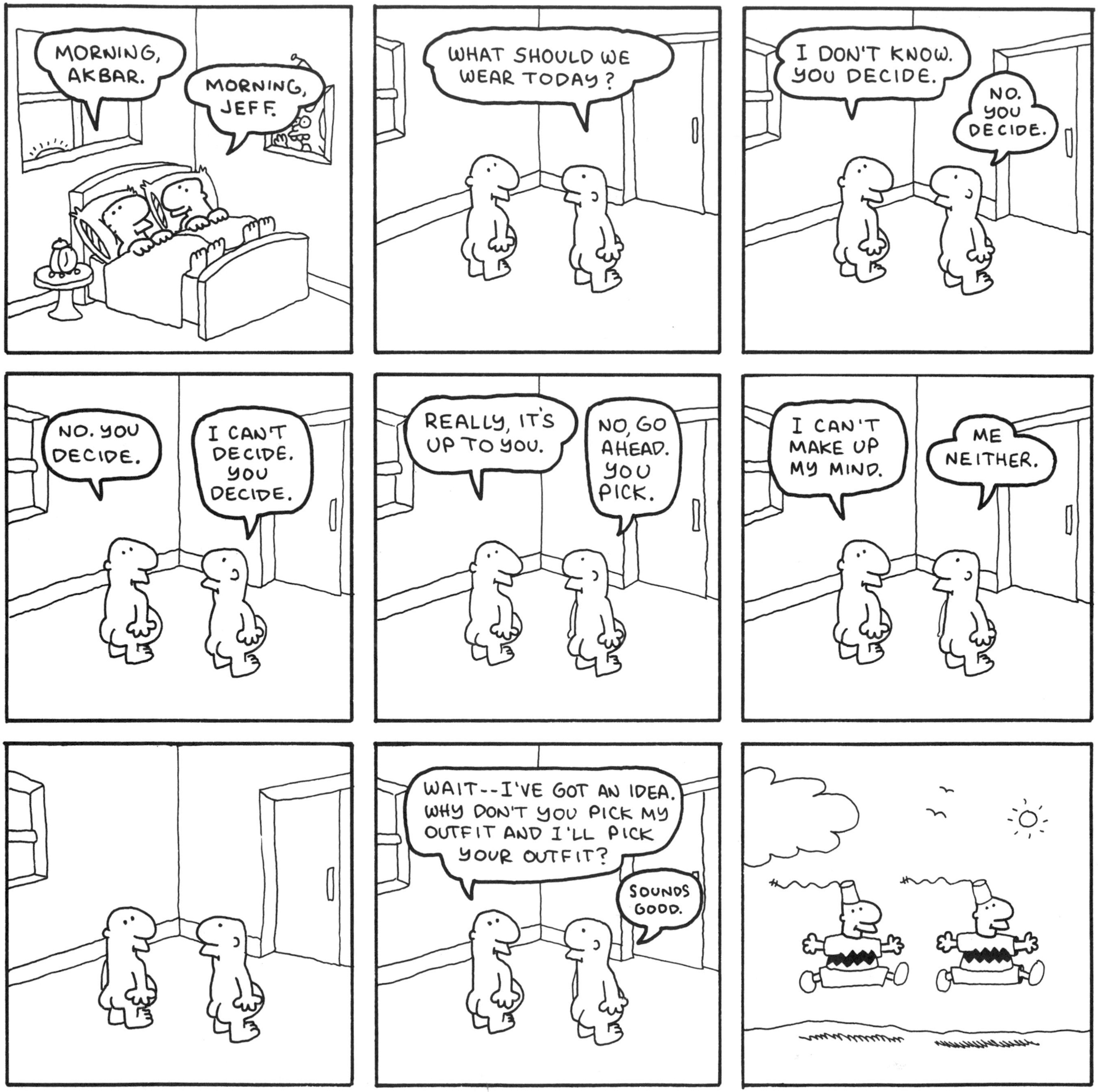
MORNING, AKBAR.
MORNING, JEFF.
WHAT SHOULD WE WEAR TODAY?
I DON'T KNOW. YOU DECIDE.
NO. YOU DECIDE.
NO. YOU DECIDE.
I CAN'T DECIDE. YOU DECIDE.
REALLY, IT'S UP TO YOU.
NO, GO AHEAD. YOU PICK.
I CAN'T MAKE UP MY MIND.
ME NEITHER.
WAIT--I'VE GOT AN IDEA. WHY DON'T YOU PICK MY OUTFIT AND I'LL PICK YOUR OUTFIT?
SOUNDS GOOD.

LIFE IN HELL

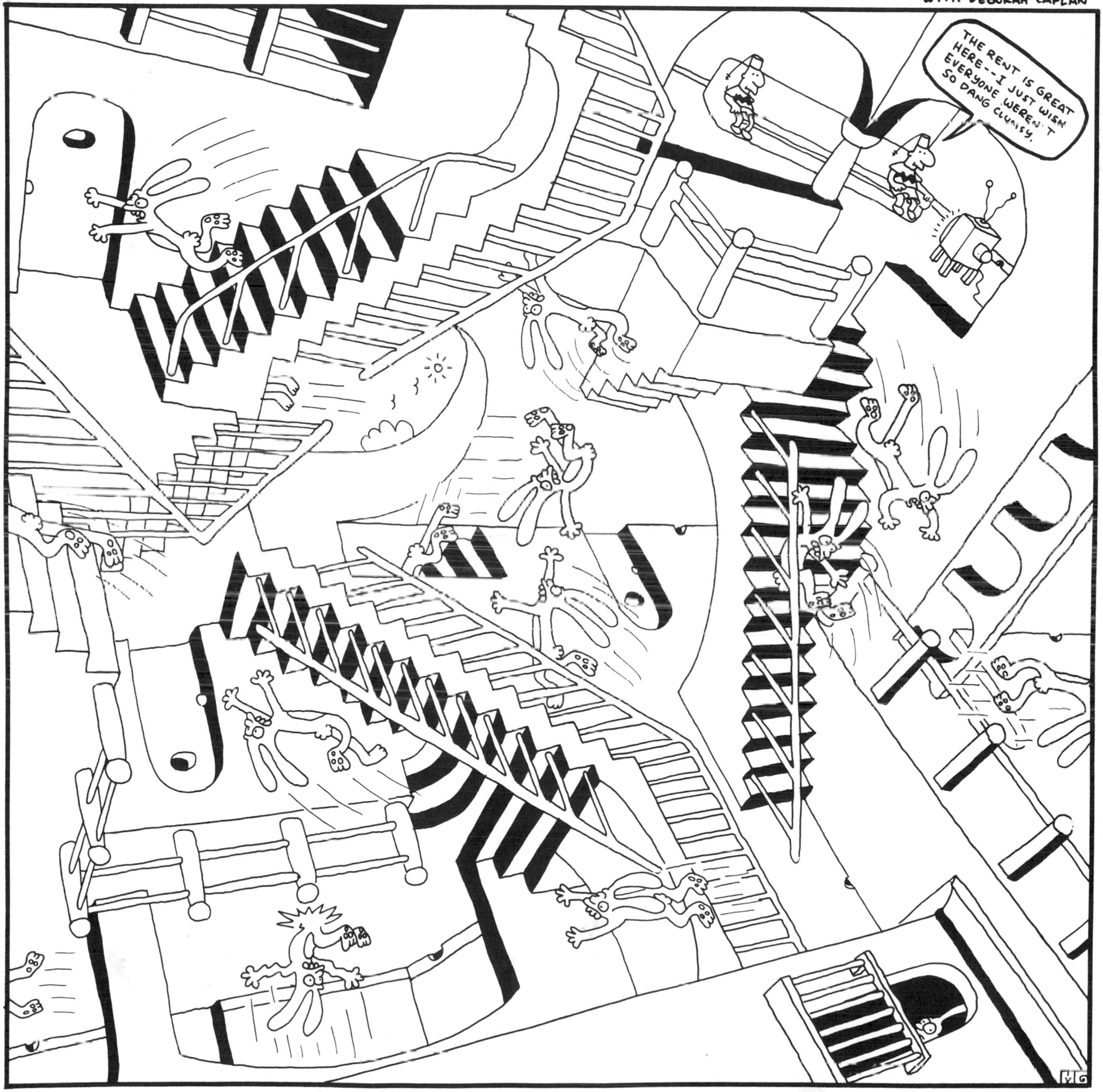
THE RENT IS GREAT HERE--I JUST WISH EVERYONE WEREN'T SO DANG CLUMSY.
MG

LIFE IN HELL

©1987 BY MATT GROENING

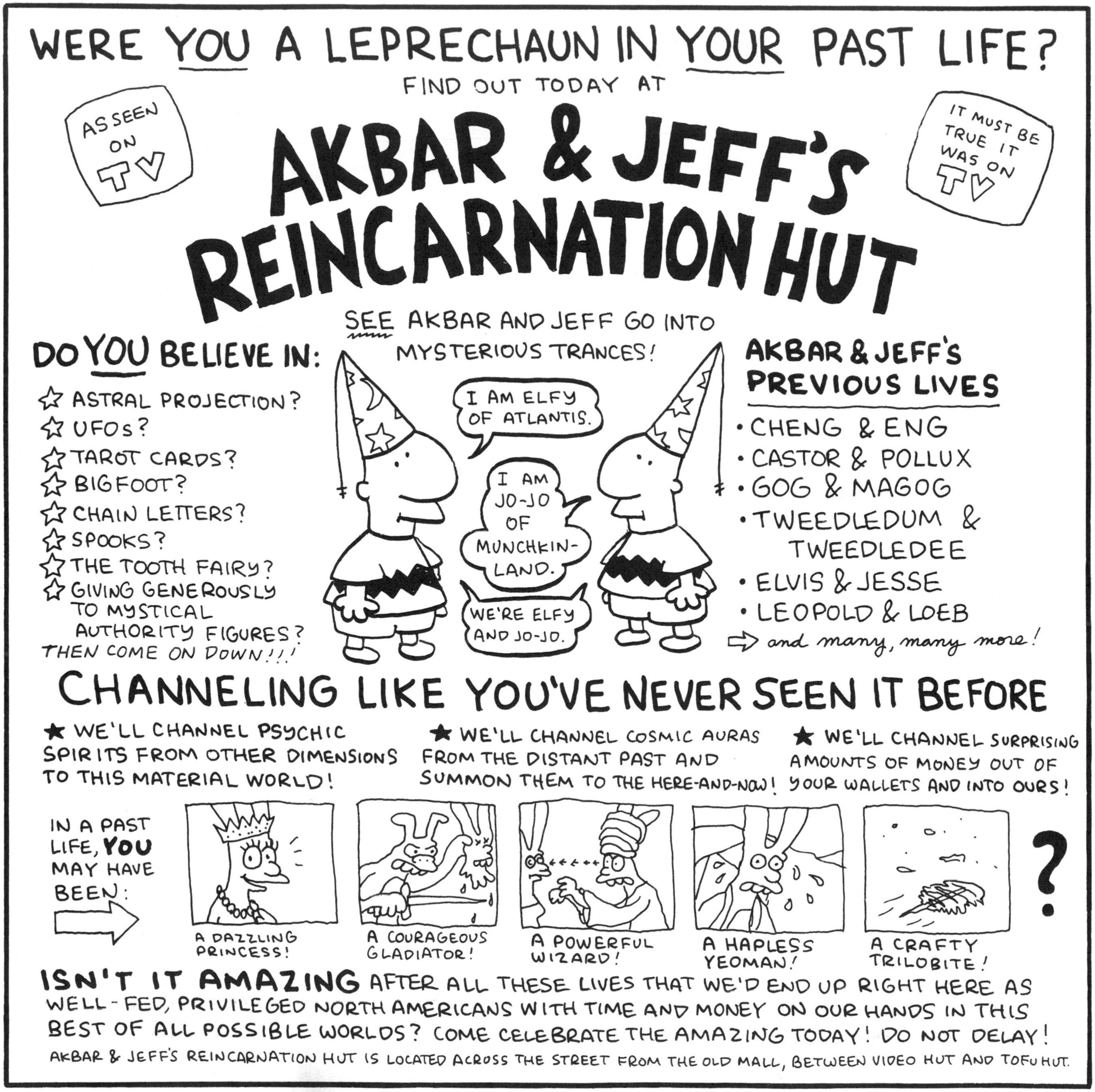

WERE YOU A LEPRECHAUN IN YOUR PAST LIFE?
FIND OUT TODAY AT
AS SEEN ON TV
IT MUST BE TRUE IT WAS ON TV
AKBAR & JEFF'S REINCARNATION HUT
SEE AKBAR AND JEFF GO INTO MYSTERIOUS TRANCES!
DO YOU BELIEVE IN:
ASTRAL PROJECTION?
UFOs?
TAROT CARDS?
BIGFOOT?
CHAIN LETTERS?
SPOOKS?
THE TOOTH FAIRY?
GIVING GENEROUSLY TO MYSTICAL AUTHORITY FIGURES?
THEN COME ON DOWN!!!
I AM ELFY OF ATLANTIS.
I AM JO-JO OF MUNCHKIN-LAND.
WE'RE ELFY AND JO-JO.
AKBAR & JEFF'S PREVIOUS LIVES
• CHENG & ENG
• CASTOR & POLLUX
• GOG & MAGOG
• TWEEDLEDUM & TWEEDLEDEE
• ELVIS & JESSE
• LEOPOLD & LOEB
and many, many more!
CHANNELING LIKE YOU'VE NEVER SEEN IT BEFORE
★ WE'LL CHANNEL PSYCHIC SPIRITS FROM OTHER DIMENSIONS TO THIS MATERIAL WORLD!
★ WE'LL CHANNEL COSMIC AURAS FROM THE DISTANT PAST AND SUMMON THEM TO THE HERE-AND-NOW!
★ WE'LL CHANNEL SURPRISING AMOUNTS OF MONEY OUT OF YOUR WALLETS AND INTO OURS!
IN A PAST LIFE, YOU MAY HAVE BEEN:
A DAZZLING PRINCESS!
A COURAGEOUS GLADIATOR!
A POWERFUL WIZARD!
A HAPLESS YEOMAN!
A CRAFTY TRILOBITE!
?
ISN'T IT AMAZING AFTER ALL THESE LIVES THAT WE'D END UP RIGHT HERE AS WELL-FED, PRIVILEGED NORTH AMERICANS WITH TIME AND MONEY ON OUR HANDS IN THIS BEST OF ALL POSSIBLE WORLDS? COME CELEBRATE THE AMAZING TODAY! DO NOT DELAY!
AKBAR & JEFF'S REINCARNATION HUT IS LOCATED ACROSS THE STREET FROM THE OLD MALL, BETWEEN VIDEO HUT AND TOFU HUT.

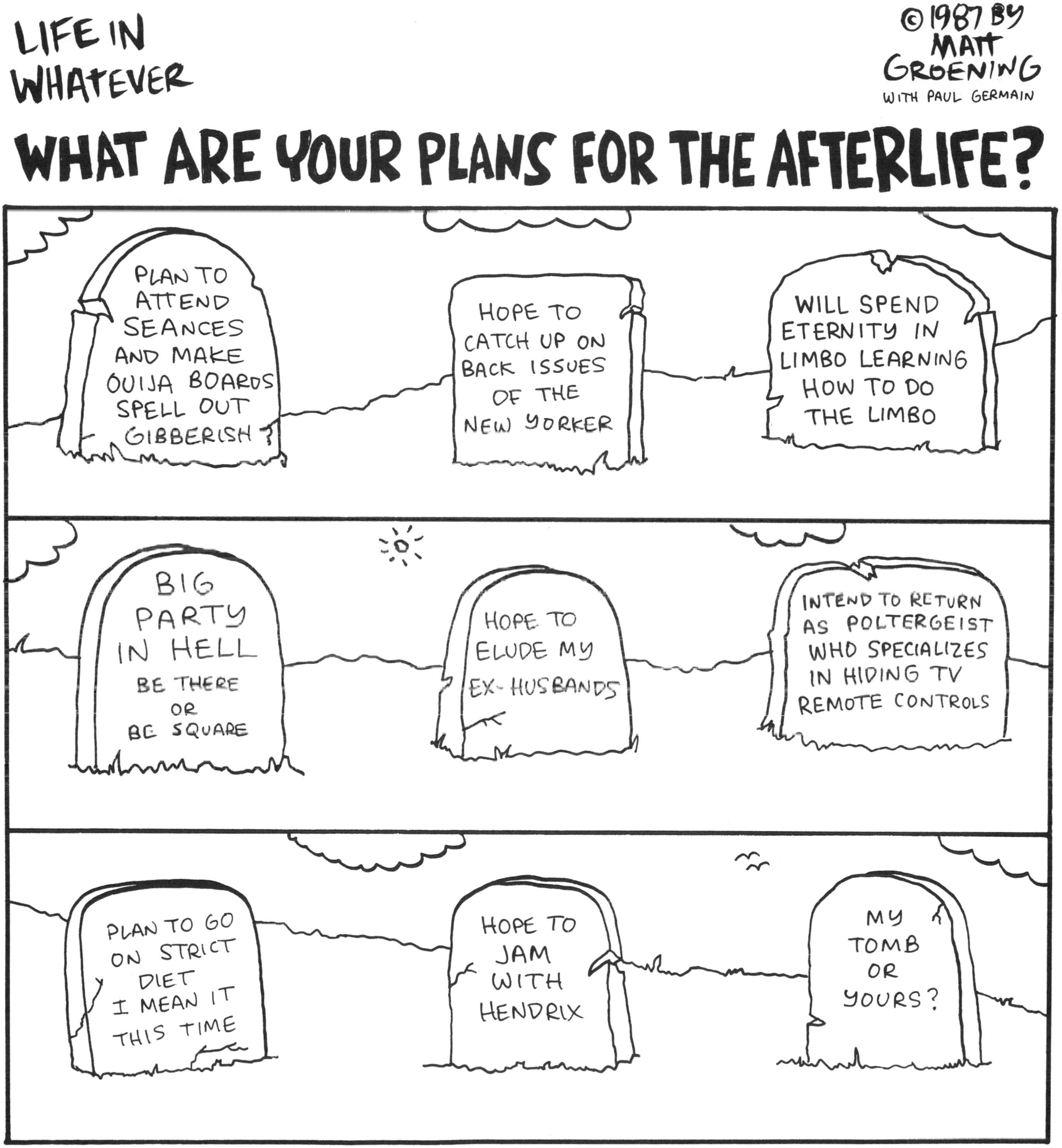
LIFE IN WHATEVER
©1987 BY MATT GROENING
WITH PAUL GERMAIN
WHAT ARE YOUR PLANS FOR THE AFTERLIFE?
PLAN TO ATTEND SEANCES AND MAKE OUIJA BOARDS SPELL OUT GIBBERISH?
HOPE TO CATCH UP ON BACK ISSUES OF THE NEW YORKER
WILL SPEND ETERNITY IN LIMBO LEARNING HOW TO DO THE LIMBO
BIG PARTY IN HELL
BE THERE OR BE SQUARE
HOPE TO ELUDE MY EX-HUSBANDS
INTEND TO RETURN AS POLTERGEIST WHO SPECIALIZES IN HIDING TV REMOTE CONTROLS
PLAN TO GO ON STRICT DIET
I MEAN IT THIS TIME
HOPE TO JAM WITH HENDRIX
MY TOMB OR YOURS?

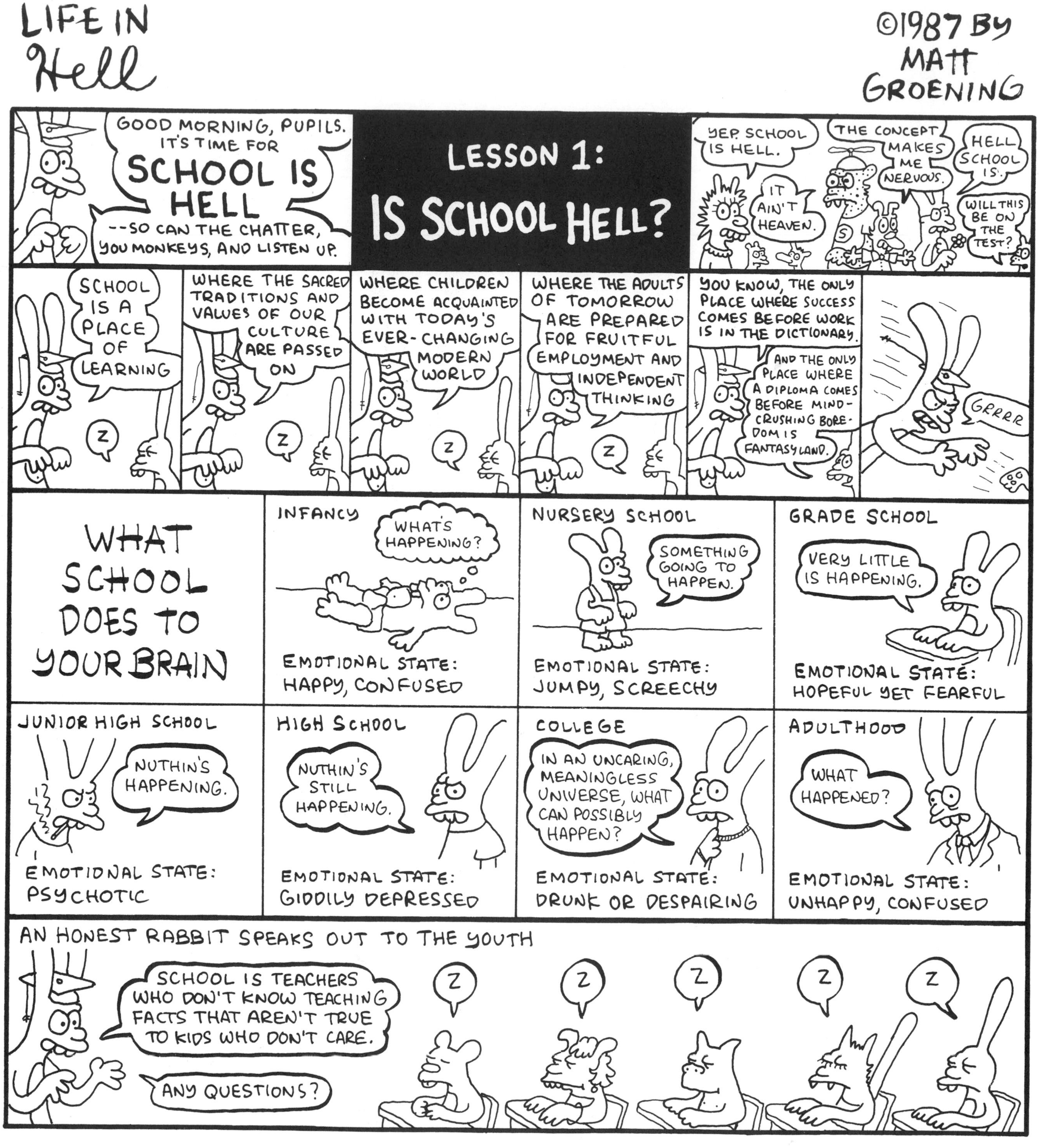

LIFE IN Hell
©1987 BY MATT GROENING
GOOD MORNING, PUPILS. IT'S TIME FOR SCHOOL IS HELL
--SO CAN THE CHATTER, YOU MONKEYS, AND LISTEN UP.
LESSON 1: IS SCHOOL HELL?
YEP. SCHOOL IS HELL.
IT AIN'T HEAVEN.
THE CONCEPT MAKES ME NERVOUS.
HELL SCHOOL IS.
WILL THIS BE ON THE TEST?
SCHOOL IS A PLACE OF LEARNING
Z
WHERE THE SACRED TRADITIONS AND VALUES OF OUR CULTURE ARE PASSED ON
Z
WHERE CHILDREN BECOME ACQUAINTED WITH TODAY'S EVER-CHANGING MODERN WORLD
Z
WHERE THE ADULTS OF TOMORROW ARE PREPARED FOR FRUITFUL EMPLOYMENT AND INDEPENDENT THINKING
Z
YOU KNOW, THE ONLY PLACE WHERE SUCCESS COMES BEFORE WORK IS IN THE DICTIONARY.
AND THE ONLY PLACE WHERE A DIPLOMA COMES BEFORE MIND-CRUSHING BOREDOM IS FANTASYLAND.
GRRRR
WHAT SCHOOL DOES TO YOUR BRAIN
INFANCY
WHAT'S HAPPENING?
EMOTIONAL STATE: HAPPY, CONFUSED
NURSERY SCHOOL
SOMETHING GOING TO HAPPEN.
EMOTIONAL STATE: JUMPY, SCREECHY
GRADE SCHOOL
VERY LITTLE IS HAPPENING.
EMOTIONAL STATE: HOPEFUL YET FEARFUL
JUNIOR HIGH SCHOOL
NUTHIN'S HAPPENING.
EMOTIONAL STATE: PSYCHOTIC
HIGH SCHOOL
NUTHIN'S STILL HAPPENING.
EMOTIONAL STATE: GIDDILY DEPRESSED
COLLEGE
IN AN UNCARING, MEANINGLESS UNIVERSE, WHAT CAN POSSIBLY HAPPEN?
EMOTIONAL STATE: DRUNK OR DESPAIRING
ADULTHOOD
WHAT HAPPENED?
EMOTIONAL STATE: UNHAPPY, CONFUSED
AN HONEST RABBIT SPEAKS OUT TO THE YOUTH
SCHOOL IS TEACHERS WHO DON'T KNOW TEACHING FACTS THAT AREN'T TRUE TO KIDS WHO DON'T CARE.
ANY QUESTIONS?
Z
Z
Z
Z
Z

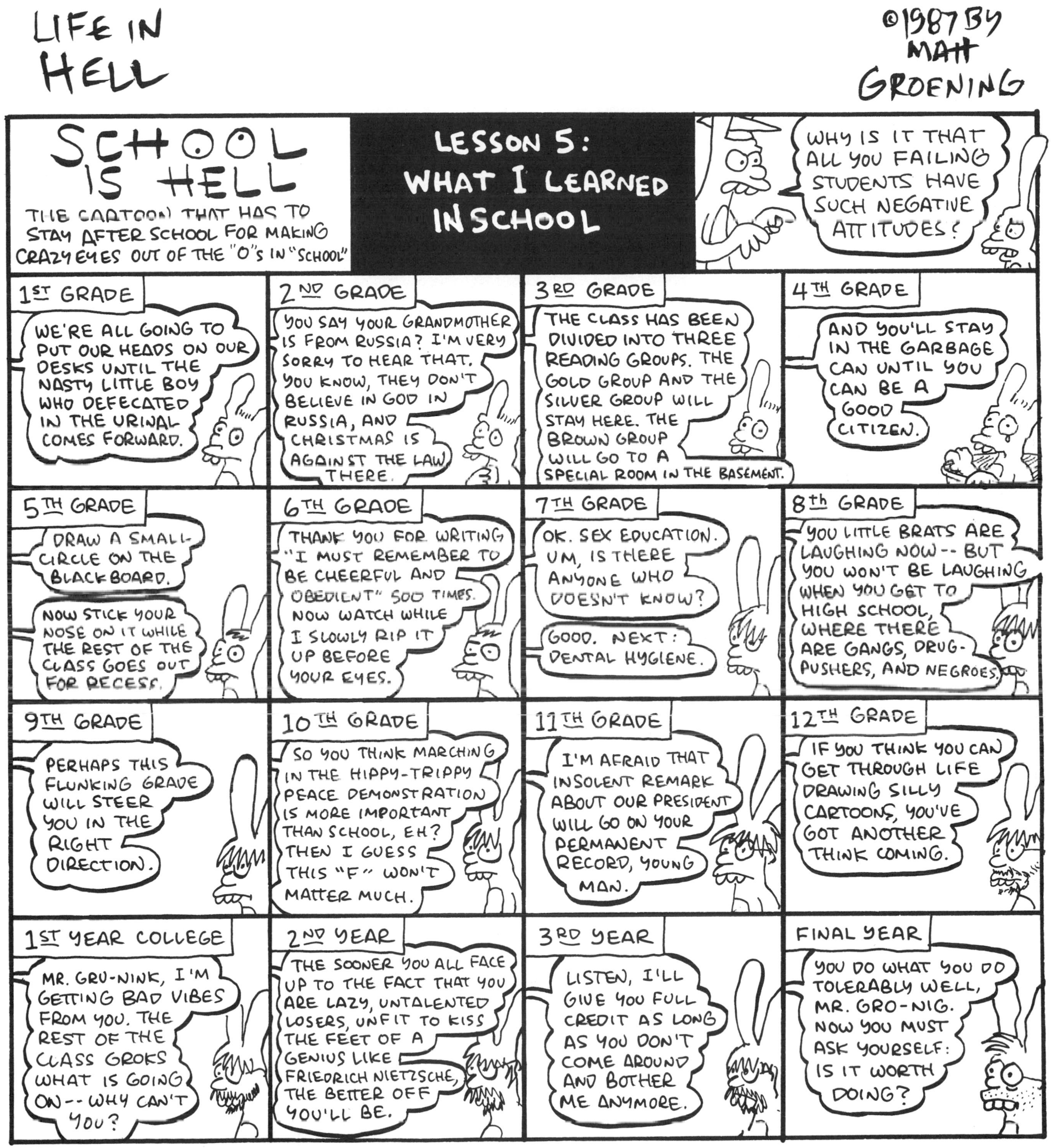
LIFE IN HELL
©1987 BY MATT GROENING
SCHOOL IS HELL
THE CARTOON THAT HAS TO STAY AFTER SCHOOL FOR MAKING CRAZY EYES OUT OF THE "O"s IN "SCHOOL"
LESSON 5: WHAT I LEARNED IN SCHOOL
WHY IS IT THAT ALL YOU FAILING STUDENTS HAVE SUCH NEGATIVE ATTITUDES?
1ST GRADE
WE'RE ALL GOING TO PUT OUR HEADS ON OUR DESKS UNTIL THE NASTY LITTLE BOY WHO DEFECATED IN THE URINAL COMES FORWARD.
2ND GRADE
YOU SAY YOUR GRANDMOTHER IS FROM RUSSIA? I'M VERY SORRY TO HEAR THAT. YOU KNOW, THEY DON'T BELIEVE IN GOD IN RUSSIA, AND CHRISTMAS IS AGAINST THE LAW THERE.
3RD GRADE
THE CLASS HAS BEEN DIVIDED INTO THREE READING GROUPS. THE GOLD GROUP AND THE SILVER GROUP WILL STAY HERE. THE BROWN GROUP WILL GO TO A SPECIAL ROOM IN THE BASEMENT.
4TH GRADE
AND YOU'LL STAY IN THE GARBAGE CAN UNTIL YOU CAN BE A GOOD CITIZEN.
5TH GRADE
DRAW A SMALL CIRCLE ON THE BLACKBOARD.
NOW STICK YOUR NOSE ON IT WHILE THE REST OF THE CLASS GOES OUT FOR RECESS.
6TH GRADE
THANK YOU FOR WRITING "I MUST REMEMBER TO BE CHEERFUL AND OBEDIENT" 500 TIMES. NOW WATCH WHILE I SLOWLY RIP IT UP BEFORE YOUR EYES.
7TH GRADE
OK. SEX EDUCATION. UM, IS THERE ANYONE WHO DOESN'T KNOW?
GOOD. NEXT: DENTAL HYGIENE.
8TH GRADE
YOU LITTLE BRATS ARE LAUGHING NOW -- BUT YOU WON'T BE LAUGHING WHEN YOU GET TO HIGH SCHOOL, WHERE THERE ARE GANGS, DRUG-PUSHERS, AND NEGROES.
9TH GRADE
PERHAPS THIS FLUNKING GRADE WILL STEER YOU IN THE RIGHT DIRECTION.
10TH GRADE
SO YOU THINK MARCHING IN THE HIPPY-TRIPPY PEACE DEMONSTRATION IS MORE IMPORTANT THAN SCHOOL, EH? THEN I GUESS THIS "F" WON'T MATTER MUCH.
11TH GRADE
I'M AFRAID THAT INSOLENT REMARK ABOUT OUR PRESIDENT WILL GO ON YOUR PERMANENT RECORD, YOUNG MAN.
12TH GRADE
IF YOU THINK YOU CAN GET THROUGH LIFE DRAWING SILLY CARTOONS, YOU'VE GOT ANOTHER THINK COMING.
1ST YEAR COLLEGE
MR. GRU-NINK, I'M GETTING BAD VIBES FROM YOU. THE REST OF THE CLASS GROKS WHAT IS GOING ON -- WHY CAN'T YOU?
2ND YEAR
THE SOONER YOU ALL FACE UP TO THE FACT THAT YOU ARE LAZY, UNTALENTED LOSERS, UNFIT TO KISS THE FEET OF A GENIUS LIKE FRIEDRICH NIETZSCHE, THE BETTER OFF YOU'LL BE.
3RD YEAR
LISTEN, I'LL GIVE YOU FULL CREDIT AS LONG AS YOU DON'T COME AROUND AND BOTHER ME ANYMORE.
FINAL YEAR
YOU DO WHAT YOU DO TOLERABLY WELL, MR. GRO-NIG. NOW YOU MUST ASK YOURSELF: IS IT WORTH DOING?

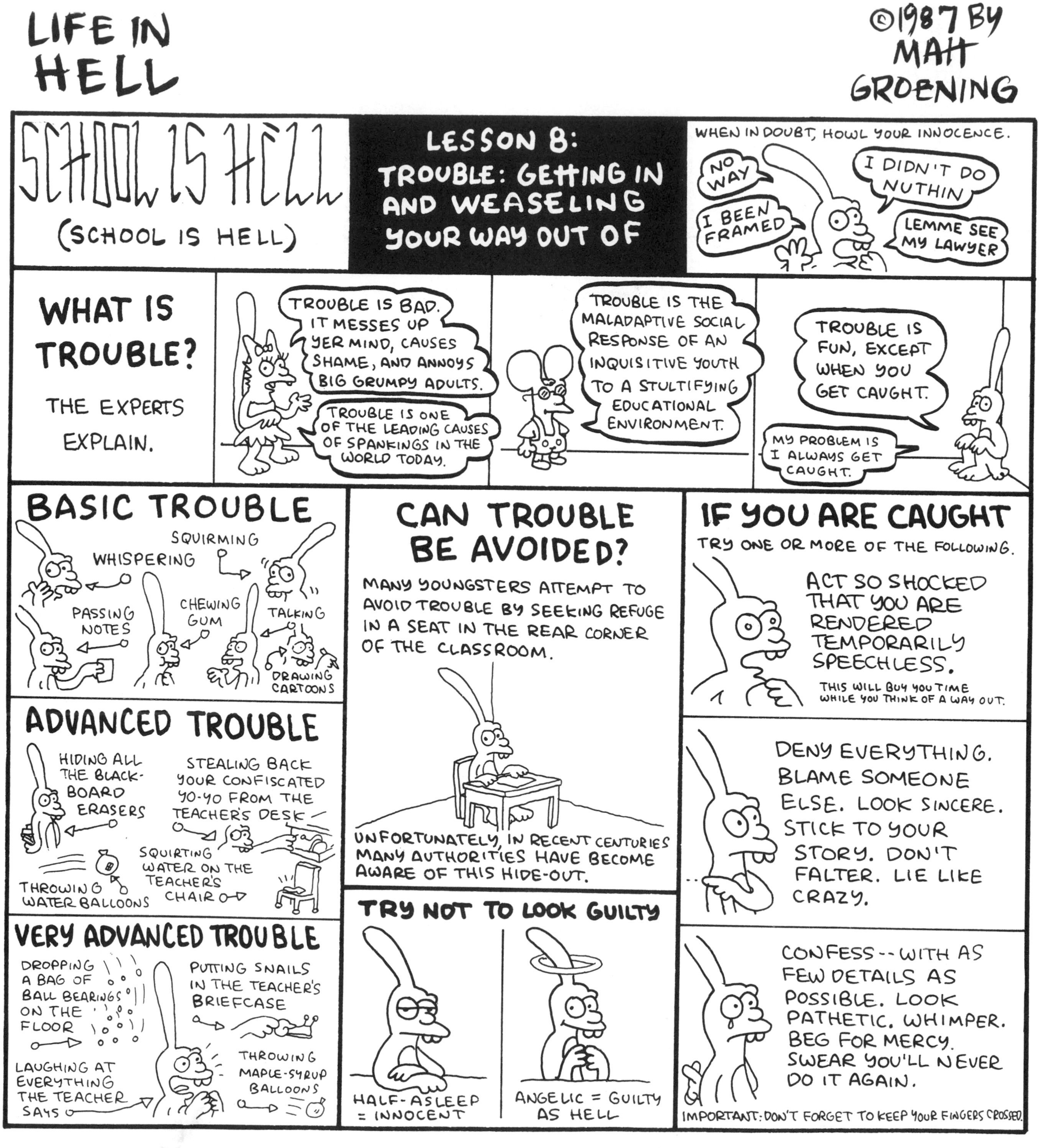

LIFE IN HELL
©1987 BY MATT GROENING
SCHOOL IS HELL
(SCHOOL IS HELL)
LESSON 8: TROUBLE: GETTING IN AND WEASELING YOUR WAY OUT OF
WHEN IN DOUBT, HOWL YOUR INNOCENCE.
NO WAY
I DIDN'T DO NUTHIN
I BEEN FRAMED
LEMME SEE MY LAWYER
WHAT IS TROUBLE?
THE EXPERTS EXPLAIN.
TROUBLE IS BAD. IT MESSES UP YER MIND, CAUSES SHAME, AND ANNOYS BIG GRUMPY ADULTS.
TROUBLE IS ONE OF THE LEADING CAUSES OF SPANKINGS IN THE WORLD TODAY.
TROUBLE IS THE MALADAPTIVE SOCIAL RESPONSE OF AN INQUISITIVE YOUTH TO A STULTIFYING EDUCATIONAL ENVIRONMENT.
TROUBLE IS FUN, EXCEPT WHEN YOU GET CAUGHT.
MY PROBLEM IS I ALWAYS GET CAUGHT.
BASIC TROUBLE
SQUIRMING
WHISPERING
PASSING NOTES
CHEWING GUM
TALKING
DRAWING CARTOONS
ADVANCED TROUBLE
HIDING ALL THE BLACKBOARD ERASERS
STEALING BACK YOUR CONFISCATED YO-YO FROM THE TEACHER'S DESK
SQUIRTING WATER ON THE TEACHER'S CHAIR
THROWING WATER BALLOONS
VERY ADVANCED TROUBLE
DROPPING A BAG OF BALL BEARINGS ON THE FLOOR
PUTTING SNAILS IN THE TEACHER'S BRIEFCASE
LAUGHING AT EVERYTHING THE TEACHER SAYS
THROWING MAPLE-SYRUP BALLOONS
CAN TROUBLE BE AVOIDED?
MANY YOUNGSTERS ATTEMPT TO AVOID TROUBLE BY SEEKING REFUGE IN A SEAT IN THE REAR CORNER OF THE CLASSROOM.
UNFORTUNATELY, IN RECENT CENTURIES MANY AUTHORITIES HAVE BECOME AWARE OF THIS HIDE-OUT.
TRY NOT TO LOOK GUILTY
HALF-ASLEEP = INNOCENT
ANGELIC = GUILTY AS HELL
IF YOU ARE CAUGHT
TRY ONE OR MORE OF THE FOLLOWING.
ACT SO SHOCKED THAT YOU ARE RENDERED TEMPORARILY SPEECHLESS.
THIS WILL BUY YOU TIME WHILE YOU THINK OF A WAY OUT.
DENY EVERYTHING. BLAME SOMEONE ELSE. LOOK SINCERE. STICK TO YOUR STORY. DON'T FALTER. LIE LIKE CRAZY.
CONFESS--WITH AS FEW DETAILS AS POSSIBLE. LOOK PATHETIC. WHIMPER. BEG FOR MERCY. SWEAR YOU'LL NEVER DO IT AGAIN.
IMPORTANT: DON'T FORGET TO KEEP YOUR FINGERS CROSSED.

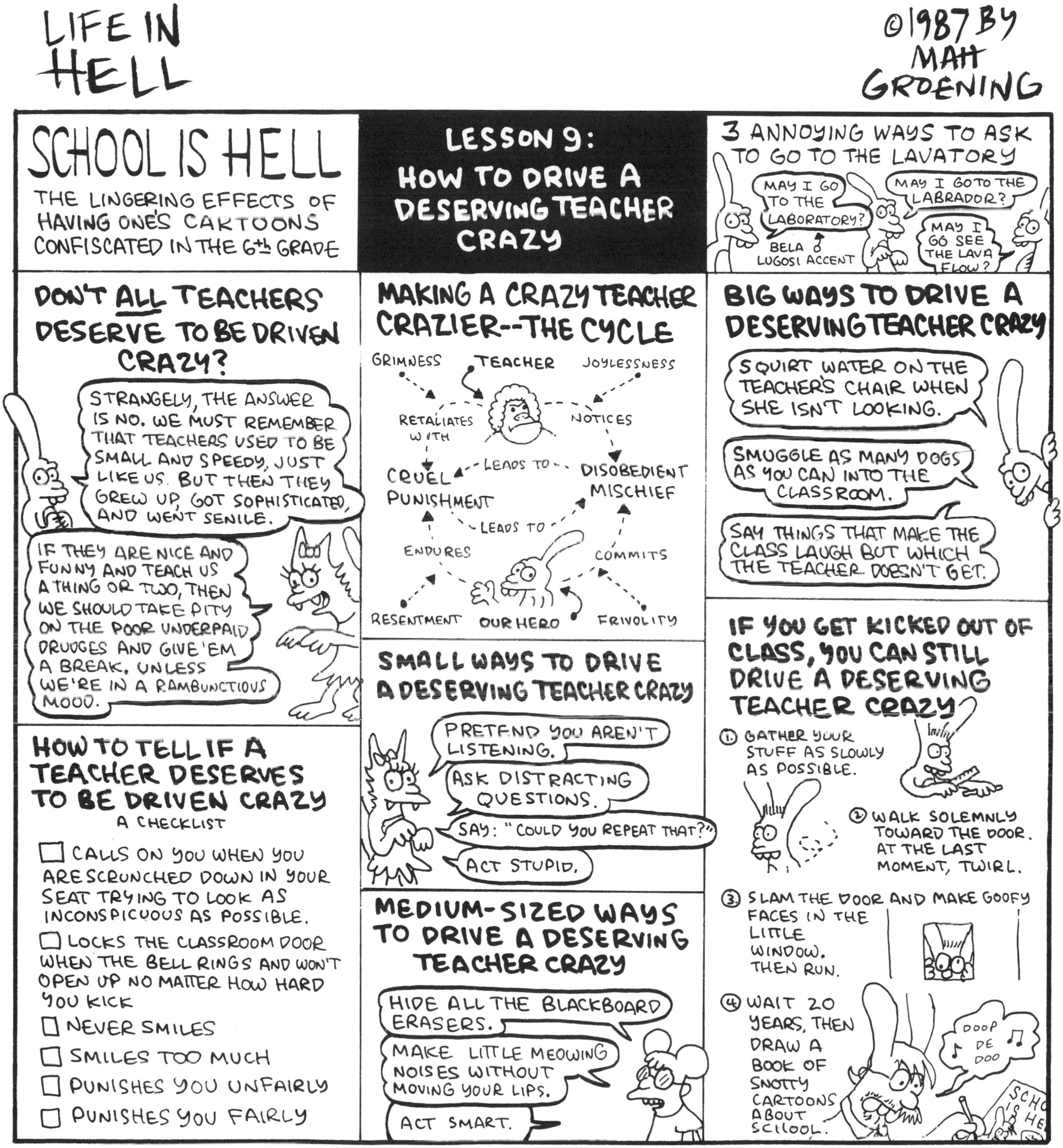
LIFE IN HELL
©1987 BY MATT GROENING
SCHOOL IS HELL
THE LINGERING EFFECTS OF HAVING ONE'S CARTOONS CONFISCATED IN THE 6th GRADE
LESSON 9: HOW TO DRIVE A DESERVING TEACHER CRAZY
3 ANNOYING WAYS TO ASK TO GO TO THE LAVATORY
MAY I GO TO THE LABORATORY?
BELA LUGOSI ACCENT
MAY I GO TO THE LABRADOR?
MAY I GO SEE THE LAVA FLOW?
DON'T ALL TEACHERS DESERVE TO BE DRIVEN CRAZY?
STRANGELY, THE ANSWER IS NO. WE MUST REMEMBER THAT TEACHERS USED TO BE SMALL AND SPEEDY, JUST LIKE US. BUT THEN THEY GREW UP, GOT SOPHISTICATED, AND WENT SENILE.
IF THEY ARE NICE AND FUNNY AND TEACH US A THING OR TWO, THEN WE SHOULD TAKE PITY ON THE POOR UNDERPAID DRUDGES AND GIVE 'EM A BREAK, UNLESS WE'RE IN A RAMBUNCTIOUS MOOD.
MAKING A CRAZY TEACHER CRAZIER--THE CYCLE
GRIMNESS
TEACHER
JOYLESSNESS
RETALIATES WITH
NOTICES
LEADS TO
CRUEL PUNISHMENT
DISOBEDIENT MISCHIEF
LEADS TO
ENDURES
COMMITS
RESENTMENT
OUR HERO
FRIVOLITY
BIG WAYS TO DRIVE A DESERVING TEACHER CRAZY
SQUIRT WATER ON THE TEACHER'S CHAIR WHEN SHE ISN'T LOOKING.
SMUGGLE AS MANY DOGS AS YOU CAN INTO THE CLASSROOM.
SAY THINGS THAT MAKE THE CLASS LAUGH BUT WHICH THE TEACHER DOESN'T GET.
SMALL WAYS TO DRIVE A DESERVING TEACHER CRAZY
PRETEND YOU AREN'T LISTENING.
ASK DISTRACTING QUESTIONS.
SAY: "COULD YOU REPEAT THAT?"
ACT STUPID.
IF YOU GET KICKED OUT OF CLASS, YOU CAN STILL DRIVE A DESERVING TEACHER CRAZY
1. GATHER YOUR STUFF AS SLOWLY AS POSSIBLE.
2. WALK SOLEMNLY TOWARD THE DOOR. AT THE LAST MOMENT, TWIRL.
3. SLAM THE DOOR AND MAKE GOOFY FACES IN THE LITTLE WINDOW. THEN RUN.
4. WAIT 20 YEARS, THEN DRAW A BOOK OF SNOTTY CARTOONS ABOUT SCHOOL.
DOOP DE DOO
HOW TO TELL IF A TEACHER DESERVES TO BE DRIVEN CRAZY
A CHECKLIST
☐ CALLS ON YOU WHEN YOU ARE SCRUNCHED DOWN IN YOUR SEAT TRYING TO LOOK AS INCONSPICUOUS AS POSSIBLE.
☐ LOCKS THE CLASSROOM DOOR WHEN THE BELL RINGS AND WON'T OPEN UP NO MATTER HOW HARD YOU KICK
☐ NEVER SMILES
☐ SMILES TOO MUCH
☐ PUNISHES YOU UNFAIRLY
☐ PUNISHES YOU FAIRLY
MEDIUM-SIZED WAYS TO DRIVE A DESERVING TEACHER CRAZY
HIDE ALL THE BLACKBOARD ERASERS.
MAKE LITTLE MEOWING NOISES WITHOUT MOVING YOUR LIPS.
ACT SMART.

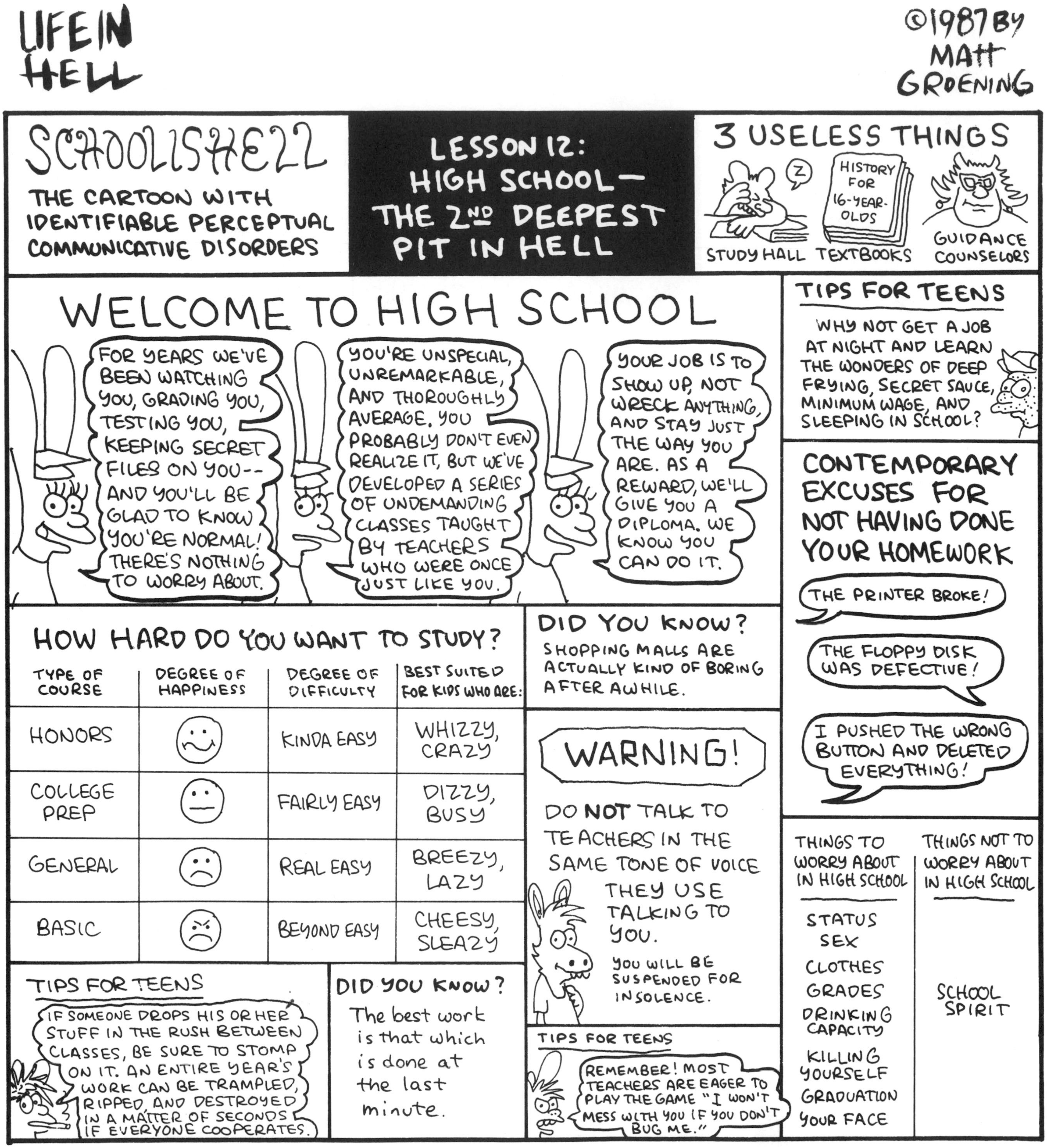
LIFE IN HELL
©1987 BY MATT GROENING
SCHOOL IS HELL
THE CARTOON WITH IDENTIFIABLE PERCEPTUAL COMMUNICATIVE DISORDERS
LESSON 12: HIGH SCHOOL— THE 2ND DEEPEST PIT IN HELL
3 USELESS THINGS
Z
STUDY HALL
HISTORY FOR 16-YEAR-OLDS
TEXTBOOKS
GUIDANCE COUNSELORS
WELCOME TO HIGH SCHOOL
FOR YEARS WE'VE BEEN WATCHING YOU, GRADING YOU, TESTING YOU, KEEPING SECRET FILES ON YOU-- AND YOU'LL BE GLAD TO KNOW YOU'RE NORMAL! THERE'S NOTHING TO WORRY ABOUT.
YOU'RE UNSPECIAL, UNREMARKABLE, AND THOROUGHLY AVERAGE. YOU PROBABLY DON'T EVEN REALIZE IT, BUT WE'VE DEVELOPED A SERIES OF UNDEMANDING CLASSES TAUGHT BY TEACHERS WHO WERE ONCE JUST LIKE YOU.
YOUR JOB IS TO SHOW UP, NOT WRECK ANYTHING, AND STAY JUST THE WAY YOU ARE. AS A REWARD, WE'LL GIVE YOU A DIPLOMA. WE KNOW YOU CAN DO IT.
TIPS FOR TEENS
WHY NOT GET A JOB AT NIGHT AND LEARN THE WONDERS OF DEEP FRYING, SECRET SAUCE, MINIMUM WAGE, AND SLEEPING IN SCHOOL?
CONTEMPORARY EXCUSES FOR NOT HAVING DONE YOUR HOMEWORK
THE PRINTER BROKE!
THE FLOPPY DISK WAS DEFECTIVE!
I PUSHED THE WRONG BUTTON AND DELETED EVERYTHING!
HOW HARD DO YOU WANT TO STUDY?
TYPE OF COURSE | DEGREE OF HAPPINESS | DEGREE OF DIFFICULTY | BEST SUITED FOR KIDS WHO ARE:
HONORS | KINDA EASY | WHIZZY, CRAZY
COLLEGE PREP | FAIRLY EASY | DIZZY, BUSY
GENERAL | REAL EASY | BREEZY, LAZY
BASIC | BEYOND EASY | CHEESY, SLEAZY
DID YOU KNOW?
SHOPPING MALLS ARE ACTUALLY KIND OF BORING AFTER AWHILE.
WARNING!
DO NOT TALK TO TEACHERS IN THE SAME TONE OF VOICE THEY USE TALKING TO YOU.
YOU WILL BE SUSPENDED FOR INSOLENCE.
THINGS TO WORRY ABOUT IN HIGH SCHOOL
STATUS
SEX
CLOTHES
GRADES
DRINKING CAPACITY
KILLING YOURSELF
GRADUATION
YOUR FACE
THINGS NOT TO WORRY ABOUT IN HIGH SCHOOL
SCHOOL SPIRIT
TIPS FOR TEENS
IF SOMEONE DROPS HIS OR HER STUFF IN THE RUSH BETWEEN CLASSES, BE SURE TO STOMP ON IT. AN ENTIRE YEAR'S WORK CAN BE TRAMPLED, RIPPED, AND DESTROYED IN A MATTER OF SECONDS IF EVERYONE COOPERATES.
DID YOU KNOW?
The best work is that which is done at the last minute.
TIPS FOR TEENS
REMEMBER! MOST TEACHERS ARE EAGER TO PLAY THE GAME "I WON'T MESS WITH YOU IF YOU DON'T BUG ME."

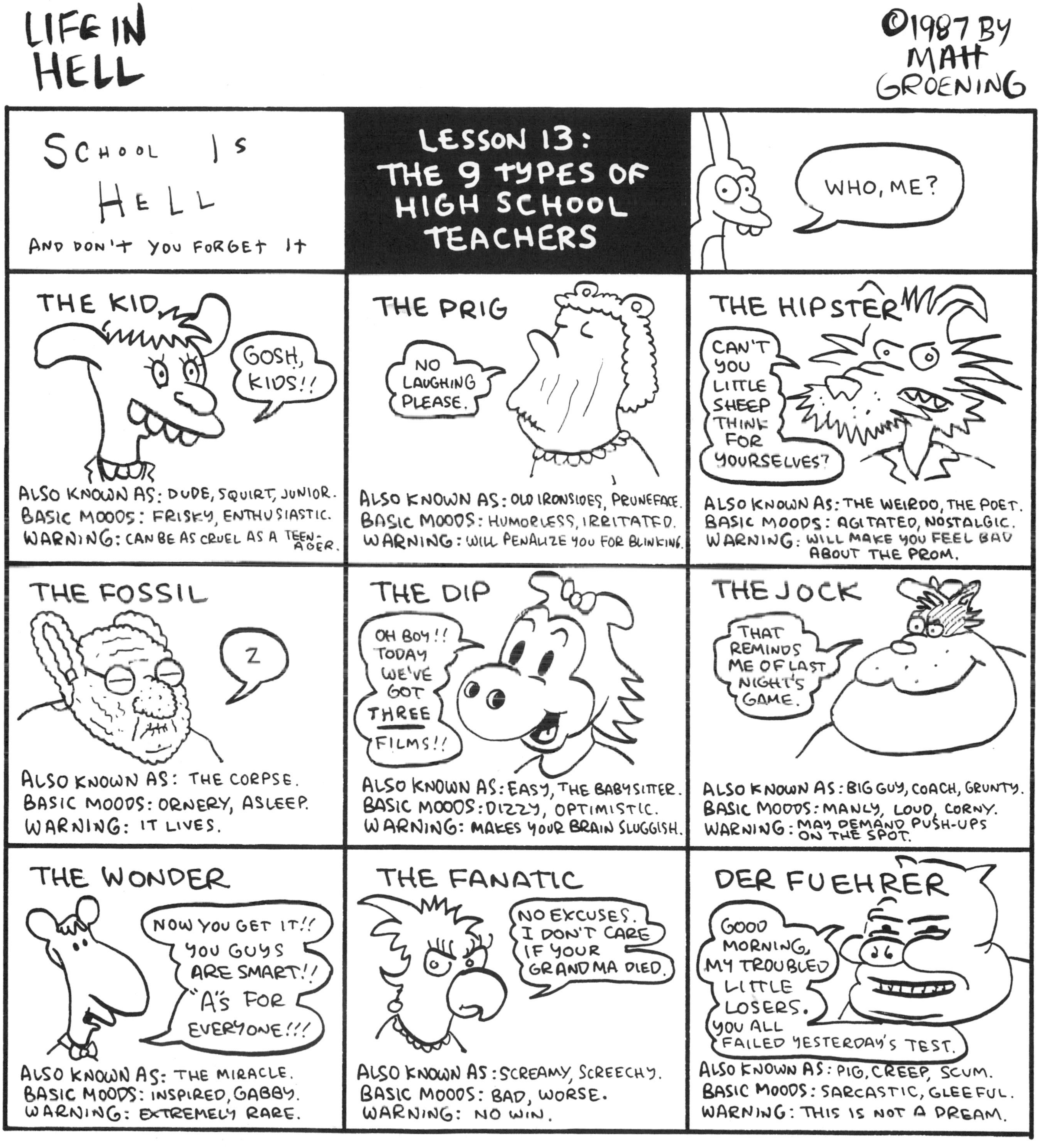
LIFE IN HELL
©1987 BY MATT GROENING
SCHOOL IS HELL
AND DON'T YOU FORGET IT
LESSON 13: THE 9 TYPES OF HIGH SCHOOL TEACHERS
WHO, ME?
THE KID
GOSH, KIDS!!
ALSO KNOWN AS: DUDE, SQUIRT, JUNIOR.
BASIC MOODS: FRISKY, ENTHUSIASTIC.
WARNING: CAN BE AS CRUEL AS A TEEN-AGER.
THE PRIG
NO LAUGHING PLEASE.
ALSO KNOWN AS: OLD IRONSIDES, PRUNEFACE.
BASIC MOODS: HUMORLESS, IRRITATED.
WARNING: WILL PENALIZE YOU FOR BLINKING.
THE HIPSTER
CAN'T YOU LITTLE SHEEP THINK FOR YOURSELVES?
ALSO KNOWN AS: THE WEIRDO, THE POET.
BASIC MOODS: AGITATED, NOSTALGIC.
WARNING: WILL MAKE YOU FEEL BAD ABOUT THE PROM.
THE FOSSIL
Z
ALSO KNOWN AS: THE CORPSE.
BASIC MOODS: ORNERY, ASLEEP.
WARNING: IT LIVES.
THE DIP
OH BOY!! TODAY WE'VE GOT THREE FILMS!!
ALSO KNOWN AS: EASY, THE BABYSITTER.
BASIC MOODS: DIZZY, OPTIMISTIC.
WARNING: MAKES YOUR BRAIN SLUGGISH.
THE JOCK
THAT REMINDS ME OF LAST NIGHT'S GAME.
ALSO KNOWN AS: BIG GUY, COACH, GRUNTY.
BASIC MOODS: MANLY, LOUD, CORNY.
WARNING: MAY DEMAND PUSH-UPS ON THE SPOT.
THE WONDER
NOW YOU GET IT!! YOU GUYS ARE SMART!! "A'S FOR EVERYONE!!!
ALSO KNOWN AS: THE MIRACLE.
BASIC MOODS: INSPIRED, GABBY.
WARNING: EXTREMELY RARE.
THE FANATIC
NO EXCUSES. I DON'T CARE IF YOUR GRANDMA DIED.
ALSO KNOWN AS: SCREAMY, SCREECHY.
BASIC MOODS: BAD, WORSE.
WARNING: NO WIN.
DER FUEHRER
GOOD MORNING, MY TROUBLED LITTLE LOSERS. YOU ALL FAILED YESTERDAY'S TEST.
ALSO KNOWN AS: PIG, CREEP, SCUM.
BASIC MOODS: SARCASTIC, GLEEFUL.
WARNING: THIS IS NOT A DREAM.

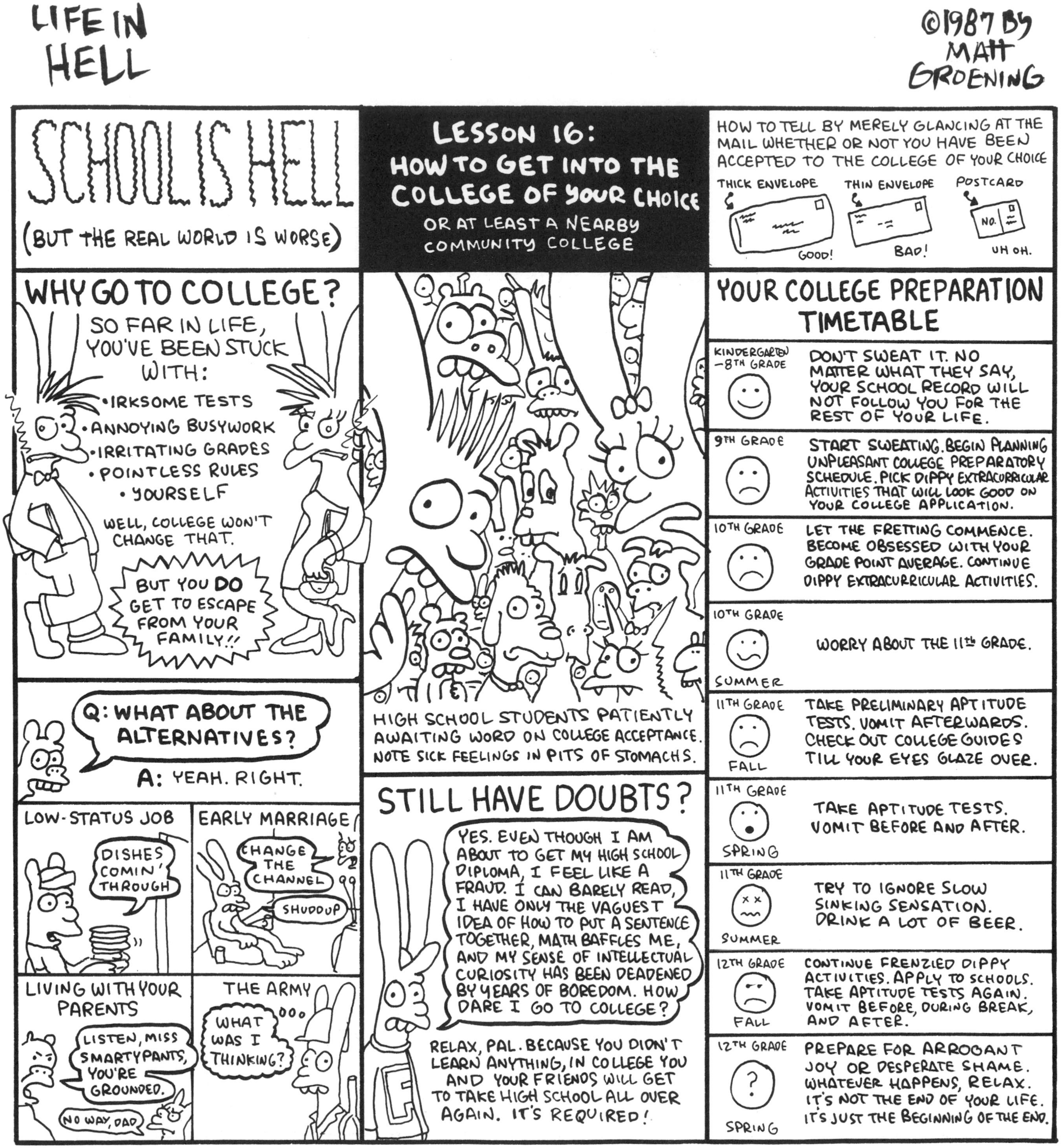
LIFE IN HELL
©1987 BY MATT GROENING
SCHOOL IS HELL
(BUT THE REAL WORLD IS WORSE)
LESSON 16: HOW TO GET INTO THE COLLEGE OF YOUR CHOICE
OR AT LEAST A NEARBY COMMUNITY COLLEGE
HOW TO TELL BY MERELY GLANCING AT THE MAIL WHETHER OR NOT YOU HAVE BEEN ACCEPTED TO THE COLLEGE OF YOUR CHOICE
THICK ENVELOPE
THIN ENVELOPE
POSTCARD
NO.
GOOD!
BAD!
UH OH.
WHY GO TO COLLEGE?
SO FAR IN LIFE, YOU'VE BEEN STUCK WITH:
•IRKSOME TESTS
•ANNOYING BUSYWORK
•IRRITATING GRADES
•POINTLESS RULES
•YOURSELF
WELL, COLLEGE WON'T CHANGE THAT.
BUT YOU DO GET TO ESCAPE FROM YOUR FAMILY!!
HIGH SCHOOL STUDENTS PATIENTLY AWAITING WORD ON COLLEGE ACCEPTANCE. NOTE SICK FEELINGS IN PITS OF STOMACHS.
YOUR COLLEGE PREPARATION TIMETABLE
KINDERGARTEN –8TH GRADE
DON'T SWEAT IT. NO MATTER WHAT THEY SAY, YOUR SCHOOL RECORD WILL NOT FOLLOW YOU FOR THE REST OF YOUR LIFE.
9TH GRADE
START SWEATING. BEGIN PLANNING UNPLEASANT COLLEGE PREPARATORY SCHEDULE. PICK DIPPY EXTRACURRICULAR ACTIVITIES THAT WILL LOOK GOOD ON YOUR COLLEGE APPLICATION.
10TH GRADE
LET THE FRETTING COMMENCE. BECOME OBSESSED WITH YOUR GRADE POINT AVERAGE. CONTINUE DIPPY EXTRACURRICULAR ACTIVITIES.
10TH GRADE SUMMER
WORRY ABOUT THE 11TH GRADE.
11TH GRADE FALL
TAKE PRELIMINARY APTITUDE TESTS. VOMIT AFTERWARDS. CHECK OUT COLLEGE GUIDES TILL YOUR EYES GLAZE OVER.
11TH GRADE SPRING
TAKE APTITUDE TESTS. VOMIT BEFORE AND AFTER.
11TH GRADE SUMMER
TRY TO IGNORE SLOW SINKING SENSATION. DRINK A LOT OF BEER.
12TH GRADE FALL
CONTINUE FRENZIED DIPPY ACTIVITIES. APPLY TO SCHOOLS. TAKE APTITUDE TESTS AGAIN. VOMIT BEFORE, DURING BREAK, AND AFTER.
12TH GRADE SPRING
PREPARE FOR ARROGANT JOY OR DESPERATE SHAME. WHATEVER HAPPENS, RELAX. IT'S NOT THE END OF YOUR LIFE. IT'S JUST THE BEGINNING OF THE END.
Q: WHAT ABOUT THE ALTERNATIVES?
A: YEAH. RIGHT.
LOW-STATUS JOB
DISHES COMIN' THROUGH
EARLY MARRIAGE
CHANGE THE CHANNEL
SHUDDUP
LIVING WITH YOUR PARENTS
LISTEN, MISS SMARTYPANTS, YOU'RE GROUNDED.
NO WAY, DAD
THE ARMY
WHAT WAS I THINKING?
STILL HAVE DOUBTS?
YES. EVEN THOUGH I AM ABOUT TO GET MY HIGH SCHOOL DIPLOMA, I FEEL LIKE A FRAUD. I CAN BARELY READ, I HAVE ONLY THE VAGUEST IDEA OF HOW TO PUT A SENTENCE TOGETHER, MATH BAFFLES ME, AND MY SENSE OF INTELLECTUAL CURIOSITY HAS BEEN DEADENED BY YEARS OF BOREDOM. HOW DARE I GO TO COLLEGE?
RELAX, PAL. BECAUSE YOU DIDN'T LEARN ANYTHING IN COLLEGE YOU AND YOUR FRIENDS WILL GET TO TAKE HIGH SCHOOL ALL OVER AGAIN. IT'S REQUIRED!

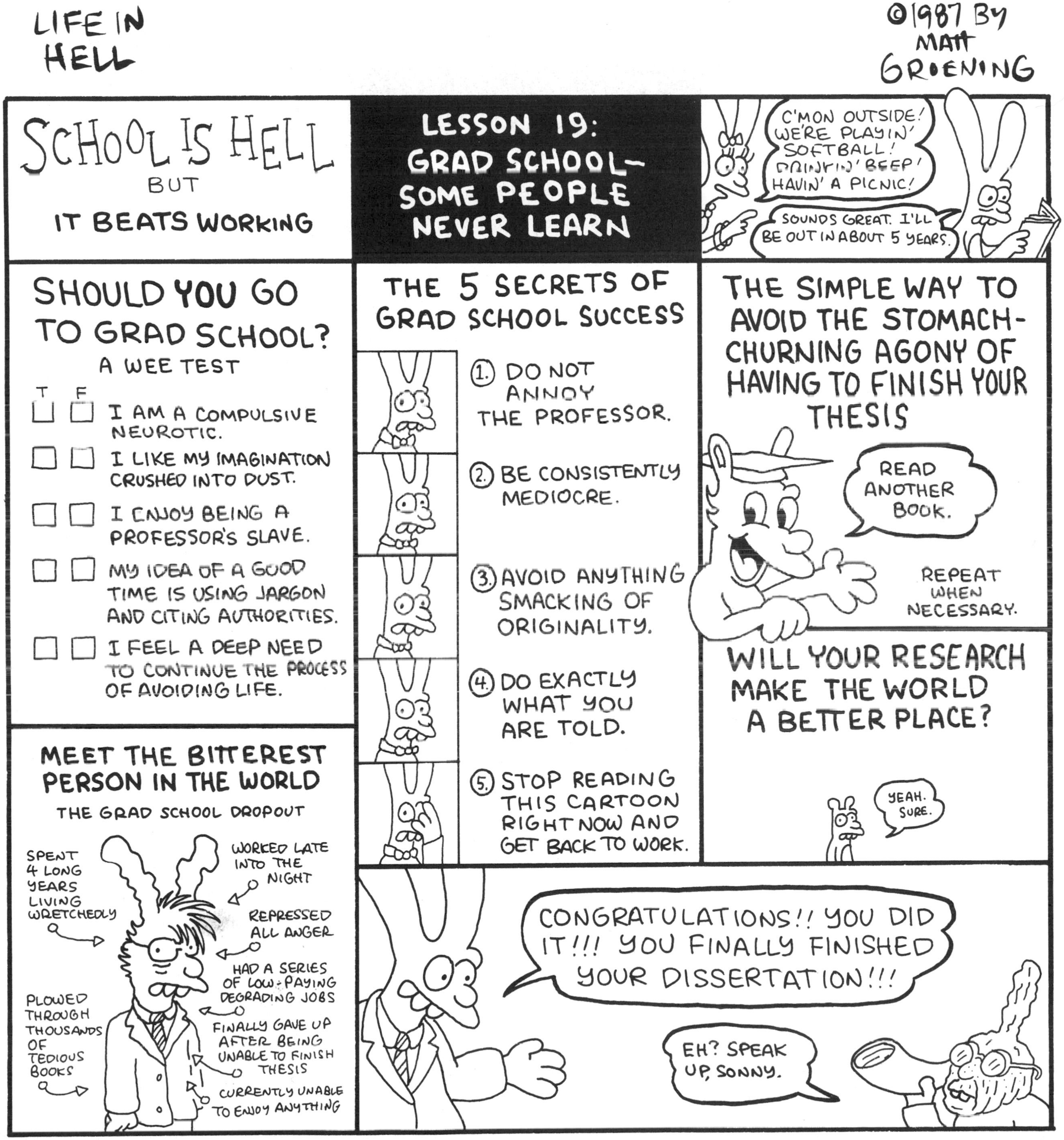

LIFE IN HELL
©1987 BY MATT GROENING
SCHOOL IS HELL BUT IT BEATS WORKING
LESSON 19: GRAD SCHOOL— SOME PEOPLE NEVER LEARN
C'MON OUTSIDE! WE'RE PLAYIN' SOFTBALL! DRINKIN' BEER! HAVIN' A PICNIC!
SOUNDS GREAT. I'LL BE OUT IN ABOUT 5 YEARS.
SHOULD YOU GO TO GRAD SCHOOL? A WEE TEST
T F
I AM A COMPULSIVE NEUROTIC.
I LIKE MY IMAGINATION CRUSHED INTO DUST.
I ENJOY BEING A PROFESSOR'S SLAVE.
MY IDEA OF A GOOD TIME IS USING JARGON AND CITING AUTHORITIES.
I FEEL A DEEP NEED TO CONTINUE THE PROCESS OF AVOIDING LIFE.
THE 5 SECRETS OF GRAD SCHOOL SUCCESS
1. DO NOT ANNOY THE PROFESSOR.
2. BE CONSISTENTLY MEDIOCRE.
3. AVOID ANYTHING SMACKING OF ORIGINALITY.
4. DO EXACTLY WHAT YOU ARE TOLD.
5. STOP READING THIS CARTOON RIGHT NOW AND GET BACK TO WORK.
THE SIMPLE WAY TO AVOID THE STOMACH-CHURNING AGONY OF HAVING TO FINISH YOUR THESIS
READ ANOTHER BOOK.
REPEAT WHEN NECESSARY.
WILL YOUR RESEARCH MAKE THE WORLD A BETTER PLACE?
YEAH. SURE.
MEET THE BITTEREST PERSON IN THE WORLD
THE GRAD SCHOOL DROPOUT
SPENT 4 LONG YEARS LIVING WRETCHEDLY
WORKED LATE INTO THE NIGHT
REPRESSED ALL ANGER
HAD A SERIES OF LOW-PAYING DEGRADING JOBS
PLOWED THROUGH THOUSANDS OF TEDIOUS BOOKS
FINALLY GAVE UP AFTER BEING UNABLE TO FINISH THESIS
CURRENTLY UNABLE TO ENJOY ANYTHING
CONGRATULATIONS!! YOU DID IT!!! YOU FINALLY FINISHED YOUR DISSERTATION!!!
EH? SPEAK UP, SONNY.

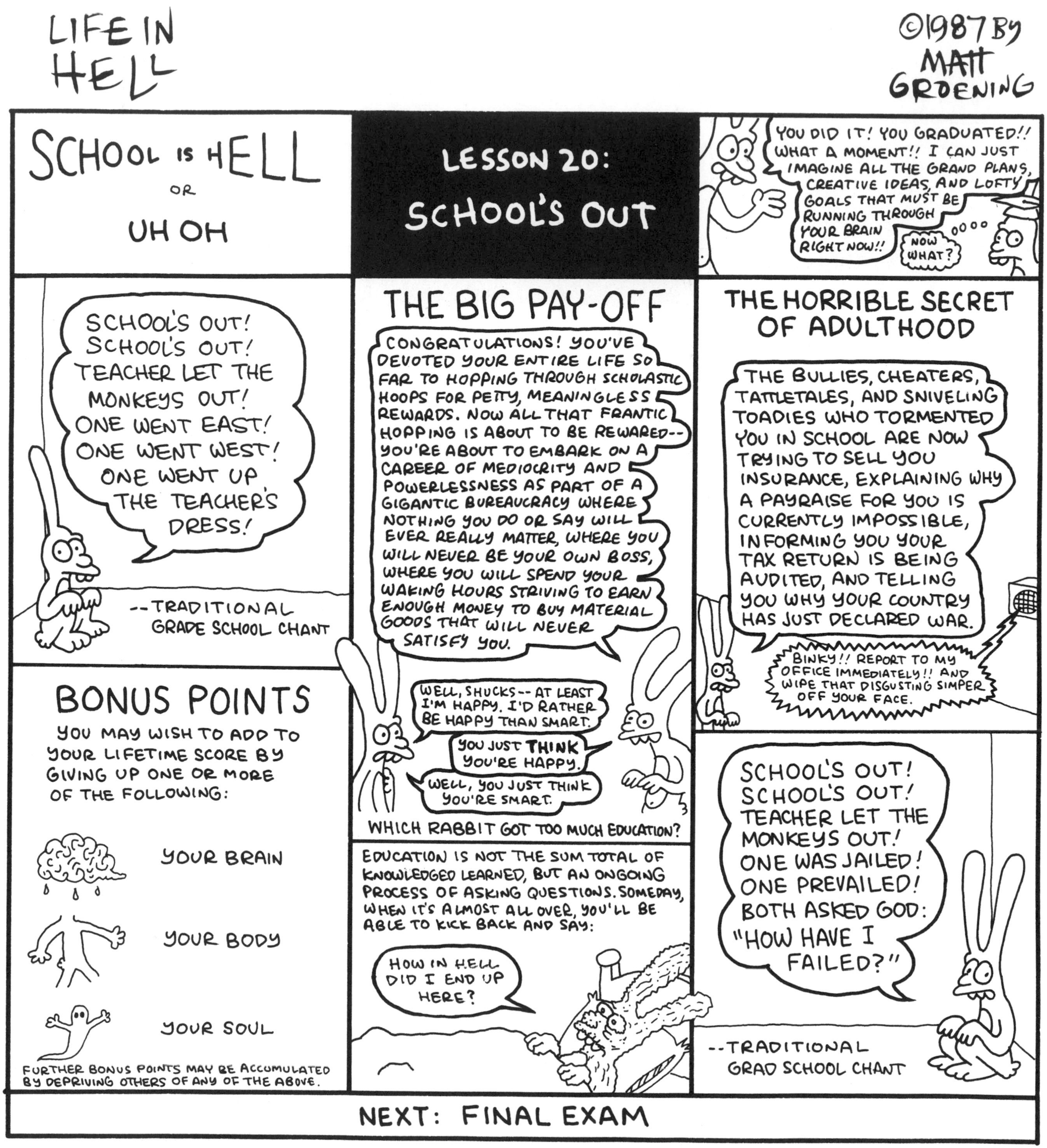
LIFE IN HELL
©1987 BY MATT GROENING
SCHOOL IS HELL
OR
UH OH
LESSON 20:
SCHOOL'S OUT
YOU DID IT! YOU GRADUATED!! WHAT A MOMENT!! I CAN JUST IMAGINE ALL THE GRAND PLANS, CREATIVE IDEAS, AND LOFTY GOALS THAT MUST BE RUNNING THROUGH YOUR BRAIN RIGHT NOW!!
OOOO
NOW WHAT?
SCHOOL'S OUT! SCHOOL'S OUT! TEACHER LET THE MONKEYS OUT! ONE WENT EAST! ONE WENT WEST! ONE WENT UP THE TEACHER'S DRESS!
--TRADITIONAL GRADE SCHOOL CHANT
THE BIG PAY-OFF
CONGRATULATIONS! YOU'VE DEVOTED YOUR ENTIRE LIFE SO FAR TO HOPPING THROUGH SCHOLASTIC HOOPS FOR PETTY, MEANINGLESS REWARDS. NOW ALL THAT FRANTIC HOPPING IS ABOUT TO BE REWARED-- YOU'RE ABOUT TO EMBARK ON A CAREER OF MEDIOCRITY AND POWERLESSNESS AS PART OF A GIGANTIC BUREAUCRACY WHERE NOTHING YOU DO OR SAY WILL EVER REALLY MATTER, WHERE YOU WILL NEVER BE YOUR OWN BOSS, WHERE YOU WILL SPEND YOUR WAKING HOURS STRIVING TO EARN ENOUGH MONEY TO BUY MATERIAL GOODS THAT WILL NEVER SATISFY YOU.
WELL, SHUCKS-- AT LEAST I'M HAPPY. I'D RATHER BE HAPPY THAN SMART.
YOU JUST THINK YOU'RE HAPPY.
WELL, YOU JUST THINK YOU'RE SMART.
WHICH RABBIT GOT TOO MUCH EDUCATION?
THE HORRIBLE SECRET OF ADULTHOOD
THE BULLIES, CHEATERS, TATTLETALES, AND SNIVELING TOADIES WHO TORMENTED YOU IN SCHOOL ARE NOW TRYING TO SELL YOU INSURANCE, EXPLAINING WHY A PAYRAISE FOR YOU IS CURRENTLY IMPOSSIBLE, INFORMING YOU YOUR TAX RETURN IS BEING AUDITED, AND TELLING YOU WHY YOUR COUNTRY HAS JUST DECLARED WAR.
BINKY!! REPORT TO MY OFFICE IMMEDIATELY!! AND WIPE THAT DISGUSTING SIMPER OFF YOUR FACE.
BONUS POINTS
YOU MAY WISH TO ADD TO YOUR LIFETIME SCORE BY GIVING UP ONE OR MORE OF THE FOLLOWING:
YOUR BRAIN
YOUR BODY
YOUR SOUL
FURTHER BONUS POINTS MAY BE ACCUMULATED BY DEPRIVING OTHERS OF ANY OF THE ABOVE.
EDUCATION IS NOT THE SUM TOTAL OF KNOWLEDGED LEARNED, BUT AN ONGOING PROCESS OF ASKING QUESTIONS. SOMEDAY, WHEN IT'S ALMOST ALL OVER, YOU'LL BE ABLE TO KICK BACK AND SAY:
HOW IN HELL DID I END UP HERE?
SCHOOL'S OUT! SCHOOL'S OUT! TEACHER LET THE MONKEYS OUT! ONE WAS JAILED! ONE PREVAILED! BOTH ASKED GOD: "HOW HAVE I FAILED?"
--TRADITIONAL GRAD SCHOOL CHANT
NEXT: FINAL EXAM

LIFE IN HELL

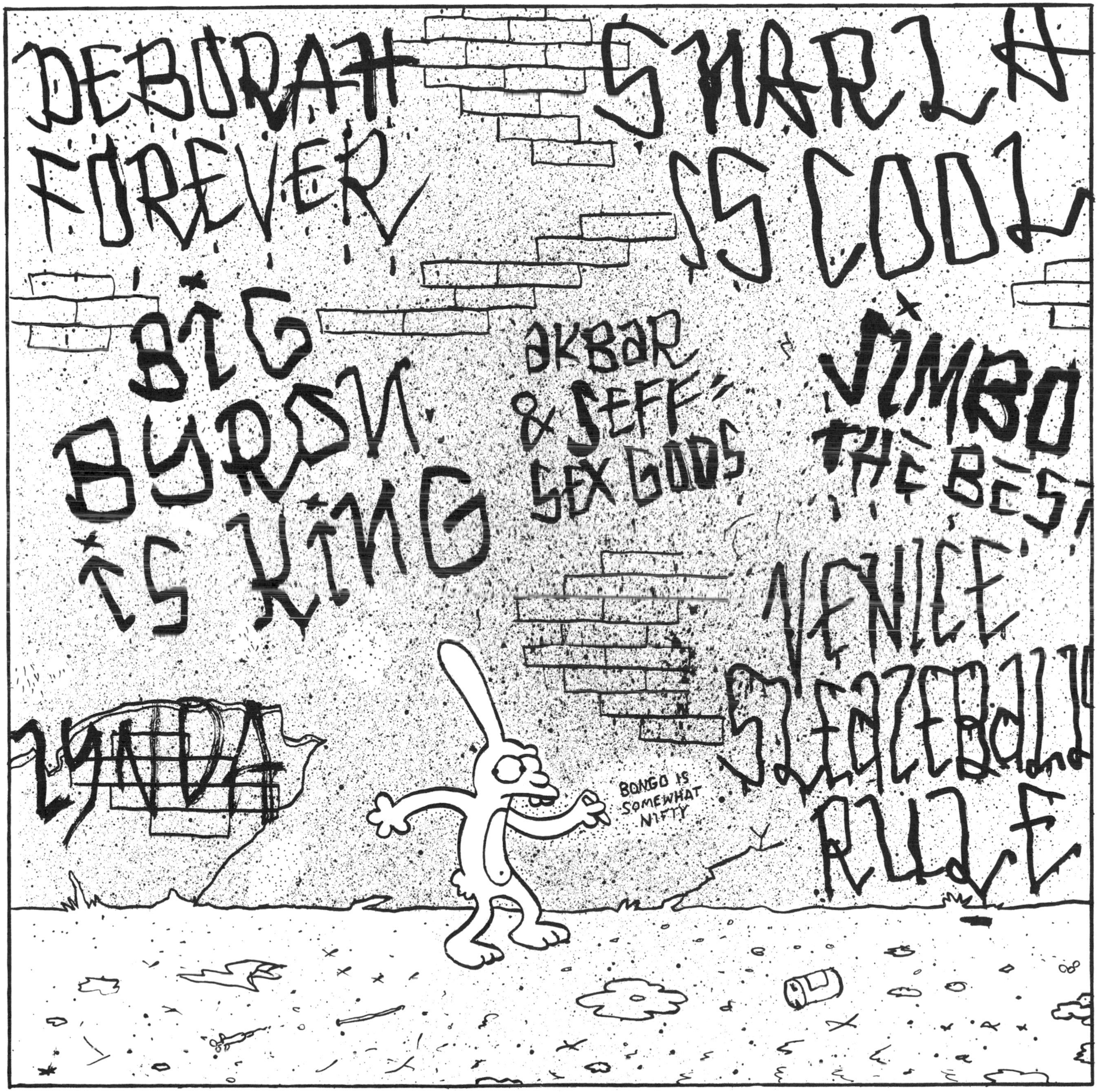
DEBORAH FOREVER
SHARLA IS COOL
BIG BYRON IS KING
AKBAR & JEFF SEX GODS
JIMBO THE BEST
VENICE SLEAZEBALLS RULE
LYNDA
BONGO IS SOMEWHAT NIFTY

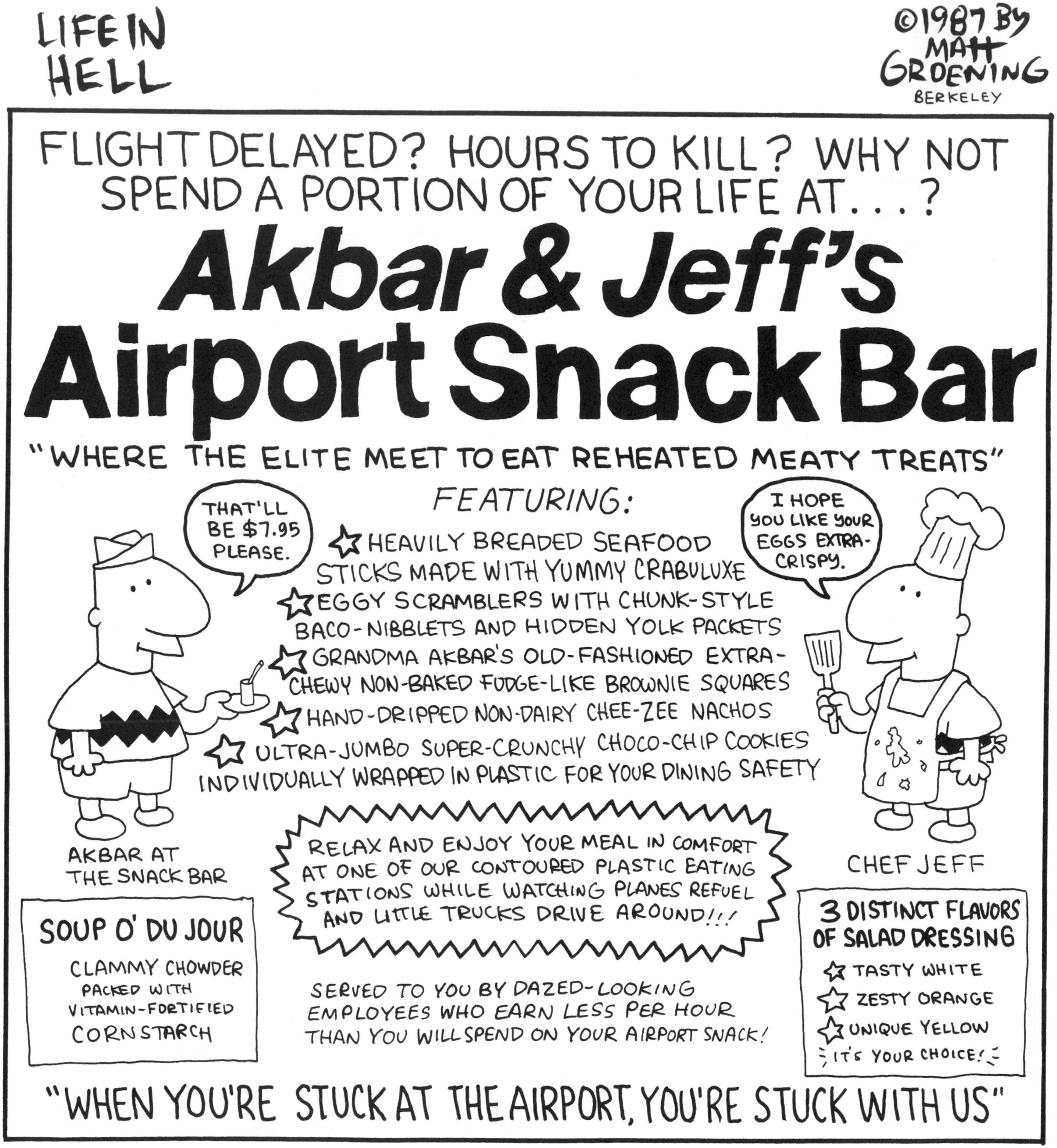
LIFE IN HELL
©1987 BY MATT GROENING
BERKELEY
FLIGHT DELAYED? HOURS TO KILL? WHY NOT SPEND A PORTION OF YOUR LIFE AT...?
Akbar & Jeff's Airport Snack Bar
"WHERE THE ELITE MEET TO EAT REHEATED MEATY TREATS"
FEATURING:
THAT'LL BE $7.95 PLEASE.
I HOPE YOU LIKE YOUR EGGS EXTRA-CRISPY.
HEAVILY BREADED SEAFOOD STICKS MADE WITH YUMMY CRABULUXE
EGGY SCRAMBLERS WITH CHUNK-STYLE BACO-NIBBLETS AND HIDDEN YOLK PACKETS
GRANDMA AKBAR'S OLD-FASHIONED EXTRA-CHEWY NON-BAKED FUDGE-LIKE BROWNIE SQUARES
HAND-DRIPPED NON-DAIRY CHEE-ZEE NACHOS
ULTRA-JUMBO SUPER-CRUNCHY CHOCO-CHIP COOKIES INDIVIDUALLY WRAPPED IN PLASTIC FOR YOUR DINING SAFETY
AKBAR AT THE SNACK BAR
RELAX AND ENJOY YOUR MEAL IN COMFORT AT ONE OF OUR CONTOURED PLASTIC EATING STATIONS WHILE WATCHING PLANES REFUEL AND LITTLE TRUCKS DRIVE AROUND!!!
CHEF JEFF
SOUP O' DU JOUR
CLAMMY CHOWDER PACKED WITH VITAMIN-FORTIFIED CORNSTARCH
SERVED TO YOU BY DAZED-LOOKING EMPLOYEES WHO EARN LESS PER HOUR THAN YOU WILL SPEND ON YOUR AIRPORT SNACK!
3 DISTINCT FLAVORS OF SALAD DRESSING
TASTY WHITE
ZESTY ORANGE
UNIQUE YELLOW
IT'S YOUR CHOICE!
"WHEN YOU'RE STUCK AT THE AIRPORT, YOU'RE STUCK WITH US"

LIFE IN HELL

THE DOG ATE "SCHOOL IS HELL" THIS WEEK

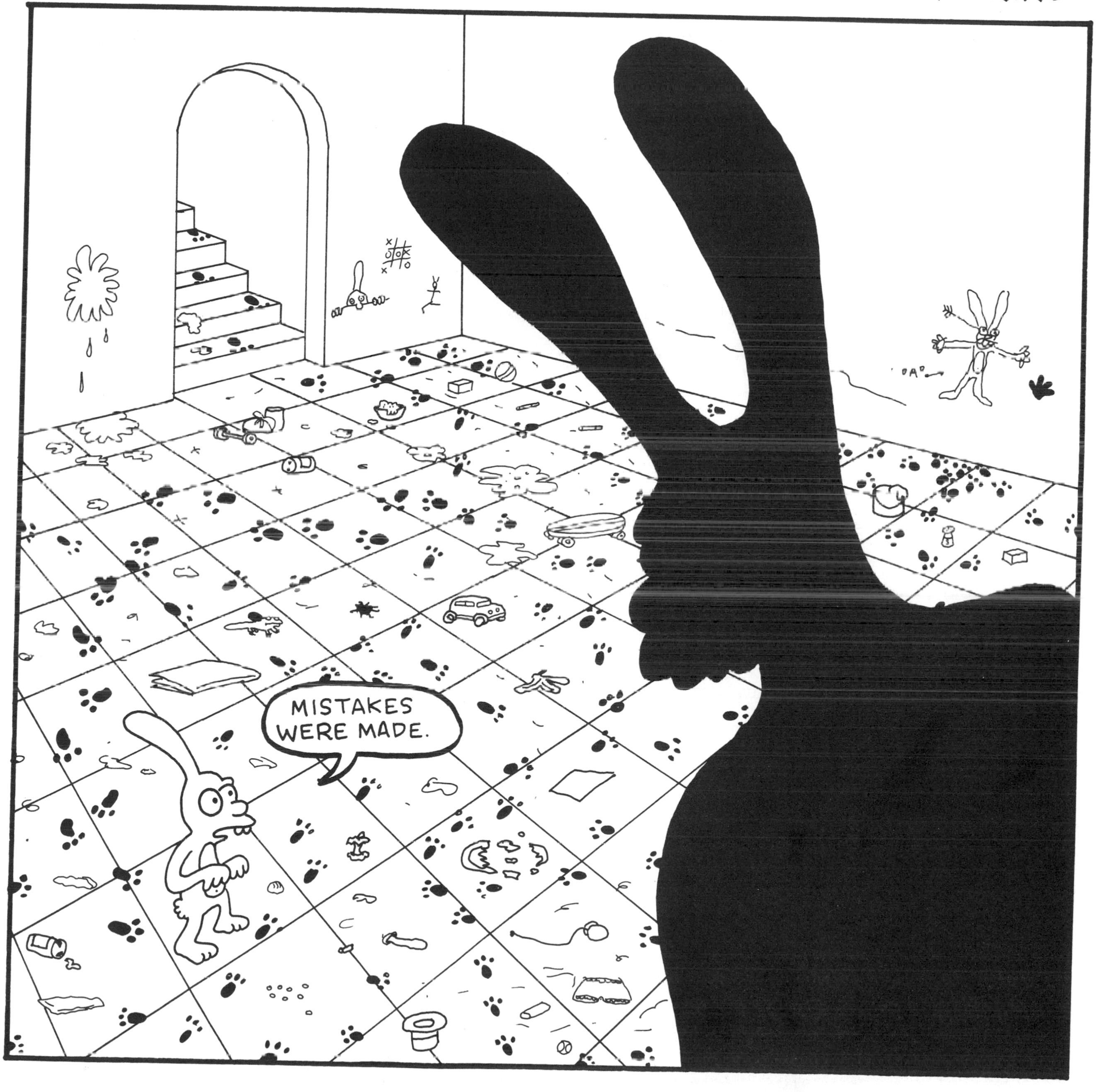
MISTAKES WERE MADE.

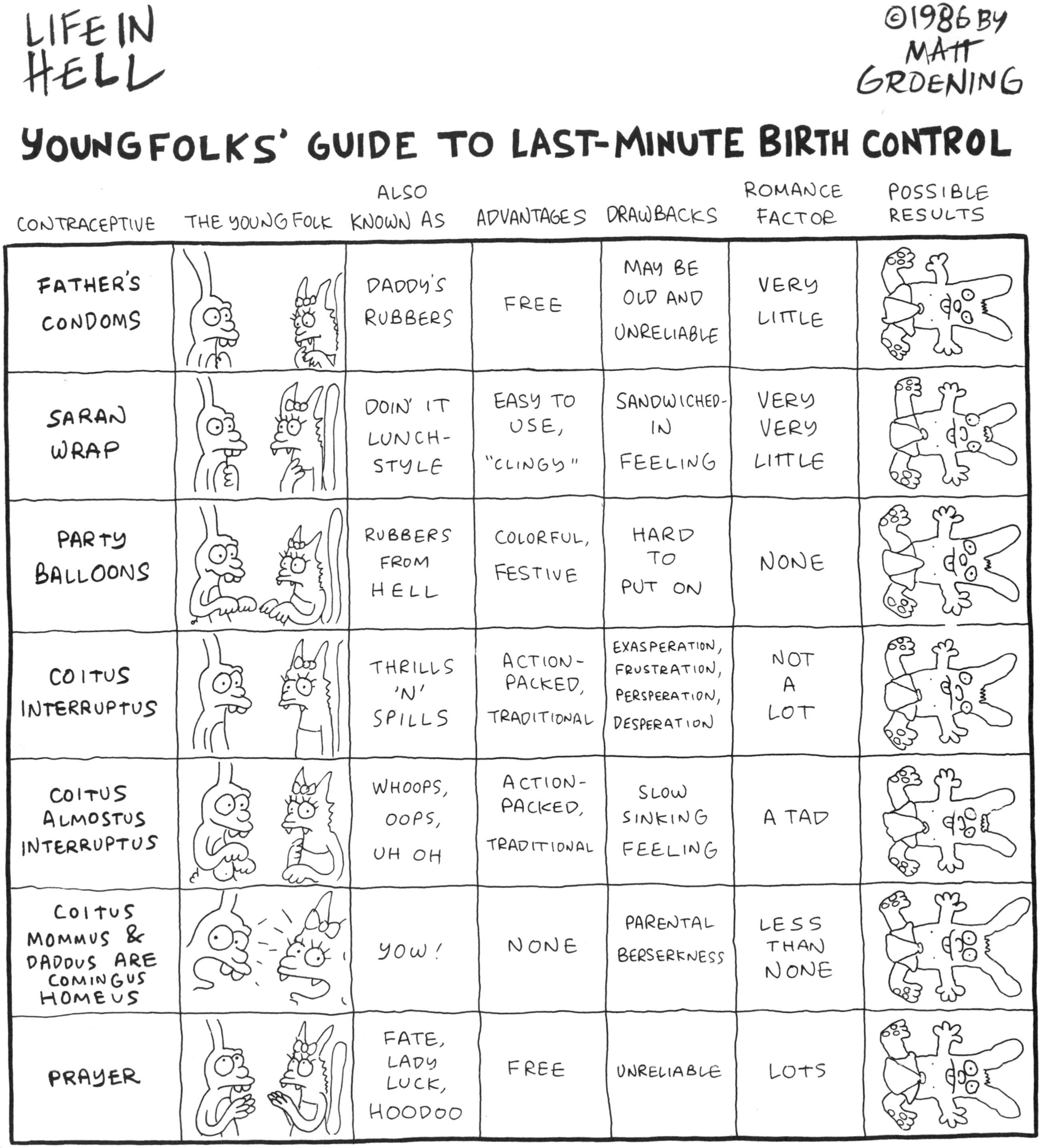
LIFE IN HELL
©1986 BY MATT GROENING
YOUNGFOLKS' GUIDE TO LAST-MINUTE BIRTH CONTROL
CONTRACEPTIVE
THE YOUNG FOLK
ALSO KNOWN AS
ADVANTAGES
DRAWBACKS
ROMANCE FACTOR
POSSIBLE RESULTS
FATHER'S CONDOMS
DADDY'S RUBBERS
FREE
MAY BE OLD AND UNRELIABLE
VERY LITTLE
SARAN WRAP
DOIN' IT LUNCH-STYLE
EASY TO USE, "CLINGY"
SANDWICHED-IN FEELING
VERY VERY LITTLE
PARTY BALLOONS
RUBBERS FROM HELL
COLORFUL, FESTIVE
HARD TO PUT ON
NONE
COITUS INTERRUPTUS
THRILLS 'N' SPILLS
ACTION-PACKED, TRADITIONAL
EXASPERATION, FRUSTRATION, PERSPERATION, DESPERATION
NOT A LOT
COITUS ALMOSTUS INTERRUPTUS
WHOOPS, OOPS, UH OH
ACTION-PACKED, TRADITIONAL
SLOW SINKING FEELING
A TAD
COITUS MOMMUS & DADDUS ARE COMINGUS HOMEUS
YOW!
NONE
PARENTAL BERSERKNESS
LESS THAN NONE
PRAYER
FATE, LADY LUCK, HOODOO
FREE
UNRELIABLE
LOTS

LIFE IN HELL

©1987 BY MATT GROENING

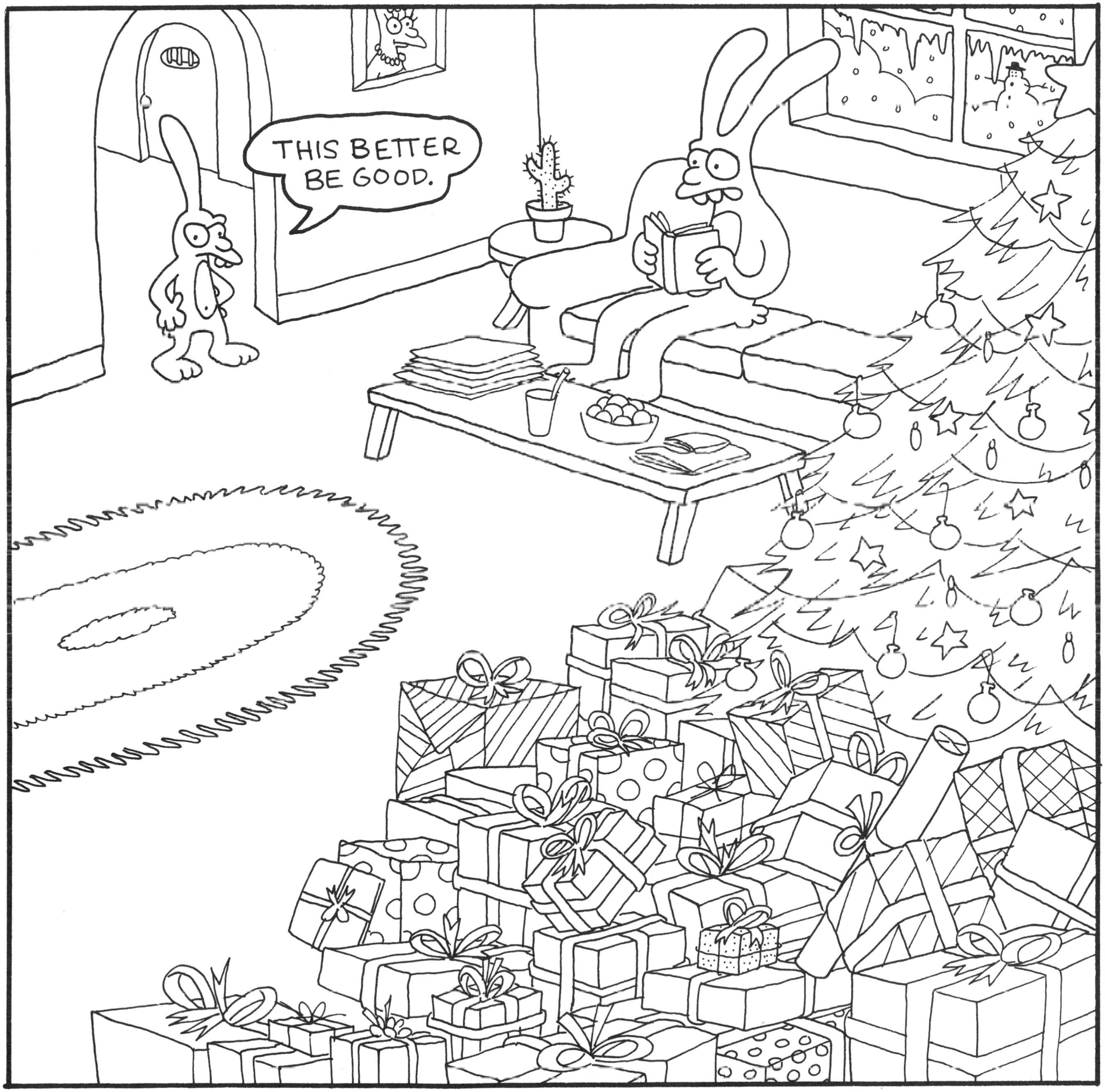
THIS BETTER BE GOOD.

XMAS IS HELL

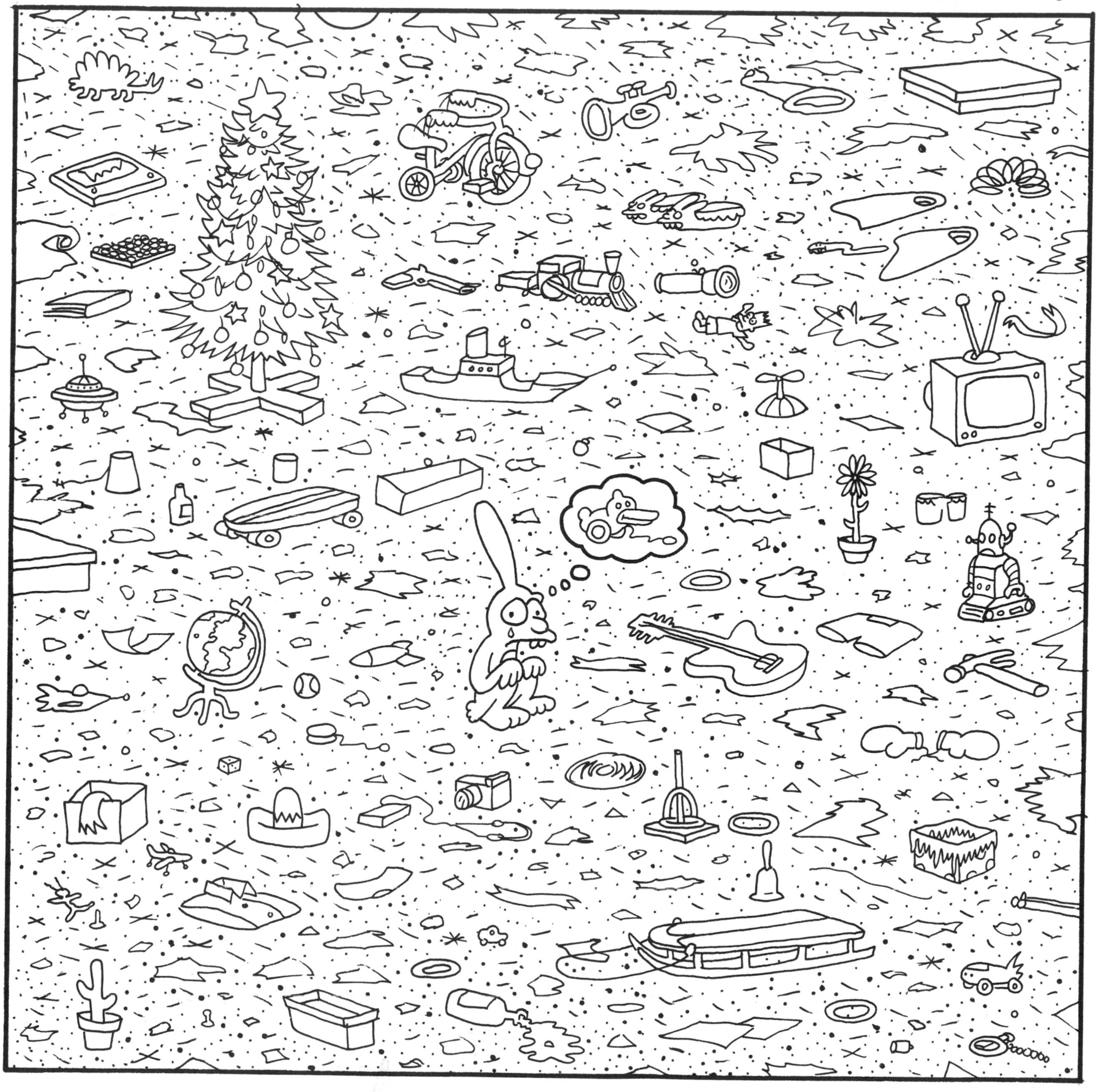

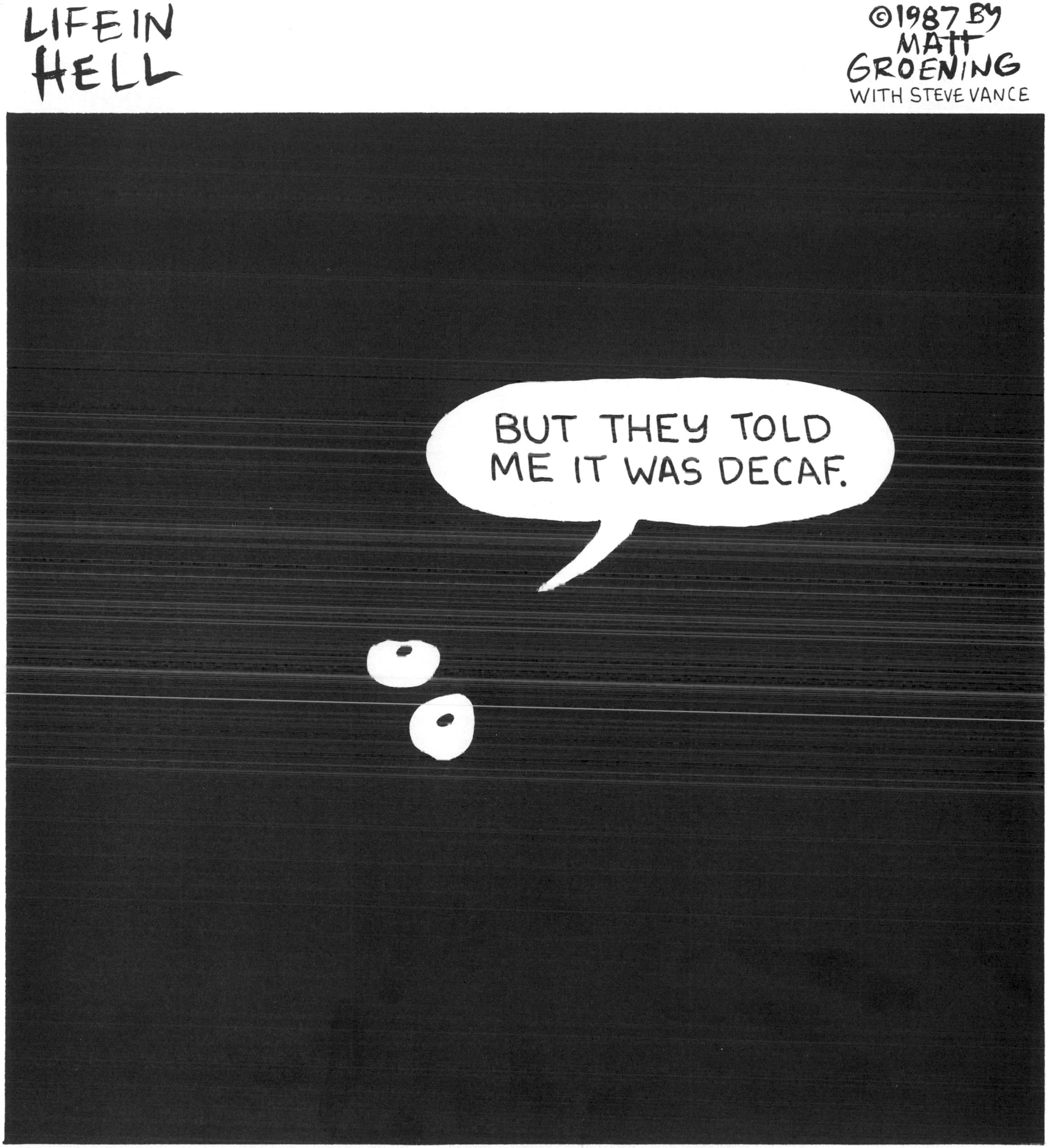
LIFE IN HELL
©1987 BY MATT GROENING
WITH STEVE VANCE
BUT THEY TOLD ME IT WAS DECAF.

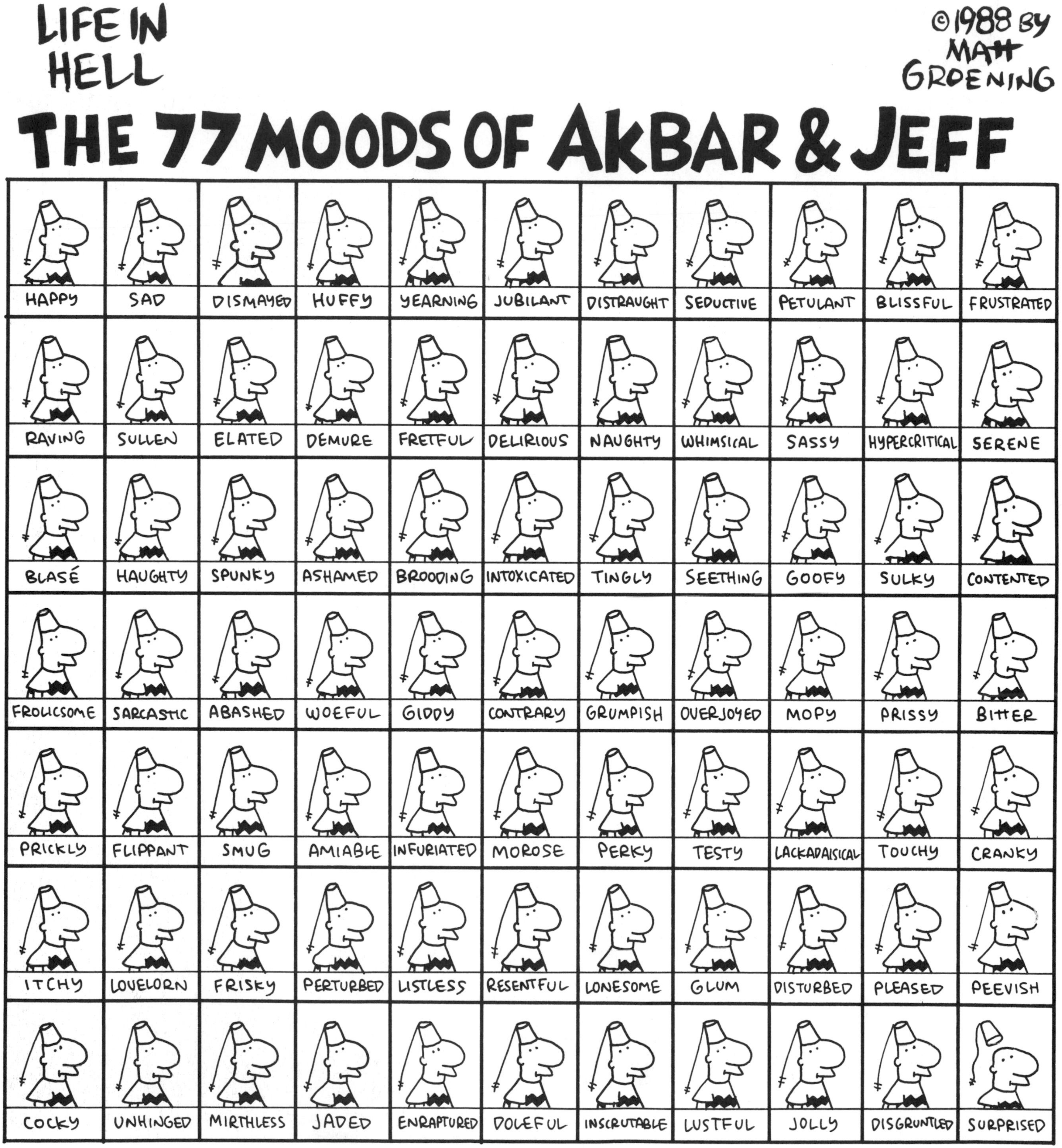
LIFE IN HELL
©1988 BY MATT GROENING
THE 77 MOODS OF AKBAR & JEFF
HAPPY
SAD
DISMAYED
HUFFY
YEARNING
JUBILANT
DISTRAUGHT
SEDUCTIVE
PETULANT
BLISSFUL
FRUSTRATED
RAVING
SULLEN
ELATED
DEMURE
FRETFUL
DELIRIOUS
NAUGHTY
WHIMSICAL
SASSY
HYPERCRITICAL
SERENE
BLASÉ
HAUGHTY
SPUNKY
ASHAMED
BROODING
INTOXICATED
TINGLY
SEETHING
GOOFY
SULKY
CONTENTED
FROLICSOME
SARCASTIC
ABASHED
WOEFUL
GIDDY
CONTRARY
GRUMPISH
OVERJOYED
MOPY
PRISSY
BITTER
PRICKLY
FLIPPANT
SMUG
AMIABLE
INFURIATED
MOROSE
PERKY
TESTY
LACKADAISICAL
TOUCHY
CRANKY
ITCHY
LOVELORN
FRISKY
PERTURBED
LISTLESS
RESENTFUL
LONESOME
GLUM
DISTURBED
PLEASED
PEEVISH
COCKY
UNHINGED
MIRTHLESS
JADED
ENRAPTURED
DOLEFUL
INSCRUTABLE
LUSTFUL
JOLLY
DISGRUNTLED
SURPRISED

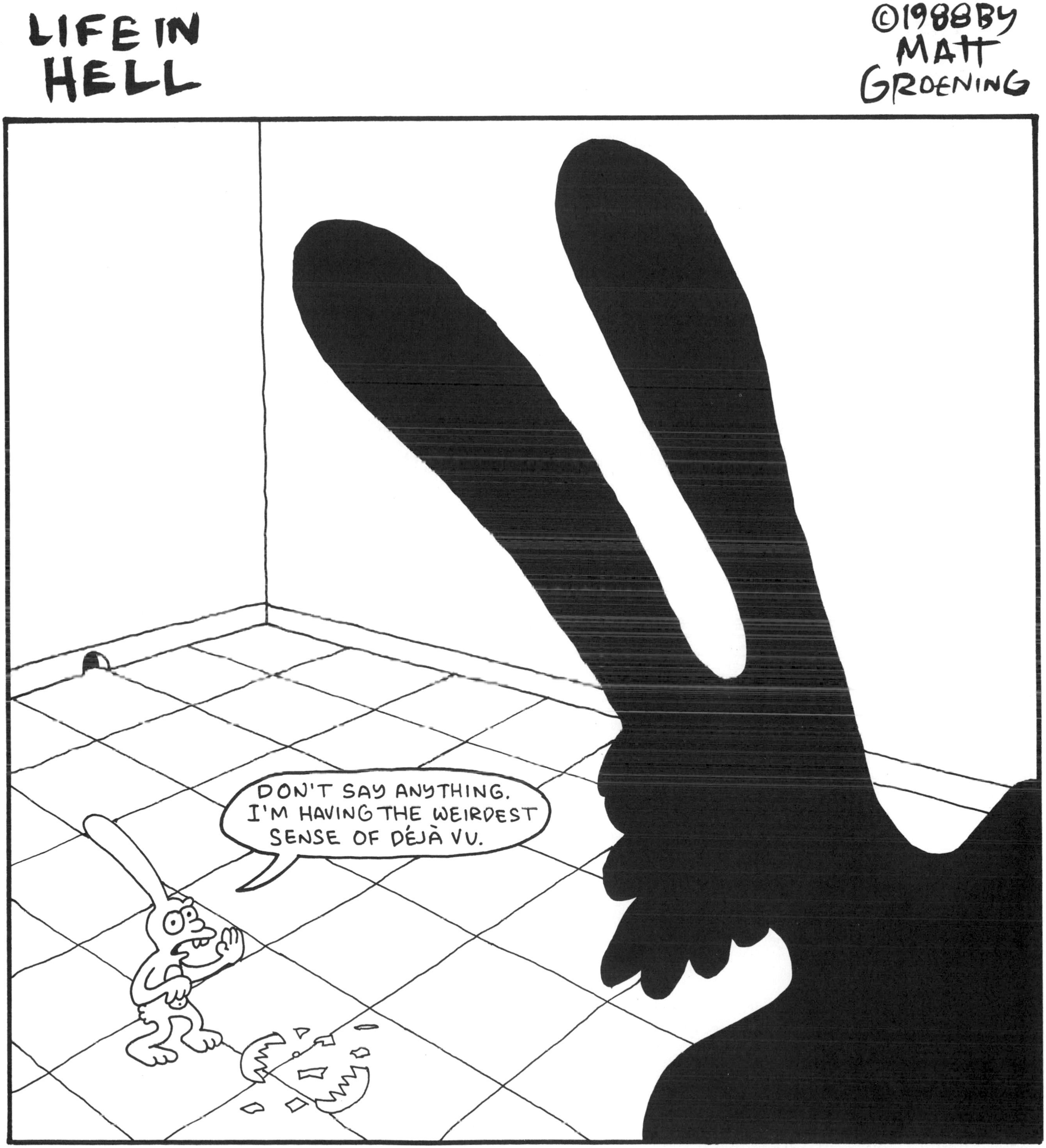
LIFE IN HELL
©1988 BY MATT GROENING
DON'T SAY ANYTHING. I'M HAVING THE WEIRDEST SENSE OF DÉJÀ VU.

LIFE IN HELL

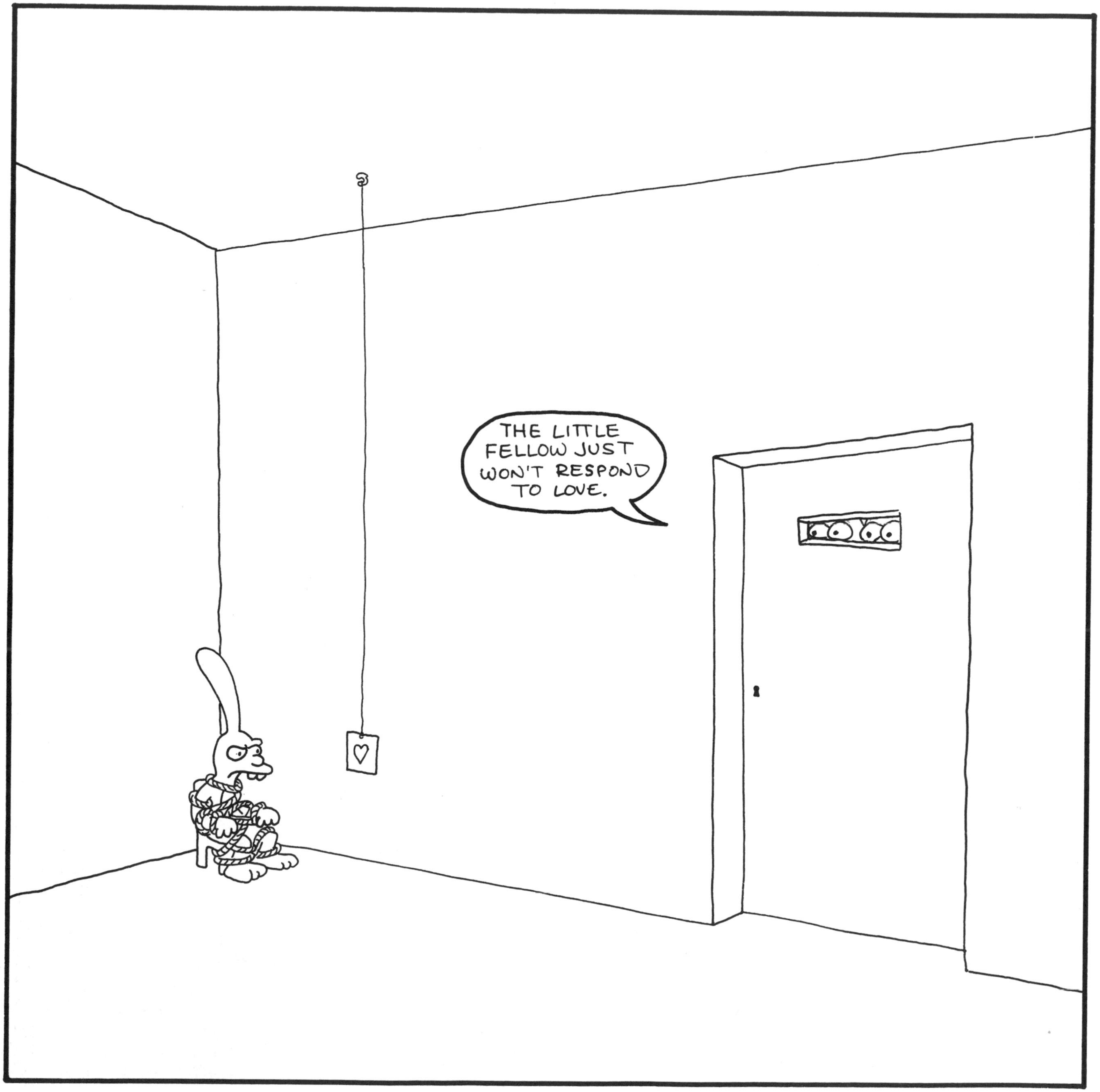
THE LITTLE FELLOW JUST WON'T RESPOND TO LOVE.

LIFE IN HELL

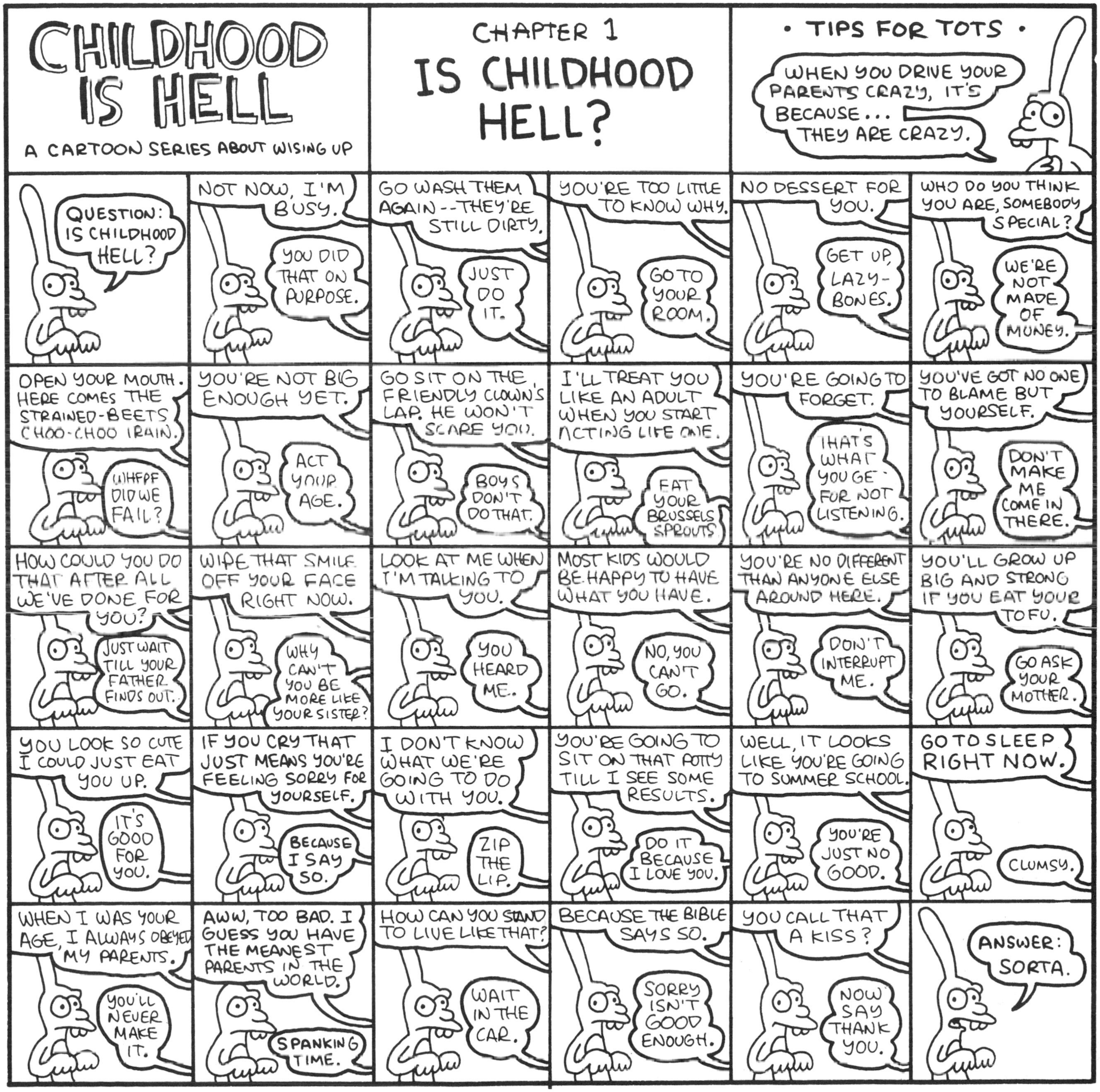
CHILDHOOD IS HELL
A CARTOON SERIES ABOUT WISING UP
CHAPTER 1
IS CHILDHOOD HELL?
• TIPS FOR TOTS •
WHEN YOU DRIVE YOUR PARENTS CRAZY, IT'S BECAUSE...
THEY ARE CRAZY.
QUESTION: IS CHILDHOOD HELL?
NOT NOW, I'M BUSY.
YOU DID THAT ON PURPOSE.
GO WASH THEM AGAIN--THEY'RE STILL DIRTY.
JUST DO IT.
YOU'RE TOO LITTLE TO KNOW WHY.
GO TO YOUR ROOM.
NO DESSERT FOR YOU.
GET UP, LAZY-BONES.
WHO DO YOU THINK YOU ARE, SOMEBODY SPECIAL?
WE'RE NOT MADE OF MONEY.
OPEN YOUR MOUTH. HERE COMES THE STRAINED-BEETS CHOO-CHOO TRAIN.
WHERE DID WE FAIL?
YOU'RE NOT BIG ENOUGH YET.
ACT YOUR AGE.
GO SIT ON THE FRIENDLY CLOWN'S LAP. HE WON'T SCARE YOU.
BOYS DON'T DO THAT.
I'LL TREAT YOU LIKE AN ADULT WHEN YOU START ACTING LIKE ONE.
EAT YOUR BRUSSELS SPROUTS
YOU'RE GOING TO FORGET.
THAT'S WHAT YOU GET FOR NOT LISTENING.
YOU'VE GOT NO ONE TO BLAME BUT YOURSELF.
DON'T MAKE ME COME IN THERE.
HOW COULD YOU DO THAT AFTER ALL WE'VE DONE FOR YOU?
JUST WAIT TILL YOUR FATHER FINDS OUT.
WIPE THAT SMILE OFF YOUR FACE RIGHT NOW.
WHY CAN'T YOU BE MORE LIKE YOUR SISTER?
LOOK AT ME WHEN I'M TALKING TO YOU.
YOU HEARD ME.
MOST KIDS WOULD BE HAPPY TO HAVE WHAT YOU HAVE.
NO, YOU CAN'T GO.
YOU'RE NO DIFFERENT THAN ANYONE ELSE AROUND HERE.
DON'T INTERRUPT ME.
YOU'LL GROW UP BIG AND STRONG IF YOU EAT YOUR TOFU.
GO ASK YOUR MOTHER.
YOU LOOK SO CUTE I COULD JUST EAT YOU UP.
IT'S GOOD FOR YOU.
IF YOU CRY THAT JUST MEANS YOU'RE FEELING SORRY FOR YOURSELF.
BECAUSE I SAY SO.
I DON'T KNOW WHAT WE'RE GOING TO DO WITH YOU.
ZIP THE LIP.
YOU'RE GOING TO SIT ON THAT POTTY TILL I SEE SOME RESULTS.
DO IT BECAUSE I LOVE YOU.
WELL, IT LOOKS LIKE YOU'RE GOING TO SUMMER SCHOOL.
YOU'RE JUST NO GOOD.
GO TO SLEEP RIGHT NOW.
CLUMSY.
WHEN I WAS YOUR AGE, I ALWAYS OBEYED MY PARENTS.
YOU'LL NEVER MAKE IT.
AWW, TOO BAD. I GUESS YOU HAVE THE MEANEST PARENTS IN THE WORLD.
SPANKING TIME.
HOW CAN YOU STAND TO LIVE LIKE THAT?
WAIT IN THE CAR.
BECAUSE THE BIBLE SAYS SO.
SORRY ISN'T GOOD ENOUGH.
YOU CALL THAT A KISS?
NOW SAY THANK YOU.
ANSWER: SORTA.

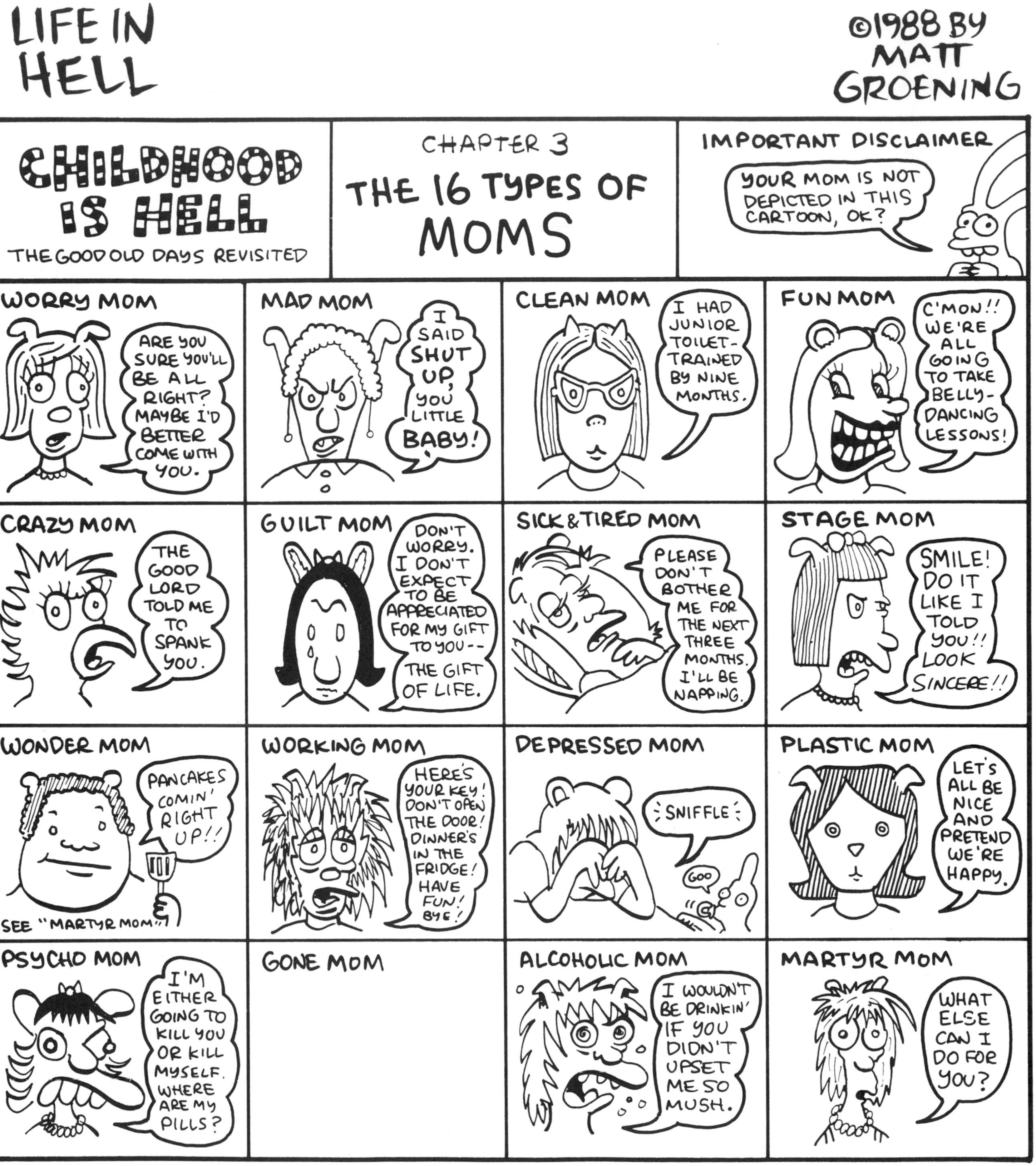
LIFE IN HELL
©1988 BY MATT GROENING
CHILDHOOD IS HELL
THE GOOD OLD DAYS REVISITED
CHAPTER 3
THE 16 TYPES OF MOMS
IMPORTANT DISCLAIMER
YOUR MOM IS NOT DEPICTED IN THIS CARTOON, OK?
WORRY MOM
ARE YOU SURE YOU'LL BE ALL RIGHT? MAYBE I'D BETTER COME WITH YOU.
MAD MOM
I SAID SHUT UP, YOU LITTLE BABY!
CLEAN MOM
I HAD JUNIOR TOILET-TRAINED BY NINE MONTHS.
FUN MOM
C'MON!! WE'RE ALL GOING TO TAKE BELLY-DANCING LESSONS!
CRAZY MOM
THE GOOD LORD TOLD ME TO SPANK YOU.
GUILT MOM
DON'T WORRY. I DON'T EXPECT TO BE APPRECIATED FOR MY GIFT TO YOU -- THE GIFT OF LIFE.
SICK & TIRED MOM
PLEASE DON'T BOTHER ME FOR THE NEXT THREE MONTHS. I'LL BE NAPPING.
STAGE MOM
SMILE! DO IT LIKE I TOLD YOU!! LOOK SINCERE!!
WONDER MOM
PANCAKES COMIN' RIGHT UP!!
SEE "MARTYR MOM"
WORKING MOM
HERE'S YOUR KEY! DON'T OPEN THE DOOR! DINNER'S IN THE FRIDGE! HAVE FUN! BYE!
DEPRESSED MOM
SNIFFLE
GOO
PLASTIC MOM
LET'S ALL BE NICE AND PRETEND WE'RE HAPPY.
PSYCHO MOM
I'M EITHER GOING TO KILL YOU OR KILL MYSELF. WHERE ARE MY PILLS?
GONE MOM
ALCOHOLIC MOM
I WOULDN'T BE DRINKIN' IF YOU DIDN'T UPSET ME SO MUSH.
MARTYR MOM
WHAT ELSE CAN I DO FOR YOU?

LIFE IN HELL

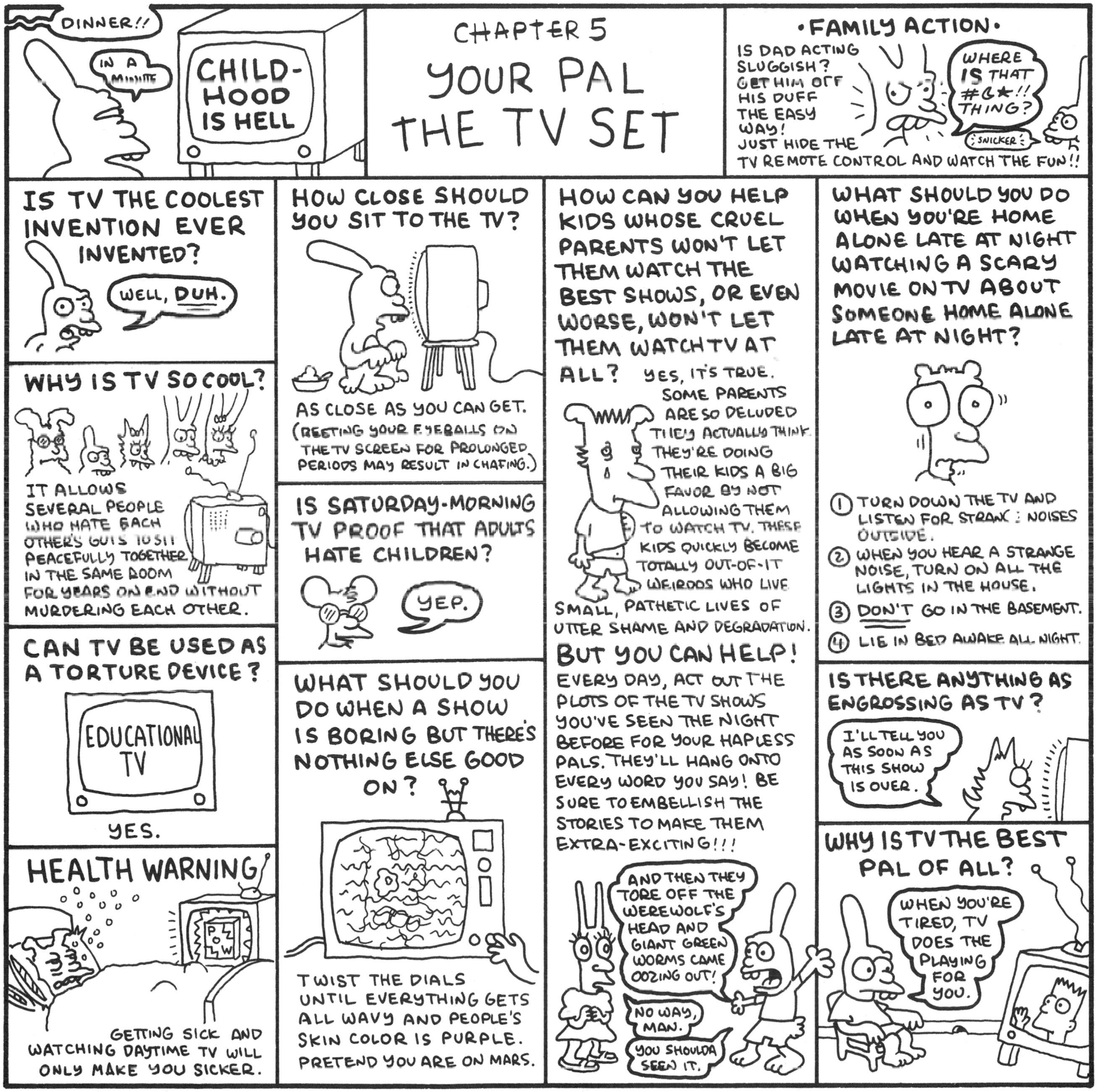
DINNER!!
IN A MINUTE
CHILD-HOOD IS HELL
CHAPTER 5
YOUR PAL THE TV SET
•FAMILY ACTION•
IS DAD ACTING SLUGGISH? GET HIM OFF HIS DUFF THE EASY WAY! JUST HIDE THE TV REMOTE CONTROL AND WATCH THE FUN!!
WHERE IS THAT #@*!! THING?
SNICKER
IS TV THE COOLEST INVENTION EVER INVENTED?
WELL, DUH.
WHY IS TV SO COOL?
IT ALLOWS SEVERAL PEOPLE WHO HATE EACH OTHER'S GUTS TO SIT PEACEFULLY TOGETHER IN THE SAME ROOM FOR YEARS ON END WITHOUT MURDERING EACH OTHER.
CAN TV BE USED AS A TORTURE DEVICE?
EDUCATIONAL TV
YES.
HEALTH WARNING
POW
GETTING SICK AND WATCHING DAYTIME TV WILL ONLY MAKE YOU SICKER.
HOW CLOSE SHOULD YOU SIT TO THE TV?
AS CLOSE AS YOU CAN GET.
(RESTING YOUR EYEBALLS ON THE TV SCREEN FOR PROLONGED PERIODS MAY RESULT IN CHAFING.)
IS SATURDAY-MORNING TV PROOF THAT ADULTS HATE CHILDREN?
YEP.
WHAT SHOULD YOU DO WHEN A SHOW IS BORING BUT THERE'S NOTHING ELSE GOOD ON?
TWIST THE DIALS UNTIL EVERYTHING GETS ALL WAVY AND PEOPLE'S SKIN COLOR IS PURPLE. PRETEND YOU ARE ON MARS.
HOW CAN YOU HELP KIDS WHOSE CRUEL PARENTS WON'T LET THEM WATCH THE BEST SHOWS, OR EVEN WORSE, WON'T LET THEM WATCH TV AT ALL?
YES, IT'S TRUE. SOME PARENTS ARE SO DELUDED THEY ACTUALLY THINK THEY'RE DOING THEIR KIDS A BIG FAVOR BY NOT ALLOWING THEM TO WATCH TV. THESE KIDS QUICKLY BECOME TOTALLY OUT-OF-IT WEIRDOS WHO LIVE SMALL, PATHETIC LIVES OF UTTER SHAME AND DEGRADATION.
BUT YOU CAN HELP!
EVERY DAY, ACT OUT THE PLOTS OF THE TV SHOWS YOU'VE SEEN THE NIGHT BEFORE FOR YOUR HAPLESS PALS. THEY'LL HANG ONTO EVERY WORD YOU SAY! BE SURE TO EMBELLISH THE STORIES TO MAKE THEM EXTRA-EXCITING!!!
AND THEN THEY TORE OFF THE WEREWOLF'S HEAD AND GIANT GREEN WORMS CAME OOZING OUT!
NO WAY, MAN.
YOU SHOULDA SEEN IT.
WHAT SHOULD YOU DO WHEN YOU'RE HOME ALONE LATE AT NIGHT WATCHING A SCARY MOVIE ON TV ABOUT SOMEONE HOME ALONE LATE AT NIGHT?
1 TURN DOWN THE TV AND LISTEN FOR STRANGE NOISES OUTSIDE.
2 WHEN YOU HEAR A STRANGE NOISE, TURN ON ALL THE LIGHTS IN THE HOUSE.
3 DON'T GO IN THE BASEMENT.
4 LIE IN BED AWAKE ALL NIGHT.
IS THERE ANYTHING AS ENGROSSING AS TV?
I'LL TELL YOU AS SOON AS THIS SHOW IS OVER.
WHY IS TV THE BEST PAL OF ALL?
WHEN YOU'RE TIRED, TV DOES THE PLAYING FOR YOU.

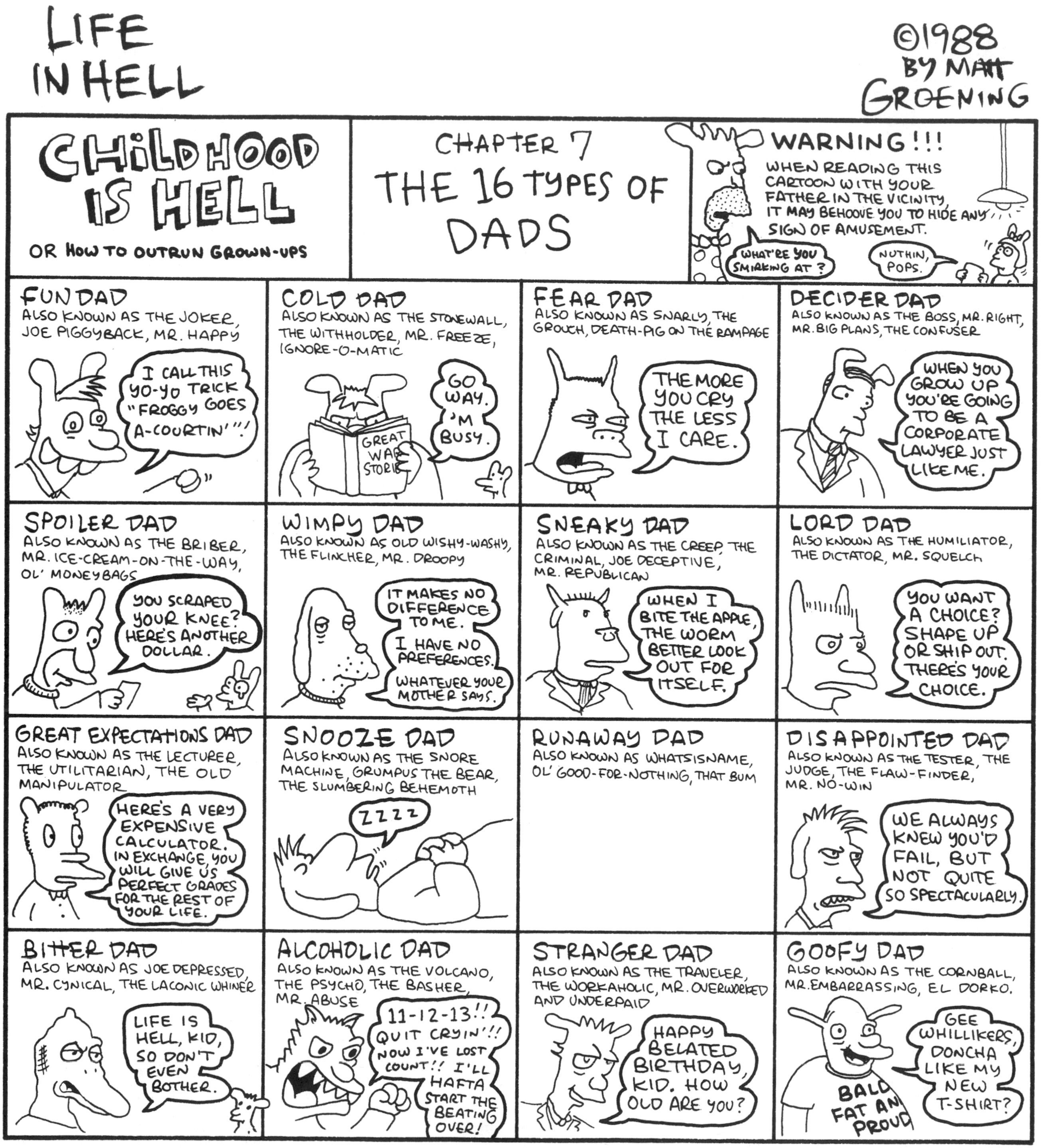
LIFE IN HELL
©1988 BY MATT GROENING
CHILDHOOD IS HELL
OR HOW TO OUTRUN GROWN-UPS
CHAPTER 7
THE 16 TYPES OF DADS
WARNING!!!
WHEN READING THIS CARTOON WITH YOUR FATHER IN THE VICINITY, IT MAY BEHOOVE YOU TO HIDE ANY SIGN OF AMUSEMENT.
WHAT'RE YOU SMIRKING AT?
NUTHIN, POPS.
FUN DAD
ALSO KNOWN AS THE JOKER, JOE PIGGYBACK, MR. HAPPY
I CALL THIS YO-YO TRICK "FROGGY GOES A-COURTIN'"!
COLD DAD
ALSO KNOWN AS THE STONEWALL, THE WITHHOLDER, MR. FREEZE, IGNORE-O-MATIC
GO WAY. 'M BUSY.
GREAT WAR STORIE
FEAR DAD
ALSO KNOWN AS SNARLY, THE GROUCH, DEATH-PIG ON THE RAMPAGE
THE MORE YOU CRY THE LESS I CARE.
DECIDER DAD
ALSO KNOWN AS THE BOSS, MR. RIGHT, MR. BIG PLANS, THE CONFUSER
WHEN YOU GROW UP YOU'RE GOING TO BE A CORPORATE LAWYER JUST LIKE ME.
SPOILER DAD
ALSO KNOWN AS THE BRIBER, MR. ICE-CREAM-ON-THE-WAY, OL' MONEYBAGS
YOU SCRAPED YOUR KNEE? HERE'S ANOTHER DOLLAR.
WIMPY DAD
ALSO KNOWN AS OLD WISHY-WASHY, THE FLINCHER, MR. DROOPY
IT MAKES NO DIFFERENCE TO ME.
I HAVE NO PREFERENCES.
WHATEVER YOUR MOTHER SAYS.
SNEAKY DAD
ALSO KNOWN AS THE CREEP, THE CRIMINAL, JOE DECEPTIVE, MR. REPUBLICAN
WHEN I BITE THE APPLE, THE WORM BETTER LOOK OUT FOR ITSELF.
LORD DAD
ALSO KNOWN AS THE HUMILIATOR, THE DICTATOR, MR. SQUELCH
YOU WANT A CHOICE? SHAPE UP OR SHIP OUT. THERE'S YOUR CHOICE.
GREAT EXPECTATIONS DAD
ALSO KNOWN AS THE LECTURER, THE UTILITARIAN, THE OLD MANIPULATOR
HERE'S A VERY EXPENSIVE CALCULATOR. IN EXCHANGE, YOU WILL GIVE US PERFECT GRADES FOR THE REST OF YOUR LIFE.
SNOOZE DAD
ALSO KNOWN AS THE SNORE MACHINE, GRUMPUS THE BEAR, THE SLUMBERING BEHEMOTH
ZZZZ
RUNAWAY DAD
ALSO KNOWN AS WHATSISNAME, OL' GOOD-FOR-NOTHING, THAT BUM
DISAPPOINTED DAD
ALSO KNOWN AS THE TESTER, THE JUDGE, THE FLAW-FINDER, MR. NO-WIN
WE ALWAYS KNEW YOU'D FAIL, BUT NOT QUITE SO SPECTACULARLY.
BITTER DAD
ALSO KNOWN AS JOE DEPRESSED, MR. CYNICAL, THE LACONIC WHINER
LIFE IS HELL, KID, SO DON'T EVEN BOTHER.
ALCOHOLIC DAD
ALSO KNOWN AS THE VOLCANO, THE PSYCHO, THE BASHER, MR. ABUSE
11-12-13!! QUIT CRYIN'!! NOW I'VE LOST COUNT!! I'LL HAFTA START THE BEATING OVER!
STRANGER DAD
ALSO KNOWN AS THE TRAVELER, THE WORKAHOLIC, MR. OVERWORKED AND UNDERPAID
HAPPY BELATED BIRTHDAY, KID. HOW OLD ARE YOU?
GOOFY DAD
ALSO KNOWN AS THE CORNBALL, MR. EMBARRASSING, EL DORKO.
GEE WHILLIKERS, DONCHA LIKE MY NEW T-SHIRT?
BALD FAT AN PROUD

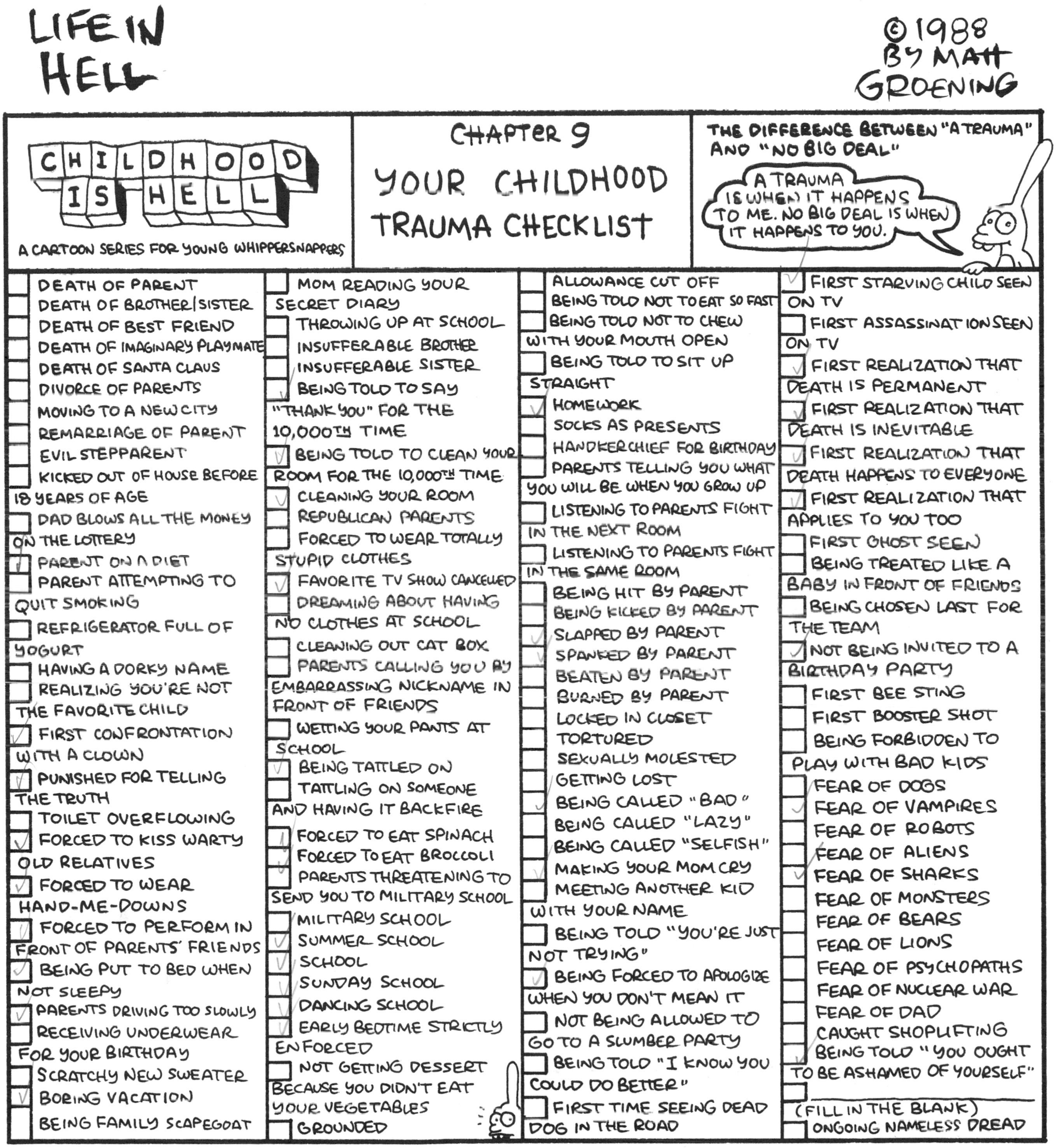
LIFE IN HELL
© 1988 BY MATT GROENING
CHILDHOOD IS HELL
A CARTOON SERIES FOR YOUNG WHIPPERSNAPPERS
CHAPTER 9
YOUR CHILDHOOD TRAUMA CHECKLIST
THE DIFFERENCE BETWEEN "A TRAUMA" AND "NO BIG DEAL"
A TRAUMA IS WHEN IT HAPPENS TO ME. NO BIG DEAL IS WHEN IT HAPPENS TO YOU.
DEATH OF PARENT
DEATH OF BROTHER/SISTER
DEATH OF BEST FRIEND
DEATH OF IMAGINARY PLAYMATE
DEATH OF SANTA CLAUS
DIVORCE OF PARENTS
MOVING TO A NEW CITY
REMARRIAGE OF PARENT
EVIL STEPPARENT
KICKED OUT OF HOUSE BEFORE 18 YEARS OF AGE
DAD BLOWS ALL THE MONEY ON THE LOTTERY
PARENT ON A DIET
PARENT ATTEMPTING TO QUIT SMOKING
REFRIGERATOR FULL OF YOGURT
HAVING A DORKY NAME
REALIZING YOU'RE NOT THE FAVORITE CHILD
FIRST CONFRONTATION WITH A CLOWN
PUNISHED FOR TELLING THE TRUTH
TOILET OVERFLOWING
FORCED TO KISS WARTY OLD RELATIVES
FORCED TO WEAR HAND-ME-DOWNS
FORCED TO PERFORM IN FRONT OF PARENTS' FRIENDS
BEING PUT TO BED WHEN NOT SLEEPY
PARENTS DRIVING TOO SLOWLY
RECEIVING UNDERWEAR FOR YOUR BIRTHDAY
SCRATCHY NEW SWEATER
BORING VACATION
BEING FAMILY SCAPEGOAT
MOM READING YOUR SECRET DIARY
THROWING UP AT SCHOOL
INSUFFERABLE BROTHER
INSUFFERABLE SISTER
BEING TOLD TO SAY "THANK YOU" FOR THE 10,000TH TIME
BEING TOLD TO CLEAN YOUR ROOM FOR THE 10,000TH TIME
CLEANING YOUR ROOM
REPUBLICAN PARENTS
FORCED TO WEAR TOTALLY STUPID CLOTHES
FAVORITE TV SHOW CANCELLED
DREAMING ABOUT HAVING NO CLOTHES AT SCHOOL
CLEANING OUT CAT BOX
PARENTS CALLING YOU BY EMBARRASSING NICKNAME IN FRONT OF FRIENDS
WETTING YOUR PANTS AT SCHOOL
BEING TATTLED ON
TATTLING ON SOMEONE AND HAVING IT BACKFIRE
FORCED TO EAT SPINACH
FORCED TO EAT BROCCOLI
PARENTS THREATENING TO SEND YOU TO MILITARY SCHOOL
MILITARY SCHOOL
SUMMER SCHOOL
SCHOOL
SUNDAY SCHOOL
DANCING SCHOOL
EARLY BEDTIME STRICTLY ENFORCED
NOT GETTING DESSERT BECAUSE YOU DIDN'T EAT YOUR VEGETABLES
GROUNDED
ALLOWANCE CUT OFF
BEING TOLD NOT TO EAT SO FAST
BEING TOLD NOT TO CHEW WITH YOUR MOUTH OPEN
BEING TOLD TO SIT UP STRAIGHT
HOMEWORK
SOCKS AS PRESENTS
HANDKERCHIEF FOR BIRTHDAY
PARENTS TELLING YOU WHAT YOU WILL BE WHEN YOU GROW UP
LISTENING TO PARENTS FIGHT IN THE NEXT ROOM
LISTENING TO PARENTS FIGHT IN THE SAME ROOM
BEING HIT BY PARENT
BEING KICKED BY PARENT
SLAPPED BY PARENT
SPANKED BY PARENT
BEATEN BY PARENT
BURNED BY PARENT
LOCKED IN CLOSET
TORTURED
SEXUALLY MOLESTED
GETTING LOST
BEING CALLED "BAD"
BEING CALLED "LAZY"
BEING CALLED "SELFISH"
MAKING YOUR MOM CRY
MEETING ANOTHER KID WITH YOUR NAME
BEING TOLD "YOU'RE JUST NOT TRYING"
BEING FORCED TO APOLOGIZE WHEN YOU DON'T MEAN IT
NOT BEING ALLOWED TO GO TO A SLUMBER PARTY
BEING TOLD "I KNOW YOU COULD DO BETTER"
FIRST TIME SEEING DEAD DOG IN THE ROAD
FIRST STARVING CHILD SEEN ON TV
FIRST ASSASSINATION SEEN ON TV
FIRST REALIZATION THAT DEATH IS PERMANENT
FIRST REALIZATION THAT DEATH IS INEVITABLE
FIRST REALIZATION THAT DEATH HAPPENS TO EVERYONE
FIRST REALIZATION THAT APPLIES TO YOU TOO
FIRST GHOST SEEN
BEING TREATED LIKE A BABY IN FRONT OF FRIENDS
BEING CHOSEN LAST FOR THE TEAM
NOT BEING INVITED TO A BIRTHDAY PARTY
FIRST BEE STING
FIRST BOOSTER SHOT
BEING FORBIDDEN TO PLAY WITH BAD KIDS
FEAR OF DOGS
FEAR OF VAMPIRES
FEAR OF ROBOTS
FEAR OF ALIENS
FEAR OF SHARKS
FEAR OF MONSTERS
FEAR OF BEARS
FEAR OF LIONS
FEAR OF PSYCHOPATHS
FEAR OF NUCLEAR WAR
FEAR OF DAD
CAUGHT SHOPLIFTING
BEING TOLD "YOU OUGHT TO BE ASHAMED OF YOURSELF"
(FILL IN THE BLANK)
ONGOING NAMELESS DREAD

LIFE IN HELL

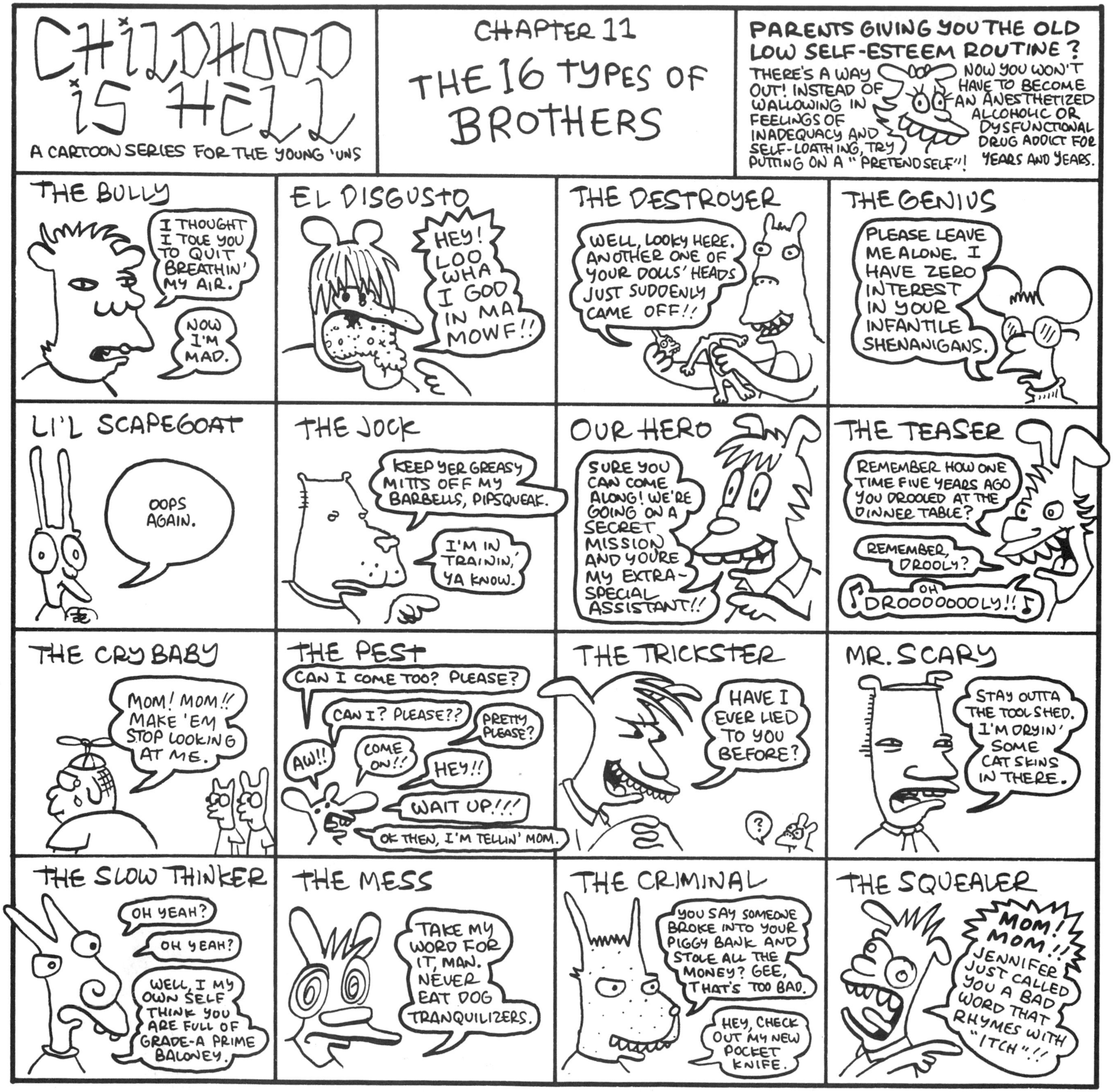
CHILDHOOD IS HELL
A CARTOON SERIES FOR THE YOUNG 'UNS
CHAPTER 11
THE 16 TYPES OF BROTHERS
PARENTS GIVING YOU THE OLD LOW SELF-ESTEEM ROUTINE?
THERE'S A WAY OUT! INSTEAD OF WALLOWING IN FEELINGS OF INADEQUACY AND SELF-LOATHING, TRY PUTTING ON A "PRETEND SELF"!
NOW YOU WON'T HAVE TO BECOME AN ANESTHETIZED ALCOHOLIC OR DYSFUNCTIONAL DRUG ADDICT FOR YEARS AND YEARS.
THE BULLY
I THOUGHT I TOLE YOU TO QUIT BREATHIN' MY AIR.
NOW I'M MAD.
EL DISGUSTO
HEY! LOO WHA I GOD IN MA MOWF!!
THE DESTROYER
WELL, LOOKY HERE. ANOTHER ONE OF YOUR DOLLS' HEADS JUST SUDDENLY CAME OFF!!
THE GENIUS
PLEASE LEAVE ME ALONE. I HAVE ZERO INTEREST IN YOUR INFANTILE SHENANIGANS.
LI'L SCAPEGOAT
OOPS AGAIN.
THE JOCK
KEEP YER GREASY MITTS OFF MY BARBELLS, PIPSQUEAK.
I'M IN TRAININ', YA KNOW.
OUR HERO
SURE YOU CAN COME ALONG! WE'RE GOING ON A SECRET MISSION AND YOU'RE MY EXTRA-SPECIAL ASSISTANT!!
THE TEASER
REMEMBER HOW ONE TIME FIVE YEARS AGO YOU DROOLED AT THE DINNER TABLE?
REMEMBER, DROOLY?
OH DROOOOOOOLY!!
THE CRYBABY
MOM! MOM!! MAKE 'EM STOP LOOKING AT ME.
THE PEST
CAN I COME TOO? PLEASE?
CAN I? PLEASE??
PRETTY PLEASE?
AW!!
COME ON!!
HEY!!
WAIT UP!!!
OK THEN, I'M TELLIN' MOM.
THE TRICKSTER
HAVE I EVER LIED TO YOU BEFORE?
?
MR. SCARY
STAY OUTTA THE TOOL SHED. I'M DRYIN' SOME CAT SKINS IN THERE.
THE SLOW THINKER
OH YEAH?
OH YEAH?
WELL, I MY OWN SELF THINK YOU ARE FULL OF GRADE-A PRIME BALONEY.
THE MESS
TAKE MY WORD FOR IT, MAN. NEVER EAT DOG TRANQUILIZERS.
THE CRIMINAL
YOU SAY SOMEONE BROKE INTO YOUR PIGGY BANK AND STOLE ALL THE MONEY? GEE, THAT'S TOO BAD.
HEY, CHECK OUT MY NEW POCKET KNIFE.
THE SQUEALER
MOM! MOM!! JENNIFER JUST CALLED YOU A BAD WORD THAT RHYMES WITH "ITCH"!!

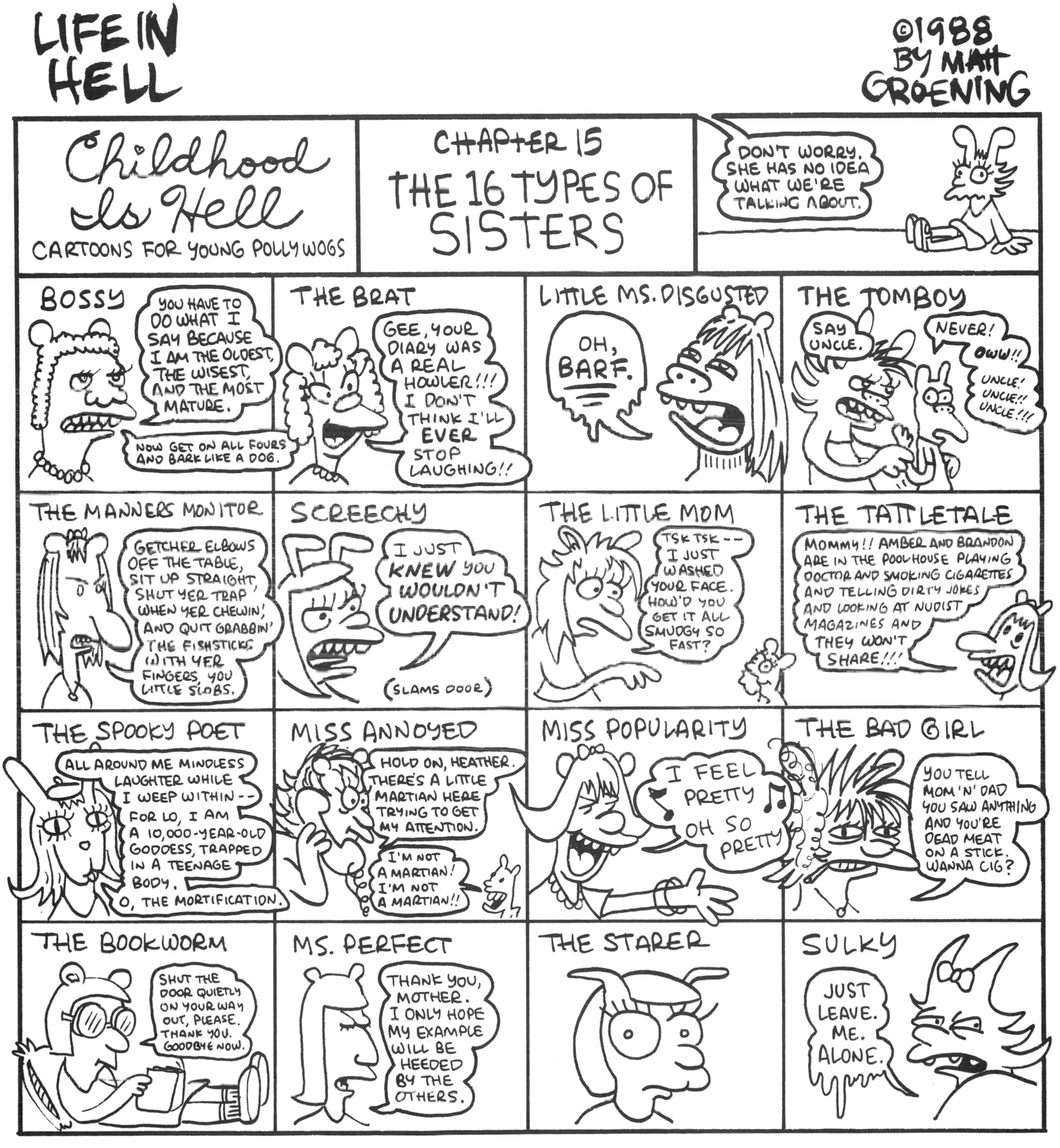

LIFE IN HELL
©1988 BY MATT GROENING
Childhood Is Hell
CARTOONS FOR YOUNG POLLYWOGS
CHAPTER 15
THE 16 TYPES OF SISTERS
DON'T WORRY. SHE HAS NO IDEA WHAT WE'RE TALKING ABOUT.
BOSSY
YOU HAVE TO DO WHAT I SAY BECAUSE I AM THE OLDEST, THE WISEST, AND THE MOST MATURE.
NOW GET ON ALL FOURS AND BARK LIKE A DOG.
THE BRAT
GEE, YOUR DIARY WAS A REAL HOWLER!!! I DON'T THINK I'LL EVER STOP LAUGHING!!
LITTLE MS. DISGUSTED
OH, BARF.
THE TOMBOY
SAY UNCLE.
NEVER!
OWW!!
UNCLE! UNCLE!! UNCLE!!!
THE MANNERS MONITOR
GETCHER ELBOWS OFF THE TABLE, SIT UP STRAIGHT, SHUT YER TRAP WHEN YER CHEWIN', AND QUIT GRABBIN' THE FISHSTICKS WITH YER FINGERS, YOU LITTLE SLOBS.
SCREECHY
I JUST KNEW YOU WOULDN'T UNDERSTAND!
(SLAMS DOOR)
THE LITTLE MOM
TSK TSK -- I JUST WASHED YOUR FACE. HOW'D YOU GET IT ALL SMUDGY SO FAST?
THE TATTLETALE
MOMMY!! AMBER AND BRANDON ARE IN THE POOLHOUSE PLAYING DOCTOR AND SMOKING CIGARETTES AND TELLING DIRTY JOKES AND LOOKING AT NUDIST MAGAZINES AND THEY WON'T SHARE!!!
THE SPOOKY POET
ALL AROUND ME MINDLESS LAUGHTER WHILE I WEEP WITHIN -- FOR LO, I AM A 10,000-YEAR-OLD GODDESS, TRAPPED IN A TEENAGE BODY.
O, THE MORTIFICATION.
MISS ANNOYED
HOLD ON, HEATHER. THERE'S A LITTLE MARTIAN HERE TRYING TO GET MY ATTENTION.
I'M NOT A MARTIAN! I'M NOT A MARTIAN!!
MISS POPULARITY
I FEEL PRETTY OH SO PRETTY
THE BAD GIRL
YOU TELL MOM 'N' DAD YOU SAW ANYTHING AND YOU'RE DEAD MEAT ON A STICK. WANNA CIG?
THE BOOKWORM
SHUT THE DOOR QUIETLY ON YOUR WAY OUT, PLEASE. THANK YOU. GOODBYE NOW.
MS. PERFECT
THANK YOU, MOTHER. I ONLY HOPE MY EXAMPLE WILL BE HEEDED BY THE OTHERS.
THE STARER
SULKY
JUST LEAVE. ME. ALONE.

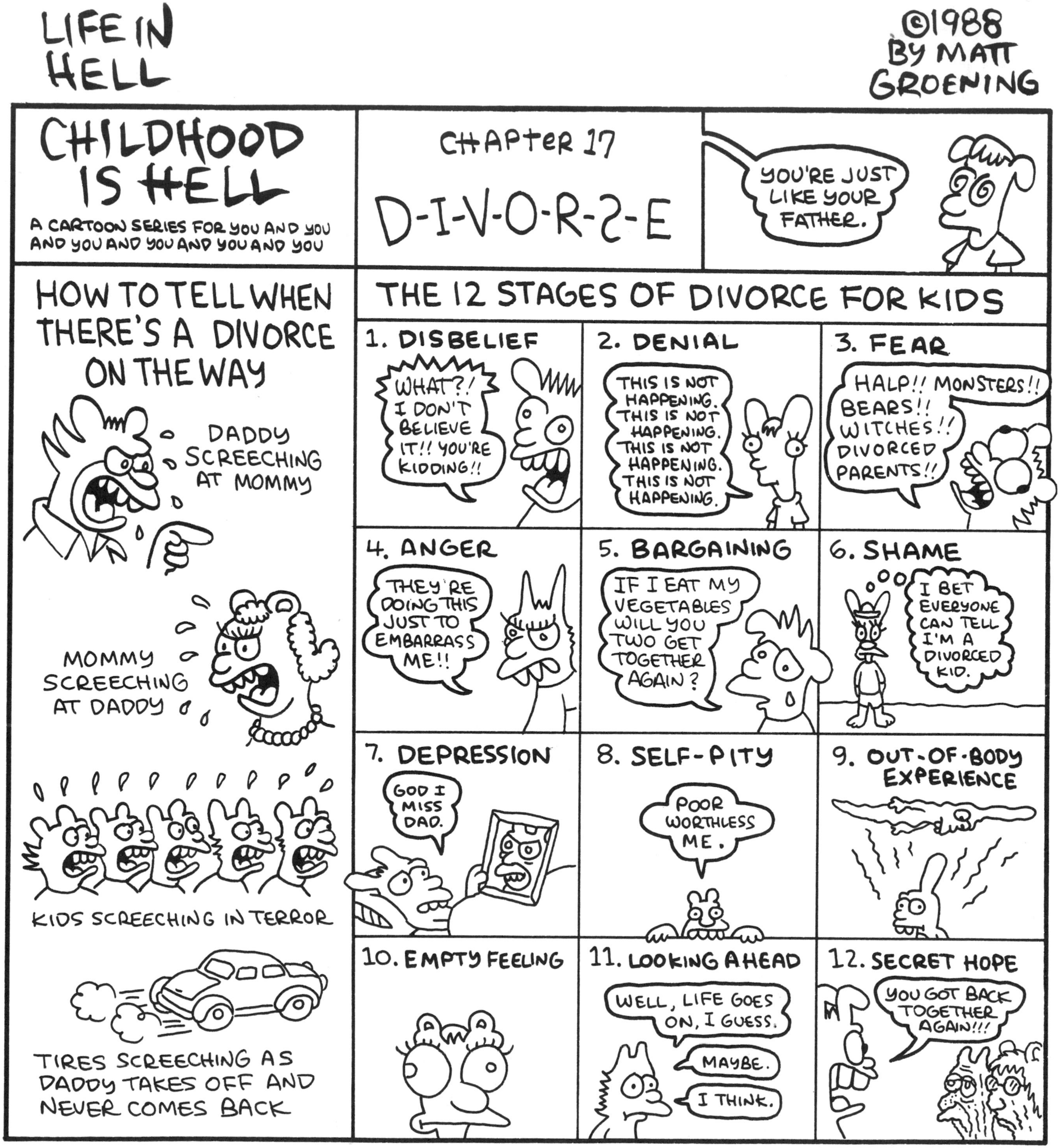

LIFE IN HELL
©1988 BY MATT GROENING
CHILDHOOD IS HELL
A CARTOON SERIES FOR YOU AND YOU AND YOU AND YOU AND YOU AND YOU
CHAPTER 17
D-I-V-O-R-S-E
YOU'RE JUST LIKE YOUR FATHER.
HOW TO TELL WHEN THERE'S A DIVORCE ON THE WAY
DADDY SCREECHING AT MOMMY
MOMMY SCREECHING AT DADDY
KIDS SCREECHING IN TERROR
TIRES SCREECHING AS DADDY TAKES OFF AND NEVER COMES BACK
THE 12 STAGES OF DIVORCE FOR KIDS
1. DISBELIEF
WHAT?! I DON'T BELIEVE IT!! YOU'RE KIDDING!!
2. DENIAL
THIS IS NOT HAPPENING. THIS IS NOT HAPPENING. THIS IS NOT HAPPENING. THIS IS NOT HAPPENING.
3. FEAR
HALP!! MONSTERS!! BEARS!! WITCHES!! DIVORCED PARENTS!!
4. ANGER
THEY'RE DOING THIS JUST TO EMBARRASS ME!!
5. BARGAINING
IF I EAT MY VEGETABLES WILL YOU TWO GET TOGETHER AGAIN?
6. SHAME
I BET EVERYONE CAN TELL I'M A DIVORCED KID.
7. DEPRESSION
GOD I MISS DAD.
8. SELF-PITY
POOR WORTHLESS ME.
9. OUT-OF-BODY EXPERIENCE
10. EMPTY FEELING
11. LOOKING AHEAD
WELL, LIFE GOES ON, I GUESS.
MAYBE.
I THINK.
12. SECRET HOPE
YOU GOT BACK TOGETHER AGAIN!!!

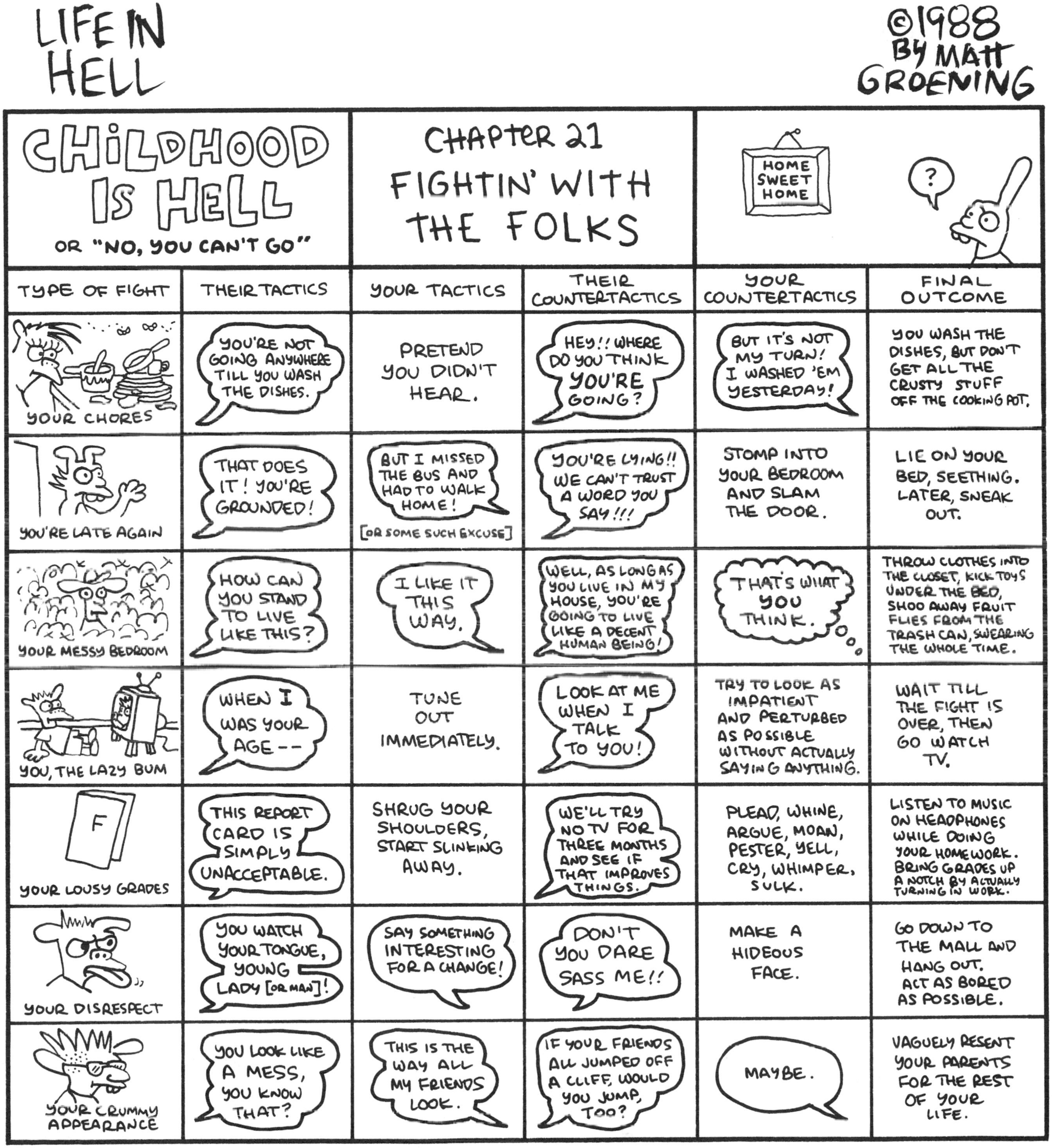
LIFE IN HELL
©1988 BY MATT GROENING
CHILDHOOD IS HELL
OR "NO, YOU CAN'T GO"
CHAPTER 21
FIGHTIN' WITH THE FOLKS
HOME SWEET HOME
?
TYPE OF FIGHT
THEIR TACTICS
YOUR TACTICS
THEIR COUNTERTACTICS
YOUR COUNTERTACTICS
FINAL OUTCOME
YOUR CHORES
YOU'RE NOT GOING ANYWHERE TILL YOU WASH THE DISHES.
PRETEND YOU DIDN'T HEAR.
HEY!! WHERE DO YOU THINK YOU'RE GOING?
BUT IT'S NOT MY TURN! I WASHED 'EM YESTERDAY!
YOU WASH THE DISHES, BUT DON'T GET ALL THE CRUSTY STUFF OFF THE COOKING POT.
YOU'RE LATE AGAIN
THAT DOES IT! YOU'RE GROUNDED!
BUT I MISSED THE BUS AND HAD TO WALK HOME!
[OR SOME SUCH EXCUSE]
YOU'RE LYING!! WE CAN'T TRUST A WORD YOU SAY!!!
STOMP INTO YOUR BEDROOM AND SLAM THE DOOR.
LIE ON YOUR BED, SEETHING. LATER, SNEAK OUT.
YOUR MESSY BEDROOM
HOW CAN YOU STAND TO LIVE LIKE THIS?
I LIKE IT THIS WAY.
WELL, AS LONG AS YOU LIVE IN MY HOUSE, YOU'RE GOING TO LIVE LIKE A DECENT HUMAN BEING!
THAT'S WHAT YOU THINK.
THROW CLOTHES INTO THE CLOSET, KICK TOYS UNDER THE BED, SHOO AWAY FRUIT FLIES FROM THE TRASH CAN, SWEARING THE WHOLE TIME.
YOU, THE LAZY BUM
WHEN I WAS YOUR AGE--
TUNE OUT IMMEDIATELY.
LOOK AT ME WHEN I TALK TO YOU!
TRY TO LOOK AS IMPATIENT AND PERTURBED AS POSSIBLE WITHOUT ACTUALLY SAYING ANYTHING.
WAIT TILL THE FIGHT IS OVER, THEN GO WATCH TV.
F
YOUR LOUSY GRADES
THIS REPORT CARD IS SIMPLY UNACCEPTABLE.
SHRUG YOUR SHOULDERS, START SLINKING AWAY.
WE'LL TRY NO TV FOR THREE MONTHS AND SEE IF THAT IMPROVES THINGS.
PLEAD, WHINE, ARGUE, MOAN, PESTER, YELL, CRY, WHIMPER, SULK.
LISTEN TO MUSIC ON HEADPHONES WHILE DOING YOUR HOMEWORK. BRING GRADES UP A NOTCH BY ACTUALLY TURNING IN WORK.
YOUR DISRESPECT
YOU WATCH YOUR TONGUE, YOUNG LADY [OR MAN]!
SAY SOMETHING INTERESTING FOR A CHANGE!
DON'T YOU DARE SASS ME!!
MAKE A HIDEOUS FACE.
GO DOWN TO THE MALL AND HANG OUT. ACT AS BORED AS POSSIBLE.
YOUR CRUMMY APPEARANCE
YOU LOOK LIKE A MESS, YOU KNOW THAT?
THIS IS THE WAY ALL MY FRIENDS LOOK.
IF YOUR FRIENDS ALL JUMPED OFF A CLIFF, WOULD YOU JUMP, TOO?
MAYBE.
VAGUELY RESENT YOUR PARENTS FOR THE REST OF YOUR LIFE.

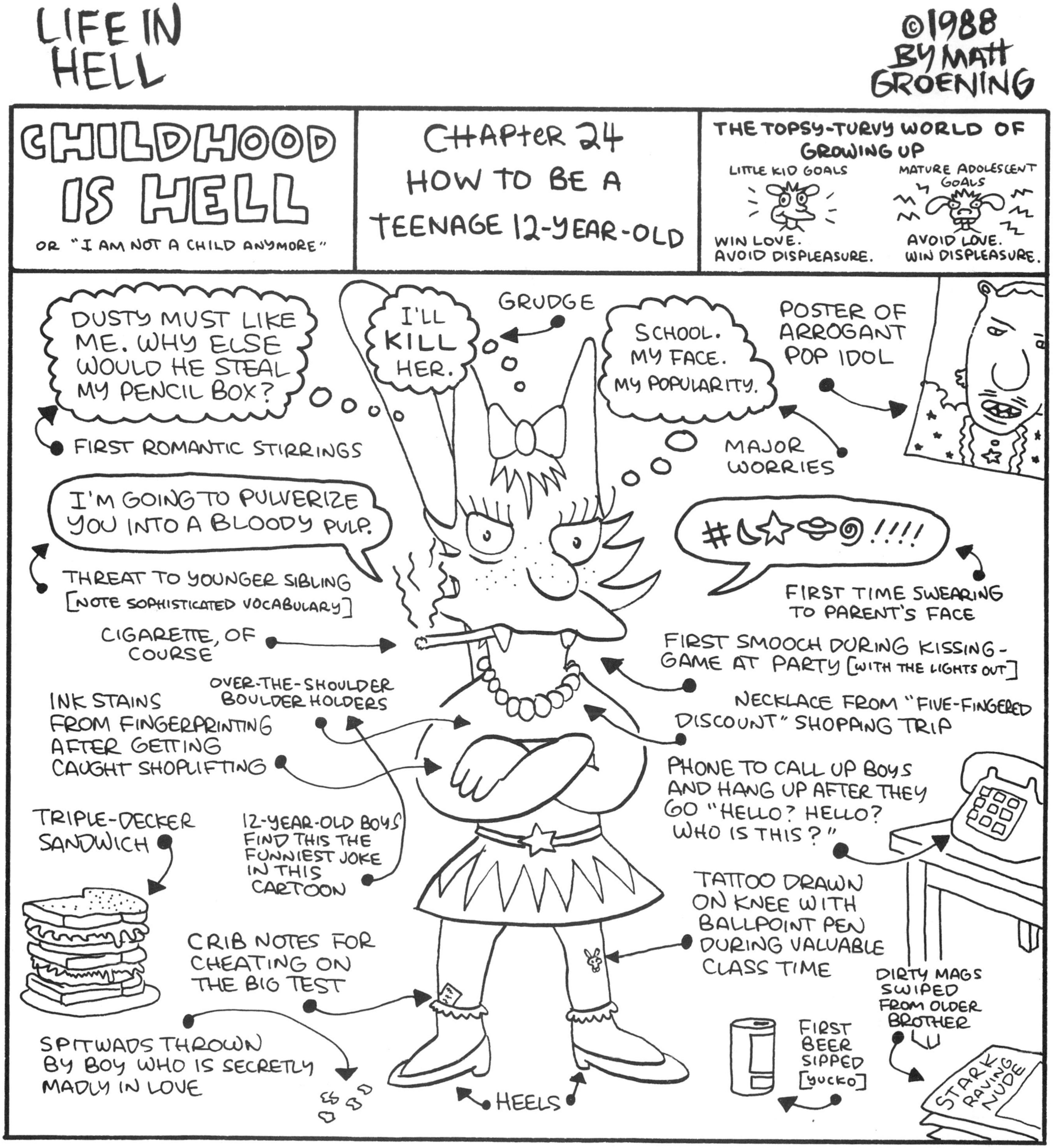
LIFE IN HELL
©1988 BY MATT GROENING
CHILDHOOD IS HELL
OR "I AM NOT A CHILD ANYMORE"
CHAPTER 24
HOW TO BE A TEENAGE 12-YEAR-OLD
THE TOPSY-TURVY WORLD OF GROWING UP
LITTLE KID GOALS
WIN LOVE. AVOID DISPLEASURE.
MATURE ADOLESCENT GOALS
AVOID LOVE. WIN DISPLEASURE.
DUSTY MUST LIKE ME. WHY ELSE WOULD HE STEAL MY PENCIL BOX?
FIRST ROMANTIC STIRRINGS
I'LL KILL HER.
GRUDGE
SCHOOL. MY FACE. MY POPULARITY.
MAJOR WORRIES
POSTER OF ARROGANT POP IDOL
I'M GOING TO PULVERIZE YOU INTO A BLOODY PULP.
THREAT TO YOUNGER SIBLING [NOTE SOPHISTICATED VOCABULARY]
#☾☆🪐◎!!!!
FIRST TIME SWEARING TO PARENT'S FACE
CIGARETTE, OF COURSE
FIRST SMOOCH DURING KISSING-GAME AT PARTY [WITH THE LIGHTS OUT]
OVER-THE-SHOULDER BOULDER HOLDERS
INK STAINS FROM FINGERPRINTING AFTER GETTING CAUGHT SHOPLIFTING
NECKLACE FROM "FIVE-FINGERED DISCOUNT" SHOPPING TRIP
PHONE TO CALL UP BOYS AND HANG UP AFTER THEY GO "HELLO? HELLO? WHO IS THIS?"
TRIPLE-DECKER SANDWICH
12-YEAR-OLD BOYS FIND THIS THE FUNNIEST JOKE IN THIS CARTOON
TATTOO DRAWN ON KNEE WITH BALLPOINT PEN DURING VALUABLE CLASS TIME
CRIB NOTES FOR CHEATING ON THE BIG TEST
DIRTY MAGS SWIPED FROM OLDER BROTHER
SPITWADS THROWN BY BOY WHO IS SECRETLY MADLY IN LOVE
HEELS
FIRST BEER SIPPED [YUCKO]
STARK RAVING NUDE

LIFE IN HELL

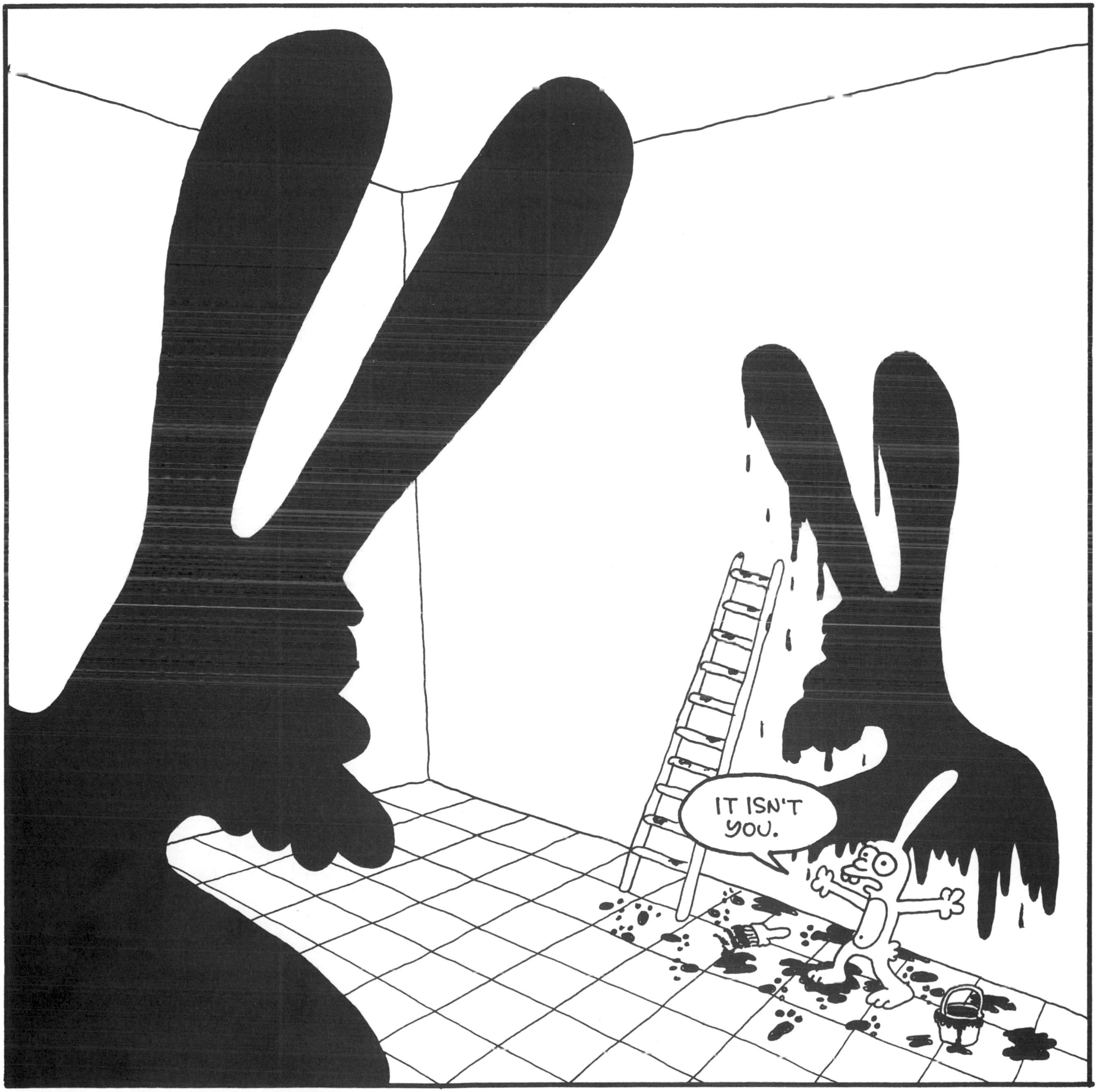
IT ISN'T YOU.

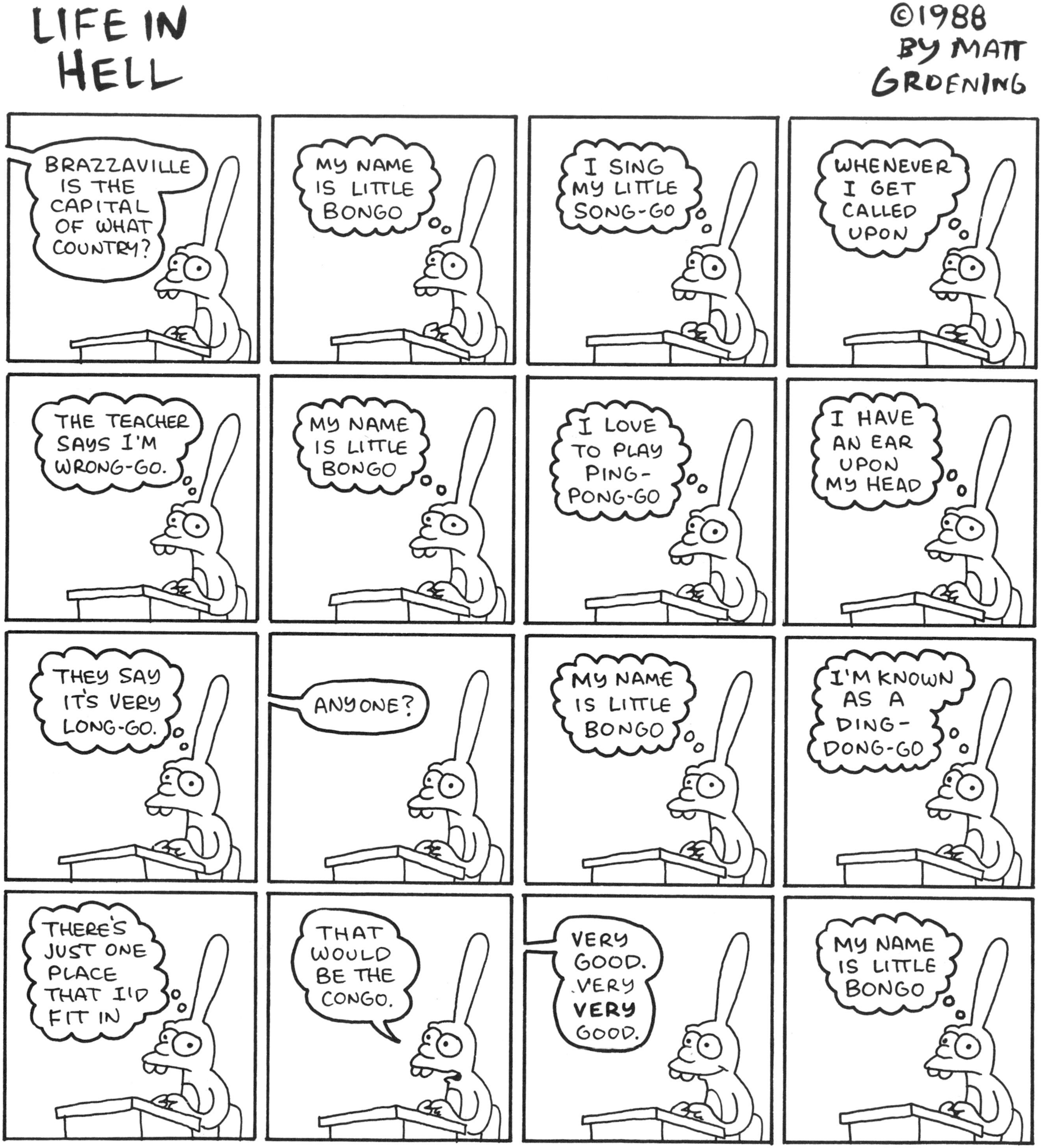
LIFE IN HELL
©1988 BY MATT GROENING
BRAZZAVILLE IS THE CAPITAL OF WHAT COUNTRY?
MY NAME IS LITTLE BONGO
I SING MY LITTLE SONG-GO
WHENEVER I GET CALLED UPON
THE TEACHER SAYS I'M WRONG-GO.
MY NAME IS LITTLE BONGO
I LOVE TO PLAY PING-PONG-GO
I HAVE AN EAR UPON MY HEAD
THEY SAY IT'S VERY LONG-GO.
ANYONE?
MY NAME IS LITTLE BONGO
I'M KNOWN AS A DING-DONG-GO
THERE'S JUST ONE PLACE THAT I'D FIT IN
THAT WOULD BE THE CONGO.
VERY GOOD. VERY VERY GOOD.
MY NAME IS LITTLE BONGO

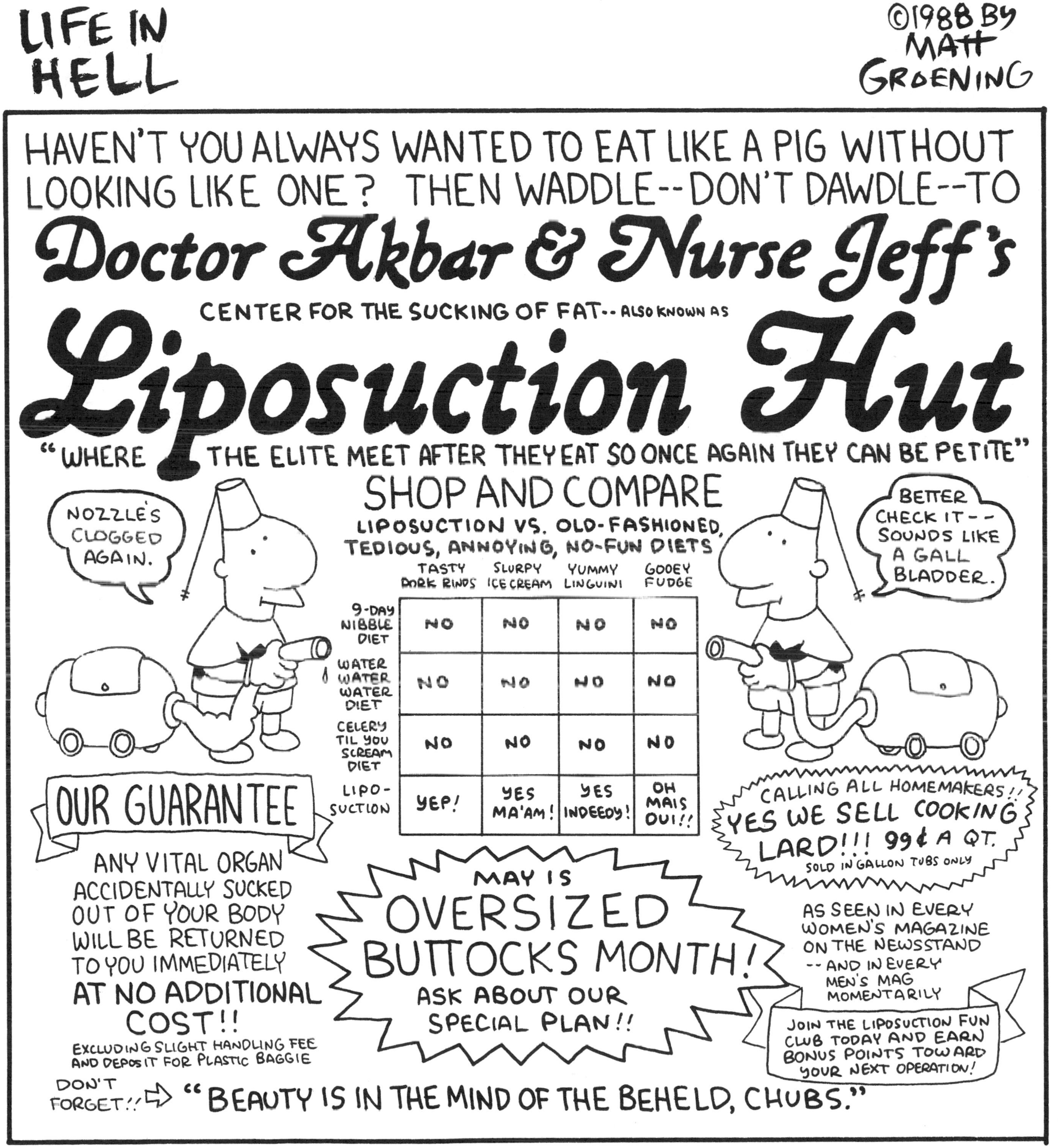
LIFE IN HELL
©1988 BY MATT GROENING
HAVEN'T YOU ALWAYS WANTED TO EAT LIKE A PIG WITHOUT LOOKING LIKE ONE? THEN WADDLE--DON'T DAWDLE--TO
Doctor Akbar & Nurse Jeff's
CENTER FOR THE SUCKING OF FAT-- ALSO KNOWN AS
Liposuction Hut
"WHERE THE ELITE MEET AFTER THEY EAT SO ONCE AGAIN THEY CAN BE PETITE"
NOZZLE'S CLOGGED AGAIN.
SHOP AND COMPARE
LIPOSUCTION VS. OLD-FASHIONED, TEDIOUS, ANNOYING, NO-FUN DIETS
BETTER CHECK IT-- SOUNDS LIKE A GALL BLADDER.
TASTY PORK RINDS
SLURPY ICE CREAM
YUMMY LINGUINI
GOOEY FUDGE
9-DAY NIBBLE DIET
NO NO NO NO
WATER WATER WATER DIET
NO NO NO NO
CELERY TIL YOU SCREAM DIET
NO NO NO NO
LIPO-SUCTION
YEP!
YES MA'AM!
YES INDEEDY!
OH MAIS OUI!!
OUR GUARANTEE
ANY VITAL ORGAN ACCIDENTALLY SUCKED OUT OF YOUR BODY WILL BE RETURNED TO YOU IMMEDIATELY
AT NO ADDITIONAL COST!!
EXCLUDING SLIGHT HANDLING FEE AND DEPOSIT FOR PLASTIC BAGGIE
CALLING ALL HOMEMAKERS!!
YES WE SELL COOKING LARD!!! 99¢ A QT.
SOLD IN GALLON TUBS ONLY
MAY IS
OVERSIZED BUTTOCKS MONTH!
ASK ABOUT OUR SPECIAL PLAN!!
AS SEEN IN EVERY WOMEN'S MAGAZINE ON THE NEWSSTAND --AND IN EVERY MEN'S MAG MOMENTARILY
JOIN THE LIPOSUCTION FUN CLUB TODAY AND EARN BONUS POINTS TOWARD YOUR NEXT OPERATION!
DON'T FORGET!!
"BEAUTY IS IN THE MIND OF THE BEHELD, CHUBS."

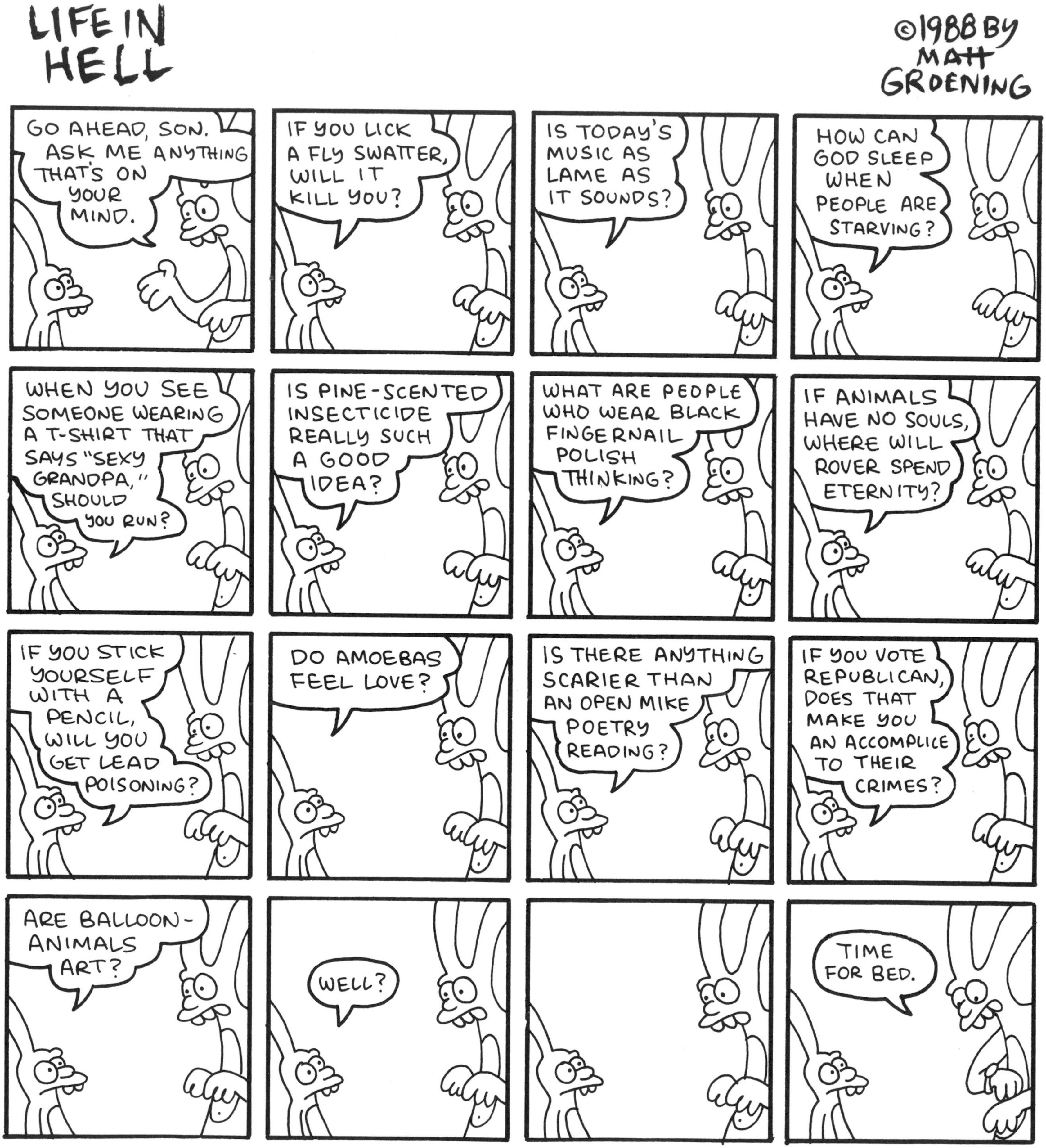
LIFE IN HELL
©1988 BY MATT GROENING
GO AHEAD, SON. ASK ME ANYTHING THAT'S ON YOUR MIND.
IF YOU LICK A FLY SWATTER, WILL IT KILL YOU?
IS TODAY'S MUSIC AS LAME AS IT SOUNDS?
HOW CAN GOD SLEEP WHEN PEOPLE ARE STARVING?
WHEN YOU SEE SOMEONE WEARING A T-SHIRT THAT SAYS "SEXY GRANDPA," SHOULD YOU RUN?
IS PINE-SCENTED INSECTICIDE REALLY SUCH A GOOD IDEA?
WHAT ARE PEOPLE WHO WEAR BLACK FINGERNAIL POLISH THINKING?
IF ANIMALS HAVE NO SOULS, WHERE WILL ROVER SPEND ETERNITY?
IF YOU STICK YOURSELF WITH A PENCIL, WILL YOU GET LEAD POISONING?
DO AMOEBAS FEEL LOVE?
IS THERE ANYTHING SCARIER THAN AN OPEN MIKE POETRY READING?
IF YOU VOTE REPUBLICAN, DOES THAT MAKE YOU AN ACCOMPLICE TO THEIR CRIMES?
ARE BALLOON-ANIMALS ART?
WELL?
TIME FOR BED.

LIFE IN HELL

©1988 BY MATT GROENING

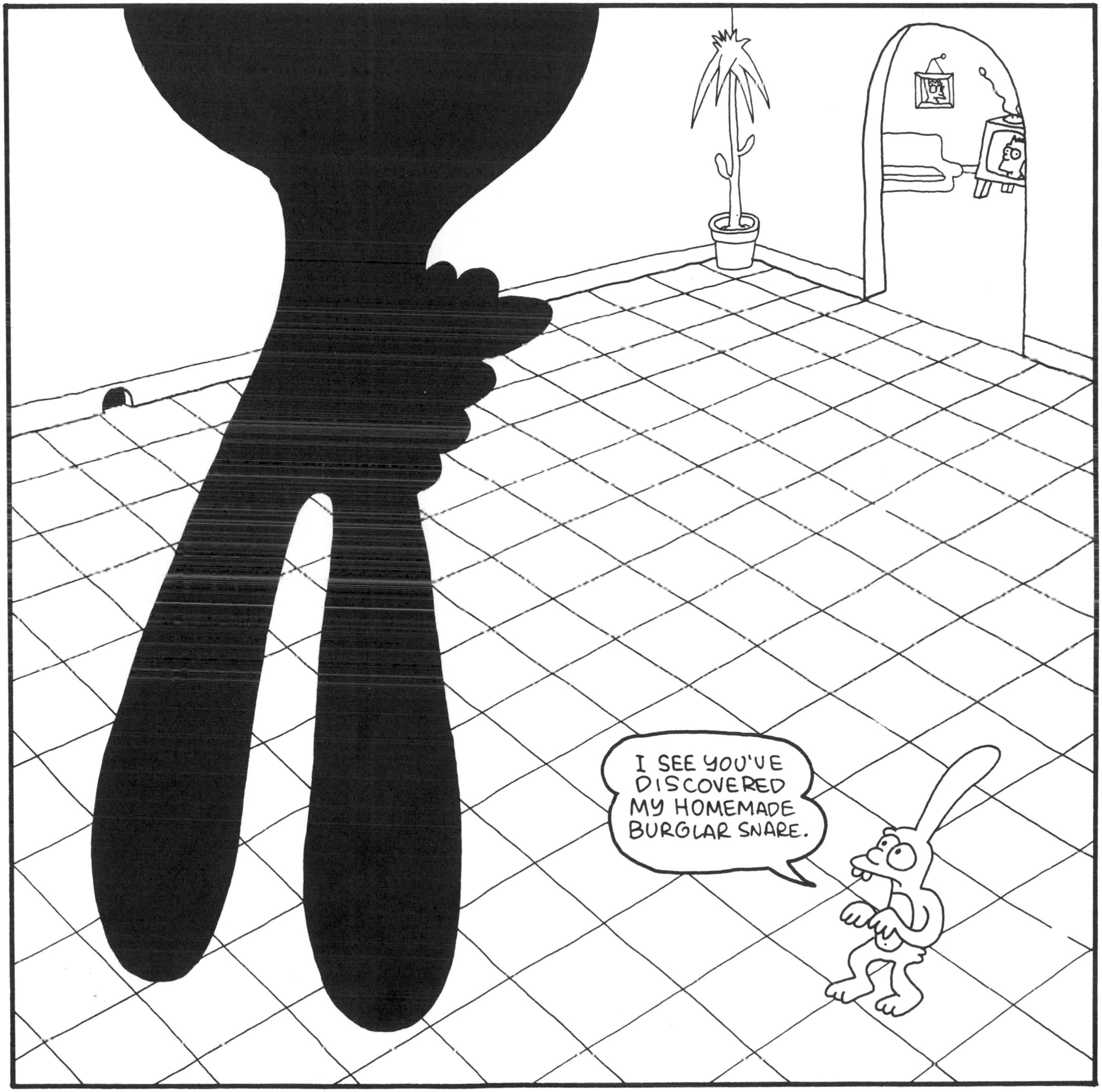
I SEE YOU'VE DISCOVERED MY HOMEMADE BURGLAR SNARE.

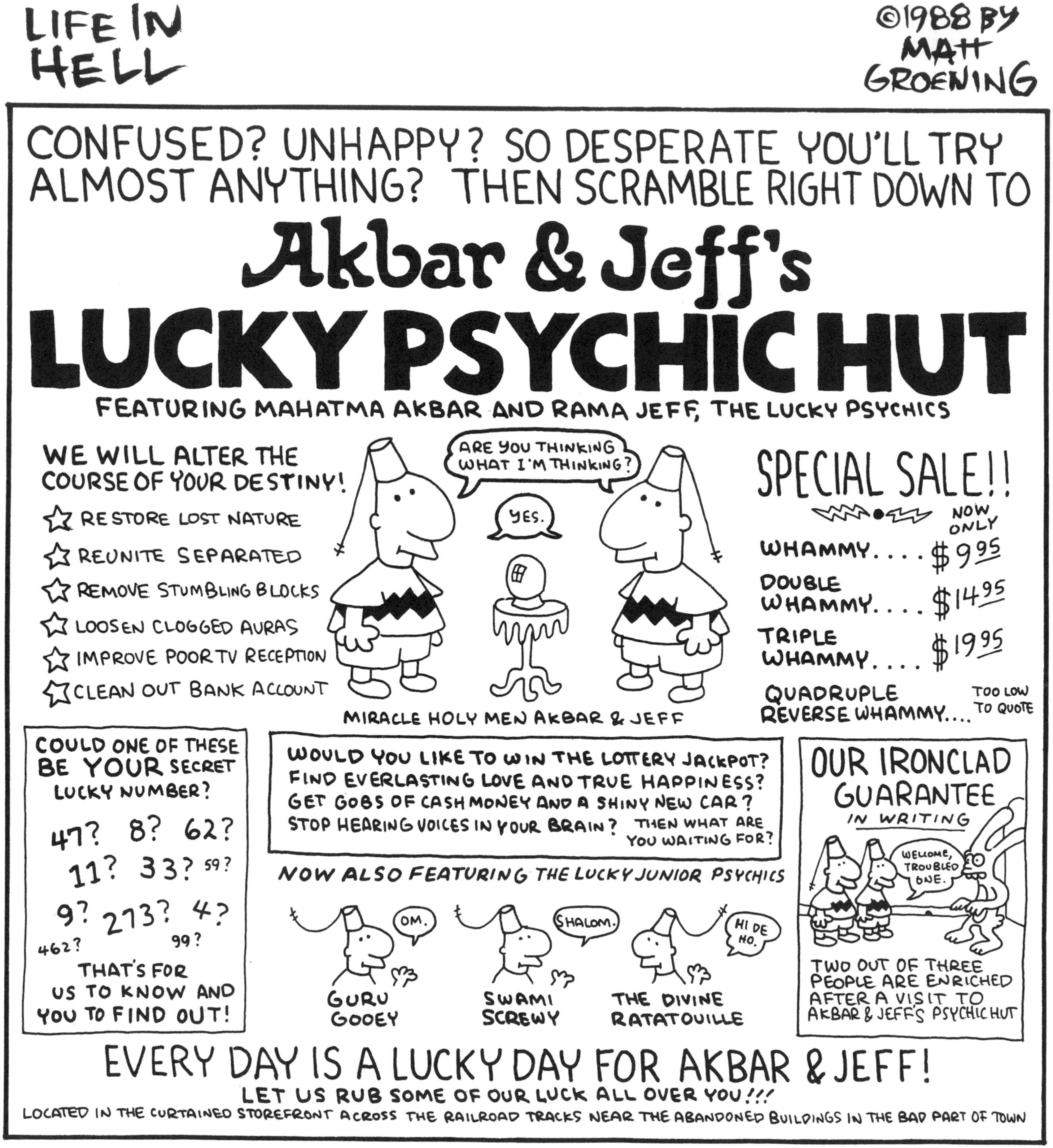
LIFE IN HELL
©1988 BY MATT GROENING
CONFUSED? UNHAPPY? SO DESPERATE YOU'LL TRY ALMOST ANYTHING? THEN SCRAMBLE RIGHT DOWN TO
Akbar & Jeff's
LUCKY PSYCHIC HUT
FEATURING MAHATMA AKBAR AND RAMA JEFF, THE LUCKY PSYCHICS
WE WILL ALTER THE COURSE OF YOUR DESTINY!
RESTORE LOST NATURE
REUNITE SEPARATED
REMOVE STUMBLING BLOCKS
LOOSEN CLOGGED AURAS
IMPROVE POOR TV RECEPTION
CLEAN OUT BANK ACCOUNT
ARE YOU THINKING WHAT I'M THINKING?
YES.
MIRACLE HOLY MEN AKBAR & JEFF
SPECIAL SALE!!
NOW ONLY
WHAMMY.... $9.95
DOUBLE WHAMMY.... $14.95
TRIPLE WHAMMY.... $19.95
QUADRUPLE REVERSE WHAMMY.... TOO LOW TO QUOTE
COULD ONE OF THESE BE YOUR SECRET LUCKY NUMBER?
47? 8? 62?
11? 33? 59?
9? 273? 4?
462? 99?
THAT'S FOR US TO KNOW AND YOU TO FIND OUT!
WOULD YOU LIKE TO WIN THE LOTTERY JACKPOT? FIND EVERLASTING LOVE AND TRUE HAPPINESS? GET GOBS OF CASH MONEY AND A SHINY NEW CAR? STOP HEARING VOICES IN YOUR BRAIN? THEN WHAT ARE YOU WAITING FOR?
NOW ALSO FEATURING THE LUCKY JUNIOR PSYCHICS
OM.
GURU GOOEY
SHALOM.
SWAMI SCREWY
HI DE HO.
THE DIVINE RATATOUILLE
OUR IRONCLAD GUARANTEE IN WRITING
WELCOME, TROUBLED ONE.
TWO OUT OF THREE PEOPLE ARE ENRICHED AFTER A VISIT TO AKBAR & JEFF'S PSYCHIC HUT
EVERY DAY IS A LUCKY DAY FOR AKBAR & JEFF!
LET US RUB SOME OF OUR LUCK ALL OVER YOU!!!
LOCATED IN THE CURTAINED STOREFRONT ACROSS THE RAILROAD TRACKS NEAR THE ABANDONED BUILDINGS IN THE BAD PART OF TOWN

LIFE IN HELL

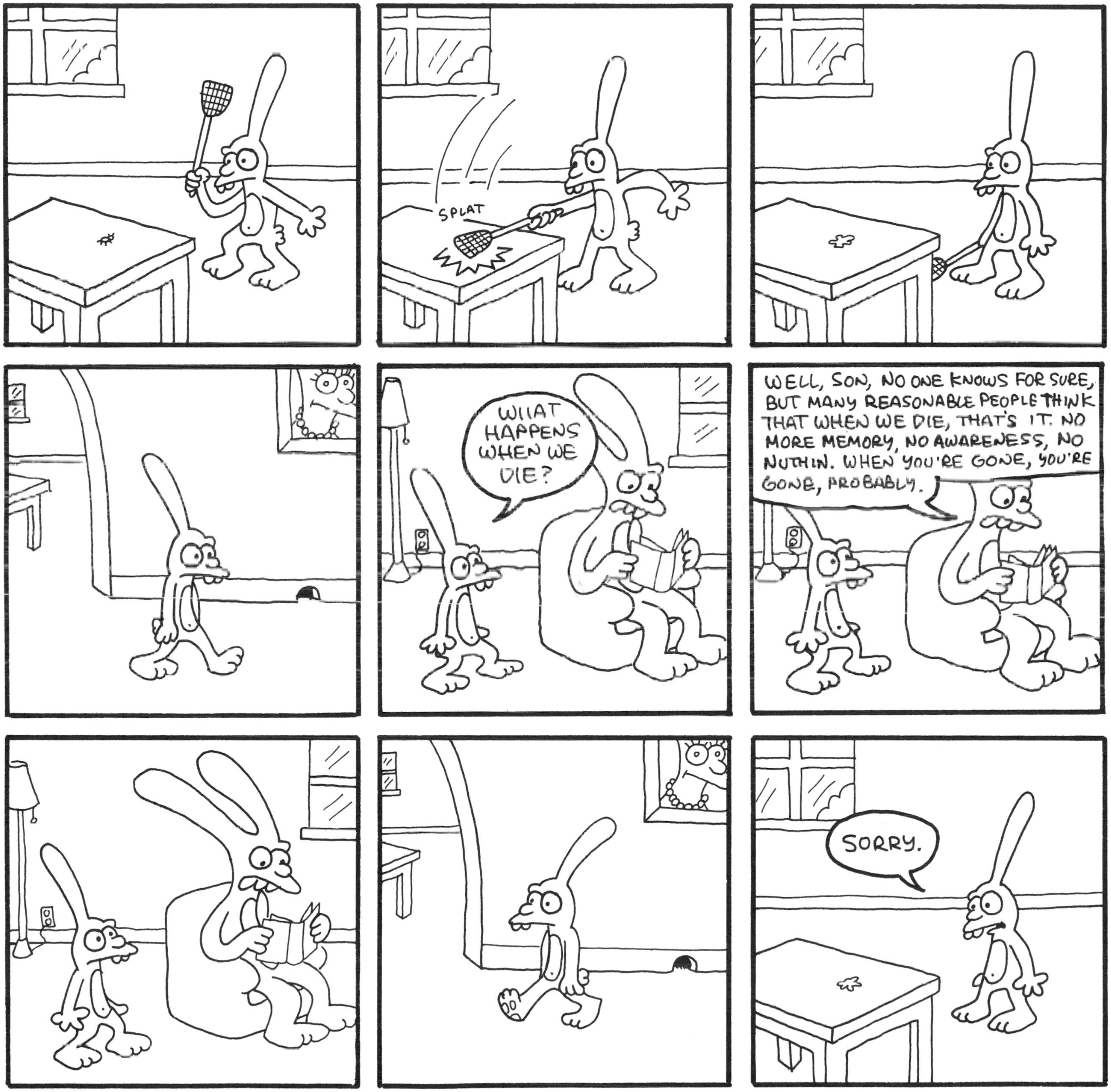
SPLAT
WHAT HAPPENS WHEN WE DIE?
WELL, SON, NO ONE KNOWS FOR SURE, BUT MANY REASONABLE PEOPLE THINK THAT WHEN WE DIE, THAT'S IT. NO MORE MEMORY, NO AWARENESS, NO NUTHIN. WHEN YOU'RE GONE, YOU'RE GONE, PROBABLY.
SORRY.

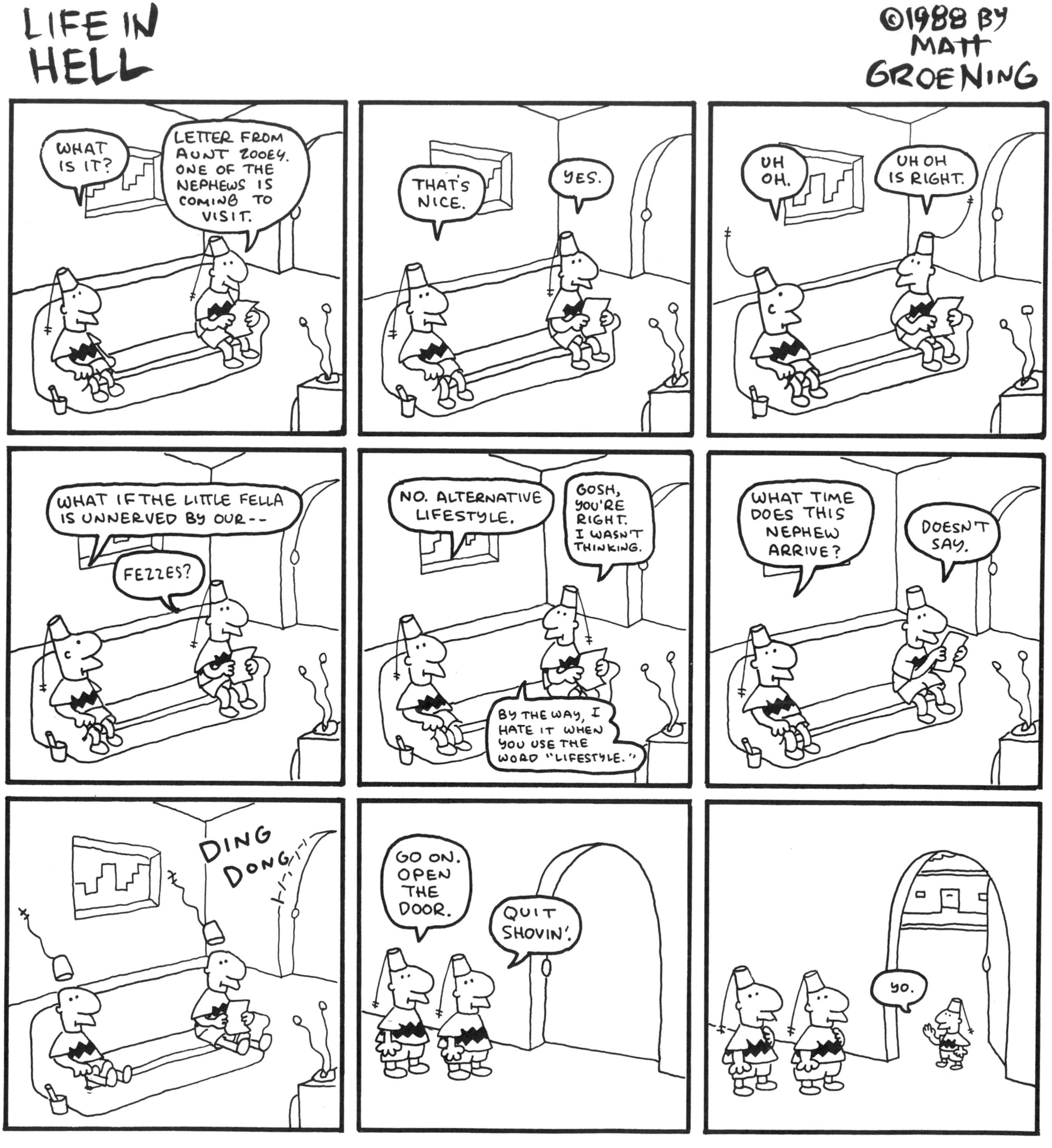
LIFE IN HELL
©1988 BY MATT GROENING
WHAT IS IT?
LETTER FROM AUNT ZOOEY. ONE OF THE NEPHEWS IS COMING TO VISIT.
THAT'S NICE.
YES.
UH OH.
UH OH IS RIGHT.
WHAT IF THE LITTLE FELLA IS UNNERVED BY OUR--
FEZZES?
NO. ALTERNATIVE LIFESTYLE.
GOSH, YOU'RE RIGHT. I WASN'T THINKING.
BY THE WAY, I HATE IT WHEN YOU USE THE WORD "LIFESTYLE."
WHAT TIME DOES THIS NEPHEW ARRIVE?
DOESN'T SAY.
DING DONG
GO ON. OPEN THE DOOR.
QUIT SHOVIN'.
YO.

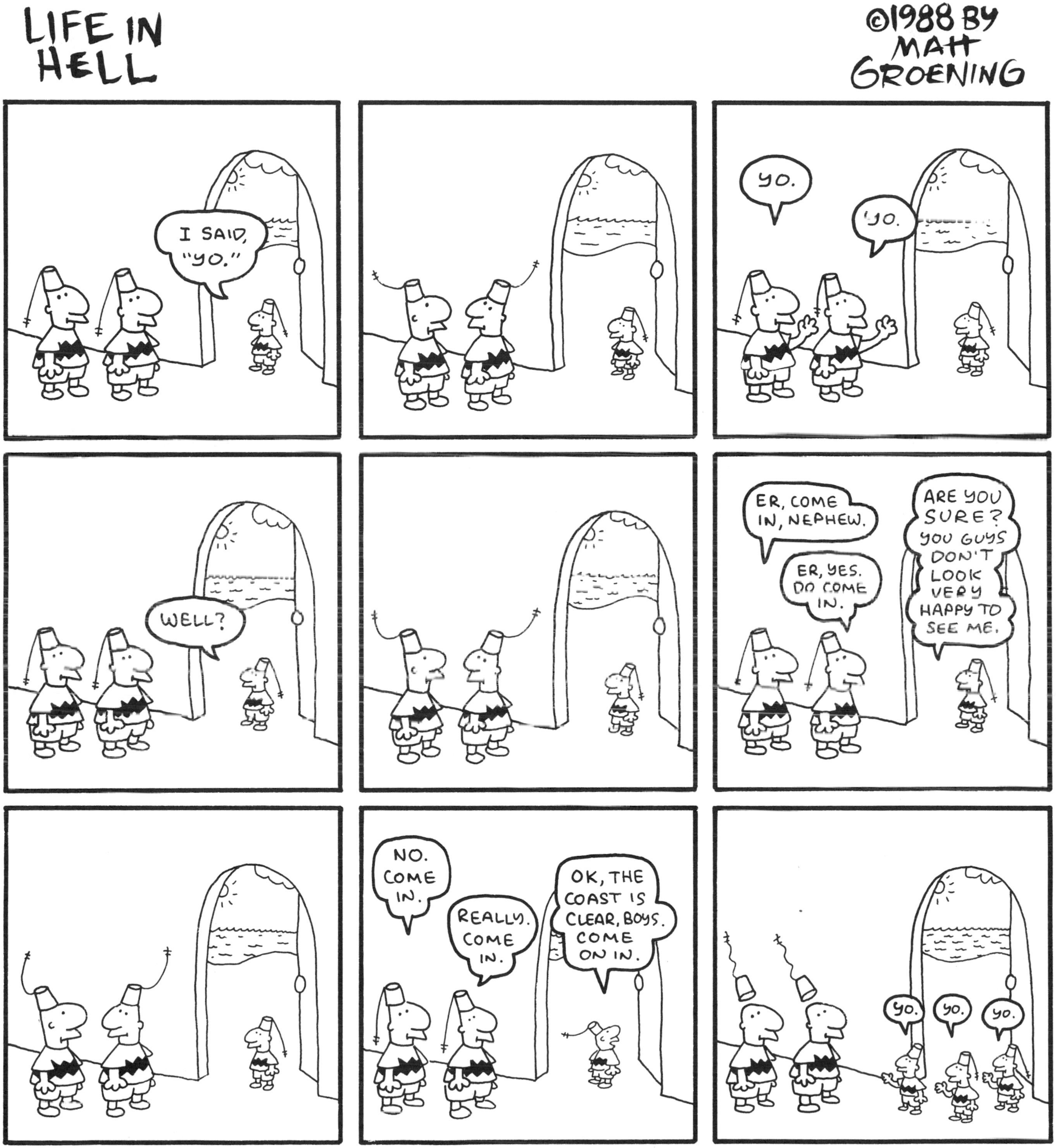
LIFE IN HELL
©1988 BY MATT GROENING
I SAID, "YO."
YO.
YO.
WELL?
ER, COME IN, NEPHEW.
ER, YES. DO COME IN.
ARE YOU SURE? YOU GUYS DON'T LOOK VERY HAPPY TO SEE ME.
NO. COME IN.
REALLY. COME IN.
OK, THE COAST IS CLEAR, BOYS. COME ON IN.
YO.
YO.
YO.

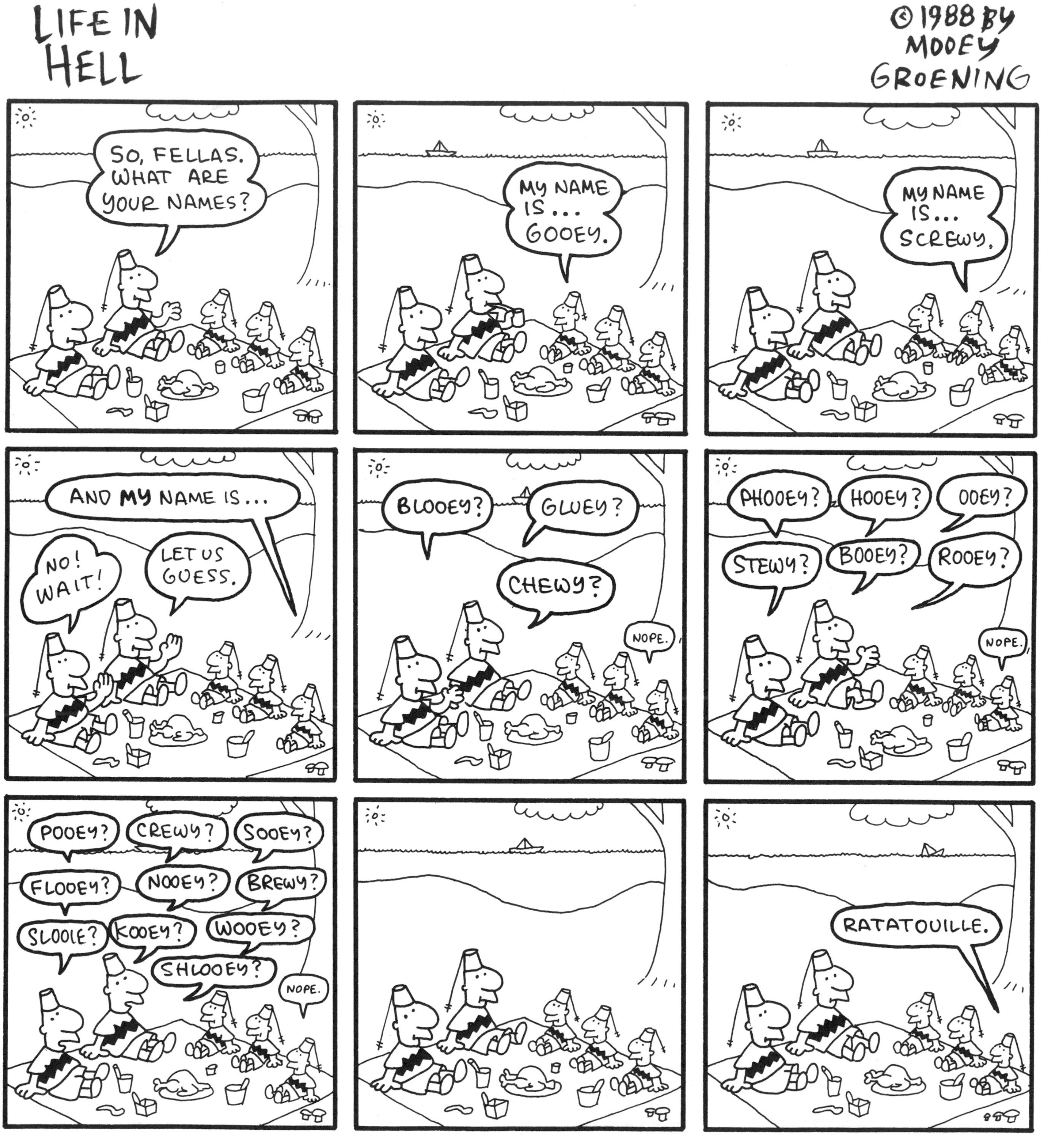
LIFE IN HELL
© 1988 BY MOOEY GROENING
SO, FELLAS. WHAT ARE YOUR NAMES?
MY NAME IS... GOOEY.
MY NAME IS... SCREWY.
AND MY NAME IS...
NO! WAIT!
LET US GUESS.
BLOOEY?
GLUEY?
CHEWY?
NOPE.
PHOOEY?
HOOEY?
OOEY?
STEWY?
BOOEY?
ROOEY?
NOPE.
POOEY?
CREWY?
SOOEY?
FLOOEY?
NOOEY?
BREWY?
SLOOIE?
KOOEY?
WOOEY?
SHLOOEY?
NOPE.
RATATOUILLE.

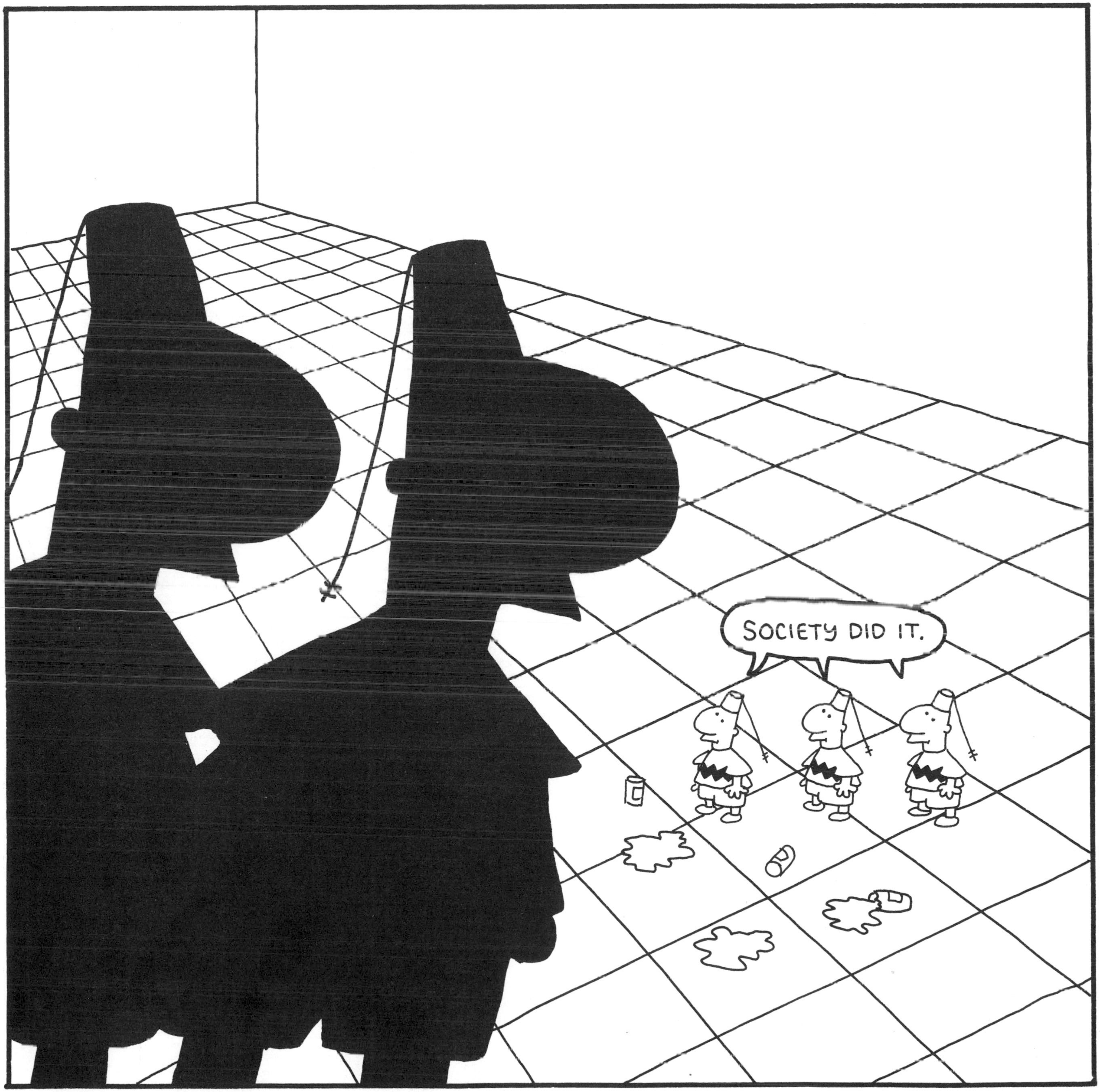
SOCIETY DID IT.

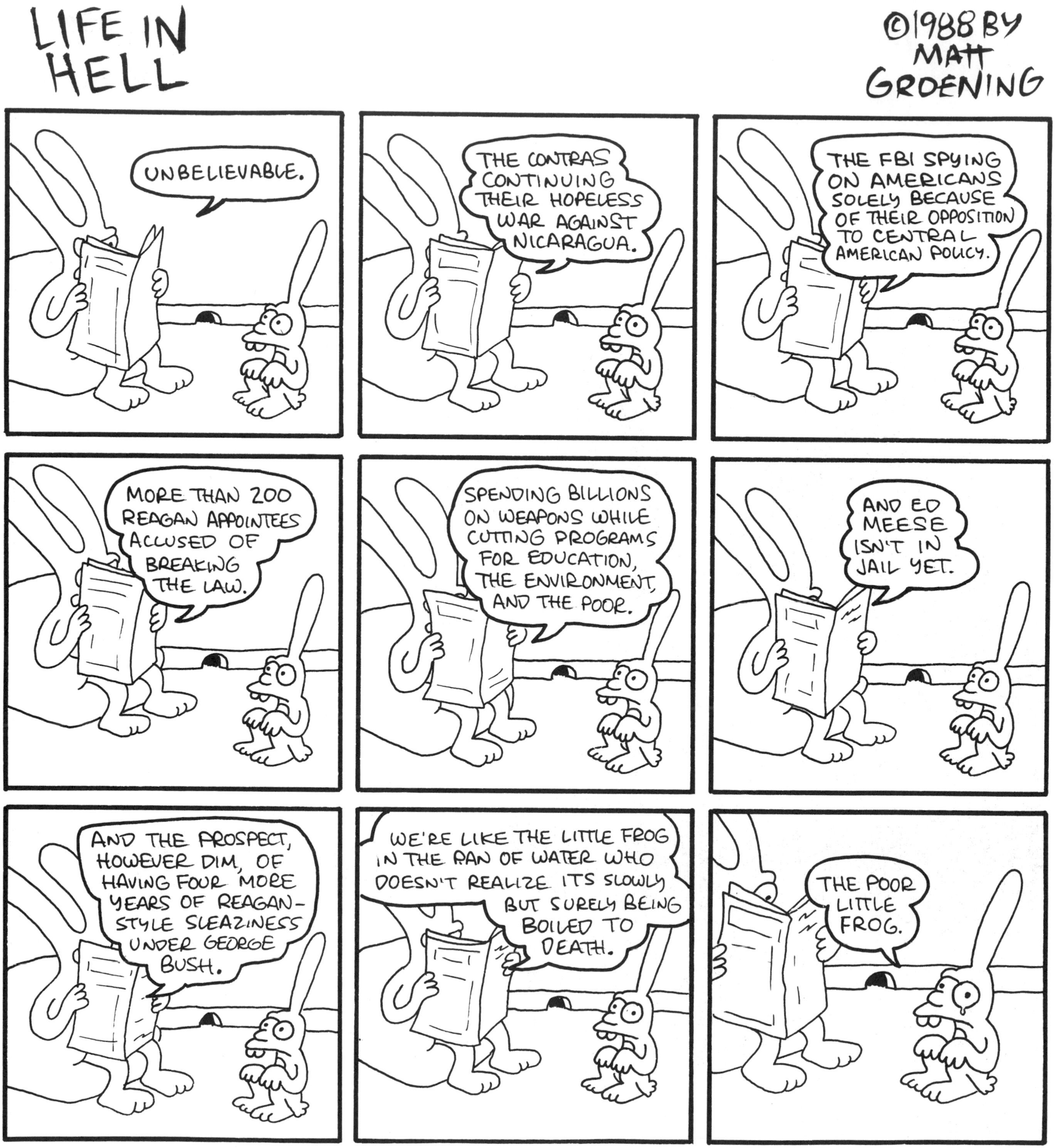
LIFE IN HELL
©1988 BY MATT GROENING
UNBELIEVABLE.
THE CONTRAS CONTINUING THEIR HOPELESS WAR AGAINST NICARAGUA.
THE FBI SPYING ON AMERICANS SOLELY BECAUSE OF THEIR OPPOSITION TO CENTRAL AMERICAN POLICY.
MORE THAN 200 REAGAN APPOINTEES ACCUSED OF BREAKING THE LAW.
SPENDING BILLIONS ON WEAPONS WHILE CUTTING PROGRAMS FOR EDUCATION, THE ENVIRONMENT, AND THE POOR.
AND ED MEESE ISN'T IN JAIL YET.
AND THE PROSPECT, HOWEVER DIM, OF HAVING FOUR MORE YEARS OF REAGAN-STYLE SLEAZINESS UNDER GEORGE BUSH.
WE'RE LIKE THE LITTLE FROG IN THE PAN OF WATER WHO DOESN'T REALIZE ITS SLOWLY BUT SURELY BEING BOILED TO DEATH.
THE POOR LITTLE FROG.

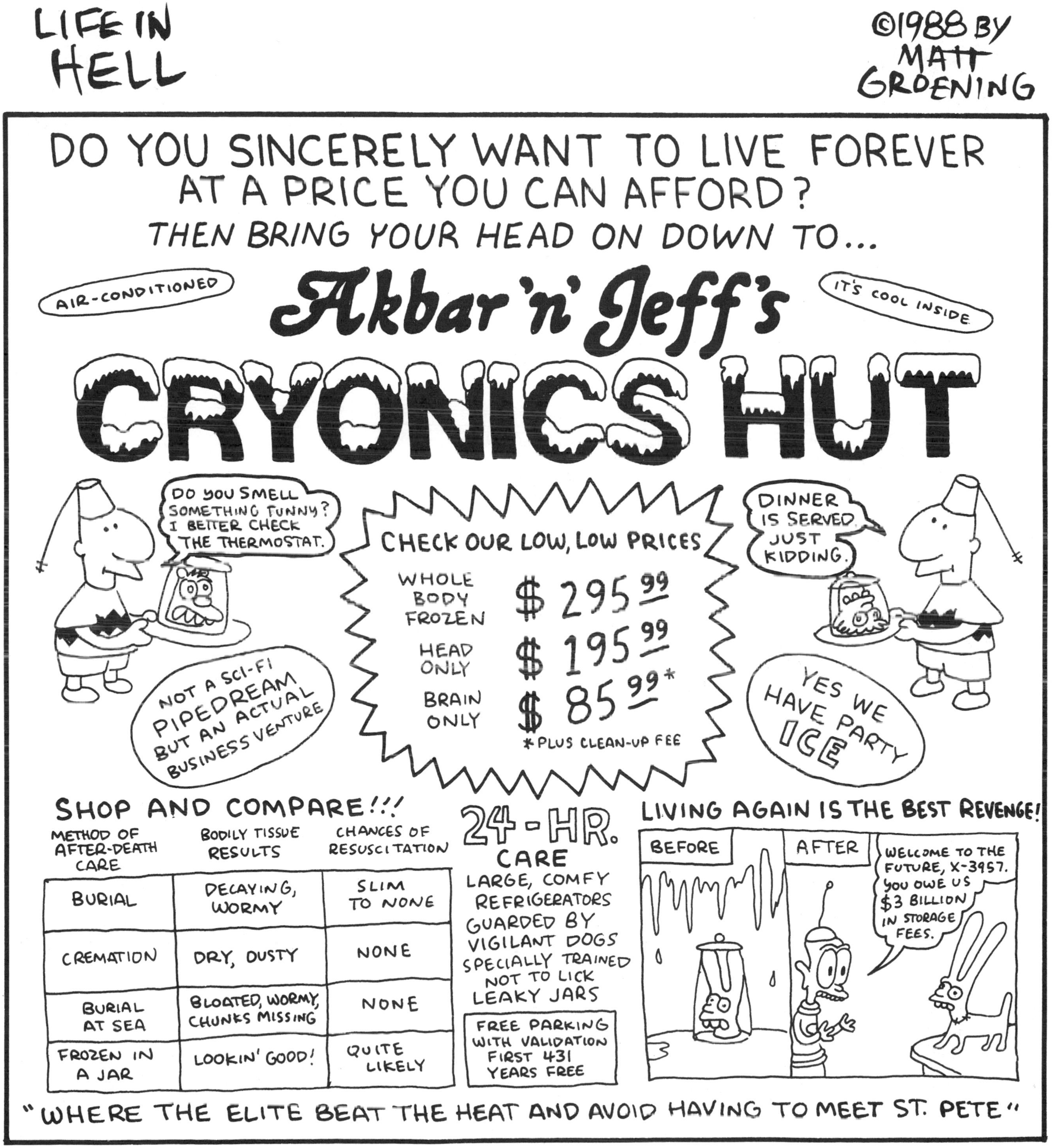
LIFE IN HELL
©1988 BY MATT GROENING
DO YOU SINCERELY WANT TO LIVE FOREVER AT A PRICE YOU CAN AFFORD?
THEN BRING YOUR HEAD ON DOWN TO...
AIR-CONDITIONED
IT'S COOL INSIDE
Akbar 'n' Jeff's
CRYONICS HUT
DO YOU SMELL SOMETHING FUNNY? I BETTER CHECK THE THERMOSTAT.
CHECK OUR LOW, LOW PRICES
WHOLE BODY FROZEN $ 295.99
HEAD ONLY $ 195.99
BRAIN ONLY $ 85.99*
*PLUS CLEAN-UP FEE
DINNER IS SERVED. JUST KIDDING.
NOT A SCI-FI PIPEDREAM BUT AN ACTUAL BUSINESS VENTURE
YES WE HAVE PARTY ICE
SHOP AND COMPARE!!!

METHOD OF AFTER-DEATH CARE	BODILY TISSUE RESULTS	CHANCES OF RESUSCITATION
BURIAL	DECAYING, WORMY	SLIM TO NONE
CREMATION	DRY, DUSTY	NONE
BURIAL AT SEA	BLOATED, WORMY, CHUNKS MISSING	NONE
FROZEN IN A JAR	LOOKIN' GOOD!	QUITE LIKELY

24-HR. CARE
LARGE, COMFY REFRIGERATORS GUARDED BY VIGILANT DOGS SPECIALLY TRAINED NOT TO LICK LEAKY JARS
FREE PARKING WITH VALIDATION FIRST 431 YEARS FREE
LIVING AGAIN IS THE BEST REVENGE!
BEFORE
AFTER
WELCOME TO THE FUTURE, X-3957. YOU OWE US $3 BILLION IN STORAGE FEES.
"WHERE THE ELITE BEAT THE HEAT AND AVOID HAVING TO MEET ST. PETE"

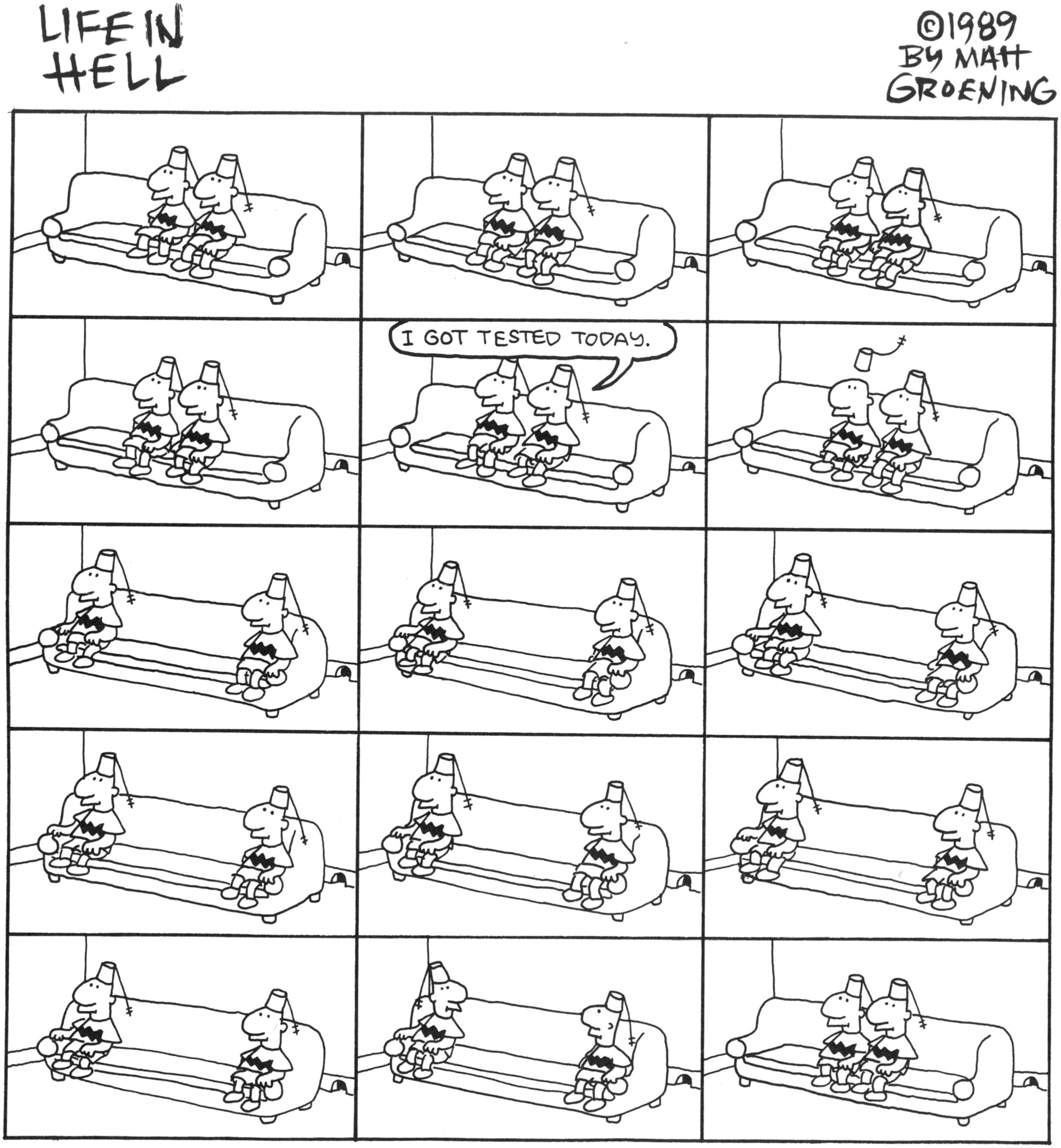
LIFE IN HELL
©1989 BY MATT GROENING
I GOT TESTED TODAY.

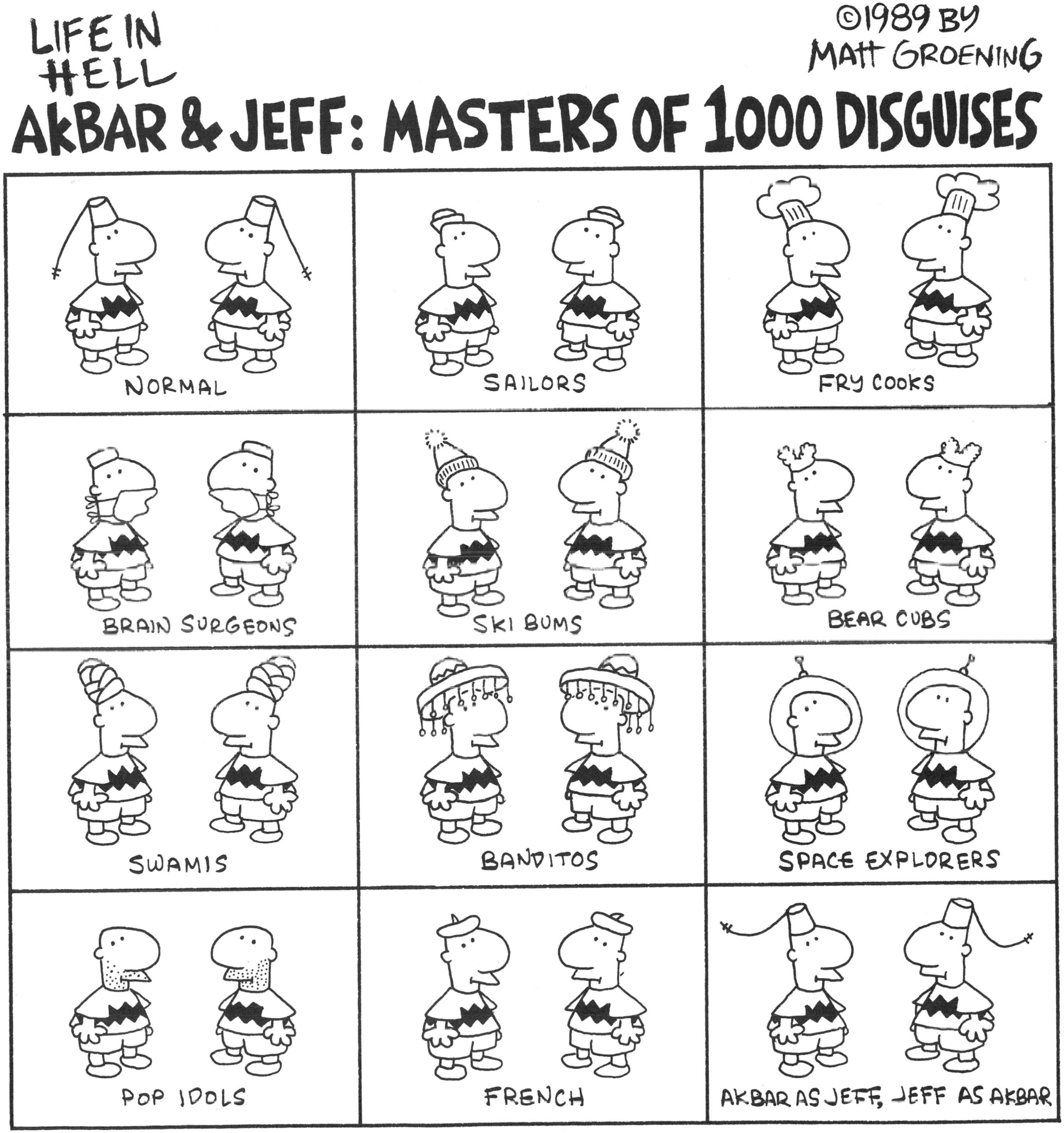
LIFE IN HELL
©1989 BY MATT GROENING
AKBAR & JEFF: MASTERS OF 1000 DISGUISES
NORMAL
SAILORS
FRY COOKS
BRAIN SURGEONS
SKI BUMS
BEAR CUBS
SWAMIS
BANDITOS
SPACE EXPLORERS
POP IDOLS
FRENCH
AKBAR AS JEFF, JEFF AS AKBAR

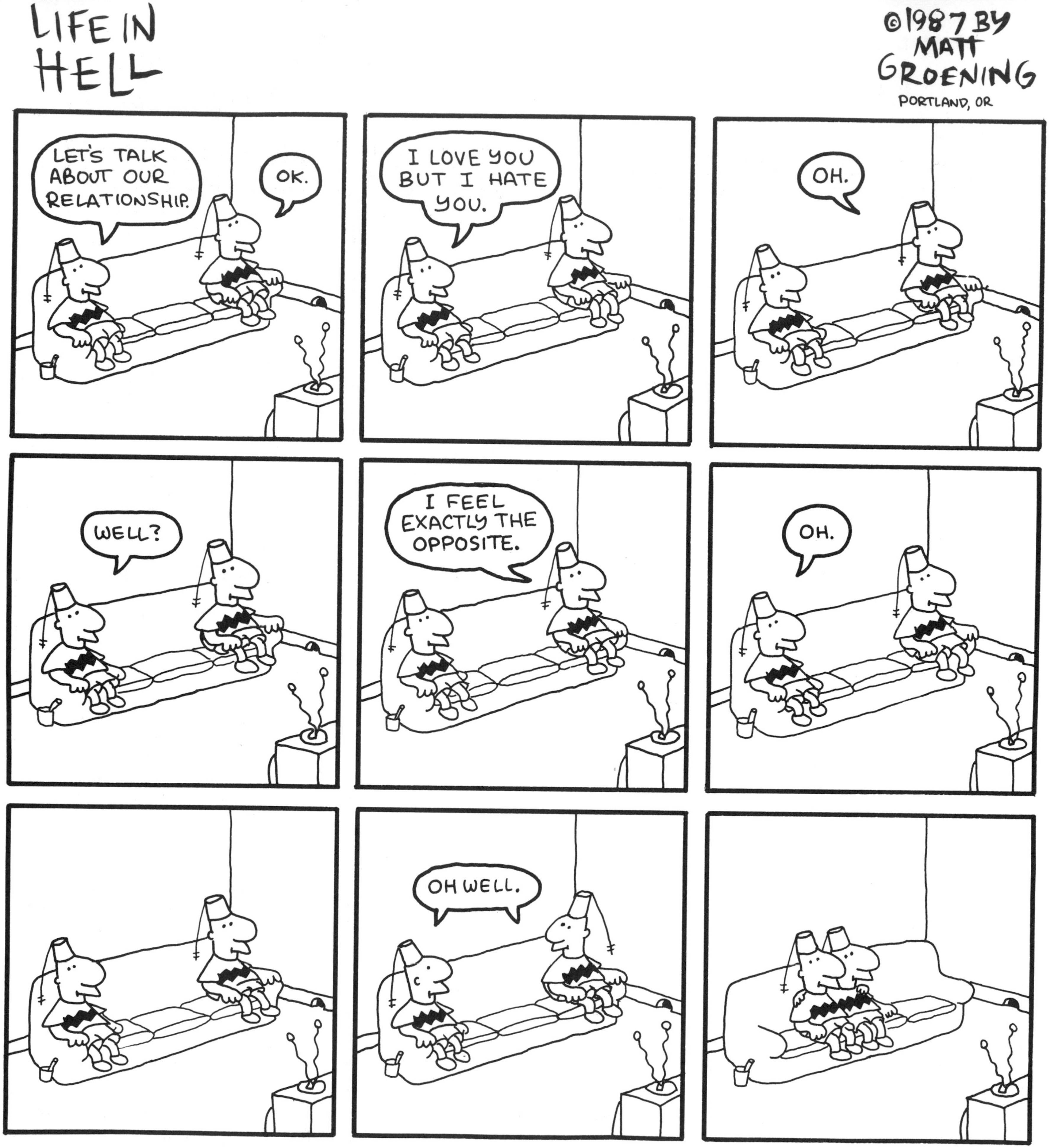
LIFE IN HELL
©1987 BY MATT GROENING
PORTLAND, OR
LET'S TALK ABOUT OUR RELATIONSHIP.
OK.
I LOVE YOU BUT I HATE YOU.
OH.
WELL?
I FEEL EXACTLY THE OPPOSITE.
OH.
OH WELL.

INDEX OF HELL

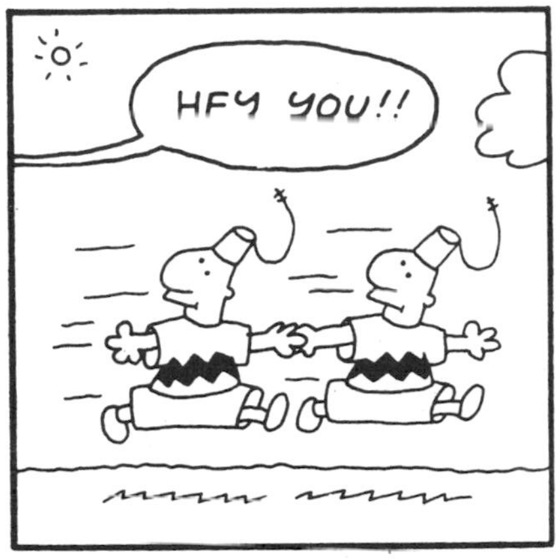

HEY YOU!!

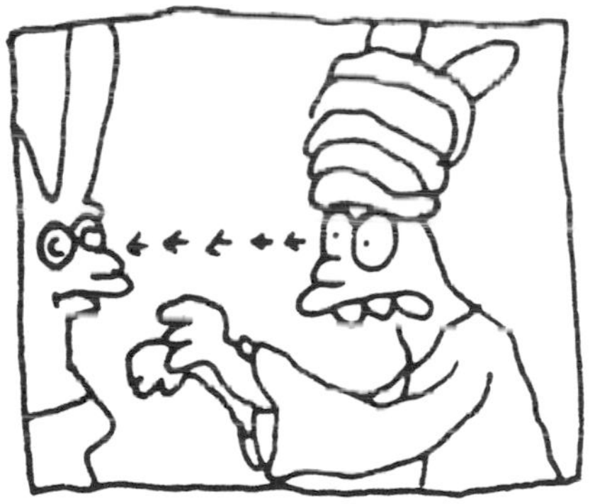

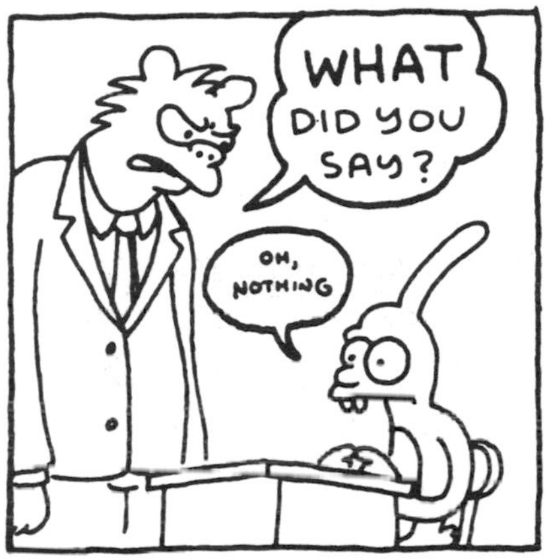

WHAT DID YOU SAY?
OH, NOTHING

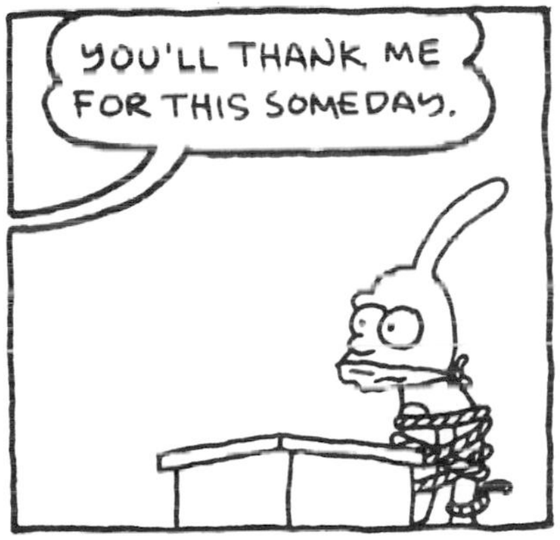
YOU'LL THANK ME FOR THIS SOMEDAY.

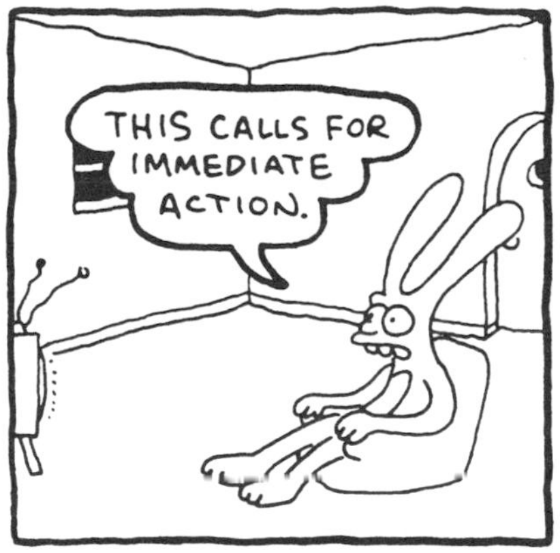
THIS CALLS FOR IMMEDIATE ACTION.

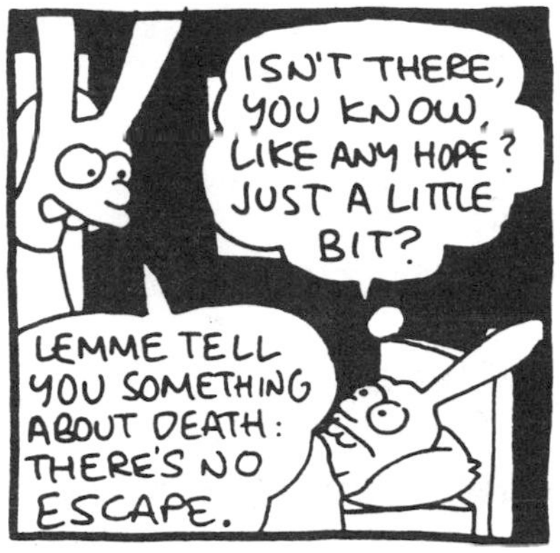
ISN'T THERE, YOU KNOW, LIKE ANY HOPE? JUST A LITTLE BIT?
LEMME TELL YOU SOMETHING ABOUT DEATH: THERE'S NO ESCAPE.

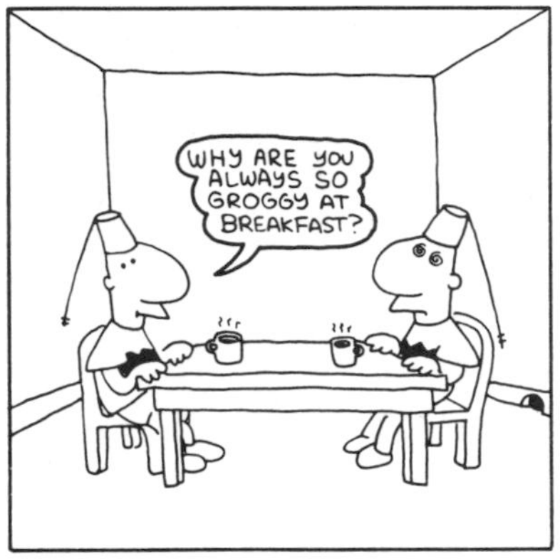
WHY ARE YOU ALWAYS SO GROGGY AT BREAKFAST?

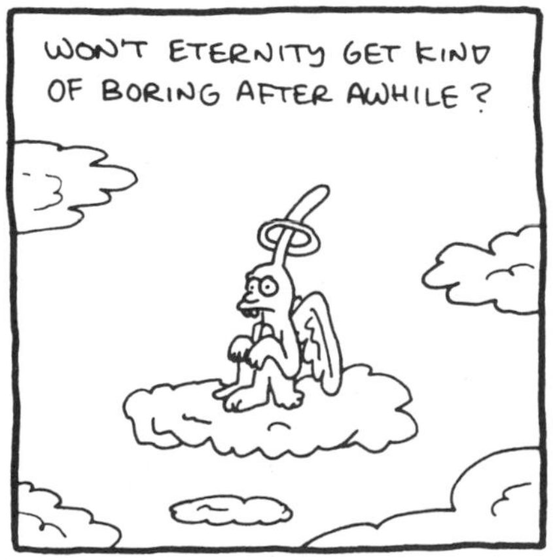
WON'T ETERNITY GET KIND OF BORING AFTER AWHILE?

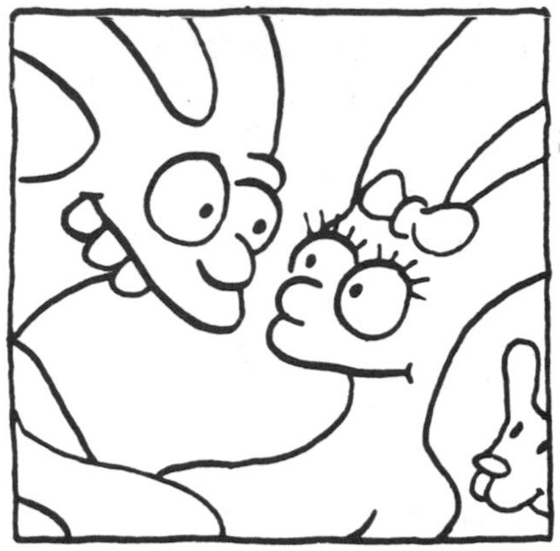

G

H

I

J

K

L

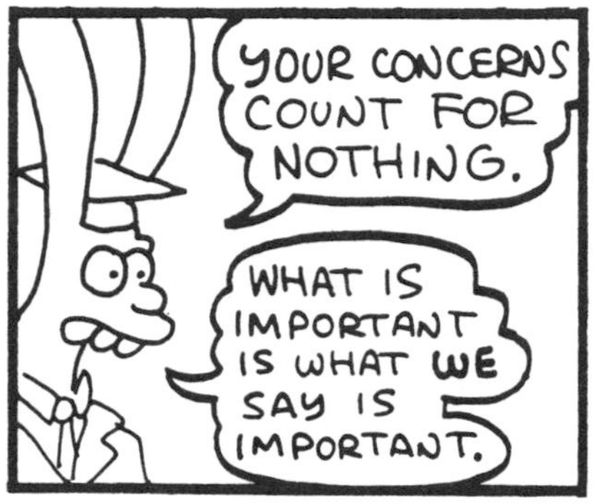
YOUR CONCERNS COUNT FOR NOTHING.
WHAT IS IMPORTANT IS WHAT WE SAY IS IMPORTANT.

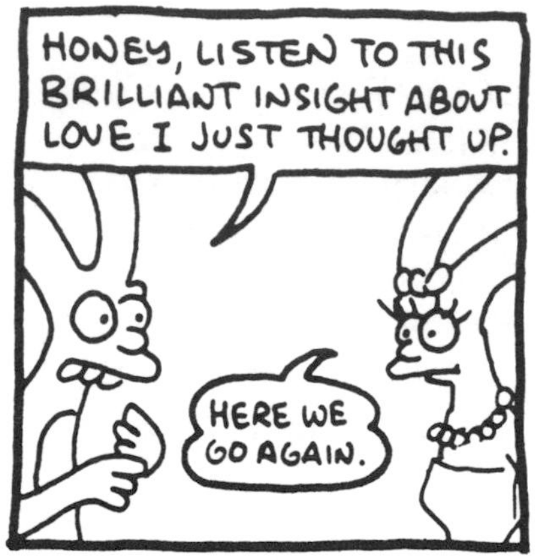
HONEY, LISTEN TO THIS BRILLIANT INSIGHT ABOUT LOVE I JUST THOUGHT UP.
HERE WE GO AGAIN.

M

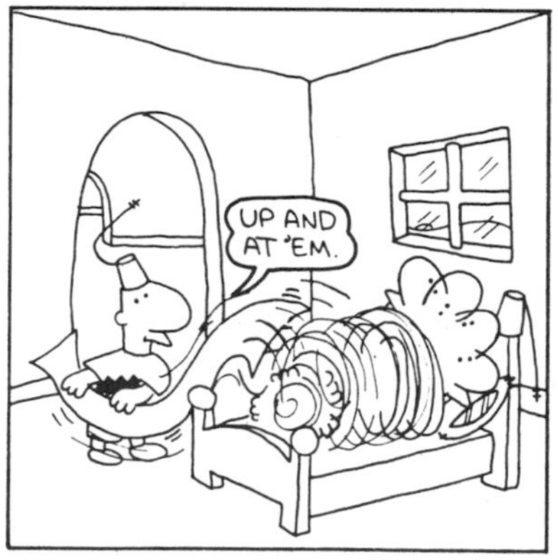
UP AND AT 'EM.

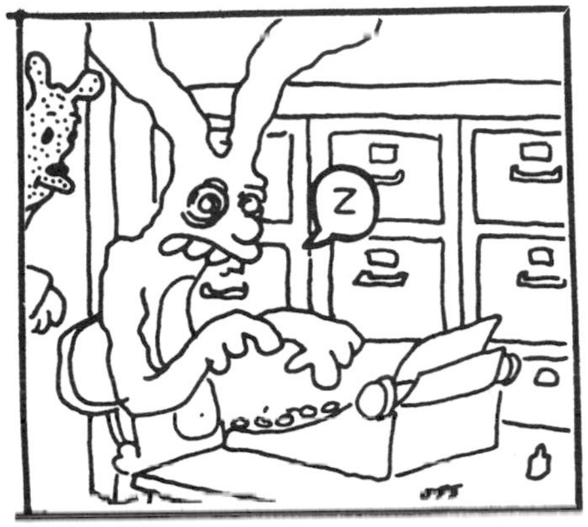
Z

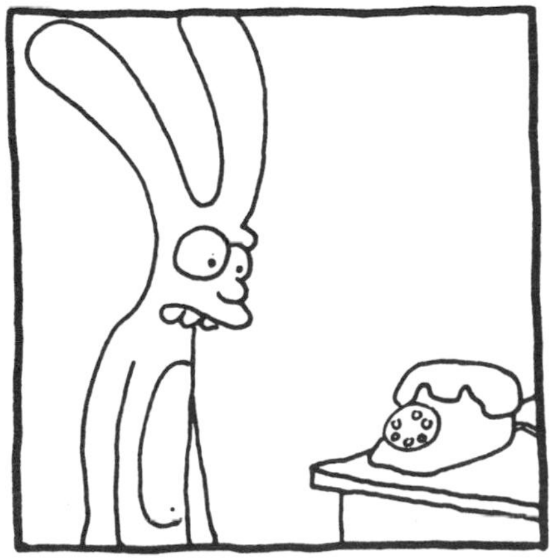

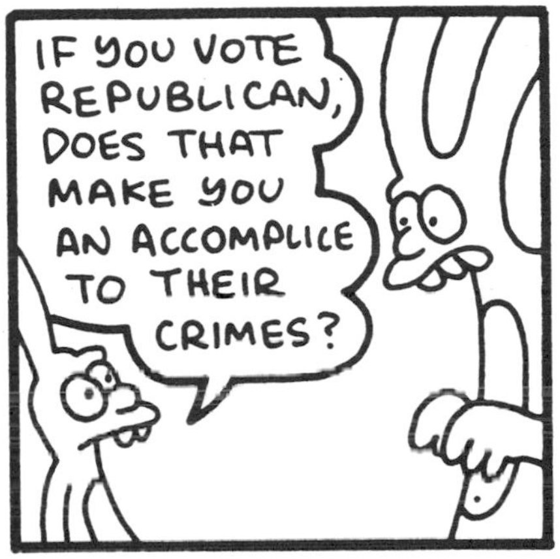
IF YOU VOTE REPUBLICAN, DOES THAT MAKE YOU AN ACCOMPLICE TO THEIR CRIMES?

FIRST OF ALL, YOU'RE LIVE ON NETWORK TV! HOW DOES THAT MAKE YOU FEEL?

U

V

W

"THE ANGRY BEHEMOTH"

I DON'T PAY YOU TO THINK. I PAY YOU TO CRINGE WHILE I SCREAM AND RANT.

X

Y

Z

ABOUT THE AUTHOR

Matt Groening was born near Beaverton, Oregon, in 1954. His father, Homer Groening, a cartoonist himself, encouraged his son's primitive doodlings. Matt enjoyed drawing from an early age, but felt a strong loathing for coloring books, mainly because he was not able to stay inside the line.

In grade school, Matt drew cartoons when he should have been paying attention, which left strange gaps in his education. To this day, he does not know his state capitals, and don't bother asking him to multiply any numbers between 7 and 13. He'll just look at you blankly.

In high school, Matt continued his frivolous ways. He drew cartoons in every class, even Physical Education, injuring himself severely in his sophomore year while doodling on the parallel bars. Until he was kicked off the staff, Matt drew cartoons for the school newspaper. Feeling the revolutionary fervor of the time, Matt and his hippie pals formed their own political party, the Teens for Decency. Responding to the campaign slogan, "If You're Against Decency, What Are You For?", his confused classmates elected Matt Student Body President and immediately regretted it.

Matt attended The Evergreen State College in Olympia, Washington, taking full advantage of the school's no-grade, no-required-courses policies. He graduated in 1977 and drove to Los Angeles, where his car broke down in the fast lane of the Hollywood Freeway just above the Vine Street exit at 2 a.m., inspiring the "Life in Hell" cartoon series. "Life in Hell" debuted in *Wet* magazine in 1978, and began its first regular weekly appearance in the Los Angeles *Reader* in 1980. The comic strip currently appears in about 250 newspapers around the world, much to Matt's amazement.

Matt has published six cartoon books, all but one with the word "Hell" in the title. He is also responsible for countless "Life in Hell" calendars, postcard books, greeting cards, posters, T-shirts, and coffee mugs. "What the hell," he explains enigmatically.

Matt's first animated work, "The Simpsons," which began as a feature on *The Tracey Ullman Show*, is now a freakishly popular weekly half-hour primetime series.

Matt lives in Los Angeles with his radiant wife, Deborah Caplan; his son, Homer; and more pet ducks than you can shake a stick at.